Constitutional Law in Belgium

Constitutional Law in Belgium

Edited by
André Alen
David Haljan
Co-editor
Willem Verrijdt

This book was originally published as a monograph in the International Encyclopaedia of Laws/Constitutional Law.

Founding Editor: Roger Blanpain
General Editor: Frank Hendrickx
Volume Editors: André Alen & David Haljan

Wolters Kluwer

Published by:
Kluwer Law International B.V.
PO Box 316
2400 AH Alphen aan den Rijn
The Netherlands
E-mail: international-sales@wolterskluwer.com
Website: lrus.wolterskluwer.com

Sold and distributed in North, Central and South America by:
Wolters Kluwer Legal & Regulatory U.S.
7201 McKinney Circle
Frederick, MD 21704
United States of America
Email: customer.service@wolterskluwer.com

Sold and distributed in all other countries by:
Air Business Subscriptions
Rockwood House
Haywards Heath
West Sussex
RH16 3DH
United Kingdom
Email: international-customerservice@wolterskluwer.com

ISBN 978-94-035-2582-2

e-Book: ISBN 978-94-035-2583-9
web-PDF: ISBN 978-94-035-2584-6

The Authors

André Alen (comprehensive content review; Nos 586–615)
Heidi Bortels (Nos 376–401; 402–414)
Benjamin Dalle (Nos 201–238)
Valérie De Schepper (Nos 1–31; 284–289)
David Haljan (compilation, language, and uniformity review)
David Keyaerts (Nos 507–541)
Frank Judo (Nos 164–200; 694–704)
Sarah Lambrecht (Nos 239; 616–645; 687–693)
Wouter Pas (Nos 296–346; 352–375)
Patrick Peeters (Nos 290–295; 347–351; 646–686)
Tim Souverijns (Nos 89–98; 99–110)
Jan Theunis (Nos 32–88)
Jeroen Van Nieuwenhove (Nos 111–163)
Arne Vandaele (Nos 542–585)
Willem Verrijdt (Nos 240–283; 415–506)

The Authors

The Editors

Prof. Em. Dr. Iur. Baron André Alen (born 25 September 1950) studied law at the Catholic University of Leuven, Belgium (1968–1973). In 1983 the University of Leuven awarded him a doctorate for a thesis on the historical and philosophical background of the Belgian Constitution.

In 1984 he was appointed Professor *Extraordinarius* at the Faculty of Law, University of Gent, Belgium, where he taught Belgian constitutional law until 1994. Between 1986 and 2001 he was also Professor of Constitutional Law, Political Institutions, and Federalism at the Faculty of Law, University of Leuven. In 2001, after his appointment to the Belgian Constitutional Court, he became Professor *Extraordinarius* of Constitutional Law with the Institute for Constitutional Law at the University of Leuven. Since 2015 he is Professor Emeritus of Constitutional Law at the Faculty of Law, University of Leuven.

Since 1978, Professor Alen has been an advisor to or a chief of staff for several Ministers of the Belgian government (including the Prime Minister between 1979–1981 and 1984–1992). In that capacity he has played a key role in the various constitutional reforms of the Belgian State, through which Belgium evolved from a unitary decentralised State to a federal State. From 1985 until 1992 he was Secretary of the Belgian Government, and from 1992 to 2001 he was an Assessor with the Legislative Division of the Belgian Council of State.

Professor Alen has participated in numerous international colloquia, including those within the framework of the OECD, and as of 2001 representing the Belgian Constitutional Court. As an expert on the Belgian federal system, he has been consulted by officials on a number of occasions regarding foreign conflicts (including Yugoslavia, South Africa, and Cyprus). He is the author of several books and articles in the field of constitutional law and administrative law, federalism, and human rights.

Professor Alen has been the President of the Belgian Constitutional Court (2014–2016 and 2018–2020). He is judge ad hoc with the European Court of Human Rights. He is also a member of the Royal Flemish Academy of Belgium for Science and the Arts.

He is also the co-editor of the *International Encyclopaedia of Constitutional Law and co-editor of the International Encyclopaedia of Sub-National Constitutional Law.*

The Editors

Dr. David Haljan is a senior research fellow with the Leuven Centre for Public Law, University of Leuven. A graduate of Osgoode Hall, Toronto, Canada, King's College London, UK, and the University of Leuven, he is the author of a number of books, articles, and notes in the field of constitutional law, public law, public international law, and commercial and administrative law. He is also a member of the Bars of Alberta and Ontario.

He is also the co-editor of the International Encyclopaedia of Constitutional Law and co-editor of the International Encyclopaedia of Sub-National Constitutional Law.

Willem Verrijdt studied law at KU Leuven (1999–2004), and since 2008 has been a law clerk (*referendaris*) at the Belgian Constitutional Court. He has been actively involved in the research and education activities of the Leuven Centre for Public Law (formerly the Institute for Constitutional Law) at KU Leuven, first as a full-time assistant (2004–2008) and later as a part-time assistant (2008–2011), an affiliated researcher (2011–2017), and a sessional lecturer (2017-present).

Table of Contents

Introduction to the 2020 Edition

Belgium initially emerged as a unitary yet decentralised State. Its 1831 Constitution opted for a hereditary monarchy and aimed at pacifying Catholics and Liberals. Many of its provisions were phrased as a reaction against Willem I, the first and only King of the United Kingdom of the Netherlands. The Belgian Constitution embraces the rule of law, democracy and the separation of powers, albeit without explicitly mentioning any of these buzzwords. Being the most modern constitution of its era, it influenced many other constitutions throughout the nineteenth century. Apart from the democratisation of the electorate, colonisation and decolonisation, and the challenges posed by two World Wars, the Belgian Constitution and Belgian constitutional practice remained very stable until the second half of the twentieth century.

From 1970 onwards, six State Reforms have transformed Belgium into a sui generis (bipolar and centrifugal) federal State, with a double set of federated entities, three Communities, and three Regions with a partly overlapping territorial jurisdiction. These reforms sought to assuage a bipolar linguistic reality and accommodate the sometimes very different policy viewpoints in the North and the South of the country. At the same time, Belgium became a Member State of several supranational and international organisations, Belgian constitutional practice displaying a significant openness towards international law and EU law. Its intricate distribution of powers between the federal State, the Communities and the Regions, and its mechanisms for the protection of minorities have resulted in one of the most complex constitutions in the world.

Describing this unique system, which is still very much a work in progress, is a daunting task. The first edition of this overview in the *International Encyclopaedia of Laws* series appeared in 1992, only one year before the 1993 Fourth State Reform. The second edition was published in 2013, only one year before the 2014 Sixth State Reform. This Sixth State Reform was very extensive, and impacted on the composition, competences and financing of many institutions. Therefore, this third edition on Belgian Constitutional Law represents yet again an entirely revised work, extensively amending the prior edition. I cannot predict whether further State Reforms will take place any time soon, but I do hope that this third edition will remain up-to-date a tad bit longer than both prior editions.

The many changes in this edition, however, cannot diminish the fact that this new third edition remains indebted to the authors of both prior editions. I must therefore take this opportunity to thank them yet again. The 1992 edition came into being with the help of Bernard Tilleman, Jan Clement, Frank Meersschaut, Patrick Peeters,

Geneviève Vander Stichele, and Geert van Haegendoren. The 2013 edition was written with the help of editor David Haljan, co-editors Patrick Peeters and Stef Feyen, and the authors Jan Clement, Elke Cloots, Benjamin Dalle, Erlinde De Lange, Stef Feyen, Philippe Gérard, David Haljan, Evelyne Maes, Wouter Pas, Patrick Peeters, Steven Peeters, Karel Van Geyt, Luc Vermeire, and Willem Verrijdt. Many of them have also contributed to this third edition. The imprint mentions which chapters each author has rewritten.

This work reflects the Belgian constitutional structure up to 31 March 2020.

André Alen
Leuven, April 2020

List of Abbreviations

A.J.T.	Algemeen Juridisch Tijdschrift
Cass.	Court of Cassation (Hof van Cassatie / Cour de Cassation)
Cons.	Constitutional Court (Grondwettelijk Hof / Cour Constitutionnelle)
ECJ	European Court of Justice
ECR	European Court Reports
ECommHR	European Commission of Human Rights
EConvHR	European Convention on Human Rights
ECtHR	European Court of Human Rights
ECtHR (GC)	European Court of Human Right, Grand Chamber
EU	European Union
ICCPR	International Covenant on Civil and Political Rights
ICESCR	International Covenant on Economic Social and Cultural Rights
Gazette	*Belgisch Staatsblad /- Moniteur Belge* (Belgium Gazette)
J.T.	Journal des Tribunaux
Pas.	Pasicrisie
R.W.	Rechtskundig Weekblad
T.B.P.	Tijdschrift voor Bestuurswetenschappen en Publiekrecht
TFEU	Treaty on the Functioning of the European Union

List of Abbreviations

Note on Caselaw

Judgments of the Constitutional Court may be found at the Court's website: www.const-court.be.
Judgments of all courts, legislation and editions of the *Belgian Gazette* may be found through the Belgian legal portal: www.belgielex.be (materials in English may be limited).
The *Belgium Gazette* is available at www.staatsblad.be / www.moniteur.be .

Note on Caselaw

General Introduction

§1. An Outline of Belgian Constitutional History

1. Often it is said that the first mention of 'Belgians' was by Julius Caesar in his *Commentarii de bello Gallico*. The 'Belgians' were the inhabitants of *Gallia Belgica* (North Gallia), a territory that partly covered modern Belgium. During the Middle Ages the term '*Belgica*' disappeared with the territory of what is now Belgium being split up into various autonomous entities (principalities), such as counties (e.g., the County of Flanders), principalities of a Prince-Bishop (e.g., the Prince-Bishopric of Luik/Liège), duchies (e.g., the Duchy of Brabant), seigniories (e.g., the Seigniory of Mechelen/Malines), and powerful cities.

Through marriage and conquest, the Dukes of Burgundy pursued a 'centralization policy', by which they acquired power in the fifteenth and sixteenth centuries in most of those autonomous principalities. From 1543, this (personal) union of principalities was called the 'Seventeen Provinces' and covered the territory of what are now Belgium, the Netherlands, Northern France, and the Grand-Duchy of Luxembourg.[1] Even though this Burgundian State was not a state in the modern sense of the term, the Seventeen Provinces were not only united by personal, dynastic bonds, but also by common political institutions (e.g., the Estates General).

This unification policy was continued by the House of Habsburg, which succeeded the Burgundians, and especially by the Gent born Holy Roman Emperor Charles V, who unified the political institutions of the Netherlands. His son, Philip II, had the same aspirations, but his centralistic, absolutist policy was less successful. Philip II, more a Spaniard than a Belgian, had less understanding of the political sensibilities of the Provinces. Furthermore his unquestioning belief in, and unqualified support for, the Roman Catholic Church did not correspond with the northern, Protestant, mentality. In 1568, the seven northern protestant provinces rebelled against Spanish rule, leading to the creation of the independent Republic of the Seven United Netherlands (the Netherlands today) in 1588, and thus to the separation of the Seventeen Provinces.

In the seventeenth century, the southern provinces remained under (harsh) Spanish rule which restricted religious and intellectual freedoms. The blockade of the port of Antwerp, the exodus of the intelligentsia to the 'free northern provinces', and the many wars with France (under Louis XIV) resulted in the substantial economic decline of the southern provinces, while the Republic of the Seven United Netherlands experienced a 'golden age'.

1. But the principality of the Prince-Bishop of Luik/Liège was not part of the Seventeen Provinces.

In 1713 with the Peace of Utrecht, the Spanish Habsburgs were succeeded by the Austrian Habsburgs, establishing Austrian rule in the southern Netherlands until 1794. In 1795, France conquered the southern Netherlands and the Principality of the Prince-Bishop of Luik/Liège, and annexed Belgium to France. While France may have given Belgium its Civil Code, French rule only lasted until the Battle of Waterloo (1815).

At the Congress of Vienna (1814–1815), the Allied Powers, especially Prussia and Great Britain, promoted the creation of a United Kingdom of the Netherlands, reuniting the old Seventeen Provinces and the Principality of the Prince-Bishop of Luik/Liège. This new State was designed to impede French imperialism. However, this new State did not last long: unifying the different southern and northern mentalities into one State proved to be impossible, in particular under the rule of the King, Willem I.

2. Willem I, the first and only King of the United Kingdom of the Netherlands (1815–1830), was an enlightened despot. His industrial and economic policy was progressive and beneficial for the country. For example, he founded the Generale Maatschappij / Société Générale, designed to invest in the southern provinces of the Kingdom.

Although the Constitution of the United Kingdom of the Netherlands was one of the most liberal constitutions of the time, it fed the enlightened despotism of Willem I.[2] It endowed the King with very wide, personal powers without political or ministerial responsibility. Minsters were responsible only to the King, not to Parliament. It also lacked provisions on residuary powers, allowing the King to lay claim to them. The King therefore assumed he exercised all powers save those formally attributed to another body, and was thus able to regulate autonomously by decree those matters which the Constitution did not formally attribute to the Legislature. Regulation was therefore generally promulgated by Royal Decrees. Consequently, the reign of Willem I was labelled 'decree government'. And since judicial review of administrative acts would impede efficient government, the King refused any sort of judicial review of his acts. He decreed that the judiciary lacked jurisdiction to review any administrative act or proceeding where the government was an interested party.

The (Dutch) King could not, however, maintain this authority because he had lost the confidence of the two main political movements in the South: the Catholics and the Liberals. The Catholics did not agree with the interventionist policy in religious matters (the King demanding a say in the training of priests and in the appointment of bishops), nor with his education policy. The foundation of schools needed his royal approval and he favoured the foundation of 'public' schools, namely schools created by the government. His education policy was designed to weaken the (strong) influence of the Catholic Church and to secularise the educational system. This convinced the Catholics of the benefits of the principle of separation of church and state, and of the constitutional liberties of religion and education as a means to prevent royal intervention in these areas. The Liberals, namely the French-speaking

2. See, e.g., A. Alen, A.W. Heringa, D. Heirbaut & C.J. Rotteveel Mansveld (eds.), *De Grondwet van het Verenigd Konninkrijk der Nederlanden van 1815* (Boom Jur. 2016).

middle class, were displeased with the language policy of Willem I who enforced the use of the Dutch language by the administration and, to some extent, in the schools. Also, the many restraints on liberties, such as press censorship and limitations on the right of association, vexed the Liberals.

3. This shared displeasure united the Catholics and Liberals, traditionally each a foe of the other, into a 'Monster Coalition' (*monsterverbond*) against the absolutist reign of Willem I, strikingly described by Thorbecke as a 'Napoleonic State with a constitutional façade'.

Initially, this Monster Coalition of Catholics and Liberals opposed the King within the limits of the law, aiming at institutional reforms within the constitutional framework, and not at separatism. The working class, however, was more willing to rebel: they faced greater suffering in miserable living conditions brought on by unemployment and food shortages, and they were influenced by the successful July-Revolution in France. The opera, 'La Muette de Portici', performed in Brussels on 25 August 1830 on the King's 59th birthday, and glorifying the fight for independence by Napoleon against Spanish rule, sparked riots against Willem's reign. The reaction of Willem I was, at first, hesitant and, then, unsuccessful. Furthermore, because European powers wanted to avoid at all costs another European war, Willem I found no support with them. The leaders of the official opposition then became revolutionaries. In September 1830, a provisional government was formed, proclaiming the independence of Belgium on 4 October 1830. It also appointed a committee of lawyers to draw up a constitution and issued decrees guaranteeing rights and liberties and prohibiting restrictions on them.

On 3 November 1830, the National Congress was elected by 30,000 electors (approximately 1% of the Belgian population). It debated the draft constitution for two and a half months. The National Congress also proclaimed the independence of Belgium and denied the House of Oranje-Nassau any authority over Belgium in perpetuity. On 22 November 1830, the Congress proclaimed Belgium to be a 'constitutional, representative and hereditary monarchy'. The German prince, Leopold of Saxe-Coburg Gotha, was asked to be the first King of Belgium and was sworn in on 21 July 1831.

On 7 February 1831, the Constitution was promulgated by the National Congress, entering into force on 25 February 1831. About 40% of the constitutional provisions are more or less copies of the 1815 Constitution of the United Kingdom of the Netherlands. About 35% stem from the French Charter of 1830 and 10% from the 1791 French Constitution. Not more than 10% of the constitutional provisions were new or original. Nevertheless, at that time the Belgian Constitution was innovative due to the way of combining those diverse constitutional texts into one, unique, Belgian Constitution. It therefore served as an example for many other constitutions of the time, such as those of Spain (1837), Greece (1844 and 1864), Italy, the Netherlands, and Luxemburg (all 1848), Prussia (1850) and Romania (1866).

4. The Belgian Constitution cannot hide from its heritage as a reaction against the absolutist reign of Willem I. It establishes a parliamentary monarchy, where the King does not bear any political responsibility, but has to act under ministerial responsibility (Article 88 Constitution). All acts and decrees issuing from the King must therefore be countersigned by a Minister (Article 106 Constitution). New for that time was the severe curtailment of the powers of the King, for he has no other powers than those attributed to him by the Constitution or by specific Acts (Article 105 Constitution). The King must execute and implement Acts without suspending them (Article 108 Constitution). The Legislature, considered as the emanation of the Nation by being elected, has the residual powers. The Constitution reposes great confidence in the Judicial Branch, making it independent of the Executive Branch, and establishing it as a third power in the constitutional framework. The courts have jurisdiction to decide all disputes concerning individual rights, irrespective of the nature of the parties (government or citizens). The judiciary also has jurisdiction to review administrative acts: courts and tribunals may only enforce regulations or orders which are in accordance with the law (Article 159 Constitution). It is not for the King, as under the reign of Willem I, but for the highest court of ordinary jurisdiction, the Court of Cassation (*Hof van Cassatie / Cour de Cassation*), to settle jurisdictional disputes between the ordinary courts and the administrative authorities or courts.

5. One of the oldest constitutions still in force, the Belgian Constitution was quite stable from a formal point of view. It was amended for the first time in 1893. Since then it has undergone several changes, with substantial amendments beginning to occur in the latter decades of the twentieth century and carrying through into the twenty-first century.

The first two modifications (1893, 1920–1921) democratised the Belgian Constitution. In 1830, the National Congress deemed that only certain people were capable of participating in political life. In accordance with the mentality of the time, only those who held property were said to have rights needing defence against the State. Consequently, the electoral system of 1831 conferred the right to vote on those who paid at least a set amount of taxes. In 1848, the franchise was broadened by reducing this minimum requirement.

The revolutionary spirit in Europe, and street riots and political strikes organised by the Socialist Party, convinced the Belgian government to modify the Constitution and reform further the electoral system. The implementation in 1893 of universal suffrage (for men at least 25 years old) appeased the working class for a few decades. The electoral system, however, still upheld the right of plural voting and thus the political control by the upper-middle class: persons having a certain level of wealth (according to property or taxes paid), persons having a diploma of higher education, or those occupying certain offices could receive up to two additional votes. Voting was compulsory, for it was assumed that this would benefit the moderate parties.

The working class would not accept this right of plural voting for much longer, however. After the First World War, a government of national unity (the Catholic, the Liberal and the Socialist Parties) implemented the principle of 'one man, one vote'. In 1919, the first elections under a universal, single vote system were organised. The Constitution was changed only in 1921 to reflect the de facto situation guaranteeing the universal single vote system for men only. Nevertheless this constitutional provision also provided that a statute, passed by a two-thirds' majority in Parliament, could enfranchise women under the same universal single vote system. This occurred in 1948.

The constitutional reforms of 1893 and 1921 also democratised the rather elitist composition of the Senate. Table 1 outlines these evolutions to the Belgian electorate.

Table 1 Evolution of the Electorate

	Population	*Registered Voters*	*Seats (Representatives)*	*Seats (Senators) (excl. senators by right)*
1831	4,079,519	46,000	102	51
1848	4,359,090	79,076	108	54
1892	6,195,355	136,775	152	76
1894	6,341,958	1,354,891 (total votes: 2,111,127)	152	102
1919	7,577,027	2,102,710	186	120
1946	8,388,526	2,724,796	202	167
1949	8,625,084	5,635,452	212	175
1978	9,837,413	6,366,652	212	181
1981	9,848,647	6,878,141	212	181
1985	9,858,895	7,001,297	212	183
1987	9,864,751	7,044,202	212	183
1991	9,978,681	7,144,884	212	184
1995	10,139,372	7,199,010	150	71
1999	10,213,752	7,343,464	150	71
2003	10,309,725	7,570,580*	150	71
2007	10,584,534	7,720,796**	150	71
2010	10,839,905	7,767,552***	150	71
2014	11,132,269	8,008,776****	150	60
2019	11,413,203	8,167,709*****	150	60

Source: Min. Internal Affairs.
* incl. 114,620 Belgian nationals residing abroad
** incl. 122,150 Belgian nationals residing abroad
*** incl. 42,089 Belgian nationals residing abroad
**** incl. 128,902 Belgian nationals residing abroad
***** incl. 177,907 Belgian nationals residing abroad

Four full constitutional restructurings ('State Reforms') (1970, 1980, 1988 and 1993), a fifth State Reform in 2001 without a corresponding amendment to the Constitution, and a Sixth State Reform in 2014 have transformed Belgium from a unitary, decentralised State into a federal State sui generis. This federal State ensures the autonomy and peaceful coexistence of two different cultures while safeguarding the rights of linguistic and ideological minorities. As a result of six significant restructurings of the State in forty years, the Constitution may have lost its characteristic as 'stable', arguably undermining its authority as the supreme rule in the Belgian constitutional system.[3] But an enduring characteristic of the Belgian Constitution is that it enumerates the fundamental principles of the constitutional system in a concise way. Through an evolutionary and teleological interpretation, the Constitution has acquired the necessary flexibility to adjust to changing political circumstances.[4]

Due to those fundamental institutional reforms, the Constitution as a document was becoming quite unreadable. In 1994 a parliamentary co-ordination committee reviewed and formally renumbered the Constitution, producing the (current) version, consolidated as of 17 February 1994.

§2. Characteristics of the Belgian State

6. In 1831, Belgium was declared to be: (i) a *rechtsstaat* (a 'state under the rule of law'), (ii) upholding the principle of the separation of powers as well as (iii) the concept of national sovereignty. It was (iv) a parliamentary monarchy, and (v) a unitary, decentralised State. Constitutional reform in the late nineteenth and twentieth centuries transformed Belgium into a democratic, federal State. The following is a brief outline of those basic features of the Belgian constitutional system, to be developed further in succeeding chapters.

I. Rechtsstaat, Constitutionalism and the Rule of Law

7. Belgium is said to be a '*Rechtsstaat*', a rather difficult term to translate into a single English word. Broadly, it means a state where all governmental actions must have a basis, a foundation, in valid law. It ensures that citizens are subject not to arbitrary rules, but to fixed, general, impersonal and predictable ones. In this sense, the term approaches the English legal concept of the 'rule of law'. Originally, the *Rechtsstaat* concept aimed to protect citizens against excesses by the Executive Branch, obliging the Executive to act within the limits of the Constitution and the law. Nowadays, this concept demands that all three branches of State

3. Since 2003, governments have wanted to change even the amending process of the Constitution (Art. 195, Constitution), to facilitate constitutional reforms. A transitional arrangement to the amending procedure of the Constitution (limited in time and only applicable to the implementation of the Sixth State Reform) was also inserted in 2012.
4. A striking example of this flexibility is the evolution in the powers of the King: Belgium evolved from an 'orleanistic monarchy', in which the King exercised personal power, to a constitutional monarchy in which he has only influence, but no power.

power, Executive, Legislative and Judicial, comply with the law, of which the Constitution is the highest. The aim of the *Rechtsstaat* concept is the safeguarding of the fundamental rights and liberties of citizens.[5] Therefore, it implies the necessity of respecting the separation of powers (ii) and the hierarchy of legal rules, since those institutional principles also aim at guaranteeing the fundamental rights and liberties of citizens. Since Title II (Belgians and Their Rights) precedes Title III (Organs of State), the structure of the Belgian Constitution implies a priority of rights and liberties in the institutional framework and the obligation of all organs of State to respect fundamental rights.

The 1831 Constitution guaranteed the classic liberal political and civil liberties, primarily used as a protection against the State. The 1831 Constitution was quite innovative: rights and liberties were incorporated into the text of the Constitution itself to make them binding law. In other contemporary constitutions, a separate Bill of Rights contained those rights and liberties, enumerating 'philosophical' principles. The 1831 Constitution was undoubtedly inspired by the English Constitution; so much that A.V. Dicey called it 'an admirable summary of the leading maxims of English constitutionalism'.[6] Distrust of the Executive Branch led to conferring the power of enforcement of these rights and liberties on the Legislature and the Judiciary. The Legislative Branch has the power to regulate the use of these fundamental rights. The Judicial Branch is entitled – and even obliged – to refuse to apply any regulations or orders violating these constitutional rights (Article 159 Constitution). It may order an authority acting unlawfully, infringing on the fundamental rights of a citizen, to pay damages (Article 1382 Civil Code) and may impose any lawfully prescribed penalties for an infringement of fundamental rights.

Modern constitutions often also contain cultural, social and economic rights, compelling the State to protect its citizens or to guarantee human dignity. After several draft proposals and a long deliberation about its scope and enforceability, Article 23 of the Constitution was incorporated in 1994 guaranteeing every person the right to lead a life in dignity. The Article safeguards labour rights, rights to social security, health protection, social, legal and medical assistance, rights to proper housing, a right to a healthy environment and the right to cultural and social development, and the right to child allowance.[7] These social, economic and cultural rights cannot, however, be enforced in the same way as the classic liberal civil and political rights. Article 23 of the Constitution does not have direct application, but has a standstill effect on the State: the State is obliged to safeguard existing levels of protection of certain social, economic and cultural rights. But according to the caselaw of the Constitutional Court, only a considerable decline in protection represents an

5. See A. Alen & W. Verrijdt, 'The Rule of Law in the Case Law of the Belgian Constitutional Court: History and Challenges' in *International Conference of the Constitutional Court of the Republic of Slovenia – 25 Years* 91–120 (J. Sovdat ed., Bled 2016).
6. A.V. Dicey, *Introduction to the Study of the Law of the Constitution* (10th ed) 204–205 (E. Wade ed. and intro., MacMillan 1965).
7. Added in 2014 after the 2014 Sixth State Reform.

infringement of Article 23, one which can yet be justified by reasons of the common good.[8] For example, in 2018 the Court annulled an Act which entailed a marked reduction in the provision of legal aid and which could not otherwise be justified by reasons of the common good.[9]

8. The Legislature was always obliged to respect the fundamental rights guaranteed by the Constitution, and – until 1980 – the Belgian legal system rejected judicial review of the constitutionality of legislation. In view of the internationalisation of legal guarantees of fundamental rights, however, this principle was challenged. Belgium is a party to the EConvHR, the ICCPR, the ICESCR and several other international instruments on human rights. Belgium has thereby accepted the jurisdiction of the ECtHR. In 1971, the Court of Cassation ruled that self-executing treaties have priority over national law, implying that all courts may decline to apply Acts violating internationally guaranteed fundamental rights.[10] As Belgium developed into a federal State, the Constitutional Court was created.[11] Its authority was originally limited to reviewing the Acts of the federal Parliament and of the Region and Community Parliaments for their compatibility with the rules on the division of powers. But as of 1989, any party having the necessary standing could petition that Court to review legislation for compatibility with the division of powers, and with three exhaustively listed fundamental rights, namely the principle of equality, the principle of non-discrimination and the freedom of education. In 2003, the jurisdiction of the Court was again extended: it may review legislation for compatibility with all the rights and liberties enumerated in Title II of the Constitution, and with Articles 170, 172 and 191 of the Constitution. This evolution transformed the Court into a true 'Constitutional Court', which, since 7 May 2007, bears precisely that name. In 2014 the Court was granted jurisdiction to review statutes for violations of the principle of federal loyalty, to conduct 'a priori' reviews of the constitutionality of regional consultative referenda, and to review decisions sanctioning MPs for their exceeding campaign finance restrictions in federal elections.

In summary, Belgium is a *Rechtsstaat* limiting the powers of the organs of State through the Constitution and guaranteeing fundamental rights. Citizens can seek redress for infringements of constitutional and fundamental rights. Constitutional provisions regarding the organisation of State institutions aim at the core idea of the Constitution: to secure fundamental rights. The cornerstone of these provisions is the principle of the separation of powers.

8. See, e.g., Cons., Judgments No. 135 and 137/2006, 14 Sep. 2006; No. 182/2008, 18 Dec. 2008; No. 135/2011, 27 Jul. 2011; No. 18/2018, 22 Feb. 2018, and No 86/2018, 5 Jul. 2018.
9. Cons., Judgment No. 77/2018, 21 Jun. 2018 (first annulment in that respect based on Art. 23 Constitution).
10. Cass., 27 May 1971 (*N.V. Fromagerie Franco–Suisse Le Ski*), *J.T.*, 1971, 460.
11. Originally called the 'Arbitragehof / Cour d'arbitrage' (literally translated 'the Court of Arbitration'), but later renamed the 'Constitutional Court': *Gazette,* 8 May 2007.

II. The Separation of Powers

9. The Belgian Constituent Assembly instituted a division of tasks among the three branches of State power. Applying Montesquieu's theory on the separation of powers, it divided State functions into the Legislative, the Executive and the Judicial. This specialisation and division of tasks, enhancing 'the efficient management' of a State, prevents an excessive concentration of power in the hands of one body which might lead to violations of the fundamental rights of citizens. Furthermore, the separation of powers particularly matched the prevailing liberal economic and political philosophy, which held that (wealthy) citizens were to enhance their welfare themselves, and which generally considered any intervention by the State to be undesirable, and a strong unified central power to be potentially dangerous.

10. A prime feature of most modern constitutions, the principle of the separation of powers of course has its place in the Belgian constitutional system. In Belgian law, the separation of powers is an unwritten binding general principle of law, underlying various constitutional provisions. Unlike the 1791 French Constitution, the Belgian Constitution implemented the 'separation' of powers as a form of 'equilibrium' of powers[12]: the principle that each power is independent in its own sphere of operation, yet is not absolutely so. Firstly, there is no rigid delimitation of an 'exclusive sphere for each power' in which the other powers have no authority to act. A separation of powers only means that the Legislature, the Executive and the Judiciary exercise mainly those tasks which are inherent in their principal function. Secondly, the 'independence' of each power within its principal function is relative because an optimal functioning of the State presupposes a close co-operation of all three powers. These powers are indeed interdependent by nature. In the Belgian constitutional system, the King is head of the Executive and is one of the branches of the Legislature, since legislative authority is exercised collectively by the King and by (at least one House of) Parliament. The Constituent Assembly considered the King to be a stabilising factor in the three constitutional powers. Thirdly, the separation of powers involves the principle of checks and balances. Each branch of the State is independent in its own sphere but is subject to review by another branch. The Executive is accountable to Parliament. Article 159 of the Constitution forbids a judge to apply any regulation or order which violates constitutional rights.

11. The Constituent Assembly had already maintained a nuanced principle of the separation of powers, and this subtlety increased with the subsequent fundamental changes to the Belgian political and constitutional system. In present constitutional practice, the principle of the 'equilibrium' of powers outweighs by far the principle of the 'separation' of powers. This latter principle has indeed lost most of its importance in the relation between the Legislative and the Executive Branches. As in other countries, power has shifted from the Legislative to the Executive. For the Executive, the principle of the separation of powers implies that it is bound by the rule of law; that it can only act upon a constitutional or legislative basis, and that, while implementing an Act, it is confined to the limits set by the Legislature. In the

12. Cass., 28 Sep. 2006 (*Ferrara*), *J.T.*, 2006, 594.

nineteenth century, 'His Majesty's Government' and Parliament opposed each other vigorously. But as the effective power of the King waned, the Executive Branch came to represent simply a parliamentary majority. As the liberal State attending to but a limited number of tasks made way for the welfare State, the Executive Branch was soon considered to be the more appropriate body to solve increasingly complex problems (e.g., balancing the interests of the various pressure groups). Nowadays most legislation originates from the Executive Branch, and is quite often adopted without any amendments. This shift in power culminated in the mid-1980s and mid-1990s, when the government was temporarily granted legislative powers in broad areas to tackle economic problems, or to satisfy the Euro-criteria and to become part of the Eurozone. The government issued 'Special Royal Decrees', avoiding hereby 'cumbersome' legislative procedures. In the 'existential' debate on the contemporary role of Parliament following, most constitutionalists agreed that Parliament was mainly a body for monitoring government activities.

12. The contemporary meaning of the separation of powers is still strongest in the relation between the Legislative and the Executive Branches on the one hand, and the Judicial on the other. We stressed above that, in response to previous excesses, the National Congress had drafted a number of constitutional provisions to guarantee the real independence of the Judiciary. The constitutional provision explicitly authorising and compelling courts and tribunals to refuse the application of regulations and orders which are illegal (Article 159 Constitution) is probably the best example of the meaning of the system of 'checks and balances' which a separation of powers implies.

13. As Belgium evolved from a unitary decentralised State into a federal State, the principle of the separation of powers acquired an extra 'vertical' dimension: powers were further divided between the Legislature, the Executive and the Judiciary at the federal level, and between the Legislature and the Executive at the level of the federated entities, namely the Communities and the Regions.

III. National Sovereignty

14. One of the cornerstones of Belgian democracy is the constitutional provision that all powers stem from the Nation (Article 33 Constitution). It refers to the 'metaphysical' foundation of the Belgian constitutional system: the concept of national sovereignty. Sovereignty refers to the supreme authority within the State having the power to determine its form of government, its constitutional system. In Belgium, this authority is exercised by 'the Nation', an abstract, indivisible collectivity comprising the citizens of the past, the present, and the future. The branches of government may only act as 'representatives' of the Nation, in the name and on behalf of the Nation. They indeed are not sovereign because they cannot set the limits to their authority on their own, being subordinate to the Constitution. The sovereignty of the Nation is exclusive, since no other branch or organ besides those attributed with authority by the Constitution may claim to exercise sovereignty.

'Sovereignty is indivisible, inalienable and not subject to any limitation.' Fundamentally, sovereignty belongs to the Nation as such, who may always reconfigure it through a revision of the Constitution. Article 33 also holds that public power must be exercised in the manner laid down by the Constitution, thereby prohibiting a delegation by the *trias politica* of the core of their functions. The national sovereignty doctrine was a reaction against previous constitutional systems lacking sufficient safeguards for the freedoms and fundamental rights of the citizens. In those systems, all powers stemmed from the King, who claimed that sovereignty was bestowed on him by the grace of God. As the State can no longer be identified with the King, he being but a constitutional body of the State, this concept implies that the King has no other powers than those vested in him by the Constitution and that his actions are subject to the rule of law.

15. Furthermore, the sovereignty of the Nation, based on Sieyès' ideas, is different from the sovereignty of the people. The latter implies that each citizen takes part in the collective power, either directly, by way of a referendum, or indirectly, by way of orders to the parliamentary representative he elects. The 1831 National Congress did not have such a broad view of democracy as Rousseau's concept of 'the sovereignty of the people' would automatically entail. The Constituent Assembly did not consider the franchise to be a right, but rather a function which had to be exercised in the interests of the Nation. According to liberal philosophy, only the people who had an interest to defend against the State were entitled to exercise the franchise.

The Constitution further ensures the interest of the Nation by protecting it from the (short-term) interests of the electorate. Parliamentarians are not representatives of the voters, of the people, but of the Nation: they decide freely. The electorate thus cannot give any specific orders to its representatives in Parliament and the Constitution excludes any implementation of direct democracy. A specific feature of this is laid down in the constitutional provision stipulating that Members of Parliament represent the Nation and not only those who elected them (Article 42 Constitution). This provision was a reaction against the 'regionalism' which had been one of the important causes of the failure of a previous attempt to set up a Belgian State in a revolution against the Austrian Emperor Joseph II. Members of Parliament have to bear in mind the interests of the Nation rather than those of the individual constituencies as the ground of their decisions.

But the process of federalisation has impaired this principle, because the Members of both Houses of Parliament are divided into French and Dutch language groups (Article 43 Constitution). For the adoption of Special Majority Acts, Members of Parliament represent both the Belgian Nation and their particular language group. Since the 2014 Sixth State Reform, fifty (of the sixty) senators are now appointed by and from out of the Parliaments of the federated entities, namely the Communities and the Regions (Article 67 Constitution). As such, they are above all representatives of their respective linguistic communities.

On the basis of its residuary powers, Parliament has only once taken the exceptional step of authorising a consultative referendum. It occurred in 1950 and concerned the 'Monarchy Crisis' which plunged the country into a deep crisis. Constitutionally, there is an irrefutable presumption that the decisions of Parliament reflect the will of the Nation, therefore decisions of Parliament cannot be challenged by way of a referendum. Later the Constitution authorised the Regions, the provinces and the municipalities to organise consultative referenda (Articles 39*bis* and 41 Constitution). Although 'the representatives of the sovereign Nation' cannot turn themselves into 'sovereign representatives of the Nation', since they must act within the limits set by the Constitution, it should be stressed that the interpretation of the Constitution by Parliament carries great weight. Unlike the Executive, the Legislative Branch has only been subjected to constitutional review from 1980. Also on the basis of its residuary powers, Parliament has more than once filled certain 'gaps' in the Constitution.

16. Increased internationalisation and the creation of supranational public law organisations (such as the EU) have further undermined the concept of national sovereignty. A partial delegation of national sovereignty was incompatible with Article 33 of the Constitution, therefore necessitating the incorporation of a new provision (Article 34) in the Constitution. This article allows a treaty or an Act to charge institutions under international public law with the exercise of a part of national sovereignty. It should be stressed that the exercise of sovereignty may be conferred only as to some matters. These matters have to be spelled out precisely in the relevant treaty or Act. Only under these conditions can the constitutional provisions dealing with the powers affected be held in suspense.[13] Sovereignty itself is not delegated, so that if the international institution disappears, the powers will automatically revert to the Nation. According to the Constitutional Court, Article 34 of the Constitution does not permit a discriminatory derogation from national identity enshrined in fundamental constitutional and political structures or from the core values of the protections provided by the Constitution.[14]

IV. A Constitutional Monarchy

17. The Provisional Government and the Constituent Assembly almost unanimously preferred a monarchy to a republic, thus avoiding offence to the superpowers of the day – all being monarchies. A consolidation of Belgian independence would only succeed if it had their support or consent. The National Congress chose the German Prince Leopold von Saxe-Coburg Gotha, widower of the English Crown Princess Charlotte – an ideal compromise acceptable to both England and Prussia. The National Congress further opted for a hereditary monarchy, the monarchy being considered as the living symbol of the continuity of the Nation as opposed to the (ever) alternating representatives of the Nation. To ensure the continuity of the monarchy, the person of the King was held to be inviolable on the civil, criminal and political levels; only his Ministers would be accountable (Article 88 Constitution). Under Article 106 of the Constitution, no act of the King, having

13. See Council of State, Legislative Division, Opinion of 18 Jan. 2008, *Parliamentary Documents (Senate)* 2007–08, No. 4–568/1, 339–340 (regarding approval of the Lisbon Treaty).
14. Cons., Judgment No. 62/2016, 28 Apr. 2016, para. B.8.7.

direct or indirect political repercussions, would be effective unless a Minister assumed the political responsibility for it in Parliament. There were and are no exceptions to this rule.

18. This does not mean that the King has a purely representative function. Undoubtedly, the first Belgian kings did have considerable power in certain areas. King Leopold I, whose second wife was the daughter of the French King, almost unilaterally determined his government's foreign policy. His privileged contacts with the royal courts and influential foreign political circles of the day were vital for the survival of the Belgian State. As long as there were no strong political parties with well-defined programs, the King also determined the composition of 'his' government. As political parties emerged and developed over the 1880s, the need to respect the parliamentary majority limited his power to appoint and dismiss Ministers (Article 96 Constitution). This led to the disappearance of the 'antagonism' between Parliament and government: government and Parliament became each other's allies, since the former was now a reflection of the parliamentary majority. Also the impact of the King on the government's agenda gradually diminished, as the role of the 'Chef de cabinet' (later, the Prime Minister) who presided over the Council of Ministers instead of the King became ever more important.

The King has the power to dissolve Parliament (Article 46 Constitution). The Constituent Assembly conferred this power on the King to enable him to settle conflicts between Parliament and the government. This power was limited in 1993 so as to increase the stability of Parliament and the government, as has the power of Parliament to dismiss a government. Nowadays it has become very infrequent for the government to find itself backed by a minority in Parliament. Governments almost invariably tender their resignation as a result of a fracturing of the government coalition.

King Leopold II retained much influence in some areas, such as town planning. He acquired a private colony, the Congo, which on his death was bequeathed to the Belgian State. King Albert I personally and successfully commanded his troops during the First World War and undertook some personal diplomatic initiatives. This led to the belief that 'foreign affairs and defence' were 'privileged areas' comparable to the doctrine of the so-called '*domaine reservé*' of the French President, a field in which a Belgian king could exercise a high degree of autonomy, or to the 'crown prerogative' in the United Kingdom. The exercise of this royal authority by King Leopold III during the Second World War created a deep conflict between the King and his government. This constitutional crisis removed the last elements of 'orleanism' still present in the Belgian monarchy. As it now stands, the 'King has no power but (only) influence.' The current constitutional role of a king in a constitutional monarchy is aptly summarised by Bagehot, 'He has the right to be consulted, to encourage and to warn.'[15] As head of the Executive Branch, the King has access to all documents regarding the decisions taken within the Council of Ministers. He is in weekly contact with the Prime Minister and frequently grants audiences to other Ministers and to prominent figures from diplomatic, academic, economic and political circles. Most of the Belgian monarchs have enjoyed long

---

15. W. Bagehot, *The English Constitution* 75 (Garland 1978).

reigns. Albert II held the throne since the death of his brother, Boudewijn, in 1993. In July 2013, Albert II abdicated (citing age-related reasons) in favour of his eldest son, Filip I / Philippe I who took the oath of office on 21 July 2013. Filip is the seventh Belgian monarch. This experience, together with the fact that the King is a neutral person not being bound by any political party, nor being part of any linguistic or cultural community, means that his advice may carry considerable weight, depending on his wisdom, experience and personality. However, his advice is not binding and the government may or may not follow it.

The King may initiate certain developments or warn against certain consequences. This role of the King may be more important than in other countries having a constitutional monarchy for two reasons. Firstly, due to the electoral system based on proportional representation, it is virtually impossible for a single party to govern alone, which means that since 1921 Belgium has almost always had coalition governments. Secondly, the cultural, political and economic differences among Belgium's linguistic communities render the King important. Because of his neutral stance, he has a central mediating, unifying role bridging the cultural, political and economic differences among those linguistic communities. To outsiders, his role is most apparent in the process of forming a government, but the King also exercises influence when there is no government crisis. Nowadays, this influence has become very discreet, since both the King and the government are bound by constitutional secrecy so as not to 'expose the Crown'.

V. From a Unitary Decentralised State to a Federal State

19. In 1831, Belgium was conceived as a unitary decentralised State. It had a central government, provinces and municipalities. The Constituent Assembly, afraid of the excesses of Jacobin centralism, created the provinces and municipalities as not purely territorial subdivisions but also as (subordinate) governments. Their general, unspecified jurisdiction over 'all matters of provincial and municipal concern' (Articles 41 and 162 Constitution) has been defined more and more strictly by the higher-level authorities exercising administrative supervision over all acts of these subordinate governments.

Belgium is no longer a unitary State. It has joined that group of nations which have tried to solve internal conflicts caused by linguistic-cultural differences by granting greater autonomy to those different groups. Belgium has peacefully evolved into a federal State with federated entities (Communities, Regions), each having its own legislature, executive, and civil service, and having jurisdiction over educational, cultural and economic matters.

20. Belgium is situated at the intersection of the Latin and the Germanic cultures, and has been divided along by a language boundary since 5 AD. This divides the nation into two different cultural and linguistic communities: the Flemish and the Walloons. The extant linguistic-cultural differences have been accentuated by the divergent economic development of the two communities. In 1831, the once-thriving region of Flanders was economically underdeveloped, whereas the then internationally renowned Walloon coal and steel industry had brought economic prosperity to the region. These socio-economic differences still exist now, but the situation has been reversed.

The socio-economic differences in turn marked out religious differences, the rural areas of Flanders being a traditional stronghold of the Catholic Church (and Party), whereas the industrial cities of Wallonia were Socialist strongholds. In 1831, this heterogeneity was not apparent at first, or at least did not clearly manifest itself politically. The leaders of the revolution were homogeneously French-speaking. This can be explained by the fact that the elite holding political power were French-speaking both in Wallonia and in Flanders, French being the cultural and political world language of the time. In Flanders, the language barrier indeed ran along social class: the upper-middle class speaking French, the lower class speaking Flemish. 'French in the parlor; Flemish in the kitchen.'[16] Because this (predominantly) French elite asserted a monopoly of political power through the electoral system, of course Belgium originated as a unitary decentralised State and as an officially French-speaking Nation. Nevertheless, it was and is a constitutional principle that the use of the languages spoken in Belgium is free and that this may be regulated only by an Act regarding the administration of public affairs and in judicial proceedings (Article 30 Constitution). This provision was originally a reaction against William I's unsuccessful attempts to stamp out the influence of French. For the National Congress, it was clear that the way would be open for future legislation to impose the exclusive use of French. And a Provisional Government Decree of 16 November 1830 did indeed make French the sole official language. It was not until 1967 that an authentic Dutch language version of the Constitution was produced. And an authentic German version of the Constitution was promulgated only in 1991.

21. In the beginning, the Flemish Movement had very moderate demands, in particular the recognition in Flanders of Dutch on an equal basis with French, under the slogan, 'The language is the whole Nation.' This moderation was partly due to the fact that political debate after the unionist period with the 'Monster Coalition' was mainly dominated by the antagonism between Catholics and Liberals and focused on the relationship between Church and State. This prevented the development of a broad pluralistic Flemish Movement. In order to appease the Flemish, certain Language Acts were passed. They imposed the use of the Dutch language in Flanders (unless the person concerned explicitly requested French) in criminal (1873) and in administrative matters (1878) as well as in education (1883). In practice, these Language Acts were rarely applied. The Flemish Movement, however, gained new momentum together with the Social Movement. Both movements are to some extent interrelated. The extension of the franchise through the 1893 and 1921 revisions of the Constitution boosted the Flemish Movement since the majority of the Belgian population was Flemish. The dominance of the French language was also a barrier to upward social mobility because French was the language in public

16. V. Lorwin, 'Belgium: Religion, Class and Language in National Politics', in *Political Oppositions in Western Democracies* 159 (R. Dahl ed., London UP 1966).

life. When, after the First World War, the trade unions and the employers (who during the time of the occupation had co-operated well with each other) concluded a 'social pact', the class issue no longer dominated the political scene and the 'Flemish question' thus became a live political issue.

22. The Equal Treatment Act of 18 April 1898, which required Acts of Parliament to be voted, assented, promulgated and published in both French and Dutch, was the first in a series of important victories for the Flemish Movement. The next step was that the teaching in and of Dutch was no longer limited to primary schools, enabling a Flemish elite to develop. Language-use legislation provoked a reaction on the part of the Walloons, and for the first time, some Walloons called for federalism. The Walloon Socialist leader, Jules Destree, presaged the danger in a lengthy 1912 letter to King Albert I which included the famous words, 'Sire, You reign over two peoples. In Belgium, there are Walloons and Flemish; there are no Belgians.'

23. The 1932 language-use legislation laid the foundations of the territoriality principle, holding that in unilingual regions the use of a given language was compulsory for all public acts, regardless of the level of government they issued from. After the Second World War, the Flemish Movement was temporarily restrained, because of Belgian national feeling fuelled by the war, and because the Flemish Movement was discredited by the collaboration of a minority of Flemish activists with the Germans. The three issues dividing Belgian political life, namely class, religion and language, merged dangerously during the Monarchy Crisis in which the country had to decide upon the return of the King, Leopold III, who had resided abroad during the war. In a consultative referendum, an overwhelming majority of the conservative Catholic Flemish favoured the return of King, as against the majority of the Walloon Socialists opposing it. It brought the country to the brink of civil war. Ultimately, a 'Belgian compromise' was worked out: the King abdicated and the monarchy remained as an institution.

Belgian political life is truly characterised by a long-standing 'elitist consensus', the majority (almost) always trying to find a solution acceptable to the minority and not hampering the latter's vital interests. Whenever this political rule of thumb is violated, very pointed conflicts arise. This is clearly illustrated by the Monarchy Crisis and the subsequent Schools Conflict which concerned the respective roles of the State and the Church in education. In the latter dispute, Catholics on the one hand and Socialists and Liberals on the other tried to impose their point of view. Eventually peace was achieved by virtue of the 'Schools Pact'. Appeasement in both class and religion issues brought once more the language issue to the political forefront in the early 1960s.

24. The 1962–1963 language laws demarcated a language boundary which would no longer be changed by periodic 'language census'. Such a recurring census was prejudicial to the Flemish because the many French-speaking people moving to the originally Flemish outskirts of Brussels led to a 'Frenchification' of the Brussels suburbs. The language laws redefined the administrative boundaries of provinces, administrative districts and municipalities accordingly, and divided the country into four language regions. There were three unilingual language regions: the Dutch language region, the French language region, and the German language region. The fourth was the bilingual Brussels-Capital region. In theory, all public acts in the unilingual regions had to be implemented solely in the language proper to that region. Only in the bilingual Brussels-Capital region were French and Dutch on a completely equal footing.

25. The division of Belgium into four language regions was enshrined in the 1970 Constitution. Any modification of the boundaries to these regions now requires a Special Majority Act (Article 4 Constitution). Until 1970, the language boundary was not very relevant in terms of the institutional framework. Subsequent amendments of the Constitution, however, gradually established federated entities: three Communities competent for educational and for cultural matters (thus meeting the Flemish demand for cultural autonomy), and three Regions competent in economic matters (meeting the demands on the part of the Walloons). The need for economic autonomy must be understood against the backdrop of a changed pattern of economic development in the Regions. Whereas the formerly prosperous Wallonia gradually declined economically, Flanders became an economically thriving region. Combined with divergent ideas held by the regional political parties on the economic policies to be pursued, this ultimately led the Walloons to believe that it would be better to take their economic future into their own hands. In order to allay Walloon fears of ending up in a permanent minority position, important safeguards were provided in national decision-making, in the spirit of the 'elitist consensus' so typical of Belgian politics. The resulting complex new institutional framework will be dealt with below in Pt. III.

§3. State Territory

26. Belgium is a small, densely populated European country bordering on the Netherlands, Germany, Luxembourg and France, and has a rather short North Sea coast (65 km / 40 miles). It covers an area of 30,686 km^2 (the continental shelf and territorial waters having an area of 2,017 km^2). Under the provisions of the Montego Bay Treaty of 10 December 1982 on the new Law of the Sea, Belgium delimited its territorial waters at 12 nautical miles (22.224 km).[17] Belgium has also demarcated its continental shelf[18] and has reserved a fishery zone for the Belgian and EU fishing fleet as well.[19] Though the territorial waters and the continental shelf as such are not part of the territory of the Belgian State, it does exercise a limited sovereignty over them. Since 1 January 1989, the Flemish Region is entitled to carry out such works and activities in territorial waters and on the continental shelf as may be required for the exercise of its jurisdiction over public works and transport (Article 6 X, Special Majority Act on Institutional Reform).

17. Act of 6 October 1987, *Gazette*, 22 Oct. 1987.
18. Act of 13 June 1969, *Gazette*, 8 Oct. 1969.
19. Act of 10 October 1978, *Gazette*, 28 Dec. 1978.

27. It was not until 1839 that the boundaries of Belgian territory were fixed, this being at the signing of the Peace Treaty of London between the Kingdom of the Netherlands and Belgium. According to its provisions, to which Belgium had no choice but to adhere, part of the Province of Limburg was attached to the Netherlands; Belgium retained only the Walloon part of Luxembourg, and the other part became a Grand-Duchy within the German Confederation. After World War I, Germany had to give up neutral Moresnet and the districts of Eupen, Malmedy and Sankt-Vith in accordance with the provisions of the 1919 Versailles Treaty. Eupen, Sankt-Vith and Moresnet (now Kelmis) are now part of the small Belgian German language region (of some 77,000 inhabitants).

28. In 1893, a fourth paragraph was added to Article 1 of the Constitution stating, 'The colonies, overseas possessions or protectorates that Belgium may acquire, are subject to specific Acts. Belgian troops raised for their defence, may only be recruited on the basis of voluntary enlistment.' On a personal initiative of Leopold II, Belgium acquired the colony of Congo, which was subsequently renamed the Republic of Zaire and later adopted its former name, the Democratic Republic of Congo. The sovereignty of Leopold II over the territory of Congo was internationally recognised at the Congress of Berlin in 1885. The Belgian Parliament subsequently granted permission as required by Article 87 of the Constitution for the King to become also the Head of another State. King Leopold II thus became Head of State of the 'Association internationale du Congo.' In 1908, just before the King's death, a Treaty transferred sovereignty over Congo to Belgium, which would exercise this right until the independence of Congo on 30 June 1960.

Under the terms of the 1919 Versailles Treaty, Belgium acquired the protectorate Rwanda-Urundi. This legal status was ratified by the League of Nations (31 August 1923) and by the Trust Agreement of 13 December 1946 concluded between Belgium and the United Nations. The territories became independent on 1 July 1962. As a result of the independence of its Congo colony and of its Rwanda protectorate, the fourth paragraph of Article 1 of the Constitution was deleted in 1970.

29. The main territorial subdivisions of the Belgian State are as follows:

(i) As a unitary State, Belgium was originally divided into nine provinces (Antwerp, Brabant, East Flanders, Hainaut, Liège, Limburg, Luxembourg, Namur, West Flanders). This was a legacy of the French occupation, for the provinces coincided with the French departments set up by the French central authorities. The provinces still exist but have become less important. In 1995, the Province of Brabant was divided in two: Flemish Brabant and Walloon Brabant. Brussels is no longer part of a province. As a consequence, Belgium now has ten provinces, five (Antwerp, Limburg, East Flanders, West Flanders, and Flemish Brabant) in the Flemish Region, and five (Hainaut, Liège, Luxembourg, Namur, and Walloon Brabant) in the Walloon Region (Article 5 Constitution). The provinces themselves are split up into several administrative districts with no political significance. These districts should not be confused with electoral districts or with judicial districts. The administrative districts themselves mostly consist of various municipalities. Currently some

581 out of the original 2,359 municipalities subsisting after the restructuring (which took place in 1975) do play an important role in local matters. The process of federalisation has further complicated this picture, with all previous territorial subdivisions still subsisting. The 2014 Sixth State Reform, however, made it possible for the Flemish Region and the Walloon Region to abolish by Special Majority Act the provinces and replace them with other supra-municipal authorities (Article 41 Constitution).

(ii) As noted earlier, Belgium is composed of four language regions (Article 4 Constitution): the French language region (the Provinces of Hainaut, Luxembourg, Namur, and Walloon Brabant, as well as the Province of Liège, except for the German-speaking municipalities); the Dutch language region (the Provinces of Antwerp, East Flanders, Flemish Brabant, Limburg, and West Flanders); the German language region (nine municipalities in the Province of Liège), and the bilingual Brussels-Capital region (nineteen municipalities, including the City of Brussels) (Figures 1 and 2). The concept of 'language region' is important because it indirectly determines the territorial jurisdiction of the federated entities of Belgium.

Figure 1 Language regions (north and central)

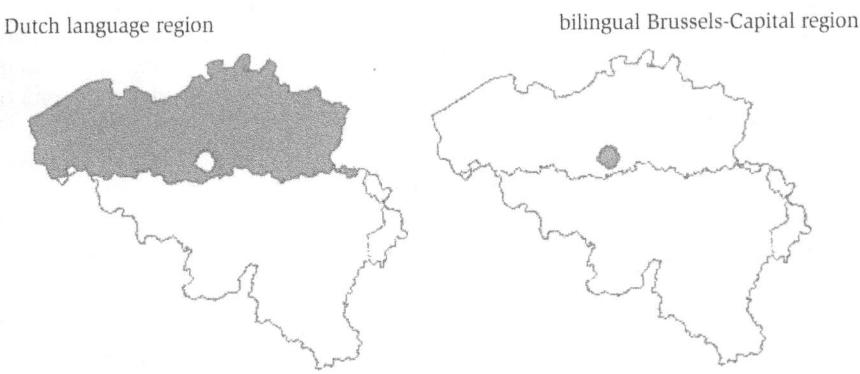

Figure 2 Language regions (south and east)

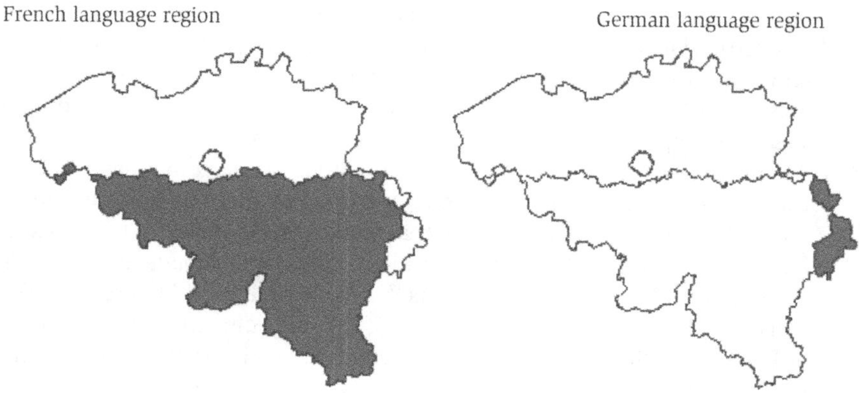

(iii) Belgium has three Communities, mainly competent for educational, cultural and person-related matters (Article 2 Constitution): the Flemish Community, the French Community and the German Community. The three Communities have exclusive jurisdiction in their respective unilingual language region (Figure 3). The Flemish Community and the French Community, on their part, also have jurisdiction in the bilingual Brussels-Capital region, depending on whether or not the relevant matter is related exclusively to the one or the other Community.

Figure 3 Communities

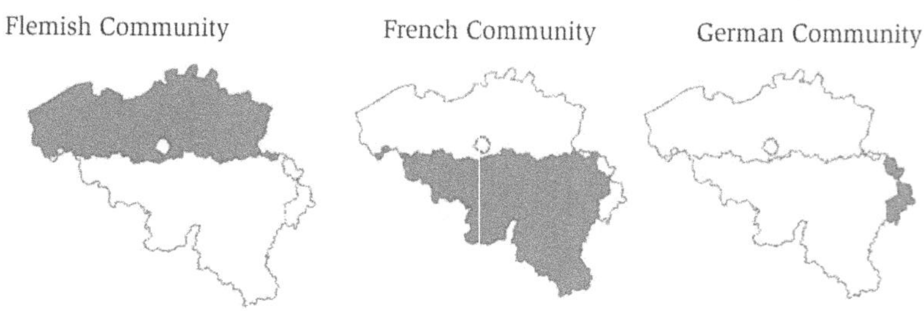

(iv) Belgium comprises three Regions having broadly defined jurisdiction in economic matters (Article 3 Constitution): the Walloon Region governing the French language region and the German language region, the Flemish Region governing the Dutch language region, and the Brussels-Capital Region governing the bilingual Brussels-Capital region. The three Regions have a territorial jurisdiction as illustrated in the map below (Figure 4).

Figure 4 Regions

§4. POPULATION AND DEMOGRAPHICS

30. The National Register of Citizens as of 1 January 2019 shows that the total population is 11,413,203, divided as follows: 6,582,788 in the Flemish Region (57.70%), 3,630,093 in the Walloon Region (and including some 77,471 making up the German Community) (31.80%) and 1,200,322 in the bilingual Brussels-Capital region (10.52%).

31. The number of foreigners living in Belgium is 1,391,425 on 1 January 2019 (12.17% of the population). The large majority thereof are EU citizens (925,140 or 66.49% of foreigners in Belgium). Some 27.12% live in Flanders; 19.32%, in Wallonia, and 20.05%, in Brussels.

Part I. Sources of Constitutional Law

32. This Part outlines the hierarchy of rules applied in the Belgian legal system. Specific sections below provide a more detailed examination of the jurisdiction and operation of the institutions issuing these rules. This Part also briefly sets out how that hierarchy is maintained.

Chapter 1. Treaties

§1. The Treaty-Making Power

33. Article 2(1)(a) of the 1969 Vienna Convention on the Law of Treaties, as adopted by the Belgian Parliament in 1992[20], defines a treaty as 'an international agreement concluded between States in written form and governed by international law, whether embodied in a single instrument or in two or more related instruments and whatsoever its particular designation'. In Belgium, the King is vested with the treaty-making power. As of 2014, treaties must be approved by the House of Representatives only. The treaty-making power is, however, not confined to the federal authorities. Article 167 §3 of the Constitution expressly empowers the Communities and Regions to conclude treaties on matters within their jurisdiction. This Article was introduced in 1993 and allows the Communities and Regions to exercise this power effectively, according to the principle *in foro interno, in foro externo.*

34. The treaty-making power of the Communities and Regions is an exclusive power, but not an absolute one. In order to guarantee the coherence of Belgian international policy, the King can stop treaty proceedings run by the Communities or Regions (Article 81 §§1–4 Special Majority Act on Institutional Reform).

As for 'mixed treaties', those dealing with matters coming under the jurisdiction of both the federal government and of the Community or Region ones, all parties concerned take part in the treaty-making decisions according to the rules prescribed by the Co-operation Agreement of 8 March 1994.[21]

35. The omission of parliamentary approval (federal, Community, or Region) renders a treaty null and void in Belgian law. Consequently, courts must refuse to enforce treaties, which have not obtained the required parliamentary approval. Nevertheless this approval is not required for certain 'executive agreements', namely if they provide only for the administrative or technical implementation of an existing treaty.[22] Executive agreements are concluded informally, for example by an exchange of diplomatic or ministerial notes or by way of a joint declaration, and as a rule, come into effect immediately.

§2. Hierarchy

36. Traditionally, there are two schools of thought as to the relationship between international law and national law. The dualism school maintains that a rule of

20. Approval of the Vienna Convention on the Law of Treaties Act of 10 June 1992, *Gazette,* 25 Dec. 1993.
21. See further below Pt. V. Ch. 1. §2. II.
22. See, in that respect, Council of State, Legislative Division, Opinion No. 42.631/AV, *Parliamentary Documents (Senate)* 2007–2008, No. 4–912/1, 15.

international law must be transformed into, brought into, the domestic legal system by national law as national law. The monism school, however, upholds the primacy of international law.

There is no provision in the Belgian Constitution determining the relationship between international law and national law. Relevant principles were, however, laid down by the Court of Cassation in the *Fromagerie Franco-Suisse Le Ski* case.[23] Before 1971, Belgium traditionally adhered to the dualistic theory, entailing that a treaty had the same legal force as any Act of Parliament. Pursuant to the principle *lex posterior priori derogat*, a treaty would prevail over the inconsistent provisions of any earlier Act, but not over statutes which subsequently came into effect. The dualistic vision is incompatible with EU law. In the *Le Ski* decision, the Court of Cassation ruled that a self-executing treaty prevails over both former and later statutes, rendering the latter thus subject to being declared inoperative by any court. The Court of Cassation argued that it is 'the very nature of the international law as determined by the treaty that leads to this primacy'. On the same basis, the Court has ruled that a self-executing treaty even prevails over the Constitution insofar as the Constitution does not provide for greater protections or guarantees.[24]

This has considerably strengthened the judicial protection of human rights in Belgium. Courts have a duty not to enforce domestic statutory provisions, which violate fundamental rights guaranteed by a self-executing treaty. Before applying a provision of an international treaty, courts should ascertain whether the treaty is valid and that the treaty provision is indeed self-executing, meaning that it has direct effect in the Belgian legal order. The criteria for a valid treaty are that it has come into force under international law; that Belgium has consented to be bound by the treaty, and has made no reservation about the applicable treaty provision; that the constitutionally required parliamentary approval has been obtained, and that the treaty has been published in an official journal.

A treaty provision which is self-executing creates rights and obligations for any citizen without any further intervention of the domestic government. To determine whether the treaty provision is self-executing, the caselaw takes into account two criteria: (i) principally, whether the provision is sufficiently accurate, precise and unconditioned (the 'objective criterion'), and in some cases (ii) the aim of the State parties (the 'subjective criterion'). Self-executing provisions are found in EU law, the EConvHR and the ICCPR.

37. The Constitutional Court may review legislation for compatibility with all rights and freedoms enumerated in Title II of the Constitution. Although it has no jurisdiction to review directly any legislation for compatibility with treaties, the Constitutional Court has nonetheless held legislation to be in contravention of fundamental rights set out in certain treaties, and has also read the rights and freedoms guaranteed by the Constitution in conjunction with analogous rights and freedoms guaranteed in international legal instruments.[25] Moreover, the Constitutional Court

23. Cass., 27 May 1971 (*Fromagerie Franco-Suisse Le Ski*), *J.T.*, 1971, 460.
24. Cass., 9 and 16 Nov. 2004, *T.B.P.*, 2005, 43 and *R.W.*, 2005–2006, 387.
25. See further below Pt. II. Ch. 5. §2. II 'The Constitutional Court'.

– unlike the Court of Cassation – applies the principle of the primacy of the Constitution over international law. In the reasoning of the Court, since it may review the constitutionality of legislation, it may thus also review the compatibility of an Act approving a treaty. And it can only review the constitutionality of an approval Act by reviewing the provisions of the treaty itself that the Act covers.[26] Thus, the Court may, within the limits of its jurisdiction, annul an Act approving an international treaty on the ground of incompatibility with the Constitution. The Court nonetheless proceeds with great caution, and has indeed never had occasion to declare such a nullity.

This point of view certainly endangers the stability of Belgian international obligations. To meet these problems, Article 26 of the Special Majority Act on the Constitutional Court was amended in 2003 to provide that no preliminary rulings may be requested from the Court on the Acts by which an EU treaty, or the EConvHR or its Protocols have been approved. Yet this is not a fully satisfactory solution. First of all, it is still possible to petition for the annulment of legislation approving these Treaties, providing the filing occurs within sixty days – instead of the otherwise six months – after publication. Secondly and more importantly, preliminary rulings on Acts approving treaties other than the EU treaties, the EConvHR or its Protocols still remain possible at all times.

Even though the Constitutional Court recognises the primacy of EU law (on the basis of Article 34 of the Constitution[27]), it asserted in the *Stability Pact* case that transferring certain powers to institutions of the EU under no circumstances allows any discriminatory derogation from the national identity enshrined in fundamental constitutional and political structures or from the core values of the protections provided by the Constitution.[28] In the Court's view, however, the Acts approving the Stability Pact did not include any such infringement. The ECJ, for its part, does not allow a constitutional court – or any court for that matter – to permit broader constitutional rights protection if this would compromise the primacy, unity, and effectiveness of EU law.[29]

38. In particular, a serious problem arises when the question of a breach of fundamental rights guaranteed by the Constitution and by self-executing human rights treaties or conventions is raised before the courts. According to the Constitution, a preliminary question should be submitted to the Constitutional Court to review the constitutional validity of that legislation. According to the Court of Cassation, however, the courts have to ascertain first if the Constitution offers broader protections and then, if this was not the case, to review the incompatibility of the legislative

26. Cons., Judgments No. 26/91, 16 Oct. 1991, and 12/94, 3 Feb. 1994.
27. Cons., Judgment No. 130/2010, 18 Nov. 2010.
28. Cons., Judgment No. 62/2016, 28 Apr. 2016. See, e.g., 'Case Comment' *T.B.P.*, 2017, No. 6. The 'Stability Pact' is the European Treaty of 2 March 2012 on Stability, Coordination and Governance in the Economic and Monetary Union. It was entered into by twenty-five of the then twenty-eight Member States of the European Union in order to stabilise the eurozone after the financial crisis. The Contracting States undertook to manage their budgetary positions and limit their public debt.
29. ECJ, Case C-399/11, (*Melloni*), 26 Feb. 2013. See A. Alen, S. Lambrecht & W. Verrijdt, 'Belgique' in *Traité des rapports entre ordres juridiques* 1393–1418 (B. Bonnet ed., LGDJ 2016).

provision with the relevant human rights convention, without requesting a preliminary ruling from the Constitutional Court.

To meet this problem, a Special Majority Act has in 2009 inserted a new paragraph into Article 26 of the Special Majority Act on the Constitutional Court. The legislation has created a new 'coincidence procedure', that is, when a human right is protected in an analogous way by both Title II of the Constitution and by a provision of European or international law. In such cases, a judge is obliged in principle to submit to the Constitutional Court a preliminary question on the compatibility of the legislative provision with Title II of the Constitution. Two exceptions to these proceedings exist: (1) when it is manifestly clear that there is no violation of Title II (*acte clair*), and (2) when it follows clearly from a judgment of an international court that there has been a breach of European or international law, or from a judgment of the Constitutional Court that there has been a violation of the Constitution (*acte éclairé*). This new procedure has reinforced the Constitutional Court's exclusive jurisdiction in matters of constitutional review. It has also inspired the French procedure of a *question prioritiare de constitutionnalité*, which gave rise to an important decision of the ECJ in *Melki*.[30] There the ECJ held that any delay to a trial court's holding national legislation inconsistent with EU law and thus being inapplicable, which delay was caused by an obligation to request a preliminary ruling on constitutionality, was acceptable providing three conditions were met. First, a judge must remain free at any stage of the proceedings to refer a question to the ECJ for a preliminary ruling. Second, a judge must remain able to issue any interlocutory orders necessary to preserve the effective protection in the final judgment of rights derived from EU law. Third, even if the constitutional question is answered in the negative, a judge must retain full jurisdiction not to apply national legislation he considers to contravene EU law. In 2014 the Special Majority Act on the Constitutional Court was amended to accommodate these conditions.[31] It can therefore be reasonably concluded that, although the Belgian coincidence procedure has never been reviewed by the ECJ, it does meet the standards set out in *Melki*.[32]

30. ECJ, Cases C-188/10 and C-188/10, (*Melki and Abdeli*), 22 Jun. 2010.
31. Articles 26 §4 and 30 of the Special Majority Act on the Constitutional Court.
32. See W. Verrijdt, 'Should the EU Effectiveness Principle Be Applied to Judge National Constitutional Review Procedures?' in *Liber Amicorum M. Melchior* 543–570 (Anthemis 2010).

Chapter 2. The Constitution

§1. CHARACTERISTICS

39. Belgium, unlike for instance the United Kingdom, has a written constitution, that is, one document that may be considered to have special legal authority. The Belgian system of government is primarily laid down in the 1831 Constitution, as amended over time. Hence, it is a constitution in the material sense of the term, setting out the framework and the principal functions of the organs of government within the State, and establishing the principles by which these must operate. The authority of the main government bodies is derived from the Constitution, unlike countries having an unwritten constitution where there is no single constitutional document on which the authority of the government bodies is based. The Belgian Constitution is indeed the fountain of all constitutional powers. According to the principle of national sovereignty laid down in Article 33 of the Constitution, the Nation delegates the exercise of powers to the authorities established and organised by the Constitution.

The whole system of government of a country, however, is never embodied in a single written text. A written constitution is invariably surrounded by a whole set of customary rules and practices, which attune the Constitution to changing conditions. Because of the primacy of written constitutional provisions, those constitutional practices have only a supplementary role; hence they can never override a written constitutional provision.

40. By contrast with the situation in countries having no written constitution, the Belgian Constitution, being the highest legal rule in the internal legal order, may be described as 'formal and rigid' because of its special (rather strict) amending procedure. Yet the Belgian Constitution does have the necessary flexibility to adjust to changing political and social circumstances by virtue of an interpretation which takes into account social evolution (an 'evolutionary interpretation'), as well as one accounting for given objectives (a 'teleological interpretation'). The General Introduction mentioned the example of the Belgian monarchy, which evolved from an 'orleanistic' monarchy into a parliamentary, constitutional monarchy without any formal amendment to the written Constitution. Article 105 of the Constitution, which provides that the King has no other powers save those formally vested in him by the Constitution and by specific Acts passed in accordance with the Constitution, offers another example of how the meaning of general constitutional provisions may change without any formal revision of the Constitution. This provision was originally intended as a means of curbing royal prerogatives. Paradoxically, it was invoked later on by the Executive Branch to justify an extreme extension of said powers.[33] The General Introduction also pointed out that subsequent amendments to Belgium's state structure have rendered the Constitution much more detailed than before. Yet the more detailed a constitutional provision is, the less flexibility it may have to adapt itself to changing circumstances.

---

33. See further below Pt. II. Ch. 3. §5. 'I. Delegation of Legislative Power'.

§2. Amending the Constitution

I. Outline

A. A Three-Stage Procedure (Article 195 of the Constitution)

41. An amendment to the Constitution is initiated by common resolutions from the three branches of the Legislature – the House of Representatives, the Senate and the King – forming then the 'Pre-Constituent Assembly'. Each branch of the Pre-Constituent Assembly separately indicates which Article(s) it considers necessary to revise. Although the resolutions of both the House of Representatives and the Senate are technically not a statute, they must nevertheless be adopted by the same simple majority as required for an ordinary statute. The declaration of the King designating the Articles to be revised will, of course, need a ministerial countersignature.

42. After publication of those three resolutions in the *Gazette*, both Houses of Parliament are automatically dissolved. The act of dissolution implies an election within forty days and the convening of the newly elected Houses within three months thereafter. Although the original idea behind this automatic dissolution of Parliament was to give the electorate a say in the proposed amendments to the Constitution, constitutional amendments are not normally a major electoral issue.

43. In the third and final stage, the new Houses of Parliament may, in agreement with the King (together forming the 'Constituent Assembly'), undertake the revision of the constitutional provisions specified in the resolutions. Before an amendment becomes effective, it must be adopted by a special two-thirds majority in both Houses. Specifically, at least two-thirds of the Members of each of the Houses must be present, and no proposed amendment may be adopted unless it secures at least two-thirds majority of the total votes cast. Abstentions are taken into account to calculate quorum, but not the majority. After having been adopted, the amendment requires Royal Assent, promulgation by the King, and publication in the *Gazette*, as is the case for ordinary laws.

It should be pointed out that the Constituent Assembly may choose whether or not to amend the designated constitutional provisions. It is not bound by the intentions of the Pre-Constituent Assembly. On the other hand, the Constituent Assembly may not exercise this power beyond the period of time for which it has been elected – in principle, five years. It may revise only those provisions which have been specified in each of the above-mentioned resolutions of the Pre-Constituent Assembly.

B. Difficulties with the Procedure

44. The amending procedure has been criticised as being too rigid, in particular because a resolution calling for revision of the Constitution automatically entails a dissolution of Parliament. A leading Belgian constitutional scholar has nevertheless observed rightly that regulating the relations between the Communities and the Regions calls now more than ever for a stringent procedure for amending the Constitution.[34] In an attempt to reform the amending procedure, and in particular to avoid the automatic dissolution of both the Houses of Parliament, resolutions for the revision of Article 195 of the Constitution had been adopted in 2003, 2007 and 2010.[35] In 2012, Article 195 was amended – temporarily – to enable without a dissolution of Parliament the amendment of other constitutional provisions not inserted into the resolutions. Although this procedure (making possible the 2014 Sixth State Reform) was highly contested, the Venice Commission concluded that it was not against the Belgian Constitution or international standards.[36]

45. The phenomenon of an 'implicit' revision of the Constitution also exists. This means that a constitutional provision quite often is not formally revised but that its scope is modified indirectly as a consequence of amending some other constitutional provisions.[37] This may occur when an Article may not be revised because it had not been mentioned in the resolutions for amending the Constitution.

II. Provisions Entrenched Beyond Amendment?

46. A few Articles of the Constitution have been set in such a way that it might be argued that the Constituent Assembly held them to be unalterable. According to Article 14*bis* of the Constitution, the death penalty is abolished. Article 17 of the Constitution provides that a general confiscation of property cannot be imposed. Article 18 of the Constitution stipulates that 'civil death', a penalty that entailed the loss of legal rights upon criminal conviction, is abolished and may not be re-established. According to Article 25 of the Constitution, no form of censorship of the press may ever be established. Nevertheless all these Articles can be amended pursuant to Article 195 of the Constitution.

47. In certain circumstances, the power to revise the Constitution is partly or entirely suspended. During a regency no alteration to the Constitution may be made regarding the constitutional powers and the status of the King, the succession to the throne, and the regency (Article 197 Constitution). Likewise, no amendments to the Constitution may be initiated or pursued in time of war or when the Houses of Parliament are prevented from meeting freely on national territory (Article 196 Constitution).

34. A. Mast, *Overzicht van het Belgisch Grondwettelijk Recht* (9th) 501–502 (Story-Scientia 1987).
35. *Gazette,* 10 Apr. 2003, 2 May 2007, and 7 May 2010.
36. Venice Commission, Opinion No. 679/2012.
37. For example, former Art. 107*quater* Constitution (now Arts 3 and 39) establishing the three Regions. Although this Article has undergone no formal revision since 1970, its scope has been modified by other Articles (e.g., Arts 134, 136–139 Constitution).

III. Consolidating the Constitution

48. Because the Constitution had grown into an incoherent and illegible text following several extensive constitutional amendments, a new Article 198 was introduced during the 1993 revision of the Constitution. According to Article 198, the Constituent Assembly may adjust the text of the Constitution for certain reasons, namely, renumbering of Articles and their subdivisions, reorganising the subdivision of the Constitution into titles, chapters, and sections, bringing the terminology in unamended provisions in line with that used in newer articles, and harmonising the Dutch, French, and German versions of the Constitution. The Constituent Assembly took the opportunity to establish in 1994 a revised version of the Constitution, the *Consolidated Constitution of 17 February 1994*. As a result of this consolidation, the Constitution has become much more logical and understandable. In 2005, and after the name of the 'Community Councils' and 'Regional Councils' had been changed to the 'Community Parliaments' and 'Region Parliaments', a second adjustment harmonised all constitutional provisions with this new terminology. Finally, a third in 2007 replaced the name 'Court of Arbitration' with the more accurate name 'Constitutional Court'.

§3. Hierarchy

49. The Constitution, as noted above, is the highest internal legal rule. Nevertheless, the primacy of constitutional rules is not fully guaranteed, since it is not within the jurisdiction of the courts to rule on the constitutionality of legislation, such as federal statutes and Community and Region Acts. Ever since the founding of the Belgian State, the caselaw has held that the legislature itself, and not the courts, should ensure that legislation is not unconstitutional.

50. The introduction of the 'presumption of constitutionality' into the caselaw by the Court of Cassation has somewhat softened the impact of the application of this principle of the inviolability of the law.[38] The former means that judges should construe legislation in accordance with the Constitution as much as possible. This principle corresponds to the German concept of a *Verfassungskonforme Auslegung* (interpreting in conformity with the constitution).

The principle of the inviolability of the law was brought into question after the reforms federalising the State. This prompted the creation of the (then called) 'Court of Arbitration', which initially had jurisdiction pursuant to Article 142 of the Constitution to review legislation for compliance with the division of powers. Since then, its jurisdiction has been extended to the review of federal, Community and Region legislation for compliance with fundamental rights and freedoms guaranteed under Title II of the Constitution, as well as its Articles 143 §1 (federal loyalty), 170 (legality of taxation), 172 (equality of taxation), and 191 (protection of the person and property of foreigners).

38. Cass., 20 Apr. 1950 (*Waleffe*) *Pas*., 1950, I, 560.

Chapter 3. Legislation

§1. Types of Legislation

I. Ordinary Statutes

51. Formally speaking, a statute is the product of joint action by the various branches of the federal Legislature: primarily the King and the House of Representatives, and in a limited number of instances, the Senate too.[39] In principle, the Constitution always uses the term 'Act' in this 'formal' sense.

52. Doctrine and caselaw have added to that concept the notion of a statute in the 'material' sense, that is to say, every generally binding rule, no matter what the issuing authority is. For example, administrative regulations are understood only in this sense to be 'Acts'. Most legislation in the formal sense of the term is also legislation in the material sense, since most Acts which have been approved by Parliament, which have been given Royal Assent, and which have been promulgated by the King, contain a generally binding legal rule. Some statutes, however, are only formally 'Acts' because they are not general rules, such as those granting Belgian nationality (Article 9 Constitution), those granting a public pension to certain persons (Article 179 Constitution), those concerning the budget and State accounts (Article 174 Constitution), and those approving annually the number of military personnel on active duty (Article 183 Constitution).

53. The distinction between the 'formal' and the 'material' sense of a law is relevant in three instances:

(i) It has an impact on the jurisdiction of the Court of Cassation to assess whether judgments rendered on appeal do not violate the 'law'. According to the well-established caselaw of that Court, 'law' here must be understood in its material sense. If an appeal judgment is inconsistent with what is only formally an Act and not also materially so, the Court will declare itself without jurisdiction.
(ii) A statute in the formal sense only cannot constitute the legislative basis for administrative regulations.
(iii) Only government Bills (and certain draft regulations) in the material sense of the term have to be submitted beforehand to the Legislation Division of the Council of State for its comments.[40]

54. When the Constitution stipulates that a matter has to be regulated 'by Act', this means that the federal Legislative Branch has exclusive jurisdiction and must not delegate its power to the King. However, the Constitutional Court has permitted

39. See Arts 77–78 Constitution.
40. See further below Pt. II. Ch. 6. §1. II 'The Legislation Division of the Council of State'.

the delegation of legislative power to the King on certain essential matters and under certain conditions (in particular that parliamentary confirmation of the Royal Decree will follow shortly thereafter).[41]

In other cases, the Constitution provides that a matter should be regulated 'by authority of an Act', meaning that Parliament may delegate its regulatory powers to another authority, such as the King, who then may issue regulations within the scope of that Act.[42] Article 14 of the Constitution, under which no penalty can be imposed nor applied except by authority of an Act, provides a good example of this. In accordance with this provision, the King has been empowered by Parliament to impose penalties for non-compliance with his regulations and orders, within the limits set by the federal Legislative Branch (a minimum and maximum penalty).

Whenever the Constitution uses the term 'Act', this may imply that jurisdiction is reserved for the federal Legislative Branch, and that the Communities and the Regions cannot legislate on the matter.[43]

II. Special Majority Acts

55. As their name indicates, Special Majority Acts differ from ordinary statutes because the former have to be adopted in compliance with a qualified (language) majority requirement, namely 'a majority of the votes cast in each language group in each House, on condition that a majority of the members of each group is present, and provided that the total number of votes in favour that are cast in the two language groups is equal to at least two thirds of the votes cast'.[44] Broadly described, these Acts set out in greater detail the constitutional structure and powers of the Communities and the Regions.

Although Special Majority Acts are the main reference standards used by the Constitutional Court when reviewing legislation under the division of powers, the Court may also review, within the limits of its jurisdiction, whether Special Majority Acts themselves comply with constitutional reference standards.[45]

III. Wartime Decrees

56. As a rule, federal legislative authority is exercised collectively by the King, the House of Representatives and the Senate (Article 36 Constitution). During the First World War, however, it was impossible for Parliament to convene. Moreover, during the Second World War, the King was held captive, and was therefore unable

41. See further below Pt. II. Ch. 3. §5. I 'Delegation of Legislative Power'.
42. Parliament may also delegate its residual powers to the King: see further below Pt. II. Ch. 3. §5. I 'Delegation of Legislative Power'.
43. See further below Pt. III. Ch. 2. §3. I.
44. Article 4 para. 3 of the Constitution.
45. Cons., Judgment No. 8/90, 7 Feb. 1990. Also see further below Pt. II. Ch. 3. §4. II.

to reign. In such a case, a Regent would normally have to be appointed by Parliament (Article 93 Constitution). But this proved to be impossible because Parliament was prevented from assembling. In order to ensure the continuity of government, the King was replaced by his Ministers.

57. Thus, during the First World War, legislative authority was exercised by the King, together with his Ministers, and, during the Second World War, by the Ministers alone. Their decisions, which regulated matters that under normal circumstances could only be subject to statute, are called 'wartime decrees'. They were promulgated in the same way as Acts in the formal sense of the term. Taking into account 'force majeure', the Court of Cassation has ruled that those wartime decrees have the same force of law as ordinary statutes. This implies that they may only be amended or repealed by Act or by authority of an Act, and that they are subject to review by the Constitutional Court.

IV. Community and Region Acts

58. The three Communities, as well as the Flemish Region and the Walloon Region, were given the power to enact statutes for those matters within their jurisdiction, these Acts having the same force of law as federal statutes throughout their respective territory.[46] Community and Region Acts are not subject to judicial review by the ordinary courts. It is the Constitutional Court that has exclusive jurisdiction to determine whether or not the division of legislative powers established under the Constitution and implemented by various (Special Majority) Acts has been complied with.

59. The Brussels-Capital Region may also pass statutes[47] having force of law but which, in the hierarchy, are situated between an ordinary statute and administrative rules. Like Community and Region Acts, a Brussels-Capital Region Act may repeal, extend, amend, or replace current legislative provisions and is subject to review by the Constitutional Court. But unlike Community and Region Acts, a Brussels-Capital Region Act is also subject to limited judicial review by other courts, as well as – in certain cases – to limited administrative review by federal authorities in order to protect Brussels' international role and its function as the capital city.

---

46. For the Communities, jurisdiction is grounded in Arts 127–130 Constitution, and for the Regions, in Art. 134. Pursuant to Art. 138, the French Community has delegated some of its powers in the bilingual Brussels-Capital region to the French Community Commission. It exercises this power through Acts which have the same legal force as Community and Region Acts.
47. The Joint Community Commission also exercises its jurisdiction through statutes having the same legal force as the Brussels-Capital Region Acts, but not being subject to administrative review: see further below Pt. III. Ch. 2. §7 'Brussels Institutions'.

§2. HIERARCHY

60. The relation of legislation to treaties has been discussed above. The constitutionality of all legislation, including Special Majority Acts and the Brussels-Capital Region Acts, may be reviewed by the Constitutional Court with respect to the division of powers between the federal, the Community, and the Region Parliaments; fundamental rights and freedoms guaranteed under Title II of the Constitution, and Articles 143 §1 (federal loyalty), 170 (legality of taxation), 172 (equality in taxation) and 191 (protection of the person and property of foreigners) of the Constitution.

Moreover, the Special Majority Acts, which allocate powers among the federal State, the Communities and the Regions, are paramount over other legislation. The latter must comply with those Special Majority Acts. Only the Constitutional Court has jurisdiction to test the conformity of legislation to Special Majority Acts.

Chapter 4. Caselaw

61. Since Belgium is a country in the civil law tradition, it is generally considered that Belgian courts decide cases by referring to the legal principles and rules contained in legislation, and that they are not bound by previous decisions of other courts ruling in similar cases. The judiciary has even been explicitly prohibited from issuing general, advisory decisions (Article 6 Civil Procedure Code). As a rule, judgments do not have any binding authority over similar cases arising afterwards and between different parties. In practice, however, the judgments of higher courts do enjoy a considerable moral authority.

62. Furthermore caselaw does have in some cases a regulatory, normative, function, a 'pouvoir normatif' as Waline has aptly pointed out.[48] Belgian courts, which under no circumstances may refuse to give judgment (Article 5 Civil Procedure Code), have, for example, acknowledged the existence of unwritten general principles of law in order to resolve those situations not anticipated by the Legislature. Constitutional law is one area in which the role of 'judge-made' law has been particularly important. On several occasions, the Court of Cassation has overruled its previous decisions to take a new stand on certain issues, at a time when the matter was already being debated within the Constituent Assembly.[49] In that respect, the caselaw on tort actions against the State and that on the primacy of self-executing treaties are perfect illustrations.[50] In the latter, the position taken by the Court of Cassation has even been described as a 'judge-made revision' of the Constitution.[51] Another prominent example where the courts have filled a 'gap' in constitutional law concerns the legal force of wartime decrees. Although these wartime decrees were not issued in compliance with Article 36 of the Constitution, which prescribes the co-operation of the three parts to the Legislative Branch, the Court of Cassation and the Constitutional Court have assimilated those wartime decrees into ordinary laws.[52]

48. M. Waline, 'Le pouvoir normatif de la jurisprudence', in *La technique et les principes du droit public. Études en l'honneur de G. Scelle* 613 (Lib. Gen de droit et de jurisprudence 1950).
49. See F. Perin, 'Y a-t-il trois pouvoirs constituants?', *Ann. Fac. Dr. Liège*, 1987, 8–11.
50. Cass., 5 Nov. 1920 (*Flandria*) *Pas.*, 1920, I, 193 and Cass., 27 May 1971 (*Fromagerie Franco-Suisse Le Ski*), *J.T.*, 1971, 460. See also above Pt. I. Ch. 1. §2.
51. J. Salmon, 'Le conflit entre le traité international et la loi interne en Belgique à la suite de l'arrêt rendu le 27 mai 1971 par la Cour de Cassation', *J.T.*, 1971, 535.
52. See above Pt. I. Ch. 3. §1. III.

Chapter 5. Unwritten Law

63. A characteristic common to constitutional conventions and to the general principles of law is that they are considered to be binding rules even though they are not, or only partly, grounded on the written constitution.

§1. Conventions

I. General

64. A system of government is never exclusively based on a set of written rules. Consequently, constitutional practice and customs play an important role in the operation of Belgian government bodies. The process of forming a government, the role of the Prime Minister, Cabinet proceedings, the opening and closing of a session of Parliament, the adjournment of the Houses of Parliament, all these are determined to a large extent by constitutional convention.

On several occasions, the Council of State has referred to unwritten rules, such as those stemming from the principles and objectives underlying the Constitution. Examples here are the conventions in which an outgoing government has only restricted transitional powers, the rule of consensus decisions in the federal Cabinet, and the principle of constitutional secrecy governing the relations between the King and his Ministers.[53]

II. Hierarchy

65. Constitutional conventions do not have the same legal force as written constitutional rules. They have only a supplementary character; hence they can never override a written constitutional provision.

§2. General Principles of Law

I. General

66. In common law systems, equitable relief is considered as a 'judicial means of offering relief to individuals from hard bargains in cases of fraud, accident, mistake or trust and as a means of confining the operation of unjust and partial laws'.[54] The role of the Judicial Branch is traditionally considered to be much more limited in a civil law system, although no one would reasonably argue today that judges are confined to being merely the *bouche de la loi*. The growing power of the Executive

53. Regarding federal Cabinet decisions by consensus, see, e.g., Council of State, Administrative Tribunal Division, Case No. 243.271, 18 Dec. 2018 (*Dewinter*).
54. See, e.g., G. McDowell, *Equity and the Constitution: The Supreme Court, Equitable Relief, and Public Policy* 4 (University Chicago Press 1941).

Branch and the increase in government functions have led the courts in civil law systems more and more to restrict the discretion of public authorities. Those limitations are based on 'general principles of law' whereby the courts refer to the principles and objectives underlying the legal system for justifying the 'equitable relief' they offer. These general principles of law referred to include the obligation to give reasons for judgment, judicial independence and impartiality, the principle of continuity in public services, and the principle of non-retroactivity. Some of these judge-made general principles of law have been codified later on, but not all general principles of law have been articulated in written law, even though they are part of the general system of law.

II. Hierarchy

67. Insofar as general principles of law are not adopted from an international treaty (e.g., the principle of due process) or found in the Constitution (e.g., the principle of equality), they are subordinate norms of law. Accordingly, legislation may – at least in principle – deviate from a general principle of law. But the Executive must comply with the general principles of law (e.g., rights of defence) in order not to render its decisions null and void.

Nevertheless, according to the caselaw of the Constitutional Court, the Legislative Branch must also respect general principles of law, such as the principle of legal certainty, the personal character of penalties, the proportionality of penalty to offence and the right of review by a higher court. The Constitutional Court may review legislation under Articles 10 and 11 of the Constitution in combination with the general principles of law.

Chapter 6. Administrative Regulations and Orders

§1. Classification

I. The Federal Level

A. Royal Decrees

68. Article 108 of the Constitution empowers the King to issue those regulations and orders which are necessary for the implementation of Acts, without ever being able to suspend those statutes themselves or to dispense with their application. Article 108 not only confers a right but also imposes an obligation. The non-implementation of a statute may ground an action for damages against the State, even when that statute does not fix a deadline within which it must be implemented.[55] The concept of 'implementation of laws' should not be interpreted too restrictively. The King may choose freely how to achieve the objectives prescribed by the legislation, whenever it is silent on how it should be implemented.[56]

Further, not issuing an administrative order or regulation may ground the Administrative Tribunal Division of the Council of State imposing a sanction for this omission. Provided certain conditions are fulfilled, the Administrative Tribunal Division will hold that the authorities have taken a negative decision. Citizens may thus bring an action before the Division to annul this denial, and may further claim damages before the Council of State pursuant to Article 11*bis* of the Consolidated Council of State Act or before the ordinary courts pursuant to Article 1382 of the Civil Code.

69. Under Article 105 of the Constitution, a specific Act passed in accordance with the Constitution may attribute to the King powers other than those formally vested in him by the Constitution. On this basis, the Legislative Branch may attribute its residual powers to the King. Similarly, the Legislative Branch has authorised the Executive Branch to take 'all necessary measures' regarding some (mostly vaguely) defined matters in times of economic crisis.[57] The Legislature may also empower the King to modify, to abolish or to complete existing legislation. Such authorisations must, however, be interpreted restrictively.

70. Apart from the power to implement legislation and the powers which specific statutes have endowed the King with, the King is also vested with 'autonomous' regulatory powers in the two areas of the civil service and the 'police power'.[58] Nevertheless, these powers too must have a basis in some constitutional or legislative provision.

55. Cass., 23 Apr. 1971 (*Goffin*) *R.W.*, 1970–1971, 1793.
56. Cass., 18 Nov. 1924 (*Mertz*) *Pas.*, 1925, 1, 25.
57. See further below Pt. II. Ch. 3. §5. I 'Delegation of Legislative Power'.
58. See further below Pt. II. Ch. 4. §3. II. B 'Autonomous' Regulatory Powers'.

B. Ministerial Decrees and Decrees of the Secretaries of State

71. Because, under the Constitution, regulatory powers are attributed to the King, Ministers have in principle no regulatory powers. There are, however, exceptions to this rule, limited though they may be.[59] In practice, Ministers issue Ministerial Decrees on matters of secondary importance which are directed at individuals. Secretaries of State have only regulatory powers, with the consent of the Ministers to which they belong.

II. The Level of Communities and Regions

A. Regulations and Orders

72. The governments of the Communities and the Regions have the power to issue those regulations and orders necessary for the implementation of Community and Region Acts, without ever being able to suspend the latter. They have no powers other than those formally vested in them by the Constitution and by Acts (federal, Community, or Region) passed in accordance with the Constitution itself (Articles 20 and 78 Special Majority Act on Institutional Reform).

B. Ministerial Decrees

73. As a rule, individual Ministers of the Community and the Region governments do not exercise any regulatory power because the principle of collegial deliberation applicable to these governments requires all their decisions to be taken by that executive entity as a whole. There is only one exception to that principle: the possibility of delegating that decision-making power to individual Ministers (Article 69 Special Majority Act on Institutional Reform).

III. The Level of Subordinate (Local) Authorities

A. Provincial and Municipal Regulations and Orders

74. The jurisdiction of the provinces and the municipalities has been defined in vague, general terms. They are empowered to act in all matters of provincial or municipal interest (Articles 41 and 162 Constitution).[60]

75. Provincial jurisdiction is very limited: on the one hand, the jurisdiction of municipal authorities must not be infringed upon; on the other, provincial regulations in principle ought not concern matters addressed by a higher authority

59. See further below Pt. II. Ch. 4. §3. II. C 'Regulatory Powers of Ministers and Secretaries of State'.
60. See further below Pt. III. Ch. 3. §1 'Territorial Decentralisation'.

(i.e., the State, the Communities, or the Regions) or should not conflict with the rules of those higher executive authorities.

76. The much broader jurisdiction of municipalities is also qualified by that of those higher authorities.

B. *The Regulations and Orders of the Brussels Conurbation and of the Brussels Community Commissions*

77. Unlike provincial and municipal institutions, the Brussels Conurbation and the Brussels Community Commissions have only exhaustively enumerated powers.

§2. Hierarchy

78. All actions of administrative authorities are subject to the principle of legality. Administrative authorities may only act if and when they are explicitly empowered to do so by the Constitution or by some legislative provision.

79. Judicial review is exercised over all acts of administrative authorities. Pursuant to Article 159 of the Constitution, courts and tribunals have a duty to decline enforcing regulations and orders conflicting with the 'law', that is, higher legal norms. The Administrative Tribunal Division of the Council of State has been given the power to annul regulations and orders on the same grounds (Article 14 Consolidated Council of State Act).

80. In addition, the acts of subordinate (local) authorities are subject to administrative review by higher political authorities who review both the legality and the merits.

81. An administrative authority making any individual decision should comply with those general regulations it has already adopted previously. This principle, reflected in the maxim '*patere legem quam ipse fecisti*', is in fact an application of the principle of equality.

The Constitutional Court will hold legislation unconstitutional if (i) that legislation deprives the provinces or municipalities of the entirety of the essence of their jurisdiction, or (ii) the restrictions on their jurisdiction cannot be justified by the fact that it could be better exercised on another level.[61]

61. Cons., Judgments No. 95/2005, 25 May 2005; No. 7/2009, 15 Jan. 2009; No. 89/2010, 29 Jul. 2010; No. 16/2015, 2 Dec. 2015; No. 100/2015, 2 Jul. 2015, and No. 162/2015, 19 Nov. 2015.

Chapter 7. Codification, Interpretation and Publication

§1. Codification

82. Since Belgium is a typical civil law country, the importance of written legislation is dominant. In some branches of law, a significant degree of codification has taken place. In these areas of law the extant statutory law, customs, and caselaw have been at some time condensed into systematic form. For example, Belgium adopted the famous *Code Napoleon* as its Civil Code (1804). Other prominent examples of codification are the Civil Procedure Code (1967), the Criminal Code (1867), the Criminal Procedure Code (1878) and the more recent Business and Enterprise Code (2013). There is, however, no general and systematic Administrative Law Code. This might explain why caselaw remains particularly important in this area of law.

83. The Consolidations and Codification Act of 13 June 1961 and Article 6*bis* of the Consolidated Council of State Act lay down the procedure regulating how legislative provisions connected to the same subject matter but scattered over different Acts can be consolidated into a single Act. Consolidation of the law is thus purely an improvement of form, without altering substance. The consolidation procedure is initiated by a request of the government to the Co-ordination Office of the Council of State. This Office submits a draft to the Legislation Division of the Council of State for comment. The consolidation is finalised by government decree subject to judicial review.

Moreover, greater attention is being paid to improving the quality of legislative drafting. A parliamentary committee has been created specifically to deal with the evaluation of legislation.[62] This committee is charged with the task of looking into problems and difficulties in the implementation or application of legislation. It reports to the House of Representatives, the Senate, and the Ministers responsible. The Prosecutor-General for the Court of Cassation and the executive body of Prosecutors-General provide an annual report to this committee giving an overview of those legislative instruments which have raised difficulties of interpretation or application for all the courts. This committee also reviews on a monthly basis those decisions of the Constitutional Court which concern the efficient administration of justice.

§2. Interpretation

84. Interpretation is particularly important in constitutional law because of the vague and general character of constitutional provisions. Interpretation makes it possible to narrow the gap between the text of the Constitution and social evolution.

62. Act of 25 April 2007, *Gazette,* 11 May 2007.

85. All branches of government interpret the Constitution when applying it. The interpretation by the Executive Branch is subject to review by the Judicial Branch, which cannot issue general, advisory decisions. Although the Legislative Branch too must comply with the Constitution, it cannot be denied that, on the basis of its residual powers, it has more than once filled certain 'gaps' in the written Constitution. Although its interpretation carries more weight than that of the other branches of government, the constitutionality of legislation remains a question to be submitted to the Constitutional Court.

86. The power to issue an 'authoritative interpretation' is a privilege, which must be founded on the Constitution. Under Articles 84 and 133 of the Constitution, the authoritative interpretation of Acts (federal, Community, and Region) is the sole prerogative of the competent legislature itself. Pursuant to these Articles, the relevant legislature may enact an Interpretation Act, explaining another statute or a provision thereof. Such an Act will be retroactive: the legislation so interpreted is considered always to have had the meaning given by the Interpretation Act.[63]

§3. Publication

87. According to Article 190 of the Constitution, no statute nor administrative regulation nor order of a general, provincial, or municipal nature is binding until it has been published in the manner laid down by Act. Article 190 of the Constitution contains a general principle of law: in order to be enforceable and obligatory vis-à-vis citizens, general norms should be published. The principle also applies to the legislation and executive decrees of the Communities and the Regions, as well as to international treaties.

88. International treaties, constitutional amendments, federal legislation, Community and Region Acts, and federal, Community, and Region (administrative) regulations must be published in the *Gazette*.[64] In general, these instruments must be published in Dutch and in French[65], and they come into force ten days after their publication unless another date is specified. Constitutional amendments, as well as the Acts and regulations of the German Community and of the Walloon Region, are also published in German. Constitutional amendments take effect as of the time of their publication.

The (administrative) regulations of subordinate (local) authorities must be published in the manner specified by (Region) Act.

Legislation issuing from international institutions must, in principle, be published in the same way and under the same conditions as international treaties. However, treaty provisions sometimes allow the binding rules of the international

63. See further below Pt. II. Ch. 3. §5. II 'Legislation Having Retroactive Effect'.
64. In effect and in practice, this means published on the website of the *Gazette*: www.staatsblad.be / www.moniteur.be.
65. The most important federal Acts and regulations are also published with a German translation.

institutions concerned not to be published in the *Gazette*, but in an official journal of the international institution itself (as in the case of the EU).

Selected Further Reading

Alen, A. 'De Grondwet, hoogste rechtsnorm?'. In *En hommage à F. Delpérée* (Bruylant, 2007) 105–113.

Alen, A. & W. Verrijdt, 'La relation entre la Constitution belge et le droit international et européen'. In *Liber amicorum Rusen Ergec* edited by I. Riassetto, L. Heuschling & G. Ravarani (Pasicrisie luxembourgeoise, 2017) 31–54.

Alen, A. & W. Verrijdt. 'Le dialogue préjudiciel de la Cour constitutionnelle belge avec la Cour de justice de l'Union européenne'. In *Les visages de l'Etat. Liber amicorum Yves Lejeune* edited by P. D'Argent, D. Renders & M. Verdussen (Bruylant, 2017) 33–74.

Bossuyt, M. & W. Verrijdt. 'The Full Effect of EU Law and of Constitutional Review in Belgium and France after the Melki Judgment'. *European Constitutional Law Review* (2011): 355–391.

Delpérée, F. (ed). *La procédure de révision de la Constitution* (Bruylant, 2003).

Dumont, H. 'Coutumes constitutionnelles, conventions de la constitution et paralégalité'. In *Liber Amicorum P. Martens* (Larcier, 2007) 269–299.

Leroy, M. *Les règlements et leurs juges* (Bruylant, 1987).

Popelier, P. & C. Van de Heyning. 'The Belgian Constitution: The Efficacy Approach to European and Global Governance'. In *National Constitutions in European and Global Governance: Democracy, Rights, the Rule of Law* edited by A. Albi & S. Bardutzky (Springer, 2019) 1225–1270.

Rimanque, K. *De regel is niet steeds recht* (Kluwer, 1990).

Van Hoecke, M. (ed.). *Algemene rechtsbeginselen* (Kluwer, 1991).

Velaers, J. 'Artikel 26 §4 van de bijzondere wet op het Grondwettelijk Hof: meer en meer evenwicht tussen de rechtscolleges bij samenloop van grondrechten'. *T.B.P.* (2010): 387–410.

Verrijdt, W. 'Belgium'. In *Member States' Constitutions and EU Integration* edited by S. Griller, M. Claes, L. Papadopoulou. & R. Puff (Hart Publishing, 2020, forthcoming).

Verrijdt, W. 'Should the EU Effectiveness Principle Be Applied to Judge National Constitutional Review Procedures?' In *Liber Amicorum M. Melchior* (Anthemis, 2010) 543–570.

Wintgens, L. (ed.). *De verplichting tot bekendmaking van de norm* (die Keure, 2003).

Part II. Form of Government

Chapter 1. General

§1. Introduction

89. The Belgian State is characterised by a representative regime founded on the principle of national sovereignty. The representative character of the State manifests itself in that the citizens only indirectly take part in the exercise of State powers, through representatives, which they elect in free, secret, and periodic elections.

By enshrining the principle of national sovereignty in the Constitution, the main objective of the National Congress was to stress that only the Nation as a whole could be the source of all State powers and that no individual person or group of persons, not even the King, could claim such powers on the basis of any personal right. From a historic point of view, this aim may be explained as a reaction against any form of royal absolutism. The National Congress wanted to break with the theory claiming that all powers descend from God.

90. Article 33 of the Constitution not only states that 'all powers issue from the Nation', but also that 'they are exercised in the way specified by the Constitution'. Accordingly, the Nation delegates the exercise of State power to certain authorities created and organised by the Constitution.

Some of these powers are exercised by the federal authorities of the State. Article 36 of the Constitution states that 'the federal legislative power is jointly exercised by the King, the House of Representatives, and the Senate'; according to Article 37, 'the federal executive power as regulated by the Constitution, is vested in the King'; and 'The judicial power is exercised by the courts. Their judgments are enforced in the name of the King' (Article 40 Constitution).

Other powers are exercised by authorities that are relatively autonomous with respect to the federal authorities: the institutions of the Communities (Articles 2, 115 §1 and 121 §1 Constitution) and the Regions (Articles 3, 115 §2 and 121 §2 Constitution), and the provincial and municipal institutions (Articles 41, 162, 165 and 166 Constitution).

Only the legislative assemblies and certain organs of the subordinate authorities (i.e., the Provincial and Municipal Councils) are composed of elected representatives. However, this does not mean that the other authorities, for instance the judiciary, do not likewise emanate from the Nation.

91. As representatives of the Nation, the Members of both (federal) Houses of Parliament represent the Nation as a whole, and not only those who elect them (Article 42 Constitution).

92. The following is a brief survey of the constitutional rules governing these various authorities. Before that, attention must be drawn to the role of the so-called '*pouvoirs de fait*' in the political process (§2). Also pointed out are some of the effects resulting from the system of representative democracy, based on the principle of national sovereignty (§3).

§2. '*Pouvoirs de Fait*': Political Parties, Lobbies and Interest Groups

93. In addition to the above-mentioned authorities, which may be called '*pouvoirs de droit*', there are powers which may be called '*pouvoirs de fait*' because they have no formally stated lawmaking or executive power. Interest or pressure groups and political parties are examples of these '*pouvoirs de fait*'. Both try to influence the decisions of the public authorities in order to defend the interests they stand for. Their aims are nonetheless quite different. A political party's objective is to participate directly in the exercise of public power, while a pressure group merely tries to influence decisions of public authorities to favour their members' interests by using all direct and indirect means at their disposal: trade unions, social security funds, associations of employers, financial institutions, industrial or professional sectors, religious associations, and so on. Pressure groups may limit their intervention to a mere appeal to public opinion or may resort to direct action as in strikes, lockouts, or boycotts. Very often, they exercise their influence within the framework of formal or informal consultation procedures. Several Members of Parliament have also close links with certain interest groups.

94. Political parties may be described as organised groups of people participating in elections. Their main goal is to advance a philosophically, socially, or economically based common ideology as well as to further the interests of their members.[66]

The Belgian Constitution does not explicitly acknowledge the existence of political parties. Their existence is nevertheless implicitly recognised in several constitutional and legislative provisions, such as Article 62 of the Constitution prescribing a proportional representation system, the Elections Act, and legislation on the financing of political parties. Political parties play an important role, as we will see when discussing the electoral system, especially by determining who will figure on the party lists for an election, and by their government-making power. Governments in Belgium are almost always coalitions.

95. Because of the major role of political parties, we will give a brief outline of the main political parties currently existing in Belgium.

---

66. G. Burdeau, *Droit constitutionnel et institutions politiques* 178 (LGDJ, 1969).

Once the existence of the Belgian State was consolidated, political parties started to develop. The Liberal Party was created in 1846. Its anticlerical stance would lead to the creation of a Catholic Party. Until the introduction of the system of proportional representation in 1899 and universal single suffrage in 1919, both parties would be in power alternately, with Belgium then actually having a two-party system. Democratisation was, however, to a large extent an achievement of the Socialist Party, which was established by a radical faction having broken away from the Liberal Party. After the 1919 election, a stable political balance of power came about. The Catholic political formation has always been in the lead; its main strongholds may said to be Flanders and rural Wallonia. The Socialist Party has always come in a close second, even occasionally overtaking the Catholic Party vote between the Wars. It mainly appeals to those in Wallonia and the large Flemish cities. The Liberal Party was the main victim of the introduction of universal suffrage. It became a distant but significant third. This voting ratio made it virtually impossible for one party or one political family to form a government on its own. From the post-war period onwards, the Catholic Party has alternated in forming coalitions with either the Liberal Party or with the Socialists, while exceptionally a 'Cabinet of National Unity' has been created. The general availability of the Catholic Party for government coalitions was related to the fact that the Catholic Party was and remains a cross-class alliance within which the major wings are the 'labour wing' (related to the Catholic trade union), the agricultural/farming wing, and the middle class. Shifts in the weight of the various Catholic social groups within the party explain switches from one coalition partner to another.[67] This changed, however, at the end of the 1990s with the formation of the so-called 'purple-green coalition' (Liberal, Socialist, and Green parties) between 1999 and 2003 and, thereafter between 2003 and 2007, the formation of a 'purple coalition' (Liberals and Socialists only) at the federal level.

In the 2007 federal election, the electoral alliance between the CD&V ('Christen-Democratisch & Vlaams', the Flemish Catholic Party) and the N-VA ('Nieuw-Vlaamse Alliantie', a Flemish nationalist party) enjoyed a significant victory at the polls. In the following general elections of 2010, each party ran individual, separate campaigns, and in the outcome the N-VA became the most important political party in the country. Since 2007, and in particular since 2010, the focus has been on the relationship between the federal State and the federated entities (the Communities and the Regions). This provides some explanation for the less than stable government since 2007 and for the most difficult and longest period of forming a government in Belgian history after the general elections of 13 June 2010.[68] The difficult formation of a coalition also resulted in Belgium's 2014 Sixth State Reform which introduced a number of substantial changes to the constitutional model of Belgium's political, social, and economic structures. Despite its electoral success the N-VA was not part of this restructuring agreement, nor was it part of that new federal government. The Flemish nationalist party N-VA having failed to obtain consensus on state reforms, the opportunity to form a government was given to the

67. W. Dewachter & E. Clijsters, 'Belgium: Political Stability Despite Coalition Crises' in *Government Coalitions in Western Democracies* 187–216 (E. Browne & J. Dreijmanis eds., Longman 1982).
68. The stalemate over coalition formation went on for a record-breaking 541 days.

Walloon Socialist Party (PS) and its leader Elio Di Rupo. The PS did reach an agreement, forming a government with the Liberal, Socialist, and Christian Democratic parties from both Flanders and Wallonia. Elio Di Rupo became Prime Minister. The campaign for the 25 May 2014 general elections focused largely on socio-economic reforms: job creation and unemployment, tax reform, pensions, and so on. In that 2014 election, the N-VA strengthened its position as the largest Flemish political party. After five months of discussions, a centre-right coalition of four parties (CD&V, Open Vld, MR and N-VA) was agreed to on 7 October 2014 with the Walloon Liberal (MR) Charles Michel serving as Prime Minister. It was a historical coalition, having only one French-speaking political party (the MR), and thus without a French-speaking majority.

On 9 December 2018 the Michel government was reduced to a minority government after the N-VA quit the coalition because of objections to the UN Migration Pact. The King then accepted the resignation of the government on 21 December 2018. The subsequent federal parliamentary elections on 26 May 2019 have redrawn the political map: with the exception of Ecolo and the Green Party, all the political parties lost seats to the far-left PVDA/PTB on the one hand, and on the other, to the far-right Vlaams Belang. This result explains in some measure the current difficulties surrounding the formation of a federal government. On 17 March 2020 a new government, led by Sophie Wilmès, took the oath of office before the King. The Wilmès government is a minority government which received the temporary support of the other parties in the federal Parliament in order to take measures necessary to address the extraordinary circumstances of the Covid-19 (coronavirus) crisis.

The issue of Belgian state restructuring led to the creation of regional parties, set up for the defence of a region or of a language community. As noted above, the N-VA is at this moment Belgium's leading political party. Other nationalist parties are the 'Vlaams Belang', an extreme right-wing party striving for Flemish separatism, and the 'DéFi' ('Démocrate, Fédéraliste, Indépendant'). This Brussels party changed its name in 2016 from the FDF ('Front Démocratique des Francophones') to the DéFi. Their ideas have gained some currency and have put electoral pressure on the other parties to take a more 'regionalist' stance.

The traditional political parties have been split up, whereby their former language wings operate as autonomous parties. Nowadays no political party is organised at the federal level except for the Workers' Party of Belgium, a far-left (even communist) party, operating as a single Belgian party. Its Flemish-speaking wing is the PVDA ('Partij van de Arbeid van België') and its French-speaking wing is the PTB ('Parti du Travail du Belgique'). This is not an unimportant phenomenon, because language-oriented regional disputes before were calmed by the (national) party leadership in order to ensure the internal cohesion of the party.

In 1968, the Catholic Party split up into the 'Parti Social Chretien' (PSC), currently 'Centre Démocrate Humaniste' (CdH), and the 'Christelijke Volkspartij' (CVP), currently 'Christen-Democratisch en Vlaams' (CD&V). In 1971, the two wings within the Liberal Party similarly formed two autonomous parties: the 'Partij voor Vrijheid en Vooruitgang' (PVV), currently 'Vlaamse Liberalen en Democraten' (Open Vld), and the 'Parti Reformateur Libéral' (PRL), currently 'Mouvement réformateur' (MR). In 1978, the Socialist Party split up into the 'Socialistische

Partij' (SP), currently 'Socialisten en Progressieven anders' (sp.a), and the 'Parti Socialiste' (PS), the latter party generally enjoying a dominant position in Wallonia. The above-mentioned political parties have many associated civil society interest groups (e.g., trade unions, mutual insurance funds, cultural organisations) together forming a so-called 'pillar'.

The Communist Party was created after the First World War as a result of a split within the Socialist Party. Only for a very short time did it hold a significant number of seats within the national Parliament. From 1985 onwards, it no longer held seats in Parliament. But since 2014, its successor the PVDA/PTB is once again represented in the federal Parliament.

Since 1981, two environmentalist parties have been represented in Parliament: 'Anders Gaan Leven' (Agalev), now known as 'Groen', and 'Ecolo'.

Table 2 sets out the distribution of seats in the House of Representatives since 1946 among the various political parties.

Some observers feel that the 'pacification democracy', in which the traditional parties together set out the broad lines of the Belgian form of government, is no longer operative.

Unlike American political parties, Belgian political parties have a highly hierarchical organisation. Most Members of Parliament vote along party lines, although inevitable internal tensions and dissensions, sometimes leading to a split within the party, do occur.

Table 2 House of Representatives: Electoral Results since 1946 – Number of Seats

Party	*1946*	*1949*	*1950*	*1954*	*1958*	*1961*	*1965*	*1968*	*1971*	*1974*	*1977*	*1978*	*1981*	*1985*	*1987*	*1991*	*1995*	*1999*	*2003*	*2007*	*2010*	*2014*	*2019*
CVP-PSC	92	105	108	95	104	96	77																
CD&V[1]								50	47	50	56	57	43	49	43	39	29	22	21	30[11]	17	18	12
CdH[2]								19	20	22	24	25	18	20	19	18	12	10	8	10	9	9	5
BSP-PSB	69	66	77	86	84	84	64	59	61	59	62												
sp.a[3]												26	26	32	32	28	20	14	23	14[12]	13	13	9
PS												32	35	35	40	35	21	19	25	20	26	23	20
PVV-PLP[4]	17	29	20	25	21	20	48	47															
Open Vld[5]									20	21	17	22	28	22	25	26	21	23	25	18	13	14	12
MR[6]									11	9	14	14	24	24	23	20	18	18	24	23	18	20	14
PL									3	3	2	1											
PVDA-PTB[7]	23	12	7	4	2	5	6	5	5	4	2	4	2										
UDRT-RAD												1	3	1									
VU				1	1	5	12	20	21	22	20	14	20	16	16	10	5	8	1				
N-VA																					27	33	25
Vlaams Belang (VB)[8]												1	1	1	2	12	11	15	18	17	12	3	18
RW							2[8]	5	14	12	5	4											
DéFi[9]							3	7	10	9[9]	10	11	8[10]	3	3	3						2	2
Groen[10]													2	4	6	7	5	9		4	5	6	8

Party	*1946*	*1949*	*1950*	*1954*	*1958*	*1961*	*1965*	*1968*	*1971*	*1974*	*1977*	*1978*	*1981*	*1985*	*1987*	*1991*	*1995*	*1999*	*2003*	*2007*	*2010*	*2014*	*2019*
Ecolo													2	5	3	10	6	11	4	8	8	6	13
Lijst Dedecker																				5	1	0	0
Others	1			1		2										4	2	1	1	1	1	1	0
Total Seats	202	212	212	212	212	212	212	212	212	212	212	212	212	212	212	212	150	150	150	150	150	150	150

Source: Department of the Interior
1. Formerly 'CVP'.
2. Formerly 'PSC'.
3. Formerly 'SP'.
4. Until the 1961 election, the 'Liberale Partij/Parti Liberal'.
5. Formerly 'PVV'.
6. Formerly 'PRL', and from 1976 until 1979 'PRLW'.
7. Formerly 'KPB-PCB'.
8. Prior to 2004, 'Vlaams Blok'.
9. Formerly 'FDF'.
10. Prior to 2003, 'Agalev'.
11. The RW was constituted in 1968 through the merger of three parties.
12. Electoral alliance between the FDF and the PLDP.
13. Electoral alliance between the FDF and the RW.
14. Electoral alliance between the CD&V and the N-VA.
15. Electoral alliance between the sp.a and Spirit (a now-dissolved party).

§3. MISCELLANEOUS

I. Referendum

96. Referenda directly and decisively binding the legislative authority of Parliament cannot be held under the Belgian constitutional system because they are not compatible with the basic representative character of Belgian parliamentary democracy which is founded on the principle of national sovereignty. Individual citizens participate in the legislative authority only by electing representatives.

The constitutionality of a consultative referendum at the federal level, however, is subject to controversy. A minority hold the opinion that the Legislature has the power to organise purely advisory referenda on matters of national interest, since it has the residuary power to do everything not formally forbidden under the Constitution. The greater weight of legal doctrine, on the contrary, concurs with the opinion of the Council of State and denies that this power exists on the ground that it would be contrary to the principle of a representative parliamentary system, because consultative referenda would in practice have the same effect as decisive referenda. Therefore, consultative referenda at the federal level can only be organised after an amendment of the Constitution. The same objection applies for a consultative referendum at the level of the federated entities. For that reason, the Constitution was amended in 2014 granting the Regions (not the Communities) the competence to organise consultative referenda. Regional referenda may not deal with public finance, budgets, and matters for which a Special Majority Region Act is needed.[69] The arrangements for the consultative referenda have to be set out in a Special Majority Region Act.[70] Every regional consultative referendum is subject to a clearing review by the Constitutional Court prior to its organisation.[71]

In addition to the question as to its constitutionality, the organisation of referenda at the federal level gives rise to many problems. National referenda, for example on language issues or on matters regarding the relations between the communities, would be impossible in a bipolar Belgium where those issues are resolved along the lines of an elitist consensus, at least when acknowledging the continued operation of 'pacification democracy'.

The only time a consultative referendum was held perfectly illustrates this problem. The referendum organised on 12 March 1950 on the question whether or not King Leopold III should return from exile and take up his prerogatives again after the Second World War, produced an overwhelming majority in Flanders favouring the return of the King against a majority in the Walloon provinces being against his return (the 'Monarchy Crisis'). Although 57.68% of the total national electorate cast an affirmative vote, the political problem was not really solved. This eventually led

69. Article 39*bis* Constitution. Special Majority Region Acts require a quorum of a majority of members of the Region Parliament and a total number of votes in favour of at least two-thirds of votes cast. For the Brussels-Capital Region, the Act must also be approved by a majority of each language group.
70. Up to now, only the Walloon Region has implemented Art. 39*bis* of the Constitution via Special Majority Region Act of 19 July 2018 (*Gazette,* 28 Sep. 2018).
71. Article 142 para. 4 of the Constitution and Art. 30*ter* of the Special Majority Act on the Constitutional Court.

to the abdication of the King, which secured the continuance of the monarchy as an institution and perhaps even of the Belgian State itself.

97. Provincial and municipal authorities have the power to organise consultative referenda under the conditions prescribed by Region Act (Article 41 Constitution).[72] Only a Provincial or Municipal Council can decide to organise such referenda, yet a certain number of inhabitants can force the hand of the Council. Such a referendum may only pertain to provincial or municipal matters respectively. The sole aim of the referendum is to inform the provincial or municipal authorities. The local inhabitants cannot be obliged to participate in the referendum.

II. Delegation of Powers

98. As the authorities designated by the Constitution must exercise their powers in the manner laid down by the Constitution (Article 33 Constitution), they cannot delegate these powers to other authorities: *potestas delegata delegari non potest.*[73] Delegation of powers is forbidden. Nevertheless, the strict application of this rule would lead to public institutions functioning too rigidly. It is assumed that an authority which under the Constitution has been given some powers by the Nation may establish some subordinate authorities and charge them with the power to take secondary measures under its supervision and with its explicit or implicit approval.[74] Therefore, the King may delegate part of his regulatory powers to his Ministers, who may enact secondary measures by Ministerial Decrees within the framework established by Royal Decree.

Selected Further Reading

Delpérée, F. (ed.) *Référendums* (CRISP, 1985).
De Prins, D. *Handboek Politieke Partijen* (die Keure, 2011).
Ganshof van der Meersch, W.J. *Pouvoir de fait et règle de droit dans le fonctionnement des institutions politiques* (Eds de la Librairie Encyclopédique, 1957).

72. And the supra-municipal authorities: see further below Pt. III. Ch. 3. §1.
73. See further below Pt. II. Ch. 3. §5. I 'Delegation of Legislative Power'.
74. Cass., 4 May 1920 (*Van Houtte*) *Pas.*, 1920, I, 135.

Chapter 2. Head of State

99. The federal executive power, pursuant to the Constitution, is vested in the King (Article 37 Constitution). Because the King himself is inviolable and unaccountable, he appoints Ministers and Secretaries of State who are responsible for his acts. As a result, the constitutional notion of 'King' refers both to the person of the King himself and to the responsible Ministers and Secretaries of State. The Executive has therefore a dualistic structure.

This chapter will briefly set out the general rules governing the personal status of the King, while the rules concerning the government are dealt with in Chapter 4.

§1. Designation

100. Belgium is a hereditary and parliamentary monarchy. The constitutional powers of the King are hereditary in direct line of the natural (non-adopted), legitimate (lawfully born in wedlock) heirs of King Leopold I, in order of primogeniture (Article 85 Constitution). Pursuant to the 'Salic law', succession to the throne under the 1831 Constitution was reserved to male heirs. Since the 1991 amendments to the Constitution, succession to the throne has been extended to female descendants, who now enjoy the same rights of succession in order of primogeniture.

The Constitution provides only one case of disqualification from this hereditary right, namely where a royal successor marries without the King's consent. But the successor can be restored to his right by the King with the assent of both Houses of Parliament (Article 85 Constitution).

101. The King does not accede to the throne until he has duly sworn the constitutional oath before a joint sitting of the Houses of Parliament (Article 91 Constitution).

102. Although not explicitly mentioned in the Constitution, it is accepted that the King may abdicate. This occurred for the first time in Belgian history on 21 July 2013 when the King, Albert II, voluntarily stepped down from the throne in favour of his son, Prince Filip, who became thereby the seventh King of Belgium.[75] The other constitutional hypothesis in which the powers of the King cease before his death is the inability to reign mentioned in Article 93 of the Constitution. In these cases, there is an interregnum until a successor or the Regent has taken the oath. During this period, the constitutional powers of the King are exercised in the name of the Belgian people by the Ministers in Cabinet and under their own responsibility (Article 90 Constitution).

75. The abdication of King Leopold III on 16 July 1951 can also be referred to. But this, however, was not really a 'voluntary' abdication because he was forced to step down in very specific circumstances.

The interregnum should be as short as possible. Article 90 of the Constitution prescribes that upon the death of the King the Houses of Parliament shall meet, without being convened, at the latest on the tenth day following the date of decease. They will either administer the oath of office to the successor or make arrangements for a regency.

103. A Regent is appointed by the Houses of Parliament in joint sitting in the following three circumstances. First, the heir to the throne is a minor, being not yet 18 years old (Article 92 Constitution). Second, the King is unable to reign (Article 93 Constitution). And finally, there are no descendants of King Leopold I and the throne is vacant (Article 95 Constitution). This latter situation can be avoided by the King's nomination of his successor, with the assent of both Houses of Parliament (Article 86 Constitution). Belgium has had two Regents to date: Surlet de Chokier (1831; vacancy of the throne) and Prince Charles (1944–1950; King Leopold III unable to reign). In the latter situation, pursuant to the Act of 19 July 1945, the Houses of Parliament meeting in joint session on 20 July 1950 acknowledged that this impossibility had ended.

The Regent has the same status as the King. This applies to his powers as well as to his privileges. However, Article 197 of the Constitution provides that during a regency no amendment to the Constitution may be made regarding the constitutional powers of the King or with respect to Articles 85–88, 91–95, 106 and 197 of the Constitution, these articles dealing with the status of the King, the succession to the throne, and the regency.

104. In one rather exceptional case, no Regent was appointed despite the King being treated as unable to reign pursuant to Article 93 of the Constitution.[76] Because of conscientious objections, King Boudewijn I refused to give royal assent to a Bill, approved by both Houses of Parliament, legalising abortion. On 3 April 1990, the Ministers meeting in Cabinet established, with the consent of the King, his inability to reign under Article 93 of the Constitution, and then gave the necessary assent to the Bill pursuant to the powers under paragraph 2 of Article 90 of the Constitution. Afterwards, on 5 April 1990, a joint session of both Houses of Parliament established that the inability to reign of King Boudewijn I had come to an end. This event has already led to several proposals to limit the prerogatives of the Crown, especially in relation to the power to give or to refuse royal assent to a Private Member's Bill once approved by Parliament.

105. To avoid repeated parliamentary discussions about the monarchy, Article 89 of the Constitution prescribes that a sovereign grant, a 'civil list', is established by Act for the duration of the reign of every King. The civil list covers the totality of financial means that are put at the disposal of the King for the exercise of his duties as Head of State. Notwithstanding this constitutional rule, the Legislature has repeatedly adjusted for inflation the amount of the civil list. Moreover the House of Representatives also votes on the annual grants-in-aid to other members of the

76. See X. Mabille, *Le débat politique d'avril 1990 sur la sanction et la promulgation de la loi* (CRISP, 1990) CH No. 1275.

Royal Family. Unlike the civil list, which is mandatory under the Constitution, these grants-in-aid are optional, voluntary. There was general political agreement to restrict significantly these amounts after the reign of the former monarch, Albert II. This resulted in the Act of 27 November 2013 (only a few months after the inauguration of King Filip) which limits the beneficiaries of the grants-in-aid to the Crown heir-apparent and the former Head of State.[77] The brothers and sisters (heirs presumptive) of the Crown heir-apparent are no longer entitled to grants-in-aid.[78] The beneficiary must also justify his expenses to the First President and the President of the Office of the Auditor General. Further, the part of the sovereign grant that is considered as salary for the beneficiaries is subjected to income tax.[79] The beneficiaries also have to pay all applicable indirect taxes.

§2. Legal Status

I. Inviolability and Unaccountability

106. The rule of the inviolability of the person of the King, under Article 88 of the Constitution, is absolute. The King has immunity from any civil or criminal proceedings. This inviolability also applies to political matters. Neither the government nor Parliament can impeach the King or call him to account for any act.

II. Inability of the King to Act Alone

107. The principle of royal inviolability and immunity is only acceptable if someone else is accountable for the King's acts. For that reason, the Constitution, immediately after stating the principle of inviolability and immunity, also provides in Article 88 of the Constitution that his Ministers are accountable.

108. This ministerial responsibility is of a political sort in the sense that Ministers are accountable to the House of Representatives (Article 101 Constitution). The principle of ministerial responsibility is general, and applies to all acts of the King which might have some political impact. Hence, it is generally accepted that even the marriage of the King comes within the scope of this principle. For this reason, the children of the second marriage of King Leopold III are excluded from succession to the throne. For matters in writing, ministerial responsibility is actualised by the countersignature of a Minister who thereby renders himself responsible (Article 106 Constitution).

---

77. Act of 27 November 2013 on Royal Grants-in-Aid and other remuneration to members of the Royal Family and regarding transparency in the financing of the monarchy (*Gazette,* 30 Dec. 2013). Provision is also made for a surviving partner. Pursuant to its Art. 9, other members of the Royal Family not in receipt of a grant-in-aid may receive, on the terms and conditions specified there, reimbursement for services rendered in the public interest.
78. By way of transitional arrangement, Prince Laurent and Princess Astrid are allowed to keep their grants-in-aid.
79. The other part of the grant covers operating and personnel expenses.

Ministerial responsibility is in principle taken up on an individual, and not collective, basis. Nevertheless the Belgian parliamentary system of proportional representation – almost invariably leading to coalition governments – has entailed the development of collective responsibility. Article 96 of the Constitution prescribes that the House of Representatives can oblige the federal government to offer its resignation to the King when: (i) a majority of House members passes a motion of non-confidence which proposes a successor to the Prime Minister for appointment by the King[80] or (ii) makes such a proposal within three days after rejecting a motion of support. On that occasion, the King appoints the proposed successor as Prime Minister, who takes office at the moment of the swearing-in of the new federal government. However, the occurrence of either type of motion, the one based on passing a motion of non-confidence, and the other, on rejecting a motion of support, is rather unlikely since the formation of an alternative majority without new elections is no sinecure in the complex Belgian political landscape. Moreover, this procedure is situated within the relationship between Parliament and government. Since 1946 no government has had to offer its resignation upon the motion of Parliament. The government would rather resign voluntarily in case of irreconcilable differences of opinion.

III. The King Has No Personal Power

109. The aforesaid rules imply that no powers of the King granted under the Constitution or by statutes can be deemed to be personal. In all cases, they are to be exercised by the King together with his Ministers. The actual administration of the State is taken care of by the government, which is responsible to the House of Representatives for its policy, the State being only formally governed in the name of the King.

110. The assertion that the King has no personal power does not mean that he has no political influence. Following Bagehot, the King, under a constitutional monarchy such as the Belgian one, has three rights: the right to be consulted, the right to encourage and the right to warn. Consultations between the King and his Ministers must be kept secret in order to avoid 'exposing the Crown'.[81] If the Ministers cannot convince the King to follow their opinion, they should resign. The political influence of the King can only apply insofar as it is accepted by his Ministers and, through them, by Parliament. Although some political parties wish to abolish the Belgian monarchy completely, currently neither a political majority nor a constitutional possibility exist to deprive the King of his role in the formation of the government.

80. Regardless of the number of members present, the required majority is thus seventy-six members.
81. See also General Introduction §2 IV 'A Constitutional Monarchy'.

SELECTED FURTHER READING

Delpérée, F. 'Le Roi règne et ne gouverne pas'. *J.T.* (1990): 701–704.
Delpérée, F. 'Le Roi sanctionne les lois'. *J.T.* (1991): 593–597.
Fornoville C. 'De Belgische monarchie in een nieuw kleedje'. In *Het federale België na de Zesde Staatshervorming* edited by A. Alen, B. Dalle, K. Muylle, W. Pas, J. Van Nieuwenhove & W. Verrijdt (die Keure, 2014) 163–176.
Molitor, A. *La fonction royale en Belgique* (2nd) (CRISP, 1994).
Stangherlin, K. *Le Patrimoine Royal* (La Charte, 2004).
Stengers, J. *L'Action du roi en Belgique depuis 1831. Pouvoir et influence* (Duculot, 1992).
van den Wijngaert, M., L. Beullens & D. Brants. *België en zijn koningen. Monarchie en macht* (Houtekiet, 2000).
X, 'Rappport de la Commission chargée d'émettre un avis motivé sur l'application des principes constitutionnels relatifs à l'exercice des prérogatives du Roi et aux rapports des grands pouvoirs constitutionnels entre eux' *Belgium Gazette* (6 August 1949): 7589–7600.

Chapter 3. The Legislature

§1. The Organ of State

I. A Bicameral Parliamentary System

A. Introduction

111. The Belgian federal parliamentary system is 'bicameral', meaning that the federal Parliament consists of two distinct assemblies. The first assembly is called the 'House of Representatives', the second the 'Senate'. For a long time and until 1993, both assemblies had the same legislative powers, some exceptions notwithstanding. As a general rule, the House of Representatives as well as the Senate were involved in the legislative process. Without prior approval by both Houses of Parliament, a Bill could not receive royal assent. The 1993 State Reform and then subsequently the 2014 Sixth State Reform transformed the Senate into a parliamentary assembly representing the federated entities and with only limited legislative powers.

112. For the vast majority of the federal legislation, the federal legislative power is jointly exercised by the King and the House of Representatives only, and the Senate has no role to play. This is different, however, for legislation that concerns either the Communities or the Regions. The House of Representatives and the Senate have concurrent jurisdiction in a number of matters that are enumerated exhaustively in the Constitution: Article 77. This constitutional list includes (1) constitutional amendments, (2) federal legislation concerning the powers of the Communities and the Regions, the composition and functioning of their parliaments and governments, their financial position, the co-operation between the federation and the federated entities, and other important aspects of their internal structure and functioning, (3) federal legislation concerning the Constitutional Court, (4) federal legislation concerning the financing of political parties and the control of their election expenses, and (5) federal legislation concerning the organisation of the Senate and the status of senators. This list of matters can be expanded with a Special Majority Act. For these matters, the House and the Senate operate on equal footing as was generally the case before 1993: both the House and the Senate must adopt the same text version before the text can be submitted for royal assent.

113. Additionally, the Senate can choose to intervene in the parliamentary proceedings in some other matters that concern the Communities and the Region, albeit to a lesser degree. These matters, also enumerated exhaustively in the Constitution (Article 78), include (1) federal legislation assuring compliance by the Communities and Regions with international or supranational obligations, and (2) federal legislation regarding the Council of State and the federal administrative courts. This list of matters can equally be expanded with a Special Majority Act. In these matters, the Senate can decide to review a Bill that the House has adopted, within fifteen days after the receipt of the Bill. The Senate then, within a period not exceeding thirty days, can either decide there is no reason to amend the Bill (in which case the

Bill is immediately submitted for royal assent), or decide to adopt the Bill after amending it. In the latter case, the House takes the final decision by either passing or amending the Bill. Finally, the Senate can draw up information reports on issues which have ramifications for the respective jurisdiction of the Communities and the Regions. These reports must be adopted with a majority of the votes cast, with both language groups in the Senate casting at least one-third of all votes. These information reports can address both legislative and other matters.

B. Rationales for the Federal Bicameral System

114. The 1831 National Congress paid much attention to the bicameral system. The institution of the Senate was deemed necessary to represent the aristocracy and large landowners. In addition, a second assembly was considered crucial to handle potential conflicts between the King and the House of Representatives. Later on, especially after the extension of the franchise in 1921, the rationale for the Belgian bicameralism became rather technical than political: a second assembly might improve the legislative work of the first assembly and correct possible errors.

115. In the course of time, the deficiencies of this original bicameral system became clear. Particularly the cumbersome nature of the legislative process, due to the double examination in both assemblies which was required for the adoption of any Bill, was considered to be a serious drawback. A revision of the system seemed inevitable. The gradual federalisation of the unitary Belgian State since 1970 made a revision of the existing bicameralism all the more urgent. Indeed, an essential feature of any federal State is due representation of the federated entities in the federal Parliament. The 2014 Sixth State Reform (following a transitory system introduced in the 1993 Fourth State Reform) established a radical reorientation of the federal bicameral system with a Senate that was no longer directly elected and almost exclusively composed of representatives of the federated entities. At the same time, the Senate lost most of its legislative powers, following the logic that federated entities should only have influence over federal legislation which directly concerns the institutional framework of the federal state.[82] This implies that, for almost all legislation which pertains to the powers of the federal level, a de facto unicameral system has been introduced, since the Legislature comprises only the House of Representatives and the King. The possible shortcomings of this unicameral system – in view of the quality of the legislative work – are remedied by the introduction of the possibility of renewed deliberation after a vote on a Bill in the House of Representatives, although this possibility is seldom applied in practice.

82. This implies that the Senate, as a non-permanent body (Art. 44 Constitution), meets much less regularly than the House of Representatives.

II. Categorisation of the Members of Parliament

A. *Categorisation of the Members of Parliament by Legislative Assembly*

116. The House of Representatives is composed of 150 directly elected members (Article 63 §1 Constitution). For the election of the House of Representatives, the territory of Belgium has been divided into eleven constituencies. The borders of these constituencies track those of the provinces.[83] The only exception concerns the six Brussels periphery municipalities with special language arrangements that, although entirely situated in the Province of Flemish Brabant, constitute a separate electoral district. Voters in this electoral district can vote for candidates from the constituency of Flemish Brabant (which corresponds with the province in which the electoral district is situated) or for candidates from the constituency of Brussels-Capital. This seemingly unnecessary complication is the result of a politically very sensitive and divisive issue concerning the principle of territorial linguistic homogeneity that took several years to resolve during the 2014 Sixth State Reform. This arrangement with a separate electoral district also applies to the European Parliament elections and is entrenched in two constitutional provisions (Articles 63 §4 and 168*bis* Constitution). It can only be amended by Special Majority Act.

The seats in the House of Representatives are allocated to the constituencies in proportion to their population size (Article 63 §2), calculated according to the population figures in the National Citizens Registry (Article 63 §3). Moreover, an electoral threshold of 5% per constituency is in effect.

117. The sixty members of the Senate are divided into two categories (Article 67 Constitution).

1. Fifty Senators Representing the Federated Entities

118. Fifty senators are appointed by and from the Members of the Parliaments of the Communities and the Regions. Twenty-nine senators represent the Flemish Parliament and the Dutch-speaking language group of the Brussels-Capital Region Parliament. Ten senators represent the French Community Parliament; eight senators the Walloon Parliament, and two senators, the French-speaking language group of the Brussels-Capital Region Parliament. The German Community Parliament is represented by a single senator. The appointment of these senators is based on a system of proportional representation of the different political parties in their respective Parliament as determined by the outcome of the relevant elections to those bodies.[84] The appointed senators retain their seats in their respective Community or

83. With the exception of Brussels-Capital, not belonging to any of the ten provinces.
84. For the allocation of the seats of the twenty-nine senators representing the Flemish Parliament and the Dutch-speaking language group of the Brussels-Capital Region Parliament, the election results of the Flemish Parliament are taken into account. For the allocation of seats to the twenty senators representing the French Community Parliament, the Walloon Parliament and the French-speaking

Region Parliament (as the case may be) in line with the underlying idea that they are representing these Parliaments in the Senate.

2. Ten Co-opted Senators

119. The co-opted senators are appointed by the senators representing the federated entities. Six co-opted senators are appointed by the twenty-nine senators representing the Flemish Parliament and the Dutch-speaking language group of the Brussels-Capital Region Parliament. Four co-opted senators are nominated by the twenty senators representing the French Community Parliament, the Walloon Parliament and the French-speaking language group of the Brussels-Capital Region Parliament. The appointment of the co-opted senators is based on a system of proportional representation of the different political parties in the Senate as determined by the outcome of the elections to the House of Representatives, this last detail being slightly at odds with the concept of a Senate representing the Communities and the Regions.

B. Categorisation of the Members of Parliament by Language Group

120. For the cases provided in the Constitution, being the approval of Special Majority Acts and the alarm-bell procedure[85], almost every Member of Parliament belongs either to the Dutch or the French language group with the sole exception of the senator representing the German Community Parliament, who does not belong to any language group (Article 43 Constitution).

121. The members of the House of Representatives are divided into language groups on the basis of objective and subjective criteria which are established by statute.[86]

(i) *The objective criterion*: Does the constituency wherein the member of the House of Representatives was elected belong entirely to the Dutch or French language region? If yes, then the member of the House of Representatives belongs to the Dutch or French language group respectively. When the member is elected in the German language region, he belongs to the French language group.
(ii) *The subjective criterion*: Depending on the language in which that member swears the oath of allegiance to the Constitution, the member of the House of

language group of the Brussels-Capital Region Parliament, the cumulative election results of the Walloon Parliament and of the French-speaking electoral lists of the Brussels-Capital Region Parliament are taken into account.

85. See further below Pt. I. Ch. 3. §1. II 'Special Majority Acts' and this chapter at §4. IV 'The Alarm-Bell Procedure'.
86. Article 1, Act of 3 July 1971, *Gazette*, 6 Jul. 1971.

Representatives elected in the constituency of Brussels-Capital belongs either to the Dutch or to the French language group.

122. The division of senators into language groups is constitutionally determined (Article 43 §2). The *Dutch language group* consists of thirty-five senators comprised of the twenty-nine senators representing the Flemish Parliament and the Dutch-speaking language group of the Brussels-Capital Region Parliament, and the six co-opted senators they appoint. The *French language group* consists of twenty-four members, namely the twenty senators representing the French Community Parliament, the Walloon Parliament, and the four co-opted senators appointed by them.

III. Electoral System

A. *The Party and Electoral System: General Introduction*

123. In the Belgian legal order, political parties are usually associations without legal personality. Although the Constitution does not expressly mention political parties, the application of the constitutional principle of proportional representation implies the existence of political parties (Articles 62 and 68 §1 Constitution). Moreover, their legal position has been recognised in an increasing number of statutes. In addition, political parties are bearers of fundamental rights and freedoms, such as the freedom of assembly, freedom of speech, and the right not to be discriminated against.

In a representative democratic legal order, political parties are the necessary intermediaries between State authority and the people. The people can register their approval or disapproval of exercises of State authority at the time of elections through groups which express major social tendencies and opinions.

124. The general evolution of the Belgian party and electoral system can be summarised as follows. From 1831 to 1847, there were no real political parties, since genuine party divisions were absent. It was a period of 'unionistic' governments, freely formed by King Leopold I. This period could be referred to as the 'orleanistic regime'. From 1847 to 1894, Belgium had a two-party system comparable to the British model. The government consisted of either Catholics or Liberals, depending on which party had the majority in Parliament. After 1894, and particularly after the First World War, the two-party system broke down due mainly to the introduction of universal suffrage and the system of proportional representation for general elections. And this gradually gave way to the current multiparty representation in the Parliaments.

125. The proportional system aims at allocating parliamentary seats in proportion to the votes cast for each party. This system increases the influence of political parties in more than one respect. To begin with, the ranking of the candidates on the party lists is generally decisive for the determination of which candidates are elected.

Moreover, since no party is able any longer to secure an absolute majority in elections, coalition governments are inevitable. Accordingly, government formation after general elections is mainly the result of party negotiations. As a consequence, the electorate no longer has the final word. Finally, the splitting up of political parties along language and community lines must be borne in mind. This splitting up has resulted in a significant increase in the number of political parties as well as in the necessity of forming coalition governments across the language divide.

126. The aim of the proportional system is a Parliament whose composition reflects the will of the electorate as accurately as possible. However, the proportional system has drawbacks too, most notably the danger of a fragmentation of political parties, particularly when the system is applied throughout the entire territory and in large constituencies. For that reason, two corrections have been introduced regarding the election of the House of Representatives.

Firstly, the Belgian proportional system is applied within the constituencies and not across the territory of Belgium as a whole. As mentioned above, there are at the moment eleven constituencies, whose borders match those of the provinces.

Secondly, an electoral threshold has been introduced. Only those party-candidate lists which obtain 5% of all votes cast in a particular constituency can win seats in the House of Representatives.

B. Candidates

127. All Members of Parliament must comply with the following four conditions of eligibility (Articles 64 and 69 Constitution):

(i) having Belgian nationality;
(ii) having the benefit of civil and political rights;
(iii) having a residence in Belgium (though not in a specific constituency), and
(iv) being at least 18 years of age.

In application of Article 11*bis* of the Constitution, legislation requires candidate lists for each party (as for other public elections) to contain an equivalent number of men and women, as well as the first two candidates on each list to be of alternate gender.

The Houses of Parliament themselves decide whether or not members meet the conditions of eligibility (Article 48 Constitution). An important judgment delivered by the Grand Chamber of the European Court of Human Rights puts this rule under pressure.[87] According to the Court, the newly elected legislative chamber's exclusive power to adjudicate postelectoral complaints violates Article 3 of the First Additional Protocol EConvHR and Article 13 EConvHR, because MPs whose own mandate depends on turning down the complaints cannot be considered to be an impartial tribunal. The inaccessible and imprecise rules of procedure governing that

87. ECtHR (GC), *Mugemangango v Belgium* (10 Jul. 2020).

complaint procedure and the lack of review by a tribunal meeting the due process standards also violate these treaty provisions. That judgment did not come as a surprise, because earlier caselaw had already made clear that the ECtHR does not accept the parliaments itself as impartial judges of disputes about their composition (ECtHR, *Grosaru v Romania* (2 March 2010)). Nevertheless, this violation of the right to fair legislative elections cannot be remedied during the current legislature, as Article 48 of the Constitution is not open for amendment.

C. *Voters*

128. Voting for members of the House of Representatives occurs on the basis of the principle of universal and equal suffrage ('one person, one vote'). In order to be entitled to vote, a person must satisfy the following three conditions (Articles 8 and 61 Constitution):

(i) have Belgian nationality;
(ii) be at least 18 years old, and
(iii) not be otherwise prohibited by Act (e.g., convicted of serious criminal offences).

Belgians who live abroad also have under certain formal conditions the right – but not the obligation – to vote.

D. *The Principles of the Election Process*

129. Voting is obligatory and secret; it takes place within a municipality, subject to any exceptions prescribed by Act (Article 62 Constitution).

130. The organisation of the electorate is regulated by Act (Article 62 Constitution). For that purpose, the legislature has divided the country into eleven constituencies for the House of Representatives.

Elections occur pursuant to the system of proportional representation (the D'Hondt system), which is established by Act (Article 62 Constitution). As mentioned above, some corrections are applied to this system.

Candidates are elected according to their ranking on the electoral list established by their respective party. Political parties have important influence in the election process. Half of the votes cast for the party list as such, rather than for specific candidates, are applied as needed to pass the election threshold to the candidates in order of their ranking on their party list. Hence a candidate's ranking on a list is very decisive for their actual electability. Political parties have additional influence in the election process because they also establish a list of 'successor-candidates' who are ranked separately (but elected at the same time with all the others) and who take the place of elected Members of Parliament when they relinquish their mandate by appointment to executive office or otherwise.

Finally, Article 39*ter* of the Constitution prohibits the entry into force of new legislation concerning the basic principles of elections for the House of Representatives less than one year before the anticipated end of the current session of Parliament.[88] The entry into force of such new legislation is postponed until at least one year after its promulgation.[89]

§2. Legal Status

I. Mandate of the Member of Parliament

A. Representative Character of a Mandate

131. The representative character of the Belgian parliamentary system implies that Members of Parliament cannot be considered to be the exclusive representatives of the constituency electing them. An imperative mandate is prohibited. A Member of Parliament is not subordinated to his electorate and is not subject to any recall from office. From a legal point of view, the former cannot receive instructions from his electorate nor from the party to which he belongs. This principle is laid down in Article 42 of the Constitution: 'The Members of both Houses of Parliament represent the Nation and not only those who elected them.' In practice, however, it is difficult to deny the existence of such a subordinate relationship between a Member of Parliament and his constituency, as well as his party. Moreover, Article 43 of the Constitution provides for the division of the Members of Parliament into language groups for specific votes and procedures. In those cases a Member of Parliament formally represents not only the Nation but also the language community to which he belongs. Also, the new function of the Senate as the representative institution of the Parliaments of the Communities and the Regions further erodes the principle contained in Article 42 of the Constitution.

B. Duration of a Mandate

132. All members of the House of Representatives are elected for a term of five years. The House is subject to a general election every five years (Article 65 Constitution). Up to the present, these general elections are held on the same day as elections for the European Parliament.

The term of office for the senators representing the Parliaments of the Communities and the Regions is different from that of the members of the House, since these senators are appointed by their respective Parliaments, the election of which does not necessarily coincide with the election of the House of Representatives and the European Parliament. The term of office of these senators begins on the day of

88. Regarding the interpretation of this concept of 'basic principles', see Council of State, Legislative Division, Opinion No. 65.673/2/AV of 29 Apr. 2019.
89. This constitutional provision also applies to legislation concerning the elections for the Community and Region Parliaments.

their taking the oath in the Senate, and ends on the opening day of the first sitting of the new Parliament which had appointed them after general elections for it (Article 70 Constitution).

The term of office for the co-opted senators, on the other hand, begins on the day of their taking the oath in the Senate and ends on the opening day of the first sitting of the House after general elections for it (Article 70 Constitution).

133. The King's power to dissolve the House of Representatives, which, like any other royal power, is exercised under Ministerial responsibility, serves as a counterweight to the political responsibility of the government to the House of Representatives.[90] The resolution to dissolve includes the calling of an election within forty days and the summoning of the House of Representatives within two months. In order to ensure parliamentary stability, the House can only be dissolved in the cases exhaustively listed in Article 46 of the Constitution, namely:

(1) when the House of Representatives, by a majority of its members, rejects a motion of support of the government and does not propose within a period of three days, starting on the day of rejecting that motion, a successor to the Prime Minister for appointment by the King;
(2) when the House of Representatives, by a majority of its members, passes a motion of non-confidence in the government and does not at the same time propose to the King a successor to the Prime Minister for appointment, and
(3) in the event of the resignation of the government, after the House of Representatives has voted its assent thereto by a majority vote of its members.

The dissolution of only the House of Representatives and not of the Senate means that, unless elections for the Parliaments of the Communities and the Regions would be held on the same date as the elections for the House of Representatives, the senators representing these Parliaments continue to exercise their mandate in the Senate. The co-opted senators, on the other hand, will have to be re-elected based on the outcome of the new elections for the House of Representatives.

Pursuant to Article 195 of the Constitution, both the House and the Senate are automatically dissolved after the publication of the resolutions listing the Articles of the Constitution set for amendment. In this case, the dissolution of both Houses of Parliament, rather than only the House of Representatives, means that the Parliaments of the Communities and the Regions will have to appoint new representatives to the Senate regardless whether elections for these Parliaments occur simultaneously with the elections for the House of Representatives or not. After dissolution, both the House of Representatives and the Senate are summoned to sit within three months (Article 46 paragraph 5 Constitution).

134. A 'parliament' (or a 'legislature') extends over the entire period of time for which the Houses of Parliament are elected and exercise their authority, and must be distinguished from the notion of a 'session'. The latter term refers to the annual

90. Since the 1993 Fourth State Reform, the government is no longer politically responsible to the Senate, but only to the House of Representatives (Art. 101 Constitution).

period during which a House sits. The distinction has practical importance. At the start of a 'parliament', each House examines the credentials of its members (Article 48 Constitution); the oath is taken, and the Members are divided into language groups (Article 43 Constitution). For every session, each House appoints its own Speaker, deputy Speakers, and organises its executive committee (Article 52 Constitution). A session is also important for the operation of parliamentary immunity from prosecution.

Article 44 of the Constitution distinguishes between two types of sessions: the ordinary and the extraordinary. An ordinary session must last for at least forty days each year and starts by right each year on the second Tuesday of October, unless the King has previously convened the Houses. In practice, the term of an ordinary session covers one year since the King closes a session only a few days before the opening of the following ordinary session. Accordingly, extraordinary sessions, for which no minimum term is imposed, are no longer required, except during an election year. Finally, since the 2014 Sixth State Reform, the Senate is not a permanent body.

II. Incompatibilities, Immunities and Privileges

A. *Incompatibilities*

135. In order to guarantee the independence of Members of Parliament, both the Constitution and legislation have introduced 'incompatibilities' between functions.

In accordance with Article 49 of the Constitution, one cannot be a member of both the House of Representatives and the Senate at the same time. Neither can a member of a Community or Region Parliament be at the same time a member of the House of Representatives or a co-opted senator (Article 119 Constitution). Furthermore, a member of the federal Parliament who, after his election, is appointed as Minister and who accepts this appointment, ceases to sit in the House of Parliament but does take up his seat again when the King terminates his office as Minister (Article 50 Constitution). As long as the Minister serves in that federal office, his seat in the House of Parliament is occupied by the first candidate-successor on the relevant party list. Legislation has broadened this arrangement to those cases where a federal Member of Parliament has been appointed as Community or Region Minister.

It is important to point out that several statutes entail additional incompatibilities for members of the federal Parliament. The main statute in this respect is the Act of 6 August 1931.[91]

B. *Immunities*

136. In order to protect members of the federal Parliament in the exercise of their function, the Constitution provides for two forms of immunity (Articles 58 and

91. *Gazette,* 14 Aug. 1931. This Act stipulates that a parliamentary mandate is incompatible with, among other things, public office or mandates (State remunerated), and judicial or religious office.

59 Constitution). These cannot be waived by a Member of Parliament. They equally apply to the Members of the Community and Region Parliaments (Article 120 Constitution).

1. Parliamentary Freedom of Speech

137. According to Article 58 of the Constitution, 'No member of either House can be prosecuted or be the subject of any investigation with regard to any opinion expressed or vote cast in exercise of his duties'. If these conditions are met, the Member of Parliament enjoys an absolute immunity under civil and criminal law, both during and after the term of his mandate. This facet of parliamentary immunity aims to protect a Member's right to freedom of speech. Hence, it applies to all statements, oral and written, concerning parliamentary function, but not to acts of violence since these cannot be considered as an 'opinion' or a 'vote'. Moreover, parliamentary immunity only applies to opinions expressed in the exercise of a parliamentary function. According to the Court of Cassation, removing jurisdiction from a judge to determine whether liability may flow from an opinion expressed by a Member of Parliament or by a parliamentary committee does not disproportionately interfere with the right to access to courts.[92] This caselaw is in line with the viewpoint of the European Court of Human Rights: only if those opinions are connected to the exercise of parliamentary functions in the strict sense is there no breach of the right of access to a court.[93]

Only the Speaker of the House can intervene in the case of any abuse of that privilege. Disciplinary sanctions taken against a Member of Parliament must, however, be proportional to the severity of the alleged breach. Also, for those sanctions imposed after the fact (as opposed to immediate sanctions), certain procedural safeguards must be observed and basic reasons must be stated.[94]

2. Immunity from Prosecution

138. The immunity from prosecution established in Article 59 of the Constitution is of a different nature than parliamentary freedom of speech. To begin with, immunity from prosecution applies to criminal matters only. Furthermore, this immunity from prosecution implies that a supplementary requirement must be met for certain criminal procedure actions (e.g., a subpoena or a summons to appear in court) involving a Member of Parliament to be legal, namely the prior authorisation of the House of which he is a member. Finally, this immunity only arises during a parliamentary mandate, when Parliament is in session, and not if the Member is caught actually in the commission of an offence.

---

92. Cass., 1 Jun. 2006, *R.W.*, 2006–07, 213.
93. ECtHR, *A v UK* (17 Dec. 2002), *Cordova v Italy (No. 1 and No. 2)* (30 Jan. 2003), *Patrono, Cascini and Stefanelli v Italy* (20 Apr. 2006), and *C.G.I.L. and Cofferati v Italy* (24 Feb. 2009).
94. ECtHR, *Karácsoni et al. v Hungary* (17 May 2016).

However, the prior authorisation of the House is not required for coercive measures involving a Member of Parliament requiring a court order, even when Parliament is in session. Nevertheless, those measures, when sought during session and in a criminal matter, may only be ordered by the President of the Court of Appeal at the request of the judge seized, except for cases where the Member is caught in the commission of an offence. This decision is communicated to the Speaker of the House of Parliament concerned. Moreover, any search or seizure authorised in this way can only be executed in the presence of the Speaker of the House concerned or a Member of Parliament appointed by him. In addition, a criminal prosecution of a Member of Parliament, when Parliament is in session, can be commenced only by officers of the Public Prosecutors Office and by competent officials, and not by private individuals.

Finally, it must be pointed out that, at any stage of criminal investigation, the Member of Parliament involved therein can request of the House in which he sits, during the parliamentary session and in criminal matters, to suspend those criminal proceedings. The House of Parliament must decide on this request with a majority of two-thirds of the votes cast. The purpose of this is to hinder rash investigations.

C. *Privileges*

139. Originally, as a result of the property assessment franchise, the office of Member of Parliament was unsalaried. However, this system could no longer be upheld in a contemporary democratic system. For Members of Parliament to have a sufficient allowance, the Constitution was revised. Although the amount provided under Article 66 of the Constitution is now adjusted for inflation by the House of Representatives, the Constitution itself had not been adapted accordingly. The allowances due to members of the House and to co-opted senators are part of the operational expenses of the House and Senate respectively, included in the budget of endowments. The allowances for senators representing the Community and the Region Parliaments are determined and paid by their respective Parliaments. In addition to this indemnification, Members of Parliament have the right of free passage on all roads maintained by public authorities or given under concession within State borders. An annual supplementary allowance can be granted to the Speaker of the House of Representatives, to be debited from the subsidy covering the expenses of this assembly. The House determines the amount that can be withheld from the allowance as a contribution to retirement and pension funds which it considers desirable to establish. According to the Constitutional Court, pursuant to Article 66 of the Constitution the pensions of the members of the House of Representatives and their relevant survivors fall under the exclusive jurisdiction of the House (exercised therefore by means of standing orders), and this grant of jurisdiction being the choice of the Constituting Power, it falls outside the review powers of the Court.[95]

According to the Act of 2 May 1995 (as further filled out by the Act of 26 June 2004), Members of Parliament must provide an annual statement of all mandates,

95. Cons., Judgment No. 135/2017, 30 Nov. 2017.

offices, and positions they have occupied during the previous year.[96] This statement of offices is published in the *Gazette* and on the website of the Office of the Auditor General together with the names of the persons submitting these statements. Members must also submit on a yearly basis to the Office of the Auditor General a confidential statement of income and property.

§3. POWERS

I. Legislation

140. The enactment of statutes requires in principle the joint action of the three branches of the federal Legislature. According to Article 36 of the Constitution, federal legislative power is jointly exercised by the King, the House of Representatives, and the Senate. Article 36 must, however, be combined with Article 74 of the Constitution which provides that in all other matters than those referred to in Articles 77 and 78 of the Constitution, federal legislative power is jointly exercised by the King and the House of Representatives – thereby excluding the Senate. Those matters account for more than 95% of federal legislation, which severely restricts the role of the Senate in the legislative process, but this is in line with the role of the Senate as a representative institution of the Communities and the Regions. Save for the matters under Article 77 of the Constitution, government Bills are tabled in the House of Representatives (Article 75 Constitution).

141. The right to propose legislation refers to the right to introduce a Bill in Parliament, as well as the right to make amendments. This right is vested in each of the three branches of the federal legislature. It is, however, limited in particular cases. For example, Members of Parliament have no right of initiative as regards Acts for treaty or budget approval.

142. If a Bill is drafted and introduced by one or more members of the House of Representatives or, as the case may be, by one or more senators, this Bill is called a 'Private Member's Bill'. If the Speaker of the House in question deems the Bill admissible, it is published in *Parliamentary Documents* and distributed among the members of the House (or Senate as the case may be). The ensuing debates require that the Bill be expressly accepted by vote for further deliberation. However, in practice, this acceptance comes almost as a matter of course and a Private Member's Bill will be rejected for further deliberation only if it is manifestly unconstitutional.

If a Bill is introduced on the initiative of the King, it is called a 'government Bill'. Prior to its introduction in Parliament, a government Bill has already passed various preparatory stages. The Minister competent, assisted by civil servants, prepares a draft. After certain compulsory consultations, that draft Bill is discussed in Cabinet.

96. *Gazette,* 26 Jul. 1995 and 30 Jun. 2004. These obligations also apply to the members of the Community and Region Parliaments, as well as for the members of the government and other public office holders.

As a general rule, the government Bill in draft must be submitted to the Legislation Division of the Council of State for its non-binding advice and comments. Depending on the Division's advice, amendments to the draft Bill may be made when the draft Bill is again discussed in Cabinet. Subsequently, it is submitted to the King for signature. Upon royal signature the draft Bill is called formally a 'government Bill'. Finally, the government, by Royal Decree, sends the Bill to the executive committee of the House of Representatives. However, there is one exception to this general rule, set out in Article 75 of the Constitution: Bills relating to matters set out under Article 77 of the Constitution can be tabled in either the House of Representatives or the Senate, as chosen by the government. Unlike Private Member's Bills, a government Bill need not be expressly accepted for further deliberation. Furthermore, it must be noted that, as far as parliamentary proceedings are concerned, government Bills are generally prioritised over Private Member's Bills.

II. Supervision of and Control over the Executive

143. Parliament's function of exercising control over the government is one of the prime features of a parliamentary democracy. Many techniques of control are at Parliament's disposal. Most of them fall exclusively within the ambit of the jurisdiction of the House of Representatives: the powers relating to the criminal responsibility of the members of the Executive (Article 103 Constitution)[97], oral questions and the interpellation of the members of the Executive, the right to hold enquiries (Article 56 Constitution), the approval of federal treaties (Article 167 §2 Constitution)[98], the annual determination of the number of military personnel on active duty (Article 183 Constitution), and financial controls through the annual approval of budgets and the public accounts of the State (Article 174 Constitution). Moreover the House of Representatives can oblige the federal government to offer its resignation to the King when it passes a motion proposing a successor to the Prime Minister for appointment by the King (Article 96 Constitution).[99] The Senate cannot impose sanctions on either the government or an individual Minister, but senators can submit written questions to the government and the Senate can require the attendance of Ministers in the context of matters under Article 77 or 78 of the Constitution (Article 100 Constitution). In what follows, a brief overview is given of the different techniques of parliamentary control.

A. *The Right of Interpellation*

144. An important instrument to call the government to account is the right of interpellation. This right has been granted to the House of Representatives only, not to the Senate, and is provided for in its standing orders. Interpellation means that a member of the House submits particular questions regarding important current political affairs to one or more Ministers, or even to the government as a whole. The

97. See further below Pt. II. Ch. 2. §2 'Legal Status'.
98. See further below Pt. V. Ch. 1. §2. II 'The Treaty-Making Power'.
99. See further above Pt. II. Ch. 2. §2. II 'Inability of the King to Act Alone'.

debate following upon such questions is concluded by a vote on a motion. Members of the House can introduce a motion of non-confidence, while the government can submit a motion of support. To avoid a vote of non-confidence, members of the House who belong to the majority usually introduce a 'simple motion', which represents a parliamentary acknowledgement of the Minister's answer, so as to move to the next item of business on the Order Paper. Such a simple motion prevails over all other motions, except for the motion of support.

B. The Right to Ask Questions

145. As mentioned above, interpellation is an instrument to call the government to account for its policy and may be decisive for the future of the government or the Minister in question. Questions, on the contrary, are addressed to a specific Minister and do not engage the government's responsibility to the House. They serve to clarify legal problems, to encourage particular action on certain points, or to obtain information. The standing orders make a distinction between written questions and oral ones. Oral questions can only be submitted by members of the House, but written questions can also be submitted by senators. Whereas oral questions are answered orally, during the sitting of the House ('question time'), written questions require a written reply. Written questions and their answers are published in the *Bulletin of Questions and Answers* of the House of Representatives and the Senate respectively. Unlike the case of interpellations, the reply to an oral question is not followed by a vote on a motion.

C. The Right to Hold an Enquiry

146. According to Article 56 of the Constitution, the House of Representatives has the right to hold an enquiry. The exercise of this right to hold an enquiry is governed by the Parliamentary Enquiries Act of 3 May 1880, as amended by Act of 30 June 1996. According to this Act, the right to hold an enquiry is exercised by either the House itself or a Commission of Enquiry specially mandated for that purpose and composed of members of the House. Unlike the right to ask questions and the right of interpellation, the right to hold an enquiry is collective in nature. The decision to hold an enquiry and create a Commission therefor must be supported by a majority of the votes cast.

The right to hold an enquiry has a very wide scope: it purports to provide the House with all relevant information for the exercise of its legislative and control functions. To that end, a Commission of Enquiry will undertake an investigation of a particular issue or question (such as child abuse or human trafficking) and then will make public its report and conclusions regarding any Ministerial responsibilities and any proposed changes to legislation. On the other hand, the right to hold an enquiry is not absolute. To begin with, the principle of the separation of powers prohibits the Commission of Enquiry from infringing upon the judiciary's powers. Hence, the Commission cannot determine the guilt or innocence of a person in criminal matters. In addition, the Commission must observe constitutional and international human rights standards, in particular the right to a fair hearing. The Court of Cassation considers these rights to be breached if pursuing parliamentary enquiries and criminal investigations would hinder a judge from rendering an objective and independent decision.[100] Nevertheless a parliamentary enquiry and a criminal investigation may be conducted simultaneously. Finally, a Commission of Enquiry and its members have the benefit of parliamentary freedom of speech as guaranteed under Article 58 of the Constitution.[101]

D. *Techniques of Financial Supervision*

147. 'The power of the purse' is a traditional and efficient method for Parliament to supervise government policies. This prerogative is exercised through the annual approval of budgets and of the public accounts of the State (Article 174 Constitution). It will be dealt with in Pt. V below.

§4. The Workings of Parliament

I. Parliamentary Proceedings: Legislative Proceedings

148. Any government or Private Member's Bill (if accepted for further deliberation) is sent by the Speaker of the House in question to the relevant parliamentary committee. The parliamentary committees, the organisation and workings of which are governed by the standing orders of the House in question, are composed of a limited number of members appointed on the basis of proportional representation. Each committee carries out the preparatory work on Bills falling within its jurisdiction. The competent committee meets in the presence of the responsible Minister, assisted by members of his staff or by civil servants. In principle the meetings of the committees are open to the public.

A simple majority suffices for a committee validly to deliberate and to vote. One or more members of the committee summarise the deliberations in a report, on which the committee then takes a vote. A few days before the plenary session takes place regarding the matter at issue, the approved committee report is submitted to all the Members of the House in question. Like government Bills and Private Member's Bills, the committee report is published in *Parliamentary Documents*.

Since the Senate has lost most of its legislative powers, Article 76 §3 of the Constitution provides for the possibility of a second readings procedure by the various committees of the House of Representatives according to rules set by the House. The relevant committee may correct or amend the text adopted on first reading.

149. On the basis of the text approved by the parliamentary committee, the Bill is discussed by the relevant House in plenary session. After a general discussion of the Bill, each clause of and each amendment to the Bill is dealt with and voted on separately (Article 76 §1 Constitution). Finally, a vote is taken, by roll-call (i.e., by

100. Cass., 6 May 1993 (*Transnuclear*) *R.W.*, 1993–94, 382.
101. Cass., 1 Jun. 2006, *R.W.* 2006–07, 213. See above Pt. II. Ch. 3. §2. II. B 'Immunities'.

individual and electronically registered votes), on the government or the Private Member's Bill as a whole (Article 55 Constitution). The sessions are in principle held in public. Nevertheless, a House may sit *in camera*, on request of its Speaker or of ten members. The House decides afterwards, by majority vote, whether the sitting will resume in public to deal with the same matter (Article 47 Constitution). The debates and votes are published in a 'Summary Report', which is available in a short version the day after. The entire report of the parliamentary debates is published later on in *Parliamentary Proceedings*.

II. Quorum and Majority

150. Except for the cases expressly provided for in the Constitution, for a quorum as well as for a majority (particularly the Special Majority Acts and the revision of the Constitution), a majority of the members of the House in question must be present before the House may validly adopt a resolution. Every resolution is passed by a majority of the votes cast, except those otherwise prescribed by the standing orders of the Houses regarding elections and nominations.[102] Upon a tied vote, the tabled proposal is rejected (Article 53 Constitution). Abstentions are taken into account to calculate quorum, but not to calculate the majority of votes cast.

151. Unlike ordinary Acts, which are approved by a simple majority of the votes cast, Special Majority Acts must be passed by a majority of the votes cast in each language group in each House, on condition that a majority of the members of each group is present, and provided that the total number of votes in favour that are cast in the two language groups is equal to at least two-thirds of votes cast (Article 4 paragraph 3 Constitution). Special Majority Acts implement the constitutional rules as to the Communities and the Regions in those matters explicitly enumerated in the Constitution. A simple majority is the rule; a qualified majority, the exception. The Constitutional Court has jurisdiction to determine whether an Act has been adopted by the constitutionally required majority.[103] But the Court has held that it has no jurisdiction to determine whether in the case of a Special Majority Act the necessary special majority was in fact satisfied. This is so because the Court considers that it has no jurisdiction to review the constitutionality of how legislation is passed.[104]

III. Royal Assent, Promulgation and Publication of Acts

152. A Bill passed by the one or both Houses of Parliament, as the case may be, must in addition be approved by the King (Article 109 Constitution). The granting of royal assent is the last stage in the legislative process: it is the act by which the

102. The election and nomination of candidates are carried out by secret ballot: Art. 55 Constitution.
103. Cons., Judgment No. 18/90, 23 May 1990.
104. Cons., Judgment No. 35/2003, 25 Mar. 2003.

King, as a separate branch of the Legislature, approves the Act adopted by Parliament. As is the case for all other powers of the King, royal assent is given (or refused) under ministerial responsibility. The King still has the right to refuse assent to a Bill, although this right has fallen into abeyance since the nineteenth century. The exceptional case of the refusal by King Boudewijn I to assent to the Act legalising abortion illustrates, however, the difficulties to which the King's refusal may still give rise.[105] Moreover, there is no time limit within which the King must assent. Therefore, a considerable delay in granting royal assent could be considered as a disguised exercise of the right of veto.

The granting of royal assent must be clearly distinguished from the promulgation by the King (Article 109 Constitution). Promulgation implies that the King, as head of the Executive, solemnly confirms the existence of the Act and orders its implementation. The King thus acknowledges that the statute has been enacted in accordance with the constitutionally prescribed procedure. The judiciary has always refused to review the regularity of the lawmaking proceedings, with the exception of the Constitutional Court which reviews special majority requirements and the non-observance of co-operative procedures. Once the King has assented to the statute, promulgation is necessarily required. In practice, the King's signature constitutes both an assent to and promulgation of the Act. That signature determines the date of the Act, since the statute comes into existence on the date of promulgation.

153. To be enforceable and binding, a statute must be published in the manner laid down by Act (Article 190 Constitution). Pursuant to the Act governing the Use of Languages in Legislative Proceedings of 31 May 1961[106], a statute must, after its promulgation, be published in the *Gazette* in Dutch as well as in French, and comes into force ten days after its publication, unless the statute itself mentions another date or authorises the King to determine the date of entry into force. As of the expiry of that date, all citizens are presumed to know the law. This principle is given by the maxim *nemo censetur ignorare legem*. According to the Council of State, a statute must be published within a reasonable time unless some reasonable justification can be provided.[107] Moreover, the publication may not be deliberately delayed. The Council of State, when reviewing the legality of an administrative act based on the legislation in question, has jurisdiction to decide whether the delay is either reasonably justified or inconsistent with due administration.

IV. The 'Alarm-Bell Procedure'

154. The parliamentary process in each House can be suspended for a short period of consultation between Dutch-speaking and French-speaking politicians, according to Article 54 of the Constitution. This procedure is called the 'alarm-bell procedure', essentially protecting the French-speaking minority in both the House of Representatives and the Senate against a government Bill or a Private Member's

105. See further above Pt. II. Ch. 2. §1 'Designation'.
106. *Gazette,* 21 Jun. 1961.
107. Council of State, Administrative Tribunal Division, Judgment No. 71.761, 12 Feb. 1998 (*Beerten*).

Bill which 'can seriously endanger relations between the communities'. If, in such a case, at least three quarters of the members of one of the language groups introduce a motion supported by reasons, after the report has been submitted and prior to the final vote in plenary session, then parliamentary proceedings are suspended and the motion is referred to Cabinet. It provides a reasoned opinion on the matter within thirty days and invites the House concerned to pronounce on this opinion or on the amended public or private Bill, as the case may be.

The alarm-bell procedure is subject to two restrictions. First, the procedure is not applicable to Budget Bills and Acts for which a special majority is required, since Budget Bills guarantee the functioning of the State, and Special Majority Acts already provide sufficient protection of the minority concerned. Secondly, the 'alarm-bell procedure' can be applied only once by the members of a language group regarding the same government Bill or Private Member's Bill.

Since its introduction in the Constitution in 1970, the alarm-bell procedure has been used only twice. The first instance concerned a relatively minor incident involving the conferral of university status to a Flemish educational institute. The second case, more recently, concerned a Bill which intended to split up the constituency of Brussels-Halle-Vilvoorde.[108] In 2010, French-speaking politicians invoked the alarm-bell procedure in order to prevent this, but the procedure was not seen to its end because the government was forced to resign (for political reasons) shortly thereafter, and followed shortly thereafter by the dissolution of Parliament. The reason why the alarm-bell procedure has been used only twice in four decades is obvious. Any dispute between the communities either is solved in Cabinet, where the communities are equally represented, or leads to the resignation of the government. Hence, the 'alarm-bell procedure' has mainly a dissuasive, preventive effect.

§5. Miscellaneous

I. Delegation of Legislative Power

155. According to Article 105 of the Constitution, a Delegation Act passed under the authority of the Constitution may expressly confer on the King powers other than those formally vested in him by the Constitution. This constitutional provision enables the Legislative Branch to attribute to the Executive Branch broad regulatory powers reaching far beyond the limits of the simple implementation of statutes provided for under Article 108 of the Constitution. Originally, Article 105 of the Constitution was meant to limit in the first place the royal prerogative. However, the same provision has been invoked later on to justify an extreme extension of the King's powers. The evolution in the meaning of this constitutional provision has been confirmed by the Constitutional Court, which held that the Legislative Branch is free to delegate its powers in domains that are not reserved by the Constitution to

108. See further above Pt. II. Ch. 3. §1. II. A 'Categorisation of the Members of Parliament by Legislative Assembly'.

the Legislature itself.[109] The only constitutional requirement is that these delegations must be sufficiently precise, since Article 105 of the Constitution stipulates that the Legislative Branch 'expressly' confers these powers to the Executive Branch.

156. Delegations of legislative power can vary considerably as far as their scope is concerned. Statutes in which the Legislative Branch chooses only to determine certain guiding principles and confer the implementation of these principles upon the King are called 'Framework Acts'.

The Legislative Branch may also give the King the power formally to repeal, extend, amend, or replace existing legislation. This option is used to implement certain legislative measures taken by the Legislative Branch in other domains of legislation.

It has even become a standard procedure for the legislature to enact each year a 'Budgetary Act', regulating various matters to achieve the government's economic, social and financial goals and attributing broad regulatory powers to the Executive to realise these goals.

157. In domains that are reserved by the Constitution for the Legislature itself, by stipulating that a matter must be regulated 'by (an) Act', the Legislative Branch cannot in principle delegate the essential aspects of these matters to the Executive Branch. The Constitutional Court held that such delegations constitute a violation of the constitutional principle of equality and non-discrimination, since a certain category of citizens is deprived of the constitutional guarantee that the measure at hand would be determined by a democratically elected body.[110] Non-essential aspects can be freely delegated to the Executive Branch, as long as these delegations are sufficiently precise and relate to the execution of measures essentially regulated by the Legislature.

On the other hand, if the Legislature does delegate power to regulate essential aspects of measures constitutionally reserved for a democratically elected body, the Constitutional Court will find a violation of the constitutional guarantee of equality and non-discrimination, unless three conditions are simultaneously met:

(1) The Legislature states that it will examine the regulations issued by the Executive Branch within a short period after their publication, in order to confirm them. Without parliamentary confirmation within the prescribed period of time, those regulations are considered to be null and void.[111]

(2) Exceptional circumstances justify the legislative delegation. These circumstances must be such that it is impossible for the Legislature to reach its goal (vested in the general interest) while following the normal legislative procedure.[112]

---

109. Cons., Judgments No. 36/2012, 8 Mar. 2012; No. 107/2013, 18 Jul. 2013, and No. 56/2016, 28 Apr. 2016.
110. Cons., Judgment No. 141/2001, 6 Nov. 2001.
111. Cons., Judgment No. 53/2003, 30 Apr. 2003.
112. Cons., Judgment No. 107/2016, 7 Jul. 1016.

(3) The legislative delegation is express and unequivocal (this being a general condition for the delegation of powers by the Legislature).

158. Only if the legislative delegation does not satisfy these three conditions, will the Constitutional Court find a violation of the constitutional principle of equality and non-discrimination. However, for the sake of completeness, two further qualifications must be added. Firstly the Court applies a stricter test to legislative delegations concerning essential aspects of education and criminal law matters. Such delegations are always unconstitutional, even if they meet the three conditions listed above. Secondly, if the constitutional provision reserving certain matters to the Legislature is one which allows the Court to review compliance directly, then the Court may find a violation of that constitutional provision as such, instead of the constitutional principle of equality and non-discrimination. More precisely, the Court can examine an Act for compatibility with the provisions of Title II of the Constitution, and Articles 170, 172 and 191 of the Constitution. Many of these provisions reserve matters to the Legislature.

159. In altogether exceptional cases, mostly in times of economic and social crises, the Legislative Branch has conferred by a 'Special Delegation Act' upon the King the power to take 'all necessary measures' regarding very vaguely defined areas of social and economic activity, to achieve goals described in the same general and broad terms. Typically, but not always, these powers include the possibility to repeal, extend, amend or replace existing legislation.

Whereas ordinary Royal Decrees may, in principle, always be amended by another Royal Decree, Special Royal Decrees may only be amended by Royal Decrees for the period during which the authorisation stands. Once this period has expired, the Special Royal Decree may only be repealed, extended, amended or replaced by or by authority of an Act.

Judicial review of ordinary Royal Decrees concerns the compatibility of the Decree not only with the Act that is thus implemented, but also with other legislation and with the Constitution. On the contrary, judicial review of Special Royal Decrees is in fact limited to the review of the compatibility with the authorising Act.

160. The Legislation Division of the Council of State and the Constitutional Court have laid down the following general conditions for such a special authorisation to be consistent with Article 105 of the Constitution.

To begin with, the special authorisation from the Legislature is acceptable in 'extraordinary' crisis situations only. It falls within the province of the Houses of Parliament to evaluate the existence of such a crisis situation. However, they should not arbitrarily assume such a situation to exist.

Secondly, the special authorisation may only be given for a very limited period of time, typically six to twelve months.

Thirdly the special powers conferred upon the Executive Branch should be properly defined. Merely setting out the goals to be achieved does not suffice. In addition, the matters to be regulated should be pointed out, so as to make effective judicial review possible.

Finally, the Legislature must observe supranational and international rules and the separation of powers. The Legislature must not infringe upon the division of powers between the State, the Communities and the Regions, nor must the authorisation concern the matters reserved by the Constitution for the Legislature itself.

In practice, however, most Special Delegation Acts do not meet those conditions, in particular the requirements that the special powers conferred be properly defined and concern no matters reserved by the Constitution for the Legislature. In order to meet the constitutional requirements as much as possible, in most cases the Legislature has made the exercise of the special powers subject to subsequent parliamentary confirmation within a short period, as has been discussed above. Once the Royal Decrees have been confirmed by Act, they may only be annulled by the Constitutional Court.

II. Legislation Having Retroactive Effect

161. Although the prohibition on laws with retroactive effect is recognised as a general principle of law, the Belgian Constitution itself does not expressly prohibit the Legislature from passing retroactive legislation. However, the Legislature must take into account the following two considerations.

First, Article 7 EConvHR and Article 15 ICCPR prohibit a retroactive application of criminal law to the detriment of the accused. Since both treaty provisions are self-executing (under Belgian law), every judge is subject to a duty not to apply any statutory provision in breach of those provisions. Second, apart from criminal cases, the Constitutional Court and the ECtHR have set out limits on the validity of retroactive legislation. Thus, a retroactive Act must not infringe peremptory judicial decisions nor violate the principle of non-discrimination. Otherwise, such a statutory provision risks being found unconstitutional by the Constitutional Court.

162. Notwithstanding the case of interpretive legislation, the application of the principle of non-discrimination in the field of retroactive acts entails the following requirements:

(1) the retroactive character of the Act must be indispensable for the common good;
(2) the retroactive Act must not influence the outcome of pending judicial proceedings, unless justified by exceptional circumstances or compelling grounds of the common good, and
(3) the retroactive Act must not infringe on peremptory judicial decisions.

163. As regards interpretive legislation, however, the Constitutional Court has developed a slightly less intrusive validity test. The rationale for the Court's different approach lies in the fact that Interpretation Acts are by definition retroactive in nature (until the date on which the Act subject to the interpretation provisions came into force) and are applicable in ongoing proceedings (Article 7 Civil Procedure Code). Nevertheless these two characteristics only apply if and to the extent that the meaning of the Act subject to interpretation could reasonably be no other than the meaning set out in the interpretation statute.[113] To the extent that the Interpretation Act does not meet this condition, the same three-stage test for non-interpretive retroactive legislation applies. Even an Interpretation Act itself must not infringe on peremptory judicial decisions, or Article 7 EConvHR and Article 15 ICCPR.

SELECTED FURTHER READING

Alen, A. & J. Clement. '"Legislatuurregering" en "legislatuurparlement": politieke gadgets of een wezenlijke innovatie?'. In *Het federale België na de vierde Staatshervorming*, edited by A. Alen & L.P. Suetens (die Keure, 1993) 195–226.

Alen, A. & K. Muylle. 'Representation and Participation of the Federated Entities on the National Level'. In *Competition versus Co-operation. German Federalism in Need of Reform – A Comparative Perspective*, edited by R. Baus, R. Blindenbacher & V. Karper (Nomos, 2007) 125–135.

Detroux, L., M. El Berhoumi & B. Lombaert (eds). *La légalité. Un principe de la démocratie belge en peril?* (Larcier, 2019).

Lejeune, Y. & H. Simonart. 'L'article 78 [105] de la Constitution ou la faculté d'étendre le pouvoir réglementaire royal'. *Ann. dr.* (1980): 313–386.

Muylle, K. & J. Theunis. 'La Cour constitutionnelle comme juge de la séparation des pouvoirs: le cas des délégations et des validations'. In *Liber Amicorum M. Melchior* (Limal, 2010) 114–127.

Peeters, P. & D. Haljan, 'Belgium's Sixth State Reform: The State of the Nation(s)', *European Public Law* (2016), (411) 416–417 and 421–423.

Rezsöhàzy, A. & M. Van der Hulst (eds). *Parlementair recht en grondrechten / Le droit parlementaire et les droits fondamentaux* (die Keure / La Charte, 2010).

Van Coppernolle, T. *Intertemporeel recht* (Intersentia, 2019).

Van der Hulst, M. & Muylle, K. *Het federale Parlement* (INNI, 2017).

Verrijdt, W. 'De interpretatieve wet: retroactiviteit en rechtszekerheid' *T.B.P.* (2007): 259–280.

X, *Les élections dans tous leurs états* (Bruylant, 2001).

113. Cons., Judgment No. 102/2006, 21 Jun. 2006.

Chapter 4. The Executive

§1. The Organ of State

I. The Traditional Way of Forming a Government[114]

164. According to Article 96 of the Constitution, the King appoints and dismisses his Ministers. He also appoints and dismisses the Secretaries of State (Article 104 Constitution). Yet to a large extent the process of forming a government is subject to unwritten constitutional rules. The King plays an important role in this process, especially in appointing the person being charged with forming the government. Nevertheless, all acts of the King are subject to the principle of ministerial responsibility. In addition, the King must take into account the election results, in order to form a government based on a parliamentary majority. This implies that the 'government-making power' in fact lies with the House of Representatives and the political parties represented there.

165. The traditional process of forming a government is a complex procedure in which several stages may be discerned. At the outset, the King consults representatives of the political parties and of socio-economic interest groups. Thereafter, he appoints an '*informateur*' who is charged with examining the various coalition possibilities. If necessary, the King may appoint intermediaries and negotiators in order to complete the work of the *informateur*. In the light of the reports received, the King then appoints a '*formateur*' who is charged with forming a new government and negotiating its programme. In recent decades, this government programme has become ever more detailed, containing more and more concrete arrangements between the coalition parties regarding the policies to be pursued. The *formateur* proposes the composition of the new government, and is usually appointed Prime Minister.

166. As all acts of the King are covered by ministerial responsibility, this traditional process of forming a new government is formalised in three simultaneous Royal Decrees. A first Decree appoints the new Prime Minister and is countersigned by his predecessor. A second Decree accepts the resignation of the outgoing government, and a third and last Royal Decree appoints the other members of the new government. The latter two Royal Decrees are countersigned by the new Prime Minister.

114. That is, after a government voluntarily steps down, or after general elections. Since 1993, an additional route – but unused as of yet – is available under Art. 96 Constitution: the obligation of a government to offer its resignation to the King when the House of Representatives proposes a successor to the Prime Minister for appointment by the King. See Pt. II. Ch. 2. §2 'Head of State. Legal Status'.

II. Composition and Organisation of the Government

A. *The Cabinet: The Cabinet-in-Council – Privy Council*

167. The meetings and collective deliberation of government Ministers is referred to as 'the Cabinet'. Chaired by the Prime Minister, the Cabinet decides on government policy and is the real centre of political life and the motor of State policy. Secretaries of State do not belong to the Cabinet, and do not participate in its meetings, except in those cases in which they are called upon. The 'Cabinet-in-Council' is the meeting of all members of government – Ministers as well as Secretaries of State.

168. One of the essential provisions introduced by the 1970 amendments to the Constitution is the composition of the Cabinet on the basis of an equivalence. According to Article 99 of the Constitution, the Cabinet is to be composed of an equal number of Dutch-speaking and French-speaking Ministers, with the exception of the Prime Minister if necessary. This provision not only constitutes a formal constitutional basis for the function of Prime Minister, but also – and more importantly – introduces at the level of the federal Executive an important guarantee for the smaller of the two major communities in Belgium. The 'alarm-bell procedure' represents another guarantee for this national minority, albeit at the level of the federal Legislature.[115] A 1993 amendment added to Article 99 that the Cabinet was to consist of fifteen members. The Cabinet must also include both men and women (Article 11*bis* Constitution).

169. Besides the Cabinet and the Cabinet-in-Council, there is also the Privy Council. The Privy Council meets only in very exceptional circumstances, and is presided over by the King. It is composed of all Ministers and Ministers of State. A Minister of State is an honorary title granted by the King to persons who have distinguished themselves in public life. It does not carry any special power. The King may also appoint Royal Commissioners and charge them with an in-depth study of a given subject, such as the drafting of a law code.

170. It has also become customary in practice for the Prime Minister to be assisted by one or more Deputy Prime Ministers, usually belonging to the other parties making up the coalition. The Prime Minister and the Deputy Prime Ministers often have informal meetings, a procedure known as the 'Inner Cabinet' which involves preparing the most important government decisions.

171. Normally, each member of the government is in charge of a Ministry. Ministerial departments are staffed by civil servants, but do not have any distinct legal personality separate from the State. Ministers also have their own staff members, being the Minister's policy advisors. In contrast to civil servants, these privately appointed staff members of Ministers and Secretaries of State may be dismissed at

115. See Pt. II. Ch. 3. §4. IV 'The Alarm-Bell Procedure'.

any time. Over the past years, the growing influence on policymaking exerted by these policy advisors to the detriment of civil servants has been subject to severe criticism.

B. Secretaries of State

172. Federal Secretaries of State, appointed and dismissed by the King, are members of the federal government. They are not part of the Cabinet. The constitutional provisions governing Ministers apply to them, with the exception of those provisions on equal language representation in the Cabinet, and on the requirements of discussion in Cabinet. They are attached to a particular Minister and their powers and the limits within which they may countersign Royal Decrees are set by the King (Article 104 Constitution).

173. The Royal Decree of 24 March 1972 implementing Article 104 of the Constitution[116] stipulates that, without prejudice to specific Royal Decrees governing the relationship between a Secretary of State and the Minister he is attached to, a Secretary of State has, in the matters assigned to him, the same powers as a Minister, save for certain exceptions.

First, the relevant Minister may always decide to deal with a matter himself, or decide that any decision should be submitted to him for his approval. Second, a Secretary of State may only exercise regulatory powers with the consent of the Minister. Finally, a Secretary of State may countersign Royal Decrees, but the countersignature of the Minister he is attached to is also required for Royal Decrees of a regulatory nature, as well as for Royal Decrees introducing a government Bill in Parliament, or assenting to and promulgating a statute.

§2. Legal Status

174. Only a Belgian national may become a Minister or Secretary of State (Article 97 Constitution). No member of the Royal Family may become a Minister or Secretary of State (Article 98 Constitution). Furthermore, no one may simultaneously be a member of the federal government and a member of a Community or Region government (Article 61 Special Majority Act on Institutional Reform).

175. A member of either House of Parliament who is appointed by the King as Minister or Secretary of State and who accepts the appointment ceases to sit in the House and only takes up his mandate again when the King has terminated his office as Minister or Secretary of State (Article 50 Constitution).[117] Ministers or Secretaries of State nonetheless have admission to both Houses and they are entitled to receive a hearing there whenever they so request. The House of Representatives also can require the attendance of Ministers and Secretaries of State. The Senate can

116. *Gazette,* 28 Mar. 1972.
117. See also Pt. II. Ch. 3. §2. II. A 'Legal Status. Incompatibilities'.

require their attendance for discussion of matters under Articles 77 and 78 of the Constitution. For other matters, the Senate can ask for their attendance (Article 100 Constitution). No Minister or Secretary of State can be prosecuted for or be the subject of any investigation regarding opinions expressed in the exercise of his duties (Article 101 Constitution).

176. Members of government are subject to specific civil and criminal liability rules in order to safeguard their freedom of action. These rules do not, however, address any political responsibility.

The rules on criminal liability are set out in Article 103 of the Constitution and are implemented by the Act Regulating the Criminal Liability of Ministers of 25 June 1998.[118] Ministers and Secretaries of State are to be tried exclusively by the Court of Appeal, sitting *en banc*, for offences they may have committed in the course of holding office, and for offences which they may have committed outside their holding of public office and for which they are tried during their term of office. The criminal prosecution can only be commenced and directed by the Public Prosecutors Office attached to the Court of Appeal having jurisdiction. An appeal from the judgment of the Court of Appeal lies with the Court of Cassation sitting *en banc*. The grounds for appeal are for error of law only: the Court does not pronounce on the merits of the case. Nevertheless the consent of the House of Representatives is required for each application for directions concerning the committal for trial of a Minister or Secretary of State, for any summons of either to appear before the Court of Appeal, and for the arrest of either (except where caught in the commission of an offence).

The last paragraph of Article 103 provides that an Act determines in which cases and pursuant to what rules injured parties may commence civil proceedings against a Minister or Secretary of State. Until now, this last paragraph has not yet been implemented.

177. Article 102 of the Constitution prescribes that under no circumstances may a verbal or a written order from the King relieve a Minister or a Secretary of State of his responsibilities. The King may not pardon a Minister or a Secretary of State except at the request of the House of Representatives (Articles 103 and 111 Constitution[119]).

§3. Powers

I. The Executive Has Only Enumerated Powers

178. Although the government is the driving force of the State and although its powers are not limited to the implementation of laws, Article 105 of the Constitution prescribes that the King has no powers other than those formally vested in him

118. *Gazette,* 27 Jun. 1998.
119. Article 111 Constitution still refers to the Court of Cassation. This is inconsistent with revised Arts 103 and 125 Constitution.

by the Constitution and by specific laws passed in accordance with the Constitution itself. The meaning of this provision is thus that the powers of the Executive Branch are enumerated exhaustively by the Constitution and by-laws passed in accordance with the Constitution. The Executive Branch may only act if there is a constitutional or a legislative basis to do so.

The express enumeration of the government's powers is a fundamental characteristic of the Belgian constitutional system. The National Congress wanted to corral the policy of Willem I who considered himself vested with all powers, save those which were expressly attributed to another authority. The Belgian Constitution, by contrast, has clearly vested the residual powers in the Legislative Branch.

179. Many powers are expressly and directly attributed by the Constitution to the King in his capacity as head of the federal Executive. Among those are the implementation of laws (Article 108), the enforcement of judgments of the ordinary courts (Article 40), national defence and foreign affairs (Article 167), the appointment of Ministers and Secretaries of State (Articles 96 and 104) and of civil servants in the general administration and to foreign affairs positions (Article 107), the appointment of judges and of members of the Public Prosecutors Office (Articles 151 and 153), the conferral of military ranks (Article 107), of titles of nobility (Article 113), and of military honours (Article 114). The King also has the power to issue money (Article 112) and to issue a reprieve or to reduce the sentence imposed by the court (Article 110).

Apart from these powers directly attributed to the King by the Constitution itself, Parliament may attribute to him ordinary or special powers, in accordance with the Constitution.[120] We explained in Pt. II. Ch. 3 the role of the King as the third element of the Legislative Branch, as well as his powers regarding Parliament, in his capacity as head of the federal government. As may be deduced from the outline above, the King is clearly involved with the exercise of all three State functions.

II. Regulatory Powers

A. *Royal Regulations and Orders Necessary for the Implementation of Laws*

180. Article 108 of the Constitution empowers the King to issue those regulations and orders which are necessary for the implementation of laws, without ever being able to suspend the laws themselves or grant any exemption from their implementation. The King derives this power directly from the Constitution itself. Therefore, any legislative provision attributing those powers to the King would be totally superfluous. Moreover, the implementation of legislation is not only a right but also an obligation and this concept of implementation should not be interpreted too restrictively.

181. When implementing legislation, the King must observe the principle of legality. In its first and most general sense, this principle means that the King may

120. See Pt. II. Ch. 3. §5. I 'Delegation of Legislative Power'.

only act if and when he is explicitly empowered to do so. In its second and more specific sense – in the context of the implementation of laws – it means that the King should obey legal rules of higher ranking, such as treaties, the Constitution, and existing laws. He cannot suspend them nor grant any exemption from their application. The compliance of the King with these two aspects of the principle of legality is subject to judicial review. Courts have a constitutional obligation not to enforce regulations and orders, unless they accord with the law (Article 159 Constitution). The Administrative Tribunal Division of the Council of State also has jurisdiction to annul regulations and orders on the same grounds.

B. 'Autonomous' Regulatory Powers

182. The question has arisen whether or not the King has regulatory powers apart from the power to implement laws, pursuant to Article 108 of the Constitution, and from those attributed to him by specific Acts (Article 105 Constitution). In accordance with the first limb to the principle of legality, such regulatory powers should be based on some constitutional or legislative provision. Such regulatory powers of the King are recognised in two areas:

(i) The organisation of the departments of the general administration and setting out rules governing civil servants. The power of the King to appoint civil servants in the general administration and into foreign affairs positions (Article 107 Constitution) implies the power to organise the Executive by setting up Ministries and other services, by determining their powers, and by establishing the rules governing civil servants, their appointment and promotion, and so on.

(ii) The 'police power'. A more controversial issue is the existence of an autonomous 'police power' of the King in his capacity as head of the Executive, to issue regulations to protect law and order in the Kingdom, in the absence of any specific legal provision. Such 'police power' would then be derived from Article 37 of the Constitution vesting executive authority in the King. In any event, this power – if it does exist – is subsidiary only, because it must be exercised in compliance with the traditional police powers of the municipal authorities who are primarily responsible in this field.

C. Regulatory Powers of Ministers and Secretaries of State

183. Article 108 of the Constitution empowers only the King to issue regulations necessary for the implementation of laws. Nonetheless Acts of Parliament have often directly conferred regulatory powers on Ministers, and this delegation is in principle not subject to judicial review. It is also accepted that the King may delegate part of his regulatory power to his Ministers, who then may issue the relevant regulations within the framework established by that Royal Decree. Finally, it has become common usage for Ministers to comment on existing legislation in 'circular letters'. These Ministerial circulars may also establish general guidelines that will govern the exercise of the discretionary powers of the Minister concerned. In general, these Ministerial circulars are not binding in nature and therefore cannot be challenged in court. Nonetheless Ministers may not deviate from their own rules in an unreasonable way.

184. Regulatory powers exercised by Secretaries of State require the consent or the countersignature of the relevant supervising Minister.

III. National Defence and Foreign Affairs

A. National Defence

185. This is covered below in Pt. V. Ch. 1, 'War, Treaty and Foreign Affairs Powers'.

B. Foreign Affairs

186. 'Foreign affairs' spans a vast array of contacts between Belgium and foreign countries in economic, social or political matters. An important aspect is establishing diplomatic relations with foreign countries. Article 107 of the Constitution empowers the King to appoint persons to foreign affairs positions. It contains an implicit authorisation to organise diplomatic relations through Belgium's embassies and consulates abroad.

C. Treaty-Making Powers

187. This is covered below in Pt. V. Ch. 1, 'War, Treaty and Foreign Affairs Powers'.

IV. Powers Regarding Parliament

188. As head of the federal Executive, the King promulgates and publishes federal laws. These are the first stages of the implementation of a law.

189. In the same capacity, the King closes a session of the Houses of Parliament, and also has the right to convene an extraordinary session of those Houses (Article 44 Constitution). He may prorogue Parliament, although any adjournment must not exceed one month nor be repeated during the same session without the consent of the Houses (Article 45 Constitution). The exercise of this power of adjournment has become obsolete.

190. The King has the right to dissolve the House of Representatives, but only under the conditions mentioned in Article 46 of the Constitution.

V. Powers Regarding the Judiciary

191. The King is involved in the Judicial Branch given the powers of appointing judges (Article 151 Constitution), of appointing and dismissing members of the Public Prosecutors Office (Article 153), of enforcing judgments (Article 40), and of granting pardons or reducing sentences (Article 110). For Ministers and Secretaries of State, a pardon is only available at the request of the House of Representatives (Articles 103 and 111 Constitution).

VI. Other Powers

192. Pursuant to Article 112 of the Constitution, the King has the right to issue money in accordance with the law.

193. The King also has the power to confer i) titles of nobility 'without being able to attach any privilege thereto' (Article 113 Constitution) and ii) military honours 'subject to what the law prescribes therefor' (Article 114). As the constitutional provision only mentions military honours, Parliament has under its residual powers established civil honours also.

§4. The Cabinet

194. The organisation of the federal government in general, and of the Cabinet in particular, have been set already above. By convention, Cabinet decisions are not made by way of vote, but are reached through discussion and consensus. If a Minister cannot reconcile himself to the decision taken, he is expected to tender his resignation.

195. When the Constitution itself[121], a particular statute[122], or a Royal Decree prescribes 'discussion in Cabinet', this is a procedure in respect of administrative acts which must be observed so as not to render invalid the decision taken. In practice, all matters with some political impact are discussed in Cabinet, even when such deliberations are not prescribed. As a result, the fundamental rule of individual Ministerial responsibility has lost much of its traditional meaning.

121. See Art. 54 (the 'alarm-bell procedure'), Art. 90 (exercise of constitutional powers of the Crown during an interregnum), and Art. 93 (inability of the King to reign).
122. Many legislative provisions prescribe 'discussion in Cabinet'.

§5. MISCELLANEOUS

I. The Prerogatives of the Administration

196. The administration must pursue the public interest. Therefore, it may invoke several privileges, in particular the power to take unilateral measures, which are directly enforceable.

197. The civil service is governed by three important principles:

(i) the 'principle of flexibility', meaning that the rules governing the organisation and the operation of the civil service may at any time be modified unilaterally by the competent authority. Hence, for example, the Royal Decree governing civil servants, their remuneration, their appointment and promotion, and such like, may be amended at any time;
(ii) the 'principle of continuity', meaning that the civil service should function without interruption in a regular and stable way. The theory of 'restricted transitional powers' is based on this principle, and
(iii) the 'principle of equality', meaning that every person under the same conditions may claim the same public services on an equal basis. Every citizen has, for example, equal access to the civil service.

II. 'Restricted Transitional Powers'

198. When Cabinet tenders its resignation to the King, this will formally be accepted only at the time of appointment of a new government. In the interim, the outgoing government is entrusted with 'restricted transitional powers' in managing affairs: it is a 'caretaker government'. The powers of a caretaker government are restricted, in that its political responsibility can no longer be censured by the House of Representatives. This customary rule of a restriction on powers reconciles, on the one hand, the principle of continuity of the public service with the principles of parliamentary democracy, on the other.

199. Traditionally, the following matters come under the notion 'restricted transitional powers': the day-to-day conduct of government, urgent matters which must be settled without delay, and decisions which are the normal continuation or termination of proceedings which had been started before the resignation. Due to the political crisis after the federal elections of 10 June 2007, the outgoing government was entrusted with 'restricted transitional powers' for nearly 200 days. During this period[123], a fourth category of matters was accepted as falling under that notion, namely matters which are proposed or supported by the Houses of Parliament. This broadening of the 'restricted transitional powers' is consistent with its rationale,

123. Also during the 541 days after the federal elections of 13 June 2010 prior to the new government being formed.

inasmuch as the principle of parliamentary democracy is respected where Parliament explicitly approves the decisions taken by the King and the outgoing government. Likewise, an outgoing government would retain the power to introduce government Bills and declarations for the amendment of the Constitution (initiated by the three branches of the Legislature: the House of Representatives, the Senate and the King).

Apart from the possibility that the King may refuse to finalise the decisions of an outgoing government, such decisions are also subject to judicial review. In particular, the Council of State exercises such review, and it examines whether the decisions come under the definition of 'restricted transitional powers' taking into account the surrounding factual circumstances.

200. Apart from the hypothesis of a government tendering its resignation, there is a similar restriction on the powers of the Executive Branch when, after a declaration that there are grounds to amend the Constitution, the Houses of Representatives or the Houses of Parliament are dissolved without the federal government having tendered its resignation. The Council of State applies the same rules it employs in reviewing the 'restricted transitional powers', the reason being that no parliamentary control exists in this case either.

Selected Further Reading

Cerexhe, G. 'Les Ministres disposent-ils d'un pouvoir réglementaire?'. *A.P.T.* (1984): 177–192.

Craenen, G. 'De positie van een demissionair kabinet in België'. *T.B.P.* (1977): 10–27.

Ganshof van der Meersch, W.J. 'Le conseil des ministres au sein du pouvoir exécutif en droit constitutionnel belge'. *Rapports belges au Xle CIDC* (Bruylant, 1985) I, 117–175.

Leroy, M. *Les règlements et leurs juges* (Bruylant, 1987).

Leus, K. *Pseudo-wetgeving* (Maklu, 1992).

Mast, A., A. Alen & J. Dujardin. *Précis de droit administratif belge* (Story-Scientia, 1989).

Moonen T., 'De Koning en de vorming van de federale Regering. Evaluatie van de langste institutionele crisis ooit' *T.B.P.* (2013): 230–249

Velaers J., 'De pariteit in de Ministeraad (artikel 99, tweede lid van de Grondwet): een vereiste met een louter taalkundige, een communautaire of ook een "taalgroep-parlementaire" betekenis?' *T.B.P.* (2015): 4–22.

Velaers, J. & Y. Peeters. 'De "lopende zaken" en de ontslagnemende regering'. *T.B.P.* (2008): 3–19.

Waleffe, B. '*Le Roi nomme et révoque ses ministers.' La formation et la démission des gouvernements en Belgique depuis 1944* (Bruylant, 1971).

Waleffe, B. *Some Constitutional Aspects of Recent Cabinet Developments in Great Britain and in Belgium: Prime Minister's Position and Cabinet Committees* (Bruylant, 1968).

Chapter 5. The Judiciary

§1. Organisation of the Judiciary

I. General Introduction

A. *Belgium's Dual Judicial Organisation: Distinguishing Between the Ordinary and the Administrative Courts*

201. Since Belgium is a State governed by the rule of law, it is essential that remedies are provided to redress infringements of a person's rights. This is the traditional safeguarding role of the judiciary. When legal rules have been violated by public authorities, different approaches are possible. On the one hand, a stringent application of the principle of the separation of powers may lead to a situation where the judiciary has no jurisdiction whenever the Executive is involved in a dispute. In that case, the matter may be referred to an administrative court. The archetype for this stringent view on the separation of powers could be found in post-revolutionary France, which reacted against the high degree of interference by the courts in France during the *ancien régime*. On the other hand, withdrawing from the jurisdiction of the court cases in which the Executive is involved may open the door to arbitrary acts on the part of the Executive. This was, for instance, illustrated by the attitude taken by the administration of Willem I under the United Kingdom of the Netherlands (1815–1830), when it considered itself to be immune from any judicial control over the legality of its acts, under the pretext that judicial review would impede efficient administration. The final decision as to what should be considered an administrative act was left to the ultimate appreciation of the King. This situation left the citizens with almost no remedy in case of an unlawful act on the part of the administration, the latter already having many privileges more as compared to citizens.

Taking into account the need to avoid these types of abuse, several legal systems submit all disputes to the judiciary, irrespective of the question whether or not the administration is involved. The Anglo-Saxon constitutional systems have been traditional examples of this approach, although several of these States have established specialised administrative courts or judicial subdivisions dealing with the administration.

202. Belgium's 'founding fathers' took up a middle position between the traditional 'Anglo-Saxon' and 'French' judicial systems. All disputes concerning 'civil rights' fall under the exclusive jurisdiction of the ordinary courts (Article 144 Constitution). Disputes concerning 'political rights' equally fall under the jurisdiction of those courts, except for the exceptions provided for by Act of Parliament (Article 145 Constitution). Hence, Belgium's constitutionally established judicial organisation implies that, in principle, the ordinary courts will have jurisdiction, whereas administrative courts having a statutorily conferred jurisdiction may be set up, but only for matters concerning 'political rights'. The legislative branch (both of the federal State and of the Communities and the Regions) thereby exercises a direct or an indirect control, having to approve either the statute establishing jurisdiction or the statute delegating authority to the Executive to create administrative law jurisdiction by way of a decree (Articles 146 and 161 Constitution). In order to ensure the equality of citizens, Article 146 of the Constitution explicitly provides that no extraordinary courts or commissions, under whatever designation, may be created. It basically bans siphoning off jurisdiction in specific matters involving specific persons. No person can be denied appearing before the judge whom the law has assigned to them (Article 13 Constitution). The Court of Cassation, Belgium's highest court of ordinary jurisdiction, is entrusted with settling all jurisdictional conflicts between the administrative courts and the ordinary courts, and thus ultimately defines the latter's jurisdiction (Article 158 Constitution).

203. Although it is hard to define the concepts 'civil' and 'political' rights, it is generally assumed that the status of persons, relations between private citizens, ordering imprisonment, and most of the fundamental rights and liberties come within the exclusive jurisdiction of the ordinary courts. On the other hand, political rights include voting rights, the right to civil service appointment and promotion, the right not to be conscripted illicitly, and the right to be exempted from illegal taxes. Because of the difficulty in defining these terms, some scholars have proposed an 'organic' criterion, which implies that a subjective right is a political right as soon as the legislature has assigned the examination of a dispute to a jurisdiction other than the ordinary courts. This point of view, which is based on a presumption of the constitutionality of statutory law, has become difficult to sustain with the establishment of the Constitutional Court. This Court affirms in its caselaw that it has jurisdiction to assess whether an Act of Parliament has rightly considered a subjective right to be a political right when it has assigned disputes concerning this subjective right to an administrative court.[124] However, the judicial review exercised by the Constitutional Court is 'marginal', implying that an Act of Parliament is only adjudged unconstitutional in the case where it confines disputes to an administrative court concerning subjective rights which are 'manifestly' civil rights.

In an important judgment, the Court of Cassation held that there are no subjective rights other than 'civil' and 'political' rights and that a remedy should exist for the infringement of each right.[125] As a rule, this remedy should be granted by the ordinary courts, except for those cases in which the legislature has conferred the settlement of disputes to another (read: 'administrative') jurisdiction.

204. In the early days of Belgium only a few administrative courts were set up. Belgium's later evolution into a welfare State has seen a diverse set of courts established and governed by a wide range of often diverging procedural rules. Administrative tribunals can only be established by, or by authority of, an Act (Articles 146 and 161 Constitution). The highest administrative court, established in 1946, is the

124. See e.g., Cons., Judgment No. 14/97, 18 Mar. 1997.
125. Cass., 21 Dec. 1956 (*Trine*) *Pas.*, 1957, I, 430.

Council of State (*Raad van State/Conseil d'Etat*). The Administrative Tribunal Division[126] of the Council of State (i) exercises legal control over lower administrative courts as the final appellate court and (ii) is competent to annul or suspend illegal administrative acts. Included among the many lower administrative courts are following. Disputes concerning asylum, access to Belgian territory, residence, and the admission and removal of foreign non-nationals are dealt with by the federal Immigration and Asylum Tribunal. The Permit Disputes Tribunal deals with municipal planning litigation in the Flemish Region. The Election Disputes Tribunal deals with cases regarding the municipal and provincial elections in the same Region. Various boards were set up to try disputes regarding various social security benefits and to impose disciplinary sanctions on members of certain professions (such as lawyers, doctors, and so on). The creation of the Labour Court (Trial Division and Appeal Division) in 1967 entailed the abolition of various administrative tribunals having jurisdiction over certain social security benefits. This meant a first step towards a rationalisation of the complicated institutional organisation of the various organs exercising administrative law jurisdiction.

The existence of a dual judicial system is generally justified by the specificity and the complexity of disputes involving matters of public law. However, it has been frequently argued that there exist in Belgium too many different administrative courts and that some general co-ordination is necessary, for instance by setting up one, single, administrative court at first instance.

B. Subdivisions Within the Courts of Ordinary Jurisdiction

205. In this section the division of labour among the various ordinary courts will be discussed very briefly. The criteria for the allocation of jurisdiction are fourfold, namely: (i) the nature of the suit, (ii) the amount of the claim, (iii) urgency, and (iv) the nature of the parties.

206. In non-criminal matters, the Courts of First Instance (*Rechtbank van Eerste Aanleg/Tribunal de Première Instance)* have general jurisdiction. These trial courts have a 'residual' jurisdiction, which means that they deal with all disputes or matters which are not explicitly assigned to other courts, save those which are referred directly to the Courts of Appeal or to the Court of Cassation (Article 568 Civil Procedure Code). In addition, they also have jurisdiction over those matters explicitly assigned to them, such as cases concerning the status of persons (as the Family

126. Apart from the Administrative Tribunal Division, the Council of State also has a Legislation Division which provides legal advice on draft legislation and regulations. See Art. 160 of the Constitution and the Consolidated Council of State Act. See also Pt. II. Ch. 6. §1 'The Council of State' and Pt. IV. Ch. 4 'Judicial Control of Administrative Action'.

Court). There is one Court of First Instance in each of the twelve judicial districts coinciding with the provinces, the separate districts of Brussels-Capital and Eupen excepted.[127]

In certain urgent cases, the President of the Court of First Instance may hear the application of a party by way of interlocutory proceedings (*kort geding/en référé*).

207. The courts having specific, limited jurisdiction are the Justices of the Peace (*Vredegerecht/Justice de paix*), the Commercial Courts and the Trial Division of the Labour Courts (Article 157 Constitution). The Justices of the Peace have jurisdiction in civil claims whose value does not exceed EUR 5,000. These judges, represented in each of the 162 cantons, were traditionally considered as mediators in disputes among neighbours. At present they have obtained, by gradual attribution, exclusive jurisdiction in various matters, such as landlord-tenant matters, irrespective of the amounts at issue.

Disputes between companies, as well as certain matters of commercial (e.g., bankruptcy, bills of exchange, intellectual property rights) and corporate law are decided on by the Business Courts. The Business Courts are organised at the district level. They are composed of a President, who is a professional judge, and two Assessors, who are lay judges.

Individual labour disputes and claims related to social security benefits are submitted to the Trial Division of the Labour Court, also organised at the district level. A striking feature of these courts is the representation of employers' organisations and trade unions on the bench, besides professional judges.

An Assignment Court, composed of the Presidents of the Court of First Instance, of the Labour Court, of the Business Court, and of the judges of the Police Courts and of Justices of the Peace decides any conflicts of jurisdiction which may arise among the ordinary courts.

208. Thus far, we have dealt with non-criminal matters only. In order to provide an understanding of the various institutions dealing with criminal law matters, it is necessary to give a very basic outline of criminal proceedings.

A criminal case starts in principle with a police investigation. On the basis of this police investigation, a Public Prosecutor decides whether or not the given circumstances of the matter require that a criminal prosecution should be initiated. In doing so, a Public Prosecutor must take into account the binding guidelines of the Minister of Justice and the College of Prosecutors-General, as well as policy considerations whether a prosecution in the given case is warranted. Criminal proceedings may also be initiated upon the request of an injured party.

From the moment the proceedings are launched, the Judiciary is necessarily involved. In the case of a felony or in the case of certain misdemeanours, a more thorough preliminary investigation is conducted by an examining magistrate. At the end of that preliminary investigation, the Committal and Bail Court (Trial Division

127. The 'essential elements' of the reforms effected for the Judicial District of Brussels-Capital – constituted as a separate judicial district by the 2014 Sixth State Reform – cannot be altered except by a Special Majority Act (Art. 157*bis* Constitution).

– *Raadkamer / Chambre du Conseil* and Appeal Division – *Kamer van Inbeschuldigingstelling / Chambre des Mises en Accusation*) decides whether or not there is sufficient evidence of guilt to put the case to trial.

If a case goes to trial, it is assigned to the competent jurisdiction. Jurisdiction in criminal matters is divided among the Police Court, the Criminal Court, and the Criminal Assizes. The jurisdiction of these criminal courts depends on the penalty set for a criminal offence. Minor offences, certain misdemeanours, as well as traffic offences, are tried by the Police Courts. Misdemeanours for which the penalty is imprisonment from eight days up to five years, or which are liable to a fine over EUR 208 are tried by the Criminal Court (*Correctionele Rechtbank / Tribunal Correctionnel*). Political and press offences, except for press offences motivated by racism or xenophobia, as well as 'serious crimes' (those offences carrying a sentence of imprisonment in excess of five years) are tried by jury in the Criminal Assizes. This Court is established in each of the ten provinces and in Brussels-Capital (Article 150 Constitution; Article 115 Civil Procedure Code). Statutory amendments to transfer from the Criminal Assizes jurisdiction over most serious crimes to the Criminal Courts were quashed by the Constitutional Court because they would effectively hollow out the concept of 'serious crime'.[128] The Courts Martial in peacetime have been abolished. Since 2003 Article 157 of the Constitution authorises the legislative branch to organise the Courts Martial in wartime.[129]

209. Since 2007, a Sentencing Administration Court (*Strafuitvoeringsrechtbank / Tribunal de l'Application des Peines*) exists in the district of each of the five Courts of Appeal.[130] This Court is empowered to deal with the implementation and conduct of prison sentences.

210. Save in exceptional cases, there is in principle a possibility of appeal.[131] By exception certain cases allow for no right of appeal from judgments rendered at first instance, such as when the value of a claim does not exceed EUR 2,500, or in case of a judgment rendered by the Criminal Assizes. Appeals from the judgments of the Court of First Instance, the Criminal Court, and the Business Court are lodged with the Court of Appeal sitting in one of five districts (Article 156 Constitution). The Court of Appeal also tries members of the federal, the Community, and the Region governments for offences they may have committed (Articles 103 and 125 Constitution).

The Courts of First Instance (civil and criminal chambers) hear appeals from decisions of the Justices of the Peace and of the Police Courts.

Judgments rendered by the Trial Division of the Labour Court are brought before its Appeal Division.

---

128. Cons., Judgment No. 148/2017, 21 Dec. 2017. See also Cons., Judgment No. 28/2018, 9 Mar. 2018.
129. See the Acts of 10 April 2003, *Gazette*, 7 May 2003.
130. Article 157 para. 4 Constitution; Act of 17 May 2006, *Gazette*, 15 Jun. 2006.
131. In proceedings before administrative courts, the possibility of appeal does not automatically exist as it depends on the statute setting up and organising the administrative court.

C. The Court of Cassation

211. In order to ensure that the courts apply and construe the law correctly, namely the Constitution, treaties, statutory law (federal Acts and Community and Region Acts), administrative Acts and any other general, provincial and local regulations, as well as the general unwritten principles of law, the National Congress established a Court of Cassation for the whole of Belgium. The Court of Cassation is Belgium's highest court of ordinary jurisdiction and its principal task is to ensure that judgments are correct in law. The Court does not adjudicate on the merits of a case, meaning that it is prevented from dealing with the facts of cases submitted to it (Article 147 Constitution). The Court must ensure only that decisions rendered on appeal have not contravened the 'law' (in the material sense of the term) nor have violated any prescribed procedures otherwise rendering a decision null and void (Article 608 Civil Procedure Code).

After quashing a decision, the Court of Cassation will remit the case either (1) back to the court which issued the decision annulled, but with a differently constituted panel, or (2) to a court seated elsewhere but equal in rank in the judicial hierarchy to that court which issued the decision in question. This latter court is obliged to comply with the judgment of the Court of Cassation on the point of law decided by that Court (Article 1110 Civil Procedure Code).

In civil cases, only a limited number of lawyers are permitted to plead before the Court of Cassation.

212. Under Belgian law, the Judiciary does not have the authority to issue binding precedents. A judgment passed in one case does not have binding effect on future cases, involving either other parties or the same parties in other cases (Article 6 Civil Procedure Code). That is, the Anglo-Saxon rule of binding precedents or *stare decisis* does not apply in Belgian law. The Constitution considers the authoritative interpretation of statutory law as the sole prerogative of the Legislature (Articles 84 and 133 Constitution). Yet, in practice, judgments given by the higher courts do enjoy considerable moral authority. As most judges do not want their judgments to be overruled, rulings of the higher courts are complied with, for the most part. Also, higher courts are not legally bound by their own decisions. These higher courts, however, generally feel very reluctant to overrule themselves so as not to endanger the predictability of the caselaw.

213. An appeal to the Court of Cassation is generally initiated on application of one of the parties involved. Unlike the UK Supreme Court or the US Supreme Court, leave to appeal is never required before the Court may hear an appeal on a judgment. Its review of legal correctness thus covers a considerable number of cases. When none of the parties involved lodges an appeal, the Prosecutor-General for the Court of Cassation may decide, exceptionally, to file an appeal where the matter at issue concerns persistent differences of interpretation on a point of law, or when the decision may negatively affect the caselaw (Articles 612 and 1089 Civil Procedure Code).

Besides its role of preserving the legal correctness of judgments, the Court of Cassation has other sorts of jurisdiction as well. It is *inter alia* empowered to determine conflicts of jurisdiction between the ordinary courts and the administrative courts (Article 158 Constitution). As a rule, a cassation appeal (i.e. final appeal and only on questions of law) against an administrative court decision is brought before the Administrative Tribunal Division of the Council of State. However, Parliament has the authority to deviate from this rule by stipulating that a cassation appeal must be brought before the Court of Cassation. The Council of State's decisions may only be quashed by the Court of Cassation on the ground of an infringement of the jurisdiction of the ordinary courts (Article 158 Constitution and Article 609 2° Civil Procedure Code).

II. Constitutional and Legal Status of the Members of the Judiciary; Judicial Independence

214. As mentioned above, administrative courts cannot be set up except by, or by authority of, an Act. The status of the members of the administrative courts is determined by legislation and is not laid down in the Constitution, as is the case with the members of the judiciary. This is equally true for the highest administrative jurisdiction, the Council of State, set up by Act of 23 December 1946. The Consolidated Council of State Act provides for guarantees which are analogous to the ones prescribed by the Constitution for the judiciary. In particular, the Constitution (i) contains provisions in order to preserve the independence of the members of the judiciary, and (ii) limits interference by the Executive with the functions of the judiciary.

A. The Independence of the Judiciary

215. In a State under the rule of law it is essential that the Judicial Branch is independent of the Executive, so that the latter can exercise no pressure on the former. The prime significance of the principle of the separation of powers nowadays lies precisely in its role of guaranteeing the real independence of the judiciary as a third power in the State. To appreciate the independence of the judiciary, it is necessary to analyse the status of its individual members in a more detailed way. Firstly, the procedures for the appointment and the promotion of judges will be discussed. Secondly, the constitutional provisions ensuring the independence of the judiciary in the exercise of their office will be examined more closely.

216. As far as the nomination and appointment of judges are concerned, Belgium has drastically changed its procedures in 1998 with the creation of the Judicial High Council (Article 151 Constitution). Previously, judges were in principle appointed directly by the King, which process had led to a politicisation of appointments. The creation of the Judicial High Council aimed to 'depoliticize' the nomination and the appointment of judges.

The Judicial High Council[132] is composed of a Dutch-speaking commission and of a French-speaking commission. Each commission has the same number of members as the other and is comprised of equal numbers of judges and officers of the Public Prosecutors Office, on the one hand, and of other members appointed by the Senate, on the other.

In each commission, there is a nomination and appointments committee, and an advice and investigation committee. The former committee nominates candidates for appointment as a judge or as an officer of the Public Prosecutors Office, for appointment to the positions of President of the Court of Cassation, of President of the Court of Appeal, of President of the Labour Court, and of President of the lower courts, and to the position of Departmental Head with the Public Prosecutors Office.

217. Judges continue to be appointed by the King. However, an appointment is based on the nomination, supported by reasons after evaluation of competence and qualifications, of the relevant appointments committee of the Judicial High Council with a two-thirds majority. The King can only reject the nomination in accordance with a number of set rules and on the basis of reasons.[133]

In the case of the appointment of a judge of the Court of Cassation or of the Court of Appeal, or of the Labour Court, the full bench of the Court concerned provides its opinion supported by reasons in advance of the nomination by the Judicial High Council. This is also the case for appointments to the position of President of the Court of Cassation, President of the Court of Appeal, or President of the Labour Court.

The Vice President of the Court of Cassation, the Presiders of its Chamber panels, the Presiders of the Chamber panels of the Court of Appeal and of the Labour Court, and the Vice Presidents of the lower courts are appointed to their positions by these courts from out of their members.

218. Since the 1998 reforms, judges, the Vice President of the Court of Cassation, the Presiders of its Chamber panels, the Presiders of the Chamber panels of the Court of Appeal and the Labour Court, the Vice Presidents of the lower courts, and the officers of the Public Prosecutors Office are subject to evaluation.[134]

219. The (professional) judges of the Labour Court are appointed by the King, upon joint nomination by the Ministers of Labour and Justice (Article 197 Civil Procedure Code), while lay judges are appointed by the King for a term of five years, upon nomination by the Minister competent for self-employed, independent traders, drawn from candidates submitted by unions and employees' organisations and by employers' associations (Articles 198 and 202 Civil Procedure Code). A similar process applies to the appointment of the lay judges in the Business Courts (Article 203 Civil Procedure Code).

---

132. See Art. 151 Constitution and Art. 259*bis*1–259*bis*22 Civil Procedure Code.
133. See Art 259*ter* Civil Procedure Code.
134. The Constitutional Court has clearly affirmed that, pursuant to Art. 151 §6 of the Constitution, the Departmental Heads of the courts (i.e., the President of the Court of Cassation, the Presidents of the Court of Appeal, and the Presidents of lower courts) are not subject to evaluation (Cons., Judgment No. 122/2008, 1 Sep. 2008).

220. For the empanelling of juries for the Criminal Assizes, a list is drawn up every four years of all persons who may be eligible to sit on a jury. Potential jurors are then selected by lot from the latest registry of voters.

221. The Constitution provides a number of guarantees for the members of the Bench so as to ensure their independence from the Executive.

1. Life Appointment

222. Article 152 of the Constitution provides that judges are appointed for life. No judge can be removed from office or be suspended except by court order. This provision implies that judges may be removed from office only as a result of a decision of the Disciplinary Tribunals, or as a result of a conviction for serious crime. In short, only a judicial decision may deprive a judge of his office or suspend him. The Executive has no authority to do so. Further, Article 152 of the Constitution explicitly provides that legislation is to determine retirement age and pension rights (Articles 383 et seq. Civil Procedure Code). On reaching retirement age, a judge is automatically deemed incapable to exercise his function. It is traditionally said that he is accorded emeritus status in order to underline that he retains the status of a judge and remains subject to disciplinary authority. In cases of an alleged criminal offence, he may only be judged by a decision rendered without appeal by the Court of Appeal. He is further subject to the other restrictions his office entails. Moreover, a judge who is no longer capable of exercising his office and who has not applied for retirement himself may be required to do so. If he persists in refusing to retire, a judicial decision on his retirement will be rendered. Besides security of tenure, Article 152 of the Constitution provides that the transfer of a judge cannot occur except by new appointment and with his consent.

2. Financial Independence from the Executive

223. Members of the judiciary are only able to function independently if they are also financially independent from the Executive. That is the reason why Article 154 of the Constitution states that the salaries of members of the judiciary and the Public Prosecutors Office are determined by Act of Parliament (Articles 355–365 Civil Procedure Code).

3. Conflicts of Interest

224. The guarantee of financial independence from the Executive Branch, provided by Article 154 of the Constitution, would be meaningless if members of the judiciary were financially dependent on the Executive because of other government positions they might hold at the same time. Hence, Article 155 of the Constitution provides that no judge may accept a salaried position from the government unless he works without remuneration and subject to the cases of incompatibility determined by Act. In this respect, Article 293 of the Civil Procedure Code provides that a judge may hold neither a remunerated political mandate nor any administrative position; nor hold the office of public notary, bailiff, practicing lawyer; nor fulfil any military function; nor be a member of the clergy. By way of exception, the King has been delegated the authority to grant an exemption so as to allow judges to hold university teaching positions or to sit on selection committees and examining boards (Article 294 Civil Procedure Code).

4. Limited Applicability

225. The above-mentioned constitutional guarantees are only applicable to the members of the ordinary courts. They do not apply to the members of the Public Prosecutors Office, nor do they apply to the members of the administrative courts or of the Constitutional Court[135] or to the lay judges of the courts having special jurisdiction (Labour Courts, Business Courts and Sentencing Administration Courts). The Acts organising those courts, however, generally provide similar guarantees.

B. Limited Interference by the Executive with the Functions of the Judiciary

226. The Judicial and the Executive Branches are not entirely independent from one another. In this section, the areas in which the Executive interferes with the functioning of the judiciary will be briefly discussed. As has been outlined above, the Executive has limited powers in the appointment of judges.

227. Judgments and orders are enforced in the name of the King in his capacity as the head of the Executive Branch (Article 40 Constitution). Indeed, that their enforcement comes within the jurisdiction of the Executive is aptly evidenced by the terms required at the end of each judicial decision pursuant to Article 1386 of the Civil Procedure Code to render it executable. The Public Prosecutors Office is thereby charged with the enforcement of judgments. In criminal matters, the Public Prosecutors Office acts ex officio; whereas in civil matters, it only acts when required to do so (Article 139 Civil Procedure Code).

228. The King has in principle the power to remit or to reduce a sentence imposed by a judge (Article 110 Constitution). The right of pardon implies that the King may exempt, partially or entirely, a person or a group of persons from serving the sentence imposed. It should be stressed that the right of pardon differs from an amnesty granted by Parliament, which retroactively removes the criminal nature of an act. Articles 103, 111, and 125 of the Constitution provide that the King cannot pardon a Minister or a member of a Community or Region government convicted

135. Although the Constitutional Court has been inserted in the Constitution, the status of its members has been fixed in a Special Majority Act in accordance with the Constitution: see below §2 II 'The Constitutional Court'.

by the Court of Appeal except on petition by the House of Representatives or by the Community or Region Parliament concerned.

229. The task and the status of the members of the Public Prosecutors Office are dualist in nature: they exercise both judicial and executive functions.

1. Functions of an Executive Nature

230. The Public Prosecutor[136] must decide whether or not a prosecution should be commenced. The Public Prosecutor may decide, even after police investigations, that criminal charges should be pursued. In civil matters, the Public Prosecutor's authority to initiate proceedings ex officio is more limited: he may launch an action, appeal a judgment, or intervene in a particular case as prescribed by Act or when the vital interests of the community so demand (Article 138*bis* §1 Civil Procedure Code). On behalf of the Executive, the Public Prosecutors Office must protect the interests of the State and of the public authorities, as well as of those of minors and missing persons, namely those for whom it is no longer certain that they may still be alive. The Public Prosecutors Office also ensures the enforcement of legislation. And the Public Prosecutors Office is also entrusted with the enforcement of judgments in criminal matters. It then acts ex officio. In civil matters, it acts upon request of a party (Article 139 Civil Procedure Code). Further, the Public Prosecutor is entrusted with the conduct of criminal investigations (Article 22 Criminal Procedure Code) and also has certain investigatory duties in civil matters. In fulfilling the above-mentioned tasks, the Public Prosecutors Office acts on behalf of the Executive. The Office thus comes under the authority of the Minister of Justice and, for labour disputes, under the authority of the Minister of Labour as well.

The Prosecutor-General for the Court of Cassation, the Prosecutors-General for the Courts of Appeal and the Federal Prosecutor (Articles 142–143 Civil Procedure Code) likewise act under the authority of the Minister of Justice and, for labour disputes, under the authority of the Minister of Labour as well. The Public Prosecutors Office thus constitutes a hierarchical body.

231. The Minister of Justice may order the start of criminal proceedings (Article 364 Criminal Procedure Code). But the Minister of Justice has no authority to order that specific cases or certain categories of criminal offence should not be pursued. This would violate the principle of separation of powers.

The Minister of Justice determines the guidelines for criminal law procedures, including those for investigations and prosecutions, on the basis of advice from the College of Prosecutors-General. All members of the Public Prosecutors Office are

136. Or a Deputy Public Prosecutor. At the levels of the Court of Appeal and the Court of Cassation, the functions of the Public Prosecutors Office are exercised by the Prosecutor-General for the Court of Appeal and the Prosecutor-General for the Court of Cassation respectively. Regarding certain crimes, the Federal Prosecutor may be responsible for prosecution: Arts 144*bis*-144*sexies* Civil Procedure Code.

bound by these directives. The Prosecutors-General are responsible for implementation of those guidelines in their respective judicial districts (Article 151 §1 Constitution; Article 143*quater* Civil Procedure Code).

232. Members of the Public Prosecutors Office do not have the same constitutional status as the members of the judiciary. Members of the Public Prosecutors Office do not enjoy security of tenure. They may be transferred, suspended, or removed from office under disciplinary measures taken by the Executive, that is, the Prosecutor-General and the Minister of Justice (who constitute the disciplinary authorities). The Constitution indeed explicitly provides that the King appoints and dismisses the members of the Public Prosecutors Office serving with the courts (Article 153 Constitution).

2. Functions of a Judicial Nature

233. It is important to stress the second function of the Public Prosecutors Office, namely the advisory role. The Public Prosecutors Office assists the judiciary in construing and implementing the law. In this capacity, the members of the Public Prosecutors Office exercise a judicial function and enjoy absolute independence from the Executive Branch.

III. Judicial Proceedings

234. As a reaction against previous abuses and excesses under the regime of King Willem I, the National Congress required that court hearings and the pronouncement of judicial decisions should be in public. (The latter rule has recently been made more flexible.) It also required that reasons for decision must be given. Nowadays, these provisions must be read in conjunction with the provisions of the EConvHR ensuring due process of law.

235. Article 148 of the Constitution provides that hearings in courts and tribunals are open to the public.

'Open court' protects the citizens against arbitrary judicial decisions. The judge is well aware that he is subject to the scrutiny of the public present in the courtroom. This guarantee is of practical importance, because some trials (particularly important criminal trials) are attended by journalists and are reported in the newspapers. Open court must also be seen as a measure to inspire confidence in the legal system because citizens can see for themselves whether the judiciary is being objective or not. Judgments in civil and commercial cases, however, are generally not reported on in the newspapers. Their annotation in law reviews may be regarded as a substitute for scrutiny by the press in criminal cases.

Article 148 of the Constitution explicitly provides a number of exceptions to the principle of public hearings, namely in those cases where public access could pose a danger to order or good behaviour. The Constitution provides that such exception requires an order of the court. In practice, some cases where the rule of public hearings may be deviated from, are explicitly laid down in statutes (such as divorce proceedings, adoption matters and child/youth protection cases). However, in cases of political offences or press offences, proceedings cannot be held *in camera* except by unanimous decision of the court.

236. Article 149 of the Constitution prescribed in 1831 the pronouncing of each judgment in open court, without exception. This rule has been subject to some criticism because it is considered as a very time-consuming burden. On 22 April 2019 that part of the Article was amended as follows, 'A judgment is to be made public in the manner prescribed by Act. In criminal cases, the verdict is pronounced in open court.'[137] The relevant implementing Act of 5 May 2019 has thus amended the Criminal Procedure Code and the Civil Procedure Code accordingly.[138] The governing principles in criminal cases and in civil cases are in large measure the same:

(i) the operative parts of the judgments, the determinative rulings/verdicts, are read out in open court;
(ii) entire, complete judgments are stored on publicly accessible electronic databases and are rendered anonymous, and
(iii) Presiders can of their own motion, or must in certain cases, read the entire full judgment in open court.

Articles 148 and 149 of the Constitution are only applicable to the ordinary courts. For the other courts, such as the administrative law courts and disciplinary courts, legislation or international human rights conventions (e.g., Article 6 §1 EConvHR), may require hearings and pronouncement of sentences to take place in public.

237. Article 149 of the Constitution provides that each judgment must be supported by reasons. This requirement has been imposed in order to enable the parties to understand the judgments. It also enables the appeal courts to review the legal correctness of lower court decisions. It protects the parties against arbitrary decisions, since judges are forced to give reasons for their rulings in a clear, consistent and unambiguous way and to consider and answer the arguments put forward by the parties. The requirement of Article 149 of the Constitution, contrary to the guarantees of Article 6 §1 EConvHR, is of a purely formal nature. Errors in law do not constitute a lack of reasons: if the reasons are consistent, there being no contradictions between the various arguments or between the ruling and the reasons for decision, a judgment may not be overturned because of a lack of reasons even if the reasons given are legally incorrect. In such a case, the judgment may well be overturned on account of errors in law, provided the relevant and necessary grounds have been invoked either by one of the parties or by the judge. The constitutional duty of providing reasons is considered to be an essential element of due process,

137. *Gazette,* 2 May 2019.
138. *Gazette,* 16 May 2019.

and hence is applicable to all the courts, those of ordinary jurisdiction and to the statutory courts, such as the administrative law courts.

238. Article 195 of the Criminal Procedure Code imposes a more stringent obligation to provide reasons in a number of criminal cases. It has been explicitly prescribed that judgments emanating from the Trial Division and the Appeal Division of the Criminal Court must justify the nature and degree of the punishment.

IV. State Liability for the Torts of Judges or of Members of the Public Prosecutors Office

239. Legislation in some countries (e.g., France, Italy, and Luxembourg) shows that in this matter the accepted view of State immunity is losing ground. Belgian jurisprudence has followed suit. In the *Anca* decisions[139], the Court of Cassation held that, under Articles 1382 and 1383 of the Civil Code, the State may be held liable by the courts of general jurisdiction for damages arising from a wrongful act committed by a judge or by a member of the Public Prosecutors Office. In order to preserve the independence of the judiciary, tort actions (including negligence) may not be brought against a judge or a member of the Public Prosecutors Office save in a restricted few cases, such as a conviction for a criminal offence, but instead have to be brought against the State.

When the act complained of is directly related to the judicial function, a claim for damages against the State will only be sustained, according to the Court of Cassation, if that act has been revoked, modified, or annulled on account of a violation of a rule of law by a definitive, final judgment. That condition poses a problem for the highest level of courts because their judgments are final. Therefore, seeking harmonisation with the *Köbler* jurisprudence of the ECJ, the Constitutional Court held that such an interpretation of Article 1382 of the Civil Code is in violation of the Constitution if it prevents the State from being held liable when there has been a 'sufficiently serious' breach of the law and an annulment of the relevant judgment rendered by the highest court is not obtainable.[140] Consequently, Article 1382 of the Civil Code must be interpreted as not preventing a judge from ruling on the liability of the State in such instances.[141] In cases where an alleged wrongful act committed by the Court of Cassation is at stake, the Constitutional Court held that sufficient guarantees exist to ensure judicial impartiality in proceedings where the Court of Cassation can review judgments of civil courts on the liability of the State for such a wrongful act.[142]

The Court of Cassation holds a twofold 'fault-concept': liability for damages arises upon (i) violation of a constitutional or a legislative rule prohibiting or compelling actions of a certain type, or (ii) upon violation of the general duty of care.

139. Cass., 19 Dec. 1991, *J.T.*, 1992, 142 and 8 Dec. 1994, *J.T.*, 1995, 497.
140. ECJ, Case C-224/01 (*Köbler*), 30 Sep. 2003.
141. Cons., Judgment No. 99/2014, 30 Jun. 2014.
142. Cons., Judgment No. 29/2017, 23 Feb. 2017.

Since 1991 the State has, however, rarely been held liable for damages for a wrongful act by or omission of a member of the judiciary.

§2. JUDICIAL REVIEW

I. Judicial Review in Belgian Constitutional Law

A. The Meaning of Judicial Review

240. In Belgian public law, a distinction should be made between, on the one hand, the judicial review of executive orders and regulations exercised by the ordinary law courts pursuant to Article 159 of the Constitution and by the Administrative Tribunal Division of the Council of State pursuant to Article 14 of the Consolidated Council of State Act[143] and, on the other hand, the judicial review of legislation, namely federal statutes and Community and Region Acts, as exercised by the Constitutional Court. Only the latter will be dealt with in this section.

B. Judicial Review of Legislation in Belgian Constitutional History

1. The Principle of the 'Inviolability of the Law'

241. Prior to 1980, constitutional review of legislation did not exist in Belgium. In 1849, the Court of Cassation ruled that, in view of the trust the National Congress had placed in the Legislative Branch, it was not up to the courts to ensure that legislation was constitutional, but instead up to Parliament itself.[144] This ruling set a de facto precedent that would be upheld for 130 years. It led to the expression that the 'law was inviolable'.

242. In 1950, the Court of Cassation introduced a 'presumption of constitutionality', ruling that if the meaning of a legal provision is open to more than one interpretation, courts may reasonably assume that the Legislature did not intend to violate the Constitution.[145] While still upholding the principle of the inviolability of the law, this ruling authorised the courts to construe the law in line with the Constitution. This technique is often applied by the Constitutional Court: declaring a legislative provision as interpreted by the referring judge to violate the Constitution, while at the same time 'discovering' that the same provision is also open to another possible interpretation which does not violate the Constitution.[146]

243. From 1948 onwards, a type of preliminary control over constitutionality has been exercised by the Legislation Division of the Council of State when it issues

143. See further below Pt. IV. Ch. 4. §2 'Judicial Review'.
144. Cass., 23 Jul. 1849, *Pas.*, 1849, 1, 443.
145. Cass., 20 Apr. 1950 (*Waleffe*) *Pas.*, 1950, 1, 560: cf. *'Verfassungskonforme Auslegung'*.
146. See, e.g., Cons., Judgment No. 24/2019, 14 Feb. 2019.

its legal opinion on draft legislation.[147] This does not, however, undercut the principle of the inviolability of the law since the legislative assemblies are not bound by this advice.

2. The Principle Qualified

244. The 1849 precedent has been qualified by the 1971 *Le Ski* case[148], in which the Court of Cassation held that courts must refuse to apply legislation which conflicts with self-executing international treaties. This led to the paradoxical situation that courts are to refuse to apply a law conflicting with fundamental rights guaranteed by a self-executing international treaty, yet cannot exercise the same authority regarding constitutionally guaranteed rights and liberties. This paradoxical situation remains notwithstanding the courts' obligation to refer to the Constitutional Court for preliminary ruling questions on the constitutionality of legislation.

245. A second qualification to the 'inviolability of the law' principle resulted from the restructuring of the State, which enabled the Communities and the Regions to enact legislation. Conflicts of jurisdiction would be inevitable in a system of a division of powers based upon mutual exclusivity. If each legislative body were left free to decide whether its own legislation was in compliance with the rules regarding the division of powers, federal and federated institutions would not be able to function properly and coherently. Since the general rule for resolving conflicts between rules of law – that a higher law prevails over a subordinate one – was rendered inapplicable by providing equal status to federal, Community, and Region Acts, a solution therefore had to be found. The institutionalisation of review for constitutionality of legislation through a specialised judicial institution – the 'Court of Arbitration' (*post* 2007, the 'Constitutional Court') – reflected the will not to depart too much from the initial principle of the 'inviolability of the law'. Because of an innate distrust of 'government by judges', the Court's jurisdiction was strictly limited to safeguarding the rules dividing legislative powers among the federal State, the Communities, and the Regions. For the same reason, a certain equilibrium was prescribed for the Court's composition. Specifically, one-half of its judges are former Members of Parliament, while the other half are senior lawyers. Moreover, the Court's membership is divided equally between the two main Belgian language groups. The 'Court of Arbitration', which was officially inaugurated on 1 October 1984 and heard its first case on 19 March 1985, has not failed in its task of striking a balance in a pluriform State.

246. Partly as a result of a growing trust in the Court, its jurisdiction and those having standing before it were broadened in the 1988 amendment of the Constitution (Article 142 Constitution) and in the 2003 amendments to its 1989 constitutive Special Majority Act. And with a 2007 constitutional amendment, the name of the

---

147. See below Pt. II. Ch. 6. §1. II 'The Legislation Division of the Council of State'.
148. Cass., 27 May 1971 (*N.V. Fromagerie Franco-Suisse Le Ski*), *J.T.*, 1971, 460. See Pt. I. Ch. 1 'Treaties'.

Court was officially changed into the 'Constitutional Court', reflecting the true role and wider tasks the Court fulfilled in the Belgian constitutional system. In 2014 the Court's jurisdiction was yet further extended.

II. The Constitutional Court

247. The Court is established by Article 142 of the Constitution. The Article's first sentence reads, 'There is for the entirety of Belgium a Constitutional Court, whose composition, jurisdiction, and functioning of which are provided for by Act of Parliament.' The primary legislation implementing this constitutional provision on the Constitutional Court is the Special Majority Act on the Constitutional Court of 6 January 1989[149], which can be found along with the Court's judgments on the Court's website: www.const-court.be.

A. *Jurisdiction*

248. The jurisdiction of the Constitutional Court is delimited in three ways:

(i) by the object of judicial review: the Court may exercise judicial review only over statutes or rules having like force of law;
(ii) by the set of constitutional reference standards the observance of which it may review, being constitutional and legal provisions on the division of powers between the federal and the federated levels, the provisions of Title II of the Constitution, and Articles 143 §1, 170, 172 and 191 of the Constitution, and
(iii) by the ways in which matters are submitted to the Court, namely applications for annulment and suspension, and requests for a preliminary ruling.

1. The Substance of Review

249. The object of judicial review as exercised by the Constitutional Court is limited to rules having force of statutory law. The most common are Special Majority Acts, ordinary Acts, and Community and Region Acts. Administrative regulations which have been confirmed by federal statute or by Community or Region Act are also considered as reviewable legislation. By contrast, the ordinary law courts and the Administrative Tribunal Division of the Council of State retain full powers to review administrative regulations and orders for constitutional conformity.

250. Between 1985 and 1988, the Constitutional Court's powers of review consisted of determining whether legislation had been enacted in compliance with the division of powers under the Constitution and implementing legislation. The prime

149. *Gazette,* 7 Jan. 1989.

– and originally sole – role of the Court resided in its arbitration of classic disputes in a federal State, hence its earlier name of the 'Court of Arbitration'. In Belgium, the division of powers between the federal State and its federated entities is based upon mutual exclusivity, concurrent legislative powers being the exception.[150] The Constitution and implementing legislation have attributed exclusive powers to the Community legislatures and to those of the Regions while entrusting the regulation of several matters to the federal legislature which also has the residual powers. In such a system of an exclusive division of powers, only one legislative body with jurisdiction *ratione materiae* as well as *ratione loci* can regulate a matter. Legislation is therefore subject to an *ultra vires* test, and liable to be struck down by the Court as such unless otherwise justified under the doctrine of implied powers.

251. Several provisions in the Constitution and in Special Majority Acts impose consultation requirements obliging the federal level and the federated entities to engage in dialogue, to ask for information or counsel, to obtain harmonisation opinions or agreements, and so on, before being allowed to exercise their individual legislative jurisdiction. According to Article 30*bis* of the Special Majority Act on the Constitutional Court, most consultation requirements are to be understood as rules distributing legislative powers among the federal level, the Communities, and the Regions. The Constitutional Court has jurisdiction to sanction legislation enacted without taking these consultation requirements into account, with the exception of the requirement to conclude co-operation agreements.

252. With the 1988 amendments to the Constitution, the jurisdiction of the Court was extended to cover compliance by legislation with three fundamental rights stemming from Title II of the Constitution, 'Belgians and Their Rights'. These are: the principle of equality (Article 10 Constitution), the principle of non-discrimination (Article 11 Constitution), and the right to and the freedom of education (Article 24 Constitution).

253. The Constitutional Court defines the principles of equality and non-discrimination in the same way as the ECtHR.[151] Articles 10 and 11 of the Constitution do not prohibit differentiated treatment in law, if there is an objective and reasonable justification to do so. The existence of such a justification must be assessed in relation to the aim and the effects of the law under scrutiny. The principle of equality is violated when there is no reasonable proportion between the means employed and the aim pursued.

Already in the Constitutional Court's first judgment related to Articles 10 and 11 of the Constitution, it explained that the principle of equality and non-discrimination has 'a general scope, forbidding all discriminations, regardless their origin: the constitutional rules on equality and non-discrimination apply to all rights and all liberties granted to the Belgians'.[152] Articles 10 and 11 of the Constitution thus operate as a go-between allowing the Court indirectly to review legislation

150. See below Pt. III. Ch. 2. §3. I. D 'An Allocation of Powers Based upon Mutual Exclusiveness'.
151. ECtHR, *Belgian Linguistic Case* (23 Jul. 1968).
152. Cons., Judgment No. 23/89, 13 Oct. 1989.

against rights and liberties set out in other constitutional provisions[153], in unwritten principles of law[154], and in international and European law.[155]

These indirect reference provisions have an important place in the Belgian Constitutional Court's jurisprudence. For example, the EConvHR is mentioned in some 30% of the Court's judgments and primary and secondary EU law is mentioned in some 10% of its judgments. When the Constitutional Court combines Articles 10 and 11 of the Constitution with provisions in the European treaties, it applies the jurisprudence of the ECtHR and of the ECJ, such as using their criteria for restricting human rights.[156] As a consequence of the Constitutional Court's ample use of EU law, it has also established an elaborate dialogue by preliminary reference with the ECJ.[157]

254. The 1988 extension of the Court's review power to cover Article 24 of the Constitution, providing a right to and a freedom of education, is linked with the 'communitarization' of education. The ideological minorities of Catholics in Wallonia and non-Catholics in Flanders feared that an attributing of legislative authority to the Communities in the field of education could jeopardise the rights they had acquired under the 'School Pact' of 1958.[158] To assuage their fears, Article 24 of the Constitution was amended to include the essential safeguards established in this political settlement, being the equality between the free (mainly Catholic) and the State school network. In addition, the Constitutional Court was empowered to review the compliance of legislation with Article 24.

255. The range of constitutional provisions subject to the Court's review powers can be extended by a Special Majority Act, as provided by Article 142 paragraphs 2, 3 and 6 of the Constitution. Parliament made use of this power in 2003 to extend the Court's review jurisdiction to all constitutional provisions under Title II (Articles 8–32), as well as to Articles 170 and 172 (taxation matters) and 191 (non-discrimination of foreign non-nationals) of the Constitution. The rationale for this widened jurisdiction lies in avoiding the intricate constructions through the prism of Articles 10 and 11 of the Constitution developed by the Court to accept cases of alleged violations of those constitutional provisions not listed in Article 142 of the Constitution.

256. In its first judgments applying the 2003 amendments, the Court developed a second technique of indirect review, one based on the fact that many domestic

153. See, e.g., Cons., Judgments No. 14/97, 18 Mar. 1997 and No. 122/98, 3 Dec. 1998.
154. Cons., Judgments No. 49/96, 12 Jul. 1996 (the principle of legal certainty); No. 46/2000, 3 May 2000 (solicitor-client privilege); No. 43/2001, 29 Mar. 2001 (the personal character of a criminal punishment); and No. 81/2007, 7 Jun. 2007 (proportionality of criminal punishment). Many of these principles are also protected in ECtHR caselaw.
155. See, e.g., Cons., Judgments No. 18/90, 2 May 1990 and No. 105/2000, 25 Oct. 2000.
156. See, e.g., Cons., Judgments No. 45/96, 12 Jul. 1996 and No. 124/2000, 29 Nov. 2000.
157. The latest example is Cons., Judgment No. 135/2019, 17 Oct. 2019, which was the 36th case referred to the ECJ. The full list of preliminary references in dialogue with the ECJ can be found on the Constitutional Court's website.
158. See further below Pt. IV. Ch. 2. §2. III. B 'Freedom of Education'.

constitutional rights have a counterpart in international and European human rights conventions. According to the Constitutional Court, such 'analogous human rights provisions' form an 'inextricable unity'. Hence, the Court must 'take into account' these analogous treaty provisions when interpreting the Constitution.[159] But the Constitutional Court does much more than merely take these treaties into account. Whenever it implements its analogy doctrine, it cites and applies all relevant jurisprudence by the ECtHR and by the ECJ, thus updating the Belgian human rights catalogue with the evolving interpretations offered by these courts. In doing so, it also maximises human rights protection: whenever a human right is guaranteed by both the Constitution and the EConvHR, the legislator may limit it only if it satisfies both the formal restriction criteria in the Constitution and the material restriction criteria of the EConvHR system.[160]

257. When using its two techniques of indirect review against international treaties, the Court can take these treaty provisions into consideration ex officio or at the request of a party. But it can do so only insofar as the violation of a constitutionally guaranteed right is asserted before the Court. Otherwise, the Court would overstep its jurisdiction granted by Article 142 of the Constitution by asserting jurisdiction to review directly the compliance of legislation with treaty provisions. For example, in a case concerning respect for privacy and family life, the Court may read Article 22 of the Constitution in the light of Article 8 EConvHR, notwithstanding that the latter provision is not explicitly invoked by the parties before the Court.[161] The inverse, however, would not be possible: the Court cannot review a legal provision directly against Article 8 EConvHR, and it could not circumvent this by invoking ex officio Article 22 of the Constitution.

258. The 2014 State Reform introduced two entirely new areas of review jurisdiction for the Constitutional Court. Neither of these has yet been invoked in any case before the Court, and thus the Court has not been able to develop any caselaw on these points.

The first new area of jurisdiction concerns the a priori review of the constitutionality of consultative Region referenda (Article 142 paragraph 4 Constitution). The new Article 39*bis* of the Constitution allows consultative referenda at the Region level provided that the question submitted to the public concerns a Region competence, with the exception of budget and financing and of matters for which a two-thirds majority is required. According to the new Article 30*ter* of the Special Majority Act on the Constitutional Court, a referendum can only be held after the Constitutional Court has determined that the proposed question falls within these substantive limits. Additionally, the Court's a priori review involves examining whether the question proposed respects the rules dividing legislative powers among the federal level, the Communities, and the Regions; the principle of federal loyalty, and the human rights guaranteed by Articles 8–30, 170, 172 and 191 of the

159. See e.g., Cons., Judgments No. 136/2004, 22 Jul. 2004; No. 189/2005, 14 Dec. 2005; No. 195/2009, 3 Dec. 2009, and No. 23/2011, 10 Feb. 2011.
160. See below Pt. IV. Ch. 2. §1. IV. B 'Conditions for Restrictions on Rights and Liberties'.
161. Cons., Judgment No. 108/2006, 28 Jun. 2006.

Constitution. The Court is also to ensure the referendum complies with the Region Act on Referenda and does not have a binding character. A consultative referendum may not be held as long as the Court has not given its fiat.

The second new area of jurisdiction concerns a rather limited review of the decisions taken by the Control Commission of the House of Representatives (Article 142 paragraph 5 Constitution). The 1989 Act on Political Party Finance limits the spending of political parties on federal election campaigns. The Control Commission, a parliamentary commission consisting of seventeen MPs and four independent experts, reviews whether the parties and the candidates have stayed within these limits. The Commission can impose sanctions on individual MPs in the forms of a warning, a limit on expense recoupment, a temporary suspension of their mandate, or even a revocation of their mandate. These decisions can be challenged before the Constitutional Court following the procedure laid down in Articles 25*bis*–25*septies* of the Special Majority Act on the Constitutional Court.

259. The 2014 State Reform also contained a modest extension of the Constitutional Court's reference standards. The Court has been granted jurisdiction to review whether statutory law violates the principle of federal loyalty, laid down in Article 143 §1 of the Constitution (Articles 1 3° and 26 §1 4° Special Majority Act on the Constitutional Court). This is not so much a new competence, but rather a confirmation of a practice developed by the Constitutional Court which had already assumed this jurisdiction by interpreting the principle of federal loyalty as a rule distributing legislative power among the federal level, the Communities, and the Regions.[162] Moreover, in the Constitutional Court's caselaw, the principle of federal loyalty coincides with the principle of proportionality inherent in all exercises of legislative power: each legislator, in the exercise of power, must ensure that the acts and decisions taken do not impede or overly hinder the exercise by other legislators of their own powers.[163]

2. Proceedings Before the Court

260. Leaving the new competences regarding consultative regional referenda and decisions by the Control Commission aside, the Constitutional Court's jurisdiction is invoked either through applications for annulment (Articles 1–25 Special Majority Act on the Constitutional Court) or through references for preliminary ruling (Articles 26–30 Special Majority Act on the Constitutional Court).

Both proceedings concern a '*contentieux objectif*', since the Court confines itself to examining whether a lower legal norm violates a higher legal norm without deciding upon the merits of claims in the pending lawsuit. Whereas annulment proceedings are indeed stand-alone actions, fully independent of any case pending before a court ('abstract norm control'), the preliminary reference procedure is initiated by a question raised in a pending lawsuit ('concrete norm control'). But even

162. Cons., Judgment No. 119/2004, 30 Jun. 2004.
163. See, e.g., Cons., Judgment No. 31/2010, 30 Mar. 2010.

when exercising its concrete norm control, the Court deals with abstract questions of constitutional law, leaving the further question of applying the law in the case itself to the referring judge.

Preliminary references make up the better part of the Constitutional Court's case-law. They have accounted for 61% of the Constitutional Court's judgments rendered between 1985 and 2018, in contrast to 34% of judgments in actions for annulment and 5% concerning petitions for suspension.

261. An application for annulment may be initiated by the executive bodies of the State, the Communities, and the Regions; by the Presidents of the federal Parliament, the Community and the Region Parliaments (at the request of two-thirds of the members of those bodies), or by any natural or legal person (Belgian or non-Belgian alike) having the necessary 'interest'. In order to demonstrate the required interest for standing, natural and legal persons must show they may be affected personally, directly, and negatively by the legislative provision challenged. The Constitutional Court applies this requirement very leniently, only very rarely deciding that a natural or legal person lacks the required interest.

Annulment applications are subject to a strict limitations period of six months following publication of the legislative provisions at issue. This time limit is shortened to sixty days after publication for challenges to legislation approving a treaty in order to enable the Constitutional Court to exercise judicial review before ratification takes place.

262. When, in a preliminary ruling, the Court decides that a legislative provision violates the Constitution, a new time limit of six months starts, enabling all possible petitioners to initiate an action for annulment. Legislation can thus be annulled a long time after its entry into force.

263. At the request of the petitioner, the application of a legislative provision may be suspended in the course of annulment proceedings, for the annulment procedure does not operate as a suspension on its own. The request to suspend legislative provisions must be submitted within three months of their publication and must be accessory to an action for annulment. The Court can consider whether the consequences of a suspension may have disproportionate effects.[164] Because such an order may constitute a major intrusion into the autonomy of the legislator, it is subject to stringent conditions: arguments in favour of the suspension must be serious and the continued application of the legislation challenged has to cause quasi irreparable prejudice. If an application for suspension is granted by the Court, it must then decide within three months upon the merits of the application, i.e. the constitutionality of the legislative provision at issue. If it does not decide within this period, the suspension order expires and ceases to have effect.

264. As is the case for annulment judgments by the Administrative Tribunal Division of the Council of State, annulment judgments rendered by the Constitutional Court operate *ex tunc* and *erga omnes*. They are final and binding on the

164. See, e.g., Cons., Judgment No. 174/2002, 27 Nov. 2002.

points of law considered, from the date of publication in the *Gazette*. They have retroactive effect unless the Court decides otherwise: the annulled legal provision is considered never to have existed within the legal system. The far-reaching consequences of an annulment of a legislative provision can, however, be alleviated and mitigated if the Court decides to maintain the consequences of the annulled legal provision, either until the date of the judgment or for a certain time after its delivery. During that period, the legislator is given the time necessary to enact new legislative provisions conforming to the Constitution.

265. Preliminary rulings are not unknown in Belgian law, being used before the ECJ and the Benelux Court. The concept of a preliminary ruling is closely linked to the concept of the unity of the legal system, and more in particular to the uniform interpretation and application of the Constitution. Judges in a given case being confronted with a question concerning the compatibility of a legal provision with one of the Court's reference standards have to refer that matter to the Constitutional Court for a preliminary ruling. Only this Court has jurisdiction to rule on the constitutionality of laws. In a centralised Kelsenian system of constitutional review, only one judicial institution is exclusively authorised to guarantee the uniform interpretation of the Constitution. The ordinary and administrative courts are denied this jurisdiction.

266. If, in the course of a lawsuit, it is alleged that legislation conflicts with one of the above-mentioned constitutional and legislative reference standards, courts must stay proceedings and refer the question to the Constitutional Court for a preliminary ruling. Exceptions to the obligatory nature of the reference depend on the hierarchical position of the judge asked to refer the question to the Constitutional Court and the context in which the question arises. Pursuant to Article 26 §§2–3 of the Special Majority Act on the Constitutional Court, all courts (from the lower courts up to the Court of Cassation and the Council of State) are exempted from referring a case to the Constitutional Court if:

(i) they have no jurisdiction in the matter or the case is inadmissible, unless the grounds of lack of jurisdiction and/or inadmissibility are themselves the object of the referral;
(ii) the Court has already ruled on the same issue (*acte éclairé*), and
(iii) the case at hand concerns urgent requests of a temporary character or custody procedures.

267. The obligation to refer is subject to further exceptions for the lower courts (i.e., the courts other than the Court of Cassation and the Administrative Tribunal Division of the Council of State). These lower courts can invoke two more grounds of exemption (Article 26 §2 Special Majority Act on the Constitutional Court):

(i) they do not consider the ruling of the Constitutional Court to be strictly necessary to decide the case;
(ii) the legislative provision in question clearly or manifestly does not violate the constitutional reference standards (*acte clair*).

It goes without saying that the slightest doubt on the constitutionality of legislation compels the lower courts to seek a preliminary ruling.

268. Since the 2003 amendments to the Special Majority Act on the Constitutional Court, one specific situation is further excluded from the preliminary ruling procedure. Preliminary rulings sought for an alleged unconstitutionality of legislation approving a 'constitutive' EU treaty, the EConvHR, or its additional protocols are no longer possible (Article 26 §1*bis* Special Majority Act on the Constitutional Court).[165] This modification was introduced in order to safeguard Belgium from international liability where the Court would declare such legislation unconstitutional. Internally, the application of the treaty would then be normatively impossible after the Court's judgment; whereas internationally Belgium would still be bound by the treaty and the obligation to observe its provisions. Nonetheless, references for preliminary rulings concerning Acts approving all other treaties still remain available.

269. The decision itself of a court to refer a case to the Constitutional Court for a preliminary ruling, ex officio or at the request of an interested party, is final and not subject to appeal.

Prior to 2014, the Constitutional Court had no explicit powers to address the consequential effects of its preliminary reference judgments holding legal provisions unconstitutional. Article 8 of the Special Majority Act on the Constitutional Court only permitted it to do so regarding judgments in petitions for annulment. The Constitutional Court has, however, extended *proprio motu* its jurisdiction to determine the consequential effects of legal provisions found unconstitutional in the former cases in a 2011 judgment, explaining that the principle of legal certainty can, in rare cases, compel it to do so.[166] Thereafter the Special Majority Legislator explicitly granted the Constitutional Court this jurisdiction, in a 2016 amendment to Article 28 of the Special Majority Act on the Constitutional Court.[167]

B. Composition of the Court

270. The twelve judges of the Constitutional Court are appointed by the King, each from a list of two candidates submitted alternately by the House of Representatives and by the Senate. Those lists must be adopted by a two-thirds majority in the House or the Senate, in order to ensure an adequate representation within the Court of political tendencies.

The criteria for appointment establish two different categories of judge. A first category is composed of six judges who have been judges on the Court of Cassation and or the Council of State, law professors, or law clerks with the Constitutional Court, each subcategory having at least one seat on the Court. The second category

165. See also Pt. I. Ch. 1. §2 'Hierarchy'.
166. Cons., Judgment No. 125/2011, 7 Jul. 2011.
167. Special Majority Act of 25 December 2016 amending Art. 28 of the Special Majority Act on the Constitutional Court, *Gazette*, 10 Jan. 2017.

is composed of six former Members of Parliament, who need not necessarily have had any legal training (although this has generally been the case), which category obviously reflects the Legislature's initial mistrust of 'government by judges'.

In addition, each category must track the lines of language parity. The Dutch-speaking and French-speaking judges each constitute their own language group. Each language group elects its own president. The office of President of the Court alternates on a yearly basis between the presidents of each language group. One of the judges must have an adequate knowledge of German. Judges must be over 40 years of age.

The Court's composition also observes a gender quota. Since 2014, the Special Majority Act on the Constitutional Court stipulates that at least four of the Court's judges must belong to the least represented gender. That requirement was only achieved in December 2019.

271. The Court is assisted by up to twenty-four law clerks (sixteen as of January 2020) and two registrars.

272. Although the Constitutional Court is not a part of the Judicial Branch in its organic sense, the independence of its members is guaranteed by providing them with legal status to a large extent informed by the constitutional provisions regarding the Judicial Branch. As with the ordinary judiciary, members of the Court are appointed for life, subject only to a legally determined retirement age of 70. Their salary is fixed by law. Their tenure of office also carries with it conflict of interest rules to prevent the holding of other offices with a risk of financial dependency.

C. *Organisation and Operation*

273. The Constitutional Court functions as a collegial body. Its judgments are delivered *per curiam* without the possibility of a dissenting opinion. Together with the secrecy of deliberations, this is viewed as a useful safeguard against any undue pressure exerted on the individual members of the Court. The Court may sit as a panel consisting of both Presidents and five other judges. To make up those panels, a list is drawn up by the presidents at the beginning of each annual session on 1 September. The Court may nonetheless sit as a plenum of twelve judges at the request of one of its presidents or of two panel members. In recent years, the Court has increasingly decided to have cases heard and decided by the full Court plenum. If one judge cannot take part in the deliberations of the plenum because of absence or because of grounds for recusal, the Court will sit as a panel of ten judges, which implies that one of the judges of the other language group, normally the least senior one, must abstain.

274. If the case is heard by a panel of seven judges, the language group of that year's President of the Court represents a majority of four judges. If the Court hears the case as a plenum of twelve judges or a panel of ten judges, the President's vote is decisive in the event of a tied vote. This system is designed to avoid a structural majority of one language group within the Court or an immobilising permanent deadlock between them. Furthermore, the system of alternating language majorities has a pluralising effect on the functioning of the Court. One year's majority knows that it will become next year's minority with the transfer of the office of President of the Court.

275. The rules of procedure before the Court aim at ensuring a fair trial. Due process of law, for example, is ensured by provisions which secure the adversarial character of the proceedings and which impose duties to render judgments within a reasonable time and to give reasons for judgment. A judge may be disqualified when there are serious reasons to believe that he is biased or that he is an interested party.

Until 2014, oral hearings had to be held in every case and the judgments had to be delivered in open court. Since then, oral hearings are only to be held if the Court considers it necessary or if one of the parties asks to be heard. Judgments are no longer pronounced in open court, their publication on the Court's website counting instead as pronouncement.

276. Proceedings before the Constitutional Court are mainly written and inquisitorial. The assistance of a lawyer is not mandatory, but due to the complex nature of the cases, legal representation is the general rule. In order to avoid groundless proceedings, the Court may switch to a simplified 'screening' procedure, whenever a case brought before the Court is manifestly without foundation or is clearly inadmissible.

277. The judgments of the Constitutional Court are final. The average time for a case to be dealt with is approximately fourteen months. Extracts of the judgments, containing the decision itself, are published in the *Gazette*. All of the Court's decisions from 1985 onwards are available in full on the Court's website.

D. The Problem of Concurring Human Rights Jurisdictions

278. The 2003 extension of the Constitutional Court's competence to review legislation as against the provisions of Title II and Articles 170, 172 and 191 of the Constitution – and more in particular the Constitutional Court's jurisprudence concerning analogous human rights review – has provoked a negative reaction from the Court of Cassation.

279. The ordinary and administrative law courts have been entitled to refuse to apply legislation considered to conflict with self-executing international treaties since the 1971 *Franco-Suisse Le Ski* decision of the Court of Cassation. The Constitutional Court's analogous human rights doctrine should not be considered as a threat to that prerogative, for it is a mere technique of interpreting the Constitution. Nevertheless, the Court of Cassation responded to the aforementioned Constitutional Court Judgment No. 136/2004 of 22 July 2004 in two of its decisions in

November 2004.[168] In these, the Court of Cassation held that, in the case of analogous human rights being guaranteed by both the Constitution and an international or European treaty, a judge may first consider whether the legal provision in issue complies with the treaty, and if it does, the judge may then decline to submit the case to the Constitutional Court for a preliminary ruling on its further compliance with the Constitution because the judge has jurisdiction to determine whether the Constitution offers more far-reaching human rights protection or not.

280. These Cassation decisions were considered to threaten the effectiveness of the Constitutional Court's human rights review, which depends on a sufficient supply of cases. More specifically, the Court of Cassation's point of view infringed Article 26 §1 of the Special Majority Act on the Constitutional Court which obliges all judges to refer cases to the Constitutional Court for a preliminary ruling if a legal provision is alleged to violate a human right guaranteed by the Constitution. In addition, the Court of Cassation contradicted the Constitutional Court's jurisprudence which considers the Constitution to be a higher norm than international treaties.

281. To bring some order to this situation, an amendment to the Special Majority Act on the Constitutional Court was adopted by Parliament and promulgated on 12 July 2009. This amendment did not settle the discussion on the hierarchy between the Constitution and international treaties. It did, however, settle the dispute concerning jurisdiction over analogous human rights review by establishing a sequence of steps when undertaking it.

The new mechanism, found in Article 26 §4, obliges all judges to send a case to the Constitutional Court for a preliminary reference when a legal provision applicable in a pending case is alleged to violate a human right laid down both in the Constitution and in an international treaty. The parties possess no choice of forum in this regard: even if they invoke only the treaty right, the judge is to examine ex officio whether that right is analogous to a right guaranteed by Title II of the Constitution. This obligation to refer is subject to three new and specific grounds to decline a referral, and these apply in all courts, including the apex ones. Judges may decline to refer a case if:

(i) the exemptions of Article 26 §2 or §3 apply;
(ii) they find that the rights in Title II of the Constitution are manifestly not violated (‘*acte clair*’);
(iii) they find that an international treaty provision is manifestly violated in light of international caselaw (‘*acte éclairé*’), and
(iv) they find that a provision of Title II of the Constitution is manifestly violated in light of the Constitutional Court's caselaw (‘*acte éclairé*’).

If the Constitutional Court decides that the legal provision under scrutiny violates the constitutional right invoked, the referring judge is obliged not to apply it.

168. Cass., 9 Nov. 2004 (P040849N), and 16 Nov. 2004 (P041127N and P040644N).

If the Constitutional Court decides that the legal provision does not violate that constitutional right, the referring judge is subsequently allowed to conduct a *Le Ski* treaty-based review.

Whether this mechanism will bring judicial harmony depends partly on the willingness of the judiciary to apply Article 26 §4 in good faith.

282. This new procedure has immediately been challenged in an EU law context. A tax judge submitted a preliminary reference to the ECJ asking whether the procedure complied with the *Simmenthal* doctrine, but the ECJ declared it inadmissible because EU law did not apply in that case.[169]

In its *Melki* judgment considering the French priority rule[170], the ECJ held that any delay of national courts in ceasing to apply national legislation not in conformity with EU law – a delay occasioned by obligations to seek preliminary rulings – was acceptable provided that the following conditions were met:[171]

(i) the ordinary or administrative judge hearing the case remains free at any stage of the proceedings to refer the matter to the ECJ;
(ii) the judge may take all provisional measures necessary to ensure the final judgment's effective protection of the parties' rights flowing from EU law;
(iii) even after a negative answer on the constitutionality question, the judge retains full jurisdiction to refuse application of all national legal provisions he considers to violate EU law, and
(iv) if the legal provision under scrutiny is a literal transposition of a Directive, a preliminary reference to the ECJ concerning that Directive's validity is mandatory.

283. Although all authors agree that Article 26 §4 meets these requirements, at least implicitly, the Special Majority Act on the Constitutional Court has been further amended in 2014 to minimise any risk of conflict. Article 30 added that judges referring a case to the Constitutional Court always have jurisdiction to order all provisional measures to ensure the effectiveness of their final verdicts. Article 26 §4 also clarified the obligation to refer a case to the Constitutional Court for a preliminary reference as not impeding the possibility of also seeking at the same time or at a later stage a preliminary reference from the ECJ.

SELECTED FURTHER READING

Alen, A. 'Twintig jaar grondwettigheidstoezicht op wetgevende normen. Krachtlijnen van de rechtspraak van het Arbitragehof van 1985 tot en met 2004'. *T.B.P.* (2005): 213–226.

Alen A., S. Lambrecht & W. Verrijdt. 'Belgique'. In *Traité des rapports entre ordres juridiques* edited by B. Bonnet (LGDJ, 2016) 1393–1141.

169. ECJ, Case C-457/09 (*Chartry v Belgium*), 1 Mar. 2011.
170. ECJ, Cases C-188/10 and C-189/10 (*Melki and Abdeli*), 22 Jun. 2010.
171. The ECJ recalling its exclusive jurisdiction over the validity of secondary EU law.

Alen, A., J. Spreutels, E. Peremans, & W. Verrijdt. 'Het Grondwettelijk Hof en het internationaal en Europees recht' *TBP* (2014): 619–652 (also published as 'Cour constitutionnelle de Belgique'. In *La coopération entre les Cours constitutionnelles en Europe. Situation actuelle et perspectives* edited by R. Huppmann & R. Schnabl (Verlag Österreich, 2014) 293–347.

Alen, A., & W. Verrijdt. 'The Dialogue Between the European Court of Human Rights and Domestic Constitutional Courts. The Belgian Example', in *Human Rights with a Human Touch. Liber Amicorum Paul Lemmens* edited by K. Lemmens, S. Parmentier and L. Reyntjens (Intersentia, 2019), 155–202.

Arts, A. et al. (eds). *Les rapports entre la Cour d'arbitrage, le Pouvoir judiciaire et le Conseil d'État* (La Charte, 2006).

Allermeersch, B., A. Alen & B. Dalle. 'Judicial Independence in Belgium'. In *Judicial Independence in Transition* edited by A. Seibert-Fohr (Springer, 2012) 307–356.

Behrendt, C. *Le juge constitutionel, un législateur-cadre positif* (Bruylant/LGDJ, 2006).

Bossuyt, M. & W. Verrijdt. 'The Full Effect of EU Law and of Constitutional Review in Belgium and France after the *Melki* Judgment'. *Eur Con. LR* (2011): 355–391.

De Visser, M. *Constitutional Review in Europe – A Comparative Analysis* (Hart Publishing, 2014).

Laenens, J., D. Scheers, P. Thiriar, S. Rutten & B. Vanlerberghe. *Handboek gerechtelijk recht* (Intersentia, 2016).

Moonen, T. *De keuzes van het Grondwettelijk Hof* (die Keure, 2015).

Peeters, P. 'The Belgian Constitutional Review Procedure under European Scrutiny'. *Eur. Pub. L* (2012): 411–422.

Popelier, P. *Procederen voor het Grondwettelijk Hof* (Intersentia, 2008).

Rigaux, M.-F. & B. Renauld. *La Cour constitutionelle* (Bruylant, 2008).

Rosoux, G. *Vers une 'dématérialisation' des droits fondamentaux?* (Bruylant, 2015).

Smets, J. & F. Debaedts. *Prejudiciële vragen aan het Grondwettelijk Hof* (Wolters Kluwer, 2016).

Souverijns, T. 'Bijzondere wetgever verduidelijkt de regeling van artikel 26, §4 van de bijzondere wet op het Grondwettelijk Hof inzake samenloop van grondrechten' *R.W.* (2013–2014): 1523–1531

Velaers, J. *Van Arbitragehof tot Grondwettelijk Hof* (Maklu, 1990).

Velaers, J. 'Het arrest *Melki – Abdeli* van het Hof van Justitie van de Europese Unie'. *R.W.* (2010–2011): 770–794.

Verdussen, M. *Les douze juges* (Eds Labor, 2004).

Verdussen, M. *Justice constitutionnelle* (Larcier, 2012)

Chapter 6. Independent Advisory or Supervisory Bodies at the Legislative and Executive Levels

§1. The Council of State

I. Historical Background

284. During the period of French rule (1795–1815), a Council of State was set up having consultative and judicial functions. The Council of State created in the United Kingdom of the Netherlands (1815–1830) was modelled after it. But because this institution was considered to be a willing instrument in the hands of the King, rather than an independent administrative jurisdiction, the National Congress did not want to introduce it into the Belgian institutional system. It considered the Judicial Branch as a safeguard against abuses on the part of the Executive Branch and its administration. The judiciary was entrusted with resolving all disputes concerning civil and political rights, save those disputes involving political rights, attributed by statute to an administrative jurisdiction.[172] In practice, however, the judiciary showed extreme reluctance in handling cases in which the administration was involved. It declared itself to have jurisdiction only for disputes between citizens, or for disputes between citizens and the government acting as a private person, but not acting as a public authority (namely, vested with the *ius imperii*). This meant that there was no judicial protection against many administrative decisions, which really was the opposite of what National Congress had intended. In its view, the Judicial Branch was always to have jurisdiction except where removed to an administrative court.

This lack of protection against abuses by the administration led to proposals to introduce a Council of State as existed in several other countries. The need for effective remedies for the citizens against arbitrary decisions became more and more urgent as the range of tasks carried out by the State – evolving from a liberal to a welfare State – increased. The judiciary tried to reverse this trend towards the setting up of a Council of State by overruling its prior decisions in what constitutes, up to now, one of the leading cases in Belgian public law: the *Flandria* case.[173] In that case, the Court of Cassation held that every civil right is entitled to judicial protection, even when violated by an administrative authority. It also recognised the exclusive jurisdiction of the ordinary law courts to grant compensatory damages for any infringement of a civil right by an administrative authority. The initiative to set up a Council of State also received the support of King Albert I who, in a letter of 3 January 1934, urged the government at the time to reform the administrative courts. In addition, many proposals and initiatives in the nineteenth and twentieth centuries have shown the necessity of a consultative body to improve the quality of

172. See Pt. II. Ch. 5. §1. I. A 'Belgium's Dual Judicial Organisation: Distinguishing Between the Ordinary and the Administrative Courts'.
173. Cass., 5 Nov. 1920 (*Flandria*) *Pas.*, 1920, 1, 193.

legislation. In the final result, the Act establishing a Council of State of 23 December 1946 was passed. A Council of State was created with two sections: (1) the Administrative Tribunal Division with a judicial function and (2) the Legislation Division with an advisory function.

285. Until 1993 the status of the Council of State derived only from statute: the Consolidated Council of State Act of 12 January 1973. Given its independence from the Executive Branch, its being the highest administrative law court, and given the authority it had gained, the Constitution in 1993 expressly confirmed in Article 160 the existence of a Council of State and its role as an administrative tribunal and advisory body.

II. The Legislation Division of the Council of State

286. Before a Bill is tabled or a regulation enacted, a preliminary opinion of certain consultative bodies regarding particular aspects of the draft law may be required. One of the most important of these advisory bodies is the Legislation Division of the Council of State.

A draft public Bill containing general binding rules has to be submitted by the federal Minister responsible for it to the Legislation Division of the Council of State for a mandatory preliminary opinion. The governments of the Communities and the Regions also have to follow this procedural requirement when they want to pass a generally binding Community or Region Act in their respective Parliaments. A draft Private Member's Bill may also be submitted by the president of the relevant Parliament for an opinion.

Draft regulations of the federal and of the Community and Region governments, except in cases of urgency as sufficiently justified with reasons given, must also be submitted to the Legislation Division for such preliminary advice. This exception is not applicable, however, where regulations repeal, extend, amend, or replace legislation.

287. The Legislation Division of the Council of State was set up as an advisory body to improve the quality of legislation and its drafting. Legislation has become increasingly complex as more and more matters come to be regulated, resulting in a steady increase of legislative rules. One of the primary tasks of the Legislation Division is to improve the technical quality of (draft) statutes and regulations. In its non-binding advice it will, for example, aim to reconcile the French version with the Dutch, both of which have equal legal status in Belgium. It will strive for uniform terminology as well as for logical structure and internal coherence in the statutes and regulations. Occasionally a proposed new regulation will affect existing regulations in other fields, and may necessitate amending their provisions. The Council of State may point this out where it has not already been taken into account. To these ends, it can employ to advantage the useful information provided by the

'Co-ordination Office' within the Council of State which keeps track of all legislative changes. The Council of State may also therefore be entrusted with the consolidation of multiple statutes with the same object into a single coherent text, or with codification, grouping together individual statutes having a similar or analogous object.

288. The Legislation Division also plays an important role in preserving the rule of law. In its advice, it will examine whether there is an adequate constitutional or legislative basis for the proposed legislation or regulation as submitted to it. This presupposes that the new law has been proposed by the competent authority. In the course of the federalisation process in Belgium, the advice of the Council of State has increased in stature because it serves as a useful interpretation of the constitutional and legislative provisions dividing powers between the federal level and the level of the federated entities. The Legislation Division will also point out whether the proposed law may conflict with a rule of higher rank.

Although, legally speaking, the advice of the Legislation Division of the Council of State is not binding, it may be rather difficult to disregard it, especially when it points out a likely breach of the Constitution or of statute. For proposed legislation, its opinions have been and are published[174], thus serving as useful information to Parliament in its control of the Executive Branch. Moreover, its opinion may also provide strong arguments for those seeking to challenge an Act before the Constitutional Court, should the Act have been passed in disregard of the advice of the Legislation Division. Additionally, its opinion points out whether the correct procedures have been complied with, such as whether any mandatory opinion has already been obtained from certain other advisory bodies. The Council of State requires, for example, the prior consent of the Budget Minister for each matter having budgetary implications.

It is important to stress that, unlike the Councils of State in other countries, the Legislation Division of the Belgian Council of State issues no policy recommendations. Its advice does not concern the appropriateness of any given legislative instrument.

289. If the preliminary advice of the Legislation Division has not been sought for a draft Bill, the sanction is purely political. If its required advice has not been sought for a draft regulation, however, either the ordinary courts may refuse to enforce that regulation, applying Article 159 of the Constitution, or the Administrative Tribunal Division of the Council of State may annul it on the grounds that the required procedure has not been complied with, thus rendering the administrative act null and void. The same judicial sanctions are applicable when the government, without sufficient justification, invokes the urgency exemption regarding a regulation. The reasons for the urgency exemption from the obligation of consultation must be well-founded and satisfactorily explained.

---

174. Since 1 January 2017 the Council of State is legally obliged to publish all opinions on its website without delay.

§2. The Office of the Auditor General

I. General

290. As is the case in all modern parliamentary democracies, each of the federal government and the Community and Region governments periodically has to submit its budget for prior approval to its respective Parliament (the federal Parliament and the Parliaments of the Communities and the Regions). The budget lists the revenues forecast and the expenditures envisaged over a certain period. Afterwards, that Parliament will control the use made of the authorisation it granted, having to approve the Public Accounts Act, being the end result of the prior budgetary period (Article 174 Constitution). This external parliamentary control should be distinguished from the internal budgetary control carried out by the Ministers, the administration itself, or by specialised services within the Executive Branch such as the Finance Inspectorate. Because of the complex nature of matters related to public expenditure, a Parliament is assisted in the examination of the draft Budget Bill, as well as in controlling the legality and regularity of implementing the budget, by a special constitutional, parliamentary, consultative body having some jurisdictional authority: the Office of the Auditor General (Article 180 Constitution). Its historical origins date back to a similar institution in the Seventeen Provinces under the reign of the Dukes of Burgundy and it is currently comparable with, for example, the French *Cour des Comptes* or the German *Bundesrechnungshof*. The legal status of the Office of the Auditor General is governed by the Auditor General Act of 29 October 1846.

291. By entrusting the verification of government accounts to the Office of the Auditor General, the National Congress wanted to ensure the Auditor's independence from the Executive Branch. The members of the Office of the Auditor General are therefore appointed by the House of Representatives for a term of office prescribed by statute (currently, six years). They may, however, be dismissed by the House of Representatives at any time. The 1846 Act specifies further a list of functions, which members of the Office of the Auditor General cannot hold on conflict of interest grounds. Salary and pension are also fixed by law.

292. Originally, the Office of the Auditor General only had jurisdiction constitutionally over national public accounts. Gradually, its authority has been extended by statute to the public accounts of the provinces and of the functionally decentralised institutions.[175] In the course of the federalisation process, statute has vested the Office of the Auditor General also with the power of verifying the budgets and accounts of the Communities and the Regions.[176] In the 2014 Sixth State Reform, Article 180 of the Constitution was supplemented with a fourth and fifth paragraph providing an explicit constitutional basis for the Special Majority legislator (and the ordinary majority legislator vis-à-vis the German Community) to empower the

175. See also further Pt. III Ch. 3 §2 'Functional Decentralisation'.
176. Article 50 *juncto* Art. 71 §1 of the Special Majority Act on Community and Region Finance of 16 January 1989.

Office of the Auditor General to examine the budgets and accounts of the Communities and the Regions as well as the other public institutions and bodies which derive from and depend on them. The Special Majority legislator (as well as ordinary majority legislator for the German Community) may also allow a Community or Region Act to regulate further this power of examination. Lastly, a federal Act of Parliament, a Community Act, or a Region one can assign further responsibilities to the Office of the Auditor General. Subject to the Office's consent, the Community or Region Act may set out what compensation the Office is to receive for undertaking these commissions. The extending of jurisdiction for the Office of the Auditor General to the Communities and Regions has led to demands to adjust the current structure of the Office of the Auditor General according to the principle that each parliamentary body should have a say in the appointment of the members of the Office assisting it in its budgetary controls. As of yet, no consensus has been reached on this matter. The Office of the Auditor General consists of two chambers, a French-speaking one and a Dutch-speaking one.

II. Powers

293. With the above point in mind then, the following remarks address specifically the powers of the Office of the Auditor General regarding the federal authorities.[177] The powers of the Office are threefold. Firstly, the prime significance of the Office of the Auditor General lies in its role of informing the legislative assemblies. In this respect, Article 180 of the Constitution provides that 'the general accounts of the State are submitted to the House of Representatives along with the comments of the Office of the Auditor General'. The Office of the Auditor General submits a yearly report to Parliament in which it comments on all the events of non-compliance with the relevant Budget Act committed by the relevant government. When dealing with urgent and important matters, the Office of the Auditor General may well decide not to wait for the yearly report and instead submit special statements to Parliament. Its observations address the legality of expenditures and their conformity with budgetary estimates. The yearly report will point out failings in management, and it may also contain suggestions on how to correct deficiencies in relevant legislation. The concrete impact of the report, enjoying extensive press coverage, is dependent on the effect given to it by Parliament. The House of Representatives can also ask the Office of the Auditor General to perform an audit of the administration, implying a review of efficiency, effectiveness, and economy. In this respect, it may be useful to point out that parliamentary budgetary control in Belgium is rather weak in comparison with other countries and occurs mainly ad hoc. The Office of the Auditor General has been increasingly involved in the drafting of the Budget Act to assist Parliament with its expertise. It will, for instance, advise the parliamentary committee on the realistic character of the estimates underlying the proposed Budget Act.

177. Recognising that the powers described in the paragraphs may also apply *mutatis mutandis* regarding the Communities and Regions.

294. Secondly, the Office of the Auditor General has an administrative task. It ensures respect for the 'principle of specialization', meaning that no item of expenditure in the budget should be exceeded and that no transfer can take place from one budget item to another.[178] The prior endorsement system, the rule that no payment voucher is accepted by the Treasury until it has received the seal of approval of the Office of the Auditor General was abolished by the 22 May 2003 amendments to the 1846 Act. In order to be able to carry out its task, the Office of the Auditor General is entitled to call for any statements, information, and explanations regarding revenues and expenditures of public funds. The body so called upon must provide the required information within one month.

295. Thirdly, although the Office of the Auditor General forms no part of the Judicial Branch and has no jurisdiction as an administrative court, it is nevertheless endowed with quasi-judicial powers in having to determine the financial liability of State accountants (civil servants) whose primary task consists in the collecting and the managing of public funds. The Office of the Auditor General examines and winds up the accounts of the general administration, as well as balances those accounts, determining in particular whether they are overall in credit or debit. In the latter case and at the request of the authority concerned, the Office of the Auditor General can determine any financial liability of the accountants, due to loss, theft, or mismanagement of public funds entrusted to them. Assessing any resultant criminal or civil liability remains, however, within the exclusive jurisdiction of the ordinary courts. If the accounts are in balance or if they are in credit, the Office of the Auditor General will release the accountant from any liability for the relevant period of time.

The judgments of the Office of the Auditor General are final and may only be quashed by the Court of Cassation on the grounds that they have contravened the law or have violated prescribed procedures, thus rendering a decision null and void. In the (rare) case that a judgment of the Office of the Auditor General is quashed by the Court of Cassation, the case will be referred to an ad hoc committee set up within the House of Representatives for final, definitive determination.

Selected Further Reading

Alen, A. 'De afdeling wetgeving van de Raad van State. Enkele kanttekeningen bij haar adviespraktijk'. In *Publiek recht, ruim bekeken: opstellen aangeboden aan prof. J. Gijssels* (Maklu, 1994) 1–28.

Alen, A. 'Le contentieux administratief français et belge. Une introduction'. In *Réforme de la procédure administrative: quo vadis?* edited by S. Lierman (Larcier, 2014) 1–5.

Coremans, H., M. Van Damme, et al. *Beginselen van wetgevingstechniek en behoorlijke regelgeving* (5th) (die Keure, 2016).

Drèze-Lebon, M. & F. Erauw. 'La Cour des comptes' *RPDB* Complément (Tome V) (Bruylant, 1977) 382–429.

178. See also Pt IV Ch 2 §1 II D 'The Principle of Non-transferability'.

Part II, Ch. 6, Advisory and Supervisory Bodies **295–295**

Quertainmont, Ph. *La Cour des comptes et sa mission juridictionnelle* (Bruylant, 1977).

Van Damme, M. 'The Council of State: Institution on the Junction of the Three Traditional Powers of the State' In *The Principle of Equality. A South African and Belgian Perspective*, edited by J. Vande Lanotte, J. Sarkin, & Y. Haeck (Maklu, 2001) 71–88.

Van Damme, M. & B. De Sutter. *Raad van State. Afdeling Wetgeving* (die Keure, 2013).

Velaers, J. *De Grondwet en de Raad van State, Afdeling Wetgeving* (Maklu, 1999).

Vijftig jaar Raad van State – Cinquante années du Conseil d'Etat, Liber memorialis 1948–1998 (Mys & Breesch, 1999).

Part III. The State and Its Subdivisions

Chapter 1. The Structure of the State: A Federal State Sui Generis

296. Belgium is traditionally known as a State fractured by linguistic and cultural divisions between two communities. Earlier, we stressed the peaceful coexistence of the Belgian communities as well as the fact that the differences between the two large communities are not only of a linguistic but also of an economic nature, and historically a religious one too. Until 1970, the heterogeneity of the Belgian population was not reflected in the institutional framework. In 1970, however, Prime Minister Gaston Eyskens stated in a famous parliamentary address, 'The unitary State, with its structure and functioning as currently regulated by the law, has been overtaken by events.' This Part attempts to give a survey of the current institutional structure of Belgium, which is a result of six successive constitutional-institutional State Reforms (1970, 1980–1983, 1988–1989, 1993, 2001, and 2012–2014). First, however, it will be necessary to outline some basic distinguishing features of Belgian federalism, since they may be helpful in providing a better understanding of the complex institutional framework, which has been set up.

297. Belgium's federalism has been characterised as 'bipolar' and 'centrifugal'. The bipolar characteristic refers to the fact that, unlike most federal systems which consist of at least eight to ten constituent subunits each having its own tradition, Belgium consists of only two large communities, the Dutch-speaking Flemish Community and the French-speaking one, plus a very small German-speaking Community. At the federal level, this bipolar character has led to a complex set of safeguards equalising in power the French-speaking minority with the Dutch-speaking majority.

The bipolar character finds an institutional expression in parity in the federal government, the language structures within the federal administration, the language groups in both Houses of the federal Parliament – on which the Special Majority Acts and the alarm-bell procedure are based – and in parity in the higher courts.

The centrifugal tendency of Belgian federalisation also constitutes an exception to normal federal practice, which is the quest for unity by the voluntary alliance of previously sovereign units. Centrifugal federalism means that the federated entities have developed out of a State, which was originally unitary or decentralised. The centripetal tendency of most federal States is the reason why most federal constitutions explicitly list the exclusive federal powers, leaving the residual powers to the federated entities. By contrast, Belgian centrifugal federalism tended instead to enumerate the powers vested exclusively in the federated entities, leaving the residual powers to the federal level. Such, indeed, is the present situation. Since 1993, however, Article 35 of the Constitution provides that residual jurisdiction is to be vested in the Communities and/or the Regions. The transitional provision in the same Article makes this – as yet not implemented – fundamental shift subject to a new provision in the Constitution enumerating the exclusive powers of the federal authorities and to a Special Majority Act laying down the conditions and procedures by which the residual jurisdiction is to be transferred.

298. A basic feature of Belgian federalism is the territoriality principle that underpins the general institutional structure. Official language legislation did eventually divide the country into four language regions (Article 4 Constitution). These three unilingual regions and one bilingual region determine the territorial jurisdiction of the Communities and the Regions, and therefore also form the territorial basis for Regional and Community elections. It is inadequate to define the Belgian Communities as such as a form of personal federalism. In fact, only within the bilingual Brussels-Capital region has a moderate form of non-territorial federalism been established. The Communities do have a clear territorial basis.[179] In Brussels both the Flemish and the French Communities have jurisdiction, but only with regard to institutions which can be considered as exclusively belonging to their Community. The Communities in Brussels have no direct jurisdiction over individual citizens or over bilingual institutions. Any form of sub-nationality is rejected.

299. The basic features of the Belgian federal structure are laid down in the Constitution. This structure is further elaborated on in Special Majority Acts passed pursuant to the Constitution. This approach is motivated by the wish to avoid the very cumbersome procedures for amendment of the Constitution and by the will to ensure that no State-institutional reform can be undertaken to which either of the country's two main population groups might possibly not assent. The Special Majority Acts must be adopted by a majority vote of each language group of each of the Houses of Parliament, provided that the majority of members of each language group is present and that the total number of votes in favour cast in each of the two language groups makes up two-thirds of the votes cast. The requirement for a Special Majority Act applies only to those cases expressly enumerated in the Constitution, all of which relate to the application of the constitutional principles on the structure of the State. Its range of application has been substantially increased during successive constitutional revisions.

Selected Further Reading

Alen, A. 'Nationalism – Federalism – Democracy. The Example of Belgium'. *Eur. Rev. Pub. L.* (1993): 41–88.

179. The territorial character of Belgian federalism was clearly confirmed by the caselaw of the Constitutional Court, the Council of State, and the ECtHR. See A. Alen & P. Peeters, 'The Competences of the Communities in the Belgian Federal State: The Principle of Exclusivity Revisited' *Eur. Pub. L* (1997) 2: 165–173; A. Alen & R. Ergec, 'Le principe de territorialité dans la jurisprudence belge et européenne – Un essai de synthèse', *J.T.* (1998) 785–790.

Part III, Ch. 1, A Federal State Sui Generis **299–299**

Alen, A., B. Dalle, K. Muylle, W. Pas, J. Van Nieuwenhove, W. Verrijdt (eds). *Het federale België na de Zesde Staatshervorming* (die Keure, 2014).

Alen, A. & R. Ergec. *Federal Belgium after the Fourth State Reform of 1993* (2nd) (Ministry of Foreign Affairs, External Trade and Development Co-operation, Texts and Documents, 1998).

Alen, A. & K. Muylle. *Handboek van het Belgisch Staatsrecht* (Wolters Kluwer, 2011).

Alen, A. & P. Peeters. 'The Belgian Federal State after the Fourth State Reform'. *Eur. Pub. L.* 1 (1995): 8–15.

Brans, M., L. De Winter & W. Swenden. *The Politics of Belgium. Institutions and Policy under Bipolar and Centrifugal Federalism* (Routledge, 2009).

Craenen, G. (ed.). *The Institutions of Federal Belgium. An Introduction to Belgian Public Law* (2nd) (Acco Press, 2001).

Delmartino, F. 'Belgium after the Fourth State Reform: Completed Federalism or Federalism in the Making?'. In *The Regions – Factors of Integration or Disintegration in Europe?*, edited by G. Färber & M. Forsyth (Baden-Baden, 1996).

Deschouwer, K. 'Kingdom of Belgium'. In *A Global Dialogue on Federalism. Volume 1. Constitutional Origins, Structure, and Change in Federal Countries*, edited by J. Kincaid & A. Tarr (McGill-Queen's University Press, 2005).

Dumont, H., M. El Berhoumi & I. Hachez. *La sixième réforme de l'Etat: l'art de ne pas choisir ou l'art du compromis?* (Larcier, 2015).

Dumont, H., N. Lagasse, M. Van der Hulst & S. Van Drooghenbroeck. 'Kingdom of Belgium'. In *A Global Dialogue on Federalism* edited by A. Majeed, R. Watts & D.M. Brown (McGill-Queen's University Press, 2006) 35–62.

Fitzmaurice, J. *The Politics of Belgium. A Unique Federalism* (London, 1996).

Goossens, J. & P. Cannoot. 'Belgian Federalism after the Sixth State Reform'. *Perspectives on Federalism* 7 (2015): 29–55.

Jacobs, D. & M. Swyngedouw. 'Territorial and Non-territorial Federalism in Belgium. The Reform of the Brussels Capital Region in 2001'. *Regional and Federal Studies* 13 (2003): 127–139.

Mörsdorf, R. *Das belgische Bundesstaatsmodell im Vergleich zum deutschen Bundesstaat des Grundgesetzes* (Frankfurt, 1995).

Pas, W. 'A Dynamic Federalism Built on Static Principles: The Case of Belgium'. In *Federalism, Subnational Constitutions, and Minority Rights*, edited by A. Tarr, R. Williams & J. Marko (London, 2004) 157–175.

Peeters, P. 'Federalism: A Comparative Perspective – Belgium Transforms from a Unitary to a Federal State'. In *Evaluating Federal Systems*, edited by B. De Villiers (Juta & Co/Nijhoff, 1994).

Peeters, P. 'The Fifth Belgian State Reform ("Lambermont"): A General Overview'. *Eur. Pub. L.* 9 (2003): 1–12.

Peeters, P. & D. Haljan. 'Belgium's Sixth State Reform: The State of the Nation(s)' *Eur. Pub. L.* 3 (2016): 411–438.

Popelier, P. & K. Lemmens. *The Constitution of Belgium. A Contextual Analysis* (Hart, 2015).

Popelier, P., D. Sinardet, J. Velaers & B. Cantillon (eds). *België, quo vadis? Waarheen na de zesde staatshervorming?* (Intersentia, 2012).

Reybrouck, K. & S. Sottiaux. *De federale bevoegdheden* (Intersentia, 2019).

Romainville, C. 'Dynamics of Belgian plurinational Federalism: A Small State under Pressure'. *Bost. Coll. Int'l & Comp. L. R.* 38 (2015): 225–250.

Romainville, C. & M. Verdussen (eds). *Les grands arrêts sur le partage des compétences dans l' Etat fédéral* (Larcier, 2019).

Sautois, J. & M. Uyttendaele (eds). *La sixième réforme de l'Etat 2012–2013* (Anthemis, 2013).

Seutin, B. & G. van Haegendoren (eds). *De bevoegdheden van de gemeenschappen* (die Keure, 2016).

Seutin, B. & G. van Haegendoren (eds). *De bevoegdheden van de gewesten* (die Keure, 2016).

Seutin, B. & G. van Haegendoren (eds). *De transversale bevoegdheden in het federale België* (die Keure, 2017).

Stangherlin, K. (ed.). *Die Deutschsprachige Gemeinschaft Belgiens* (die Keure, 2005).

Uyttendaele, M. *Trente leçons de droit constitutionnel* (3rd) (Bruylant, 2017).

Vanpraet, J. *De latente staatshervorming. De bevoegdheidsverdeling in de rechtspraak van het Grondwettelijk Hof en de adviespraktijk van de Raad van State* (die Keure, 2011).

Velaers, J. 'The Belgian Federalism/Confederalism Debate in Light of Classic Constitutional Theory'. In *(Con)federalism: Cure or Curse*? edited by K. Deschouwer & J. Poirier (2015, Re-Bel e-book 18).

Velaers J., J. Vanpraet, Y. Peeters & W. Vandenbruwaene (eds). *De zesde staatshervorming: instellingen, bevoegdheden en middelen* (Intersentia, 2014).

Vuye, H. & G. Clémer. *De zesde staatshervorming (eerste fase)* (Intersentia, 2013).

Witte, E., A. Alen, H. Dumont, & R. Ergec (eds). *Het statuut van Brussel – Bruxelles et son statut* (Larcier, 1999).

Chapter 2. An Outline of the Federated Entities: Communities and Regions

§1. The Concept of a Double Set of Federated Entities

300. In order to understand Belgian federalism, it should first be pointed out that Belgium has a dual-layered federal structure with two kinds of federated entities: the Communities and the Regions (Article 1 Constitution). The Communities and the Regions have a partly overlapping territorial jurisdiction, though their powers cover different subject matters. Moreover, both have their own institutions. 'Communitarization', the creation of the Communities, was the response to a long-standing demand of the Flemish Movement, which had been striving for genuine recognition and the development of Dutch language and culture. Hence, the Constitution acknowledged the existence of three Communities: the Flemish Community, the French Community, and the German Community (Article 2 Constitution). If 'communitarization' was principally a response to Flemish aspirations, 'regionalization' (viz., the creation of the Regions) originally sought to meet the Walloons' desire for economic autonomy. The outcome of the 1970 State Reform was the recognition of three Regions: the Flemish Region, the Walloon Region, and the Brussels Region[180] (Article 3 Constitution).

301. Belgium thus comprises six federated entities, all vested with a distinct legal personality. The prima facie conclusion that Belgium is composed of two times three sub-states, each which their own jurisdiction and institutions, is not however completely correct.[181] Other constitutional provisions make the institutional framework far more complex. For Flanders, the Community and the Region institutions have more or less 'merged' since the Community Parliament and government have been given the power to exercise Flemish Region jurisdiction (Article 137 Constitution). For Wallonia, the Constitution allows for the transfer of jurisdiction of the French Community to the Walloon Region and the French Community Commission of Brussels-Capital (Article 138 Constitution). And because the German Community has no coexistent Region, the Constitution allows for a limited transfer of jurisdiction from the Walloon Region to the German Community (Article 139 Constitution).

302. The institutional framework of the Communities and the Regions is mainly laid down in a number of Special Majority Acts, except for the German Community whose status is set out in an ordinary Act.

The basic laws governing the Communities and the Regions are:

---

180. Later on (1988) this Region was denominated as the 'Brussels-Capital Region' (Art. 136 Constitution).
181. W. Pas, 'The Equality of the Subjects of a Federation: a Necessary Precondition for a Good Working Federalism? The Belgian Example' in *Federalism: Choices in Law, Institutions and Policy. A Comparative Approach with Focus on the Russian Federation* 121–134 (K. Malfliet & L Nasyrova eds, Leuven 1998).

(i) the *Special Majority Act on Institutional Reform of 8 August 1980*, establishing the structure and powers of the Flemish Community, the French Community, and the Flemish Region and the Walloon Region;
(ii) the *Act regarding German Community Institutional Reform of 31 December 1983*, establishing the structure, powers and financial means of the German Community;
(iii) the *Special Majority Act on Brussels Institutional Reform of 12 January 1989*, providing for the structure and powers of the Brussels-Capital Region, and
(iv) the *Special Majority Act on Community and Region Finance of 16 January 1989*, providing for the financing of the Communities and the Regions, with the exception of the German Community.

§2. General Principles Regarding the Institutional Framework

303. The double set of federated entities has created a complex institutional framework. The rules regarding the institutional framework are laid down in the Constitution and in the Special Majority Acts mentioned above, except for certain instances where the Communities and Regions have the power to modify their own institutions and the rules concerning them ('institutional autonomy').

Like the federal State, each Community and Region has a legislative body, a 'Parliament', and a government, as well as its own civil service. This would mean that there are three Parliaments for the Communities and three Parliaments for the Regions. Each of them has a government. Instead of six legislative bodies and corresponding executives and administrations of the federated entities, however, there are in fact seven of them.

The reason is that, on the one hand, in Flanders the Parliament and the government of the Flemish Community exercise the powers of the Flemish Region. The Community and the Region retain both their separate legal personality, though they are organised and managed as one entity. Their Acts, while having the same legal force, have a different (territorial) scope. The Flemish Parliament and the Flemish government are constituted differently according to whether they are dealing with Community or Region matters. This system is based on a constitutional provision stating that a Special Majority Act may empower the Flemish Community or the French Community to exercise the powers respectively of the Flemish Region or of the Walloon Region. The provision, however, was only put into operation for the Flemish Community (Article 137 Constitution, Article 1 §1 Special Majority Act on Institutional Reform).

On the other hand, within the bilingual Brussels-Capital region, two more institutions have legislative powers at their disposal: the Joint Community Commission and the French Community Commission. The Joint Community Commission has a proper Council and Executive, with jurisdiction in the field of some bilingual Community matters (Article 135 Constitution, Article 63 Special Majority Act on Brussels Institutional Reform). The French Community Commission is not only an administrative organ, like the Flemish Community Commission in Brussels, but also a federated entity with legislative powers in some Community matters, more specifically those which have been transferred by the French Community. In the south of the country, a merger of institutions appeared to be impossible because the Walloon Region embraces two language regions and because of the sociological and political independence of the Brussels francophones with regard to Wallonia. Therefore some regional powers of the Walloon Region are exercised by the organs of the German Community (Article 139 Constitution), while some powers of the French Community are exercised by the organs of the Walloon Region and the French Community Commission in Brussels (Article 138 Constitution).

304. The seven Parliaments of the federated entities, except for the Parliament of the German Community, are constituted on the basis of regional elections. These elections take place every five years, on the same day as the elections for the European Parliament, with no possibility of early dissolution (Article 117 Constitution). Since the Parliament of the German Community is elected within its own language region, all Community and Region Parliaments are formed on a strict territorial basis as a logical consequence of the fact that the Communities and the Regions both have a limited territorial jurisdiction. A citizen can only participate in the election of the representative bodies which have jurisdiction over him.[182] In this way, four out of the seven Parliaments are elected directly. The three other Parliaments are derived from the first four. Directly elected are the Flemish Parliament (with members elected in the Flemish Region and the bilingual Brussels-Capital region), the Walloon Parliament, the Parliament of the German Community, and the Brussels-Capital Region Parliament. The Parliament of the French Community is composed of the members of the Walloon Region Parliament plus some members of the French language group of the Brussels-Capital Region Parliament. The Council of the Joint Community Commission is composed of the members of the Dutch and French language groups of the Brussels-Capital Region Parliament. The Council of the French Community Commission consists of the members of the French language group of the same Parliament.

The Parliaments of the federated entities are represented on the federal level through the Senate, which is composed mainly of senators appointed by the parliaments of the federated entities (Article 67 Constitution).[183]

§3. General Principles Regarding the Distribution of Powers

I. Basic Principles

A. The Powers of the Communities and the Regions Are 'Entrenched'

305. In a federal State, the distribution of powers between the central authority and the federated entities is effected by a Constitution having a fair degree of rigidity so that its basic terms are 'entrenched'; that is, they cannot be amended at the

182. Cons., Judgment No. 90/94, 22 Dec. 1994.
183. See above Pt. II. Ch. 3. §1. II 'Categorisation of the Members of Parliament'.

sole discretion of the federal authority nor by any single federated entity or combination of federated entities. Federal constitutions allocating powers between the federal authority and the federated entities traditionally may be amended only with the consent – or at least the involvement – of the federated entities. This is mostly achieved by the rule that the Constitution may only be amended by a (possibly special) majority in both Houses of Parliament, the federated entities usually being represented in the Second Chamber.

306. In fact, in Belgium the Communities and the Regions are represented in the federal Senate, which is composed almost entirely of senators appointed by the Communities and the Regions.[184] The Senate has a limited legislative power, but has the same jurisdiction as the House of Representatives over amending the Constitution and over Special Majority Acts (Article 77 Constitution). Because of the special majority requirement for adopting constitutional revisions and Special Majority Acts allocating the powers of the Communities and the Regions, as well as because of parity in the federal government, it is inconceivable that the federal Parliament could pass an Act affecting the institutional status of the Communities and the Regions against the will of one of the two language groups. An exception to this principle is the autonomy of the German Community. According to Articles 115, 118, 121, 123, 130 and 176 of the Constitution, an 'ordinary' Act regulates its structure, powers and financial means.

B. The Legislative Power of the Communities and the Regions

307. The legislative power of the Communities and the Regions is exercised by their enacting Community or Region Acts. The term for these is '*decreet*' / '*décret*'. In the case of the Brussels-Capital Region and the Joint Community Commission in Brussels, the term '*ordonnantie*' / '*ordonnance*' is used, reflecting a slightly different legal status.[185] The Community or Region Acts have force of law throughout the territory for which they are intended. They may repeal, extend, amend or replace prevailing statutory provisions in the allocated areas of jurisdiction. Jurisdictional disputes (conflicts of competence) between federal Acts of Parliament and Community or Region Acts are settled by the Constitutional Court. This Court also reviews legislation for compliance with the fundamental rights guaranteed by the Constitution.[186]

The equivalent legal status of federal, Community, and Region statutes should not be considered inconsistent with what is seen as a general principle of federalism, expressed in the maxim '*Bundesrecht bricht Landesrecht*'. This only applies to concurrent powers, and in Belgian public law these are the exception to the rule.

---

184. The Brussels-Capital Region is represented indirectly by senators appointed by the Flemish Parliament, the French Community Parliament, and the French language group of the Brussels-Capital Region Parliament (Art. 67 Constitution).
185. See below §7 'Brussels Institutions'.
186. See Pt. II. Ch. 5. §2. II 'The Constitutional Court'.

C. The Enumerated Character of the Communities' and Regions' Powers

308. As a result of the centrifugal history of Belgian federalism, the powers of the federated entities are enumerated, while the residual powers have remained until today under federal jurisdiction. However, the 1993 Constitution made the fundamental choice to turn the system of the distribution of powers upside-down. Article 35 of the Constitution states that residual jurisdiction is to be vested in the Communities and/or the Regions. The implementation of this fundamental shift is subject nonetheless to two major conditions: (i) a new provision in the Constitution enumerating the exclusive powers of the federal authorities, and (ii) a Special Majority Act laying down the conditions and procedures by which the Communities and Regions may exercise the residual powers. The profound rethinking of the enumeration of powers and of the corresponding financing system implied by this shift lets a possible implementation of Article 35 converge with the political discussions on the future of Belgian federalism.

309. The enumerated character of the powers of the Communities and the Regions does not imply a restrictive interpretation of their jurisdiction by the Constitutional Court, nor does it exclude the Communities and Regions from exercising 'implied powers'.

The powers of the Communities and the Regions, although exhaustively enumerated and allocated, are very broad. Even in the frequent cases that their powers are not attributed *in toto*, and some particular aspects are devolved neither to the Communities nor to the Regions but remain vested in the federal authority, Community and Region powers do not have to be construed narrowly. The Constitutional Court imposes a restrictive interpretation on the exceptions to Community and Region powers reserved to the federal authority so that they cannot prejudice the scope of Community and Region jurisdictions. The Court also considers that the responsibilities allocated to the Communities and the Regions should be interpreted rather broadly, in order that – the narrowly-construed exceptions aside – they should be regarded as transferred 'globally' and 'in their entirety'.[187] This broad interpretation of allocated powers allows the federated entities to use all necessary means to give *effet utile* to their powers (inherent implied powers), apart from the possibility of explicitly entering into federal jurisdiction by means of 'complementary implied powers'.

310. The broad interpretation of enumerated powers has been reinforced through curtailing 'reserved matters' by a Special Majority Act of 2001.[188] The Constitution contains various provisions reserving a regulatory power to the federal Legislature (hence 'reserved matters'). Until 2001 the reference to '*wet*' / '*loi*' stood in principle as a reference to the federal legislator. From 2001 onwards, constitutional provisions may be understood to contain an exclusive reservation of power for the benefit of that Legislature only if the provision dates from after the creation of the Communities and Regions and the start of the reforms towards a federal State

187. See, e.g., Cons., Judgment No. 25/86, 26 Jun. 1986.
188. Presently Art. 19 §1, Special Majority Act on Institutional Reform.

(1970–1980), and it arises out of the provision itself or out of the legislative *travaux préparatoires* that such a federal reservation was explicitly intended. Older provisions of the Constitution are to be considered to guarantee a principle of legality only, namely the requirement for a formal Act of Parliament.[189] Whether this Parliament is the federal, Community, or Region Parliament is not determined in the constitutional provision itself, but should be determined on the basis of the other rules regulating the division of powers.

D. An Allocation of Powers Based upon Mutual Exclusiveness

311. The devolution of powers in the Belgian system is essentially based on exclusive powers conferred on the Communities and the Regions. In principle, one and only one legislature has jurisdiction to regulate a certain matter. Combined with the equating of federal, Community, and Region legislation in terms of legal force, there are in principle no concurrent legislative powers, nor is there a supremacy clause with priority given to the central authority (*Bundesrecht bricht Landesrecht*).

This is the logical consequence of the devolutionary origin of Belgian federalism. A supremacy clause would render uncertain the transfer of powers from the federal level to the Communities and Regions. The exclusivity of powers was also considered to offer the strongest guarantee against jurisdictional conflicts.

From its very beginning, the Constitutional Court has emphasised in its judgments the exclusive nature of the powers conferred on the Communities and on the Regions, both *ratione materiae* and *ratione loci*.[190] An exclusivity of material powers implies that every matter subject to regulation can only be legislated on by one particular legislature. If a certain matter draws on several different legislative powers and seems to allow for regulation by different legislatures, under the principle of exclusivity that matter falls to be regulated by the legislature whose jurisdiction comes most close in character to it. The exclusivity of the territorial allocation of powers implies that every regulation has to be localised within the territorial area where the legislature has jurisdiction, so that every concrete situation is regulated by one and only one legislature.

312. Several techniques for the allocation of powers mitigate the basic principle of strict exclusivity, and, by way of exception, certain concurrent powers are granted:

(i) *shared exclusive powers*: when one aspect of a certain matter is attributed exclusively to one authority and another aspect to another authority (e.g., healthcare dispensed in or out of hospitals comes within the jurisdiction of the Communities, while the federal authority retains power over, among other things, basic legislation on hospitals);

189. Cons., Judgments No. 35/2003, 25 Mar. 2003; No. 115/2004, 30 Jun. 2004; and No. 95/2005, 25 May 2005.

190. Standing caselaw of the Constitutional Court, since Judgments No. 9/86 and No. 10/86, 30 Jan. 1986.

(ii) *parallel powers*: powers which are exercised by several authorities in a cumulative way and independently, as is the case for complementary powers;
(iii) *complete concurrent powers*: powers which are exercised by several authorities, with federal legislation, however, taking precedence and being authorised to abolish or to replace existing Region or Community Acts on the same matter, or to prevent any further legislative action by the federated entities. The only example in this respect is the autonomous or general taxing power of the Communities and the Regions. According to Article 170 §2 of the Constitution, federal law may repeal, if necessary, an existing Community or Region tax, while the Communities and the Regions may only levy taxes in the absence of a federal law, and
(iv) *limited concurrent powers*: where the federal legislation sets out the basic principles, leaving the power to complete these general federal rules (e.g., public contracts and consumer protection) or the power to apply the federal rules (e.g., federal technical norms for vehicles are controlled by the Regions; the federal State may enact rules on the conditions for recognition of healthcare professionals, while the Communities have jurisdiction to grant that recognition) to the Communities and the Regions. It must be noted that the Constitutional Court uses this technique in order to reconcile the need for some federal uniformity with the autonomy of the Communities and Regions in cases where there is no explicit constitutional or legal basis for these federal framework-powers (e.g., limitations on the right to privacy as mentioned in Article 22 of the Constitution).[191]

313. To the extent that the Communities and the Regions are vested with 'limited concurrent powers', it goes without saying that Community and Region rules must observe federal rules which they have to complete or to apply.

When some aspects of one power are within the exclusive purview of one authority, while other aspects of the same power come within the sole responsibility of another authority, or when the Communities and the Regions, like the federal government, have the power to enact instruments needed to exercise their powers, it is possible that cumulative and parallel measures are enacted in the same area by distinct levels of authority without any law being subordinate to another. The policy of one authority could therefore interfere with that of another, with neither acting *ultra vires*. In these cases, the Constitutional Court, as well as the Council of State, apply the principle of proportionality, which thus developed into a rule on the regulation of the division of powers. It holds that no authority may, in administering a policy entrusted to it, take such radical steps that would obstruct disproportionally another authority in the effective pursuit of the latter's own policy. The principle of proportionality is applied by the Constitutional Court with respect to all powers, even the completely exclusive ones, and is considered to be inherent in every implementation of powers, *ratione materiae* as well as *ratione loci*.[192] It serves to curtail the implementation of a given power and to impose some obligations to co-operate.[193]

191. See, e.g., Cons., Judgment No. 16/2005, 19 Jan. 2005.
192. See, e.g., Cons., Judgment No. 168/2004, 28 Oct. 2004.
193. See, e.g., Cons., Judgment No. 132/2004, 14 Jul. 2004.

The principle of proportionality to a certain extent plays the role of the principle of *Bundestreue* (federal loyalty), the latter still being formally a rule for preventing conflicts of interest in the Belgian Constitution (Article 143 §1 Constitution).[194]

E. The Principle of 'Vertical Authority' or the Separation of Government Levels

314. The above-mentioned 'limited concurrent powers' constitute an exception to the principle of the 'vertical authority' system, under which, subject to any express provisions to the contrary embodied in the Constitution or enacted by a Special Majority Act pursuant to the Constitution, the competent legislative authority – State, Community, or Region – is also the executive power and vice versa.

F. Communities and Regions Also Having Implied Powers

315. The theory of 'implied powers' of the Communities and the Regions has been explicitly enshrined in the Belgian federal system (Article 10 Special Majority Act on Institutional Reform). It provides that Community and Region Acts may contain provisions relating to matters over which the Communities or Regions have no express jurisdiction to the extent that such provisions are necessary for the exercise of their explicitly conferred powers. The recognition of implied powers is a logical consequence of the Belgian system of allocation of powers in which the federated entities have only enumerated powers.

The Constitutional Court has set the conditions for applying 'implied powers' as follows.

(i) The Communities and the Regions may regulate matters which are not enumerated only if this is 'necessary'. It is up to the Community or Region legislatures to assess and to state the reasons for this necessity. The Constitutional Court will limit its review to a marginal one, only rejecting the necessity stated when the given reasons are obviously incorrect.
(ii) The federal subject matter entered into should lend itself to a differentiated regulation, which means that it can be regulated by different authorities.
(iii) Any action taken by a Community or a Region legislature outside the normal scope of its powers can only be of an auxiliary and a supplementary nature so that the impact on the federal matter may not be more than marginal.

Initially these conditions were rigorously applied. But recent caselaw tends to accept a broader use of implied powers without prejudice to the broad interpretation

194. The 2014 Sixth State Reform has extended jurisdiction to the Constitutional Court to review legislation for conformity with the principle of federal loyalty (Arts 1 3° and 26 §1 4° of the Special Majority Act on the Constitutional Court). On the principle of federal loyalty, see, generally, A. Alen, P. Peeters & W. Pas, '"Bundestreue" im belgischen Verfassungsrecht', *Jahrbuch des öffentlichen Rechts* Neue Folge. Band 42 (1994), 439–505. See also below §4 I B 'The Principles of Belgian Co-operative Federalism'.

of the Community and Region powers by the Constitutional Court. The fact that the Court accepts a broad interpretation of powers and the use of implied powers with regard to matters expressly reserved to the federal legislator (for which a broad interpretation alone would not suffice) shows the concern for a smooth and not too rigid division of powers.

G. A General Limitation on the Powers of the Communities and the Regions: The Concept of an Economic and Monetary Union

316. In a landmark judgment on 25 February 1988, the Constitutional Court ruled that 'the new structure of the Belgian State was founded on an economic and monetary union – by which is meant that the institutional framework of an economy is built on constituent units and is characterised by an integrated market (the "economic union") and a single currency (the "monetary union").'[195] The Court argued that the concept of an economic and monetary union confined the constitutional taxing power of the Regions. Special Majority Acts in 1988 and 1989 reinforced the legal status of this concept of an economic and monetary union. In economic matters, the Regions must exercise their powers in accordance with the principles of freedom of movement of persons, goods, services, and capital, and of freedom of trade and industry, as well as in compliance with the general legal framework of the economic union and monetary unity as established by or by authority of Act, and by or by authority of international treaties (Article 6 §1 VI Special Majority Act on Institutional Reform). The same concept sets limits to the powers of the Communities and the Regions to borrow money (Article 49 Special Majority Act on Community and Region Finance).[196] It is generally assumed that the concept of an economic and monetary union constitutes a general limitation on the powers of both the Communities and the Regions. This assumption is clearly reflected in the case-law of both the Constitutional Court and of the Council of State.[197]

The Belgian concept of an economic and monetary union refers to the general framework of an economic union and monetary unity at the international level, and more precisely on the European level. The European and the Belgian economic and monetary unions are, however, not identical. National freedom of movement standards may impose stricter restrictions on the jurisdiction of the Communities and the Regions than would result from European law, while, on the other hand, European rules on the freedom of movement do not necessarily apply as such to internal, national situations.[198]

195. Cons., Judgment No. 47/88, 25 Feb. 1988.
196. See below, Pt. V. Ch. 2. §2. V 'Loans'.
197. See, e.g., Cons., Judgment No. 32/91, 14 Nov. 1991.
198. Cons., Judgment No. 11/2009, 21 Jan. 2009; Council of State, Legislative Division, Opinion No. 54.334/AV of 3 Dec. 2013, *Parliamentary Documents (Flemish Parliament)* 2013–14, No. 2340/1.

H. Complementary Powers of the Communities and the Regions

317. The Communities and the Regions have also been endowed with complementary powers, namely that jurisdiction enabling the federated entities to exercise their allocated powers.[199]

1. Scientific Research

318. The Communities and the Regions have regulatory powers over scientific research relating to matters within their own jurisdiction, including scientific research in an international framework.

The federal government has analogous jurisdiction over scientific research relating to matters within its own body of powers. Besides this parallel power, the federal government has some co-ordination jurisdiction, as well as certain powers to participate in international scientific research programmes (like the programmes of the European Space Agency). The federal government may also take initiatives, establish institutions, and allocate financial resources for scientific research in matters coming within the jurisdiction of the Communities or the Regions which are either the subject of international or supranational agreements to which Belgium is a contracting party, or relate to activities and programmes which transcend the interests of a Community or a Region. In those cases, the federal government, before taking a decision, shall first submit a proposal for co-operation to the Communities and/or the Regions (Article 6*bis* Special Majority Act on Institutional Reform).

2. Administrative Supervision

319. The Regions are empowered to organise and to exercise administrative supervision over the provinces, municipalities, supra-municipal authorities, conurbations, federations of municipalities, and municipal district governments. In matters relating to their jurisdiction, the Communities and the federal government may organise specific administrative review (Article 7 Special Majority Act on Institutional Reform).

3. Creation of an Infrastructure of Decentralised Services, Establishments and Enterprises and Acquisition of Equity Holdings

320. The Communities and the Regions may issue provisions relating to infrastructure which are necessary for the exercise of their powers (Article 8 Special Majority Act on Institutional Reform). In matters coming within their jurisdiction, they may further set up decentralised services, establishments and enterprises, and

199. The international and financial powers of the Communities and the Regions will be dealt with in Pt. V.

acquire equity holdings. By authority of a Community or Region Act, those bodies may be granted legal personality and may be authorised to acquire equity holdings. This Act also regulates their creation, composition, powers, functioning, and administrative supervision (Article 9 Special Majority Act on Institutional Reform).

4. Creation of Government Departments

321. The Governments of the Communities and the Regions have their own administration, institutions and civil servants (Article 87 Special Majority Act on Institutional Reform). The Communities and the Regions may also determine the administrative and financial status of their civil servants, with the exception of their pension schemes and trade union status. The salaries of civil servants and the operating costs of departments are chargeable to the Communities and the Regions (Article 89 Special Majority Act on Institutional Reform).

5. The Transfer of Movables and Immovables

322. State-owned personal and real property essential to the exercise of the powers of the Communities and the Regions must be transferred to them without any indemnity (Article 12 Special Majority Act on Institutional Reform). Notwithstanding some exceptions provided in Article 57 of the Special Majority Act on Community and Region Finance (e.g., education and public works), the conditions of and procedures for each transfer are fixed by Royal Decree in Council.

The governments of the Communities and the Regions may carry out any expropriation in the public interest in such cases and according to such procedures as are fixed by a Community or Region Act, and in compliance with the judicial procedures laid down by Region Act and with the principle of just and prior compensation as laid down in Article 16 of the Constitution (Article 79 §1 Special Majority Act on Institutional Reform).

6. Penalties for Failure to Comply with Region and Community Acts

323. Within the limits of the powers vested in the Communities and the Regions, Community and Region Acts may render punishable any non-compliance with their provisions, as well as establish criminal penalties. With regard to these offences and penalties, the general principles governing criminal law contained in Book I of the federal Criminal Code apply, although Community and Region Acts may contain exceptions. If a Community and Region wants to introduce a new form of criminal sanction, the prior consent of the federal government is required. Concerning criminal procedure, the Communities and the Regions exercise powers with regard to the evidential value of official reports, the availability of residential search warrants, and the conferral of police officer status on designated Community and Region officials (Article 11 Special Majority Act on Institutional Reform).

The Communities and the Regions also participate in elaborating binding guidelines for criminal policy, established by the federal Minister of Justice in accordance with Article 151 §1 of the Constitution. Moreover, the Community or Region government is authorised to request the federal Minister of Justice to order the Public Prosecutor to proceed with the prosecution of an offence punishable under a Community or Region Act (Article 11*bis* Special Majority Act on Institutional Reform).

7. The Creation of Administrative Tribunals

324. The Constitutional Court and the Legislation Division of the Council of State have recognised the jurisdiction of the Communities and Regions to create, within their respective fields of jurisdiction, specific administrative tribunals through their implied powers to enter into a matter assigned to the federal State by Article 161 of the Constitution.[200] The Administrative Tribunal Division of the Council of State, however, remains the 'cassation court' for these administrative tribunals (that is, the final appeal court, on questions of law alone).

II. The Powers of the Communities in Particular

A. *The Powers of the Communities* Ratione Materiae

325. The powers of the Communities *ratione materiae* relate broadly to cultural matters, education, 'person-related' matters, the use of languages, co-operation between the Communities, and international co-operation (Articles 127–130 Constitution).[201]

1. Cultural Matters

326. Cultural matters are broadly defined as follows (Article 4 Special Majority Act on Institutional Reform):

(1) Defence and promotion of language;
(2) Promotion of training for research workers;
(3) Fine arts;
(4) Cultural heritage, museums and other cultural and scientific institutions, with the exception of historic sites and monuments;

---

200. Cons., Judgments No. 49/2003, 30 Apr. 2003; No. 8/2011, 27 Jan. 2011; No. 53/2016, 21 Apr. 2016; Council of State, Legislative Division, Opinion 53.889/AV/1 of 17 Oct. 2013, *Parliamentary Documents (Flemish Parliament)* 2013–14, No. 2334/1.

201. And developed and implemented by Special Majority Acts; the Act on German Community Institutional Reform of 31 December 1983 renders the provisions of the Special Majority Act on Institutional Reform applicable to the German Community.

(5) Libraries, discotheques and kindred services;
(6) Audiovisual and audio media services (radio and television broadcasting) with the exception of communications by the federal government;
(7) Financial support to the written press;
(8) Youth policy;
(9) Continuing education and cultural animation;
(10) Physical education, sports and open-air activities;
(11) Leisure activities;
(12) Preschooling in nursery and day care units;
(13) Extracurricular courses and education;
(14) Artistic training;
(15) Intellectual, moral and social training;
(16) Social advancement;
(17) Professional training and retraining, and
(18) Practical learning and training on the shop floor.

2. Education

327. Since 1989, the Communities have jurisdiction in educational matters (Articles 127, 130 Constitution) except for: (i) the determination of the beginning and the end of compulsory education; (ii) establishing minimum criteria for the granting of diplomas, and (iii) pension schemes. Because the Community's jurisdiction originates directly in the Constitution, a Special Majority Act cannot curtail this power by reserving any extra federal powers within the field of education.[202]

3. Person-Related Matters

328. Person-related matters (Article 5 Special Majority Act on Institutional Reform) pertain to: (i) healthcare policy, (ii) aid given to individuals (social assistance), (iii) the houses of justice[203], (iv) family benefits, and (v) the system of movie ratings. Included under these heads are the policy on healthcare dispensed in or out of hospitals (notwithstanding several federal exceptions), the licensing of healthcare professionals and determining the license quota per specialism, as well as health and hygiene education and preventive medicine services – with the exception of certain prevention initiatives at the federal level. Also included are family policy, social welfare policy, the policy on integrating immigrants, as well as the policy on care for the disabled, care of the elderly, care and protection of minors (including correctional measures for young offenders), social assistance to prisoners and legal primary care.

202. Cons., Judgments No. 44/2005, 23 Feb. 2005; and No. 154/2005, 20 Oct. 2005.
203. The 'houses of justice' (*justitiehuizen / maisons de justice*) offer a variety of services in the criminal justice sector both for victims of crime (support, advice, mediation) and for offenders (mediation, and supervision of probation, temporary release, and non-custodial sentences).

Social security policy, however, remains almost exclusively a federal matter – with the exception of family benefits. The fact that a social benefit (like healthcare insurance) has to be categorised as a 'social security benefit' in the sense of European law does not necessarily mean it should be considered as 'social security' within the Belgian context.[204]

4. Use of Languages

329. The Flemish Community and the French Community are empowered (Articles 129–130 Constitution) to regulate the use of languages in administrative matters, in schools established, subsidised or recognised by the public authorities, and in labour relations between employer and employee, as well as in any corporate instruments and documents required by law and regulation. For the German language region, this power has remained mostly federal (except for the use of languages in schools). Likewise, the Flemish Community and the French Community are not authorised to regulate the use of languages in those municipalities with special language arrangements. In such municipalities, the federal legislation on the use of languages in the above-mentioned matters may only be amended by a Special Majority Act.

5. Co-operation Between the Communities

330. The Communities are empowered to arrange formal co-operation amongst themselves (Articles 127–128, 130 Constitution). This power has been defined in several Acts. Thus, the federal State, the Communities and the Regions may enter co-operation agreements, or the Communities and the Regions may adopt uniform Acts, particularly related to the joint creation and management of common services and institutions, the joint exercise of powers, or the development of common initiatives (Article 92*bis* and 92*bis*/1 Special Majority Act on Institutional Reform).[205]

6. International Co-operation

331. The Communities have jurisdiction regarding co-operation on the international level, within the scope of their powers (Articles 127–128, 130 Constitution). They enjoy treaty-making powers covering these matters, with a Special Majority Act detailing the procedure for making treaties. The general rules with regard to international co-operation and the treaty-making powers are laid down in Articles 167–169 of the Constitution.[206]

---

204. ECJ, Case C-212/06, 1 Apr. 2008; Cons., Judgment No. 11/2009, 21 Jan. 2009.
205. See below §4 I B 'The Principles of Belgian Co-operative Federalism'.
206. See Pt. V. Ch. 1.

B. *The Powers of the Communities* Ratione Loci

332. The powers of the Communities *ratione loci* are determined according to the concept of language regions. The three Communities have exclusive jurisdiction in their respective unilingual language region. The Flemish Community and the French Community also have jurisdiction over institutions in the bilingual Brussels-Capital region which, because of the activities concerned (cultural and educational matters) or the organisation at issue (person-related matters), must be regarded as belonging exclusively to their respective Community (Articles 4, 127–130 Constitution).

The powers of the two Communities in the bilingual Brussels-Capital region are nevertheless limited, and do not imply any jurisdiction to impose rules directly on persons. There is no 'sub-nationality' in Belgium.[207] For persons and bilingual institutions, the federal government is competent in the field of culture and education with some limited powers for the Brussels-Capital Region (Article 135*bis* Constitution);[208] the Joint Community Commission, in the field of person-related matters (Article 135 Constitution).

333. Jurisdiction over the use of languages constitutes an exception to the general principles set out above. For the bilingual Brussels-Capital region, as well as the municipalities with special language arrangements, the federal authorities still have jurisdiction (Article 129 Constitution).

III. The Powers of the Regions in Particular

A. *The Powers of the Regions* Ratione Materiae

334. The three Regions have been attributed broad powers *ratione materiae*. Their powers include area development planning, environment and water policy, rural redevelopment and nature conservation, housing, agriculture, economic affairs, energy policy, subordinate authorities, employment policy, public works and transport, animal well-being, and traffic safety policy. Article 6 §1 of the Special Majority Act on Institutional Reform delimits the Regions' powers in principle as follows:

I. area development planning
   1. municipal planning and regional land use and management;
   2. alignment plans for the municipal road network;
   3. the acquisition, development and equipment of sites for heavy industry, light industry (small business, arts and crafts) and services, or of other infrastructure to accommodate investors, including capital

207. A. Alen & J. Clement, 'Fédéralisme personel et territorial en Belgique' in *Federalism: A Tool for Conflict Management in Multicultural Societies with Regard to the Conflicts in the Near East* 59–79 (T. Fleiner ed., Fribourg 2008).
208. See Art. 4*bis* Special Majority Act on Brussels Institutional Reform.

investment for the equipment of industrial estates in the vicinity of seaports and their availability to users;
4. inner-city redevelopment;
5. redevelopment of disused industrial sites;
6. land policy;
7. monuments and heritage sites.

II. environment and water policy
1. protection of the environment, including the protection of the soil, subsoil, water and air from pollution, as well as from noise pollution and nuisance;
2. waste policy;
3. inspection and supervision of dangerous and unhealthy premises, excluding labor protection;
4. production and supply of water, including technical regulations governing drinking water; purification of effluent and sewerage;
5. financial compensation for damage caused by general disasters.

The federal government retains jurisdiction for product norms and protection against ionizing radiation, including radioactive waste.

III. rural redevelopment and nature conservation
1. regrouping of agricultural holdings and rural redevelopment;
2. protection and conservation of nature;
3. parks and greenbelts;
4. forests;
5. hunting, with the exception of the manufacture, trade in, and possession of hunting weapons;
6. fishing;
7. pisciculture;
8. agricultural water management and non-navigable waterways, including their banks;
9. drainage;
10. polders and marshland.

IV. housing
1. housing and the inspection of dwellings constituting a danger to public health and hygiene;
2. specific rules concerning residential tenancies.

V. agriculture
1. agriculture policy and offshore fishing;
2. financial compensation for damage caused by agricultural disasters;
3. specific rules concerning farming and livestock leases.

The federal government retains jurisdiction over food safety and animal health.

VI. economic affairs
1. economic policy;

2. regional aspects of credit policy, including the creation and the management of public credit institutions;
3. export policy, without prejudice to the federal powers to guarantee export-, import- and investment risks, and its powers over multilateral trade policy;
4. import, transport and export of weapons, ammunition and equipment or technology for military use or for maintaining public order. The federal State retains the power for import and export with regard to the army and the police force. The Regions have to comply with the criteria of the EU code of conduct on arms export;
5. natural resources
6. the conditions governing permits to establish a business or a profession, with the exception of the conditions for access to healthcare professions and to service-providing intellectual professions;
7. specific rules concerning commercial tenancies;
8. loans to businesses, and compensation for businesses suffering disruptions from public works;
9. tourism.

In economic matters, the Regions shall exercise their powers in accordance with a) the principles of freedom of movement of persons, goods, services, and capital, and of freedom of trade and industry; b) the general legal framework of the economic union and monetary unity as established by or by authority of an Act and by or by authority of international treaties.

To that end, the federal authorities are empowered to lay down general rules concerning:

1. public contracts;
2. consumer protection;
3. organization of the economy;
4. maximum limits for aid to companies in matters of economic expansion, which may only be altered if the Regions agree to the changes.

The federal authorities, moreover, are exclusively empowered as to:

1. monetary policy;
2. finance policy and the protection of savings, including the regulation and the supervision of credit and other financial institutions, and of insurance and similar companies, holding companies and joint investment funds, mortgage loans, consumer credit, banking and insurance law, and the creation and the management of public credit institutions;
3. price and income policy, with the exception of the regulation of prices in matters under the jurisdiction of the Communities and the Regions;
4. competition law and business practices law, with the exception of awarding quality labels and registered designations of origin having a regional or a local character;

5. commercial law and company law;
6. industrial and intellectual property;
7. quotas and licenses;
8. weights, measures, and standards;
9. confidentiality of statistics;
10. the National Investment Corporation;
11. labor law and social security.

VII. energy policy

The regional aspects of energy and in any case:

1. supply and local transmission of electricity by means of a grid with a nominal voltage less than or equal to 70,000 volts, including the supply tariffs for the electricity grid but excepting the tariffs for the transmission grids;
2. public gas distribution, including the tariffs for distribution but with the exception of the tariffs for the network of gas transport;
3. use of mine-gas and exhaust gases from blast-furnaces;
4. remote heating distribution systems;
5. development of slag heaps;
6. renewable sources of energy, excluding those derived from nuclear power;
7. recovery of energy;
8. rationalizing energy use.

The federal authorities are empowered as to matters the technical and economic indivisibility of which requires an identical treatment nationwide, namely:

1. studies on energy supply;
2. the nuclear fuel cycle;
3. major infrastructural facilities for the storage of energy, and the transmission and generation of energy;
4. rates, prices, and tariffs.

VIII. subordinate authorities

1. the composition, organization, powers, and functioning of provincial and municipal institutions, and supra-municipal authorities, with the exception of certain specific rules on language legislation and on 'language pacification' in municipalities with special language arrangements, and with the exception of policy on Civil Status Registries, on the police force, on the fire services, and on pensions schemes. The Region governments appoint and dismiss the Provincial Governors, with the prior consent of the federal government;
2. altering or correcting the boundaries of the provinces, supra-municipal authorities, and municipalities, excepting municipalities with special language arrangements;

3. the composition, organization, powers and functioning of the conurbations and federations of municipalities, with the exception of municipalities with special language arrangements;
4. elections for the organs of provincial, supra-municipal, municipal, municipal district, conurbation, and federation governments, including rules and controls on electoral expenses, with exception of specific rules on language legislation and on 'language pacification' in municipalities with special language arrangements (if a Region Act decreases the degree of proportionality in the electoral system, a special majority is required);
5. the disciplinary system with respect to mayors, and providing the possibility of a specific appeal procedure with the Council of State;
6. the administration of church property of the recognized religions (the federal State retaining the power to recognize a religion, and to finance the salaries and pensions of its respective religious functionaries);
7. cemeteries and treatment of human remains;
8. associations of provinces, supra-municipal authorities, and municipalities, excepting specific federal supervision over the fire services;
9. the general financing of municipalities, conurbations and federations of municipalities, as well as the supra-municipal authorities and provinces;
10. the financing of projects to be carried out by the municipalities, conurbations and federations of municipalities, provinces, supra-municipal authorities, and other public legal persons in matters coming within the jurisdiction of the Regions, except if those projects relate to matters coming within the jurisdiction of the federal authorities or the Communities;
11. the conditions under which, and the way in which, municipal district governments referred to in Article 41 of the Constitution may be created.

The federal authorities as well as the Communities have the power to impose specific obligations on the subordinate authorities, including financial responsibilities.

IX. employment policy
1. the finding of employment;
2. programmes for putting unemployed persons back to work;
3. the employment of persons receiving social reintegration benefits;
4. the employment of foreign workers and the application of federal rules governing the employment of workers with specific residency permits;
5. controls and sanctions regarding job-search efforts by unemployed persons, as well as prescribing exceptions for certain categories of unemployed persons;

6. reduction of certain social security contributions for specific target groups;
7. the system of service vouchers;
8. grants to promote the employment of older workers;
9. educational paid leave;
10. local employment agencies;
11. outplacement, with the exception of certain matters of labor law;
12. certain matters of temporary employment.

X. public works and transport
1. roads;
2. waterways;
3. legal statute of roads and waterways, with exception of the railways;
4. ports;
5. seawalls;
6. dykes;
7. ferries;
8. the equipment and the management of airports and public aerodromes, with the exception of Brussels National Airport;
9. city and local public transport, including specialized scheduled services, taxi services and the renting out of cars with driver;
10. pilotage and buoyage services into and out of ports, as well as sea rescue and towing services;
11. police rules regarding traffic on waterways, excluding regulations on nuclear transport, the transport of explosives, and the transport of animal substances that endanger the population;
12. rules relating to the crew and the safety of inland navigation;
13. minimum technical safety standards for the construction and maintenance of roads and waterways;
14. regulations concerning the transport of dangerous goods and exceptional road transport, excluding the regulations on nuclear transport, the transport of explosives, and the transport of animal substances that endanger the population;
15. additional financing for investments in rail infrastructure, under the condition of a co-operation agreement with the federal authorities.

The powers mentioned in points 2, 4, 5 and 10 imply the right to carry out works and activities, including dredging, necessary to the exercise of those competences, within the territorial waters and on the continental shelf.

XI. animal welfare

XII. traffic safety policy
1. the speed limits on public roads, with the exception of motorways;
2. regulations regarding the placement of and the checking of traffic signs;
3. regulations concerning the maximum permissible weight of vehicles using public roads;

4. supervision of compliance with the technical federal regulations on bringing vehicles into circulation and the technical inspection of vehicles in application of federal norms;
5. the homologation of radars and other instruments linked to regional jurisdiction;
6. regulations concerning the training and examinations for driving licenses, including the organization and approvals of driving schools and examination centers, with the exception of federal jurisdiction for determining the knowledge and skills required for driving vehicles;
7. promoting, raising awareness of, and providing information on road safety.

B. The Powers of the Regions Ratione Loci

335. Article 5 of the Constitution establishes the territory of the Flemish and Walloon Region by referring to the provinces they comprise. That part of the territory which does not belong to any of these provinces forms the Brussels-Capital Region (Article 2 Special Majority Act on Brussels Institutional Reform). The territorial jurisdiction of the Regions therefore also corresponds with the language regions: the Walloon Region governing the French language region and the German language region; the Flemish Region governing the Dutch language region and the Brussels-Capital Region governing the bilingual Brussels-Capital region.

§4. Co-operation Between the Federation and the Federated Entities and the Prevention and Settlement of Conflicts

I. Co-operation Between the Federation and the Federated Entities

A. General

336. Modern federalism has added a third principle to the classic principles of autonomy and participation, namely that of co-operation. 'Dual federalism' in which the centre and the federated entities are seen as completely juxtaposed autonomous authorities and in which the separation of the scope of their respective responsibilities has ultimately excluded co-operation in the exercise of their functions has given way to a general finding that a rigid separation of levels of authority is impossible, and that interdependence and mutual influence in the exercise of powers are inevitable. The emphasis is now more on complementary aspects and co-operation than on separation and autonomy. Public finance and the allocation of revenues have played a key role in the development of this type of 'co-operative federalism', which itself has encouraged co-operation in various often informal ways, such as intergovernmental conferences.[209] Since co-operative federalism leads not infrequently to a marginalisation of parliamentary control and to a concomitant rise in the responsibilities of the Executive Branch, some extreme examples of co-operative federalism have raised severe criticism.[210] Yet, social reality shows that, for example, in the Federal Republic of Germany, co-operation developed spontaneously and informally into a 'genuine system' before being institutionalised in certain areas by the Constitution.[211]

B. The Principles of Belgian Co-operative Federalism[212]

337. Belgium has experienced a similar development. Besides the equivalence in legal status of federal Acts and Community or Region Acts, the exclusivity of powers was considered a prerequisite to preserving the autonomy of the Communities and the Regions. The inevitable interference in the exercise of federal, Community, and Region responsibilities prompted the emergence between 1980 and 1988 of certain forms of co-operation not based on written law, such as 'management agreements' in health policy. The strict autonomy of the respective authorities, for example, has often created legal obstacles to associating agencies of one authority with the operations of the agencies of another. The merit of the Third State Reform (1988–1989) has been the elimination of certain legal objections rooted in the principle of autonomy, and an accompanying extension to the range of co-operation. In 1993, the concept of co-operation agreements received (implicit) constitutional recognition, Article 77 of the Constitution stating at that time that approval of these agreements should be given by both the House and the Senate. The 2014 Sixth State Reform emphasised intergovernmental consultation and co-operation, especially by attaching to the new powers of the Communities and Regions obligations to consult and co-operate between them and with the federal State. It also introduced certain new forms of co-operation, like 'uniform Acts' and the 'Brussels Metropolitan Community'.

338. Hence, Belgian public law, as it stands today, recognises a variety of forms of co-operation between the federal State, the Communities, and the Regions:

(i) the possibility of reciprocal representation in management and decision-making bodies (Article 92*ter* Special Majority Act on Institutional Reform);
(ii) co-operation agreements, which on occasion may even be mandatory. The federal State, the Communities, and the Regions may or must conclude co-operation agreements, particularly those related to the joint creation and

---

209. J. Anastopoulos, *Les aspects financiers du fédéralisme* 409–410 (LGDJ, 1979).
210. G. Kisker, *Kooperation im Bundesstaat. Eine Untersuchung zum kooperativen Föderalismus in der Bundesrepublik Deutschland* 229 (Mohr, 1977) referring to the danger of 'oligarchical federalism'.
211. C. Greywe–Leymarie, *Le fédéralisme coopératif en République fédérale d'Allemagne* 10 (Economica, 1981).
212. See also A. Alen, 'De samenwerking tussen de federale Staat en de deelstaten', *R.W.*, 1989–1990, 1303–1313; A. Alen & P. Peeters, 'België op zoek naar een coöperatief federaal Staatsmodel', *T.B.P.*, 1989, 343–371.

management of common services and institutions, the joint exercise of powers, or the development of common initiatives. These agreements are negotiated and concluded by the competent government, and in principle they only take effect after having been approved by an Act of the federal, Community, or Region Parliament (Article 92*bis* Special Majority Act on Institutional Reform);

(iii) a multitude of co-operative procedures, more particularly at the executive level, ranging from mere 'consultation' to 'agreement' (see in particular Article 6 §§2–8 Special Majority Act on Institutional Reform). The non-observance of those procedures for certain legislation and administrative rules may entail judicial sanctions, in particular annulment either by the Constitutional Court (Article 30*bis* Special Majority Act on the Constitutional Court) or by the Administrative Tribunal Division of the Council of State (Article 14*bis* Consolidated Council of State Act);

(iv) an Intergovernmental Consultation Committee, constituting the centrepoint for consultation, co-operation, and co-ordination among the federal State, the Communities, and the Regions in order to achieve individual or joint objectives (Articles 31 and 31/1 Act on Institutional Reform of 9 August 1980). This Committee can set up inter-ministerial conferences (IMCs) composed of members of the federal government and of the governments of the Communities and the Regions (Article 31*bis* Act on Institutional Reform of 9 August 1980). Most IMCs have no decision-making power: they only prepare the decisions of the respective governments by trying to achieve co-ordinated policies. The only IMC with an explicit legal basis and with decision-making power is the Inter-ministerial Conference on Foreign Policy;

(v) the adoption of 'uniform Acts' by the Communities and the Regions (*not* the federal State) (Article 92*bis*/1 Special Majority Act on Institutional Reform). This technique of co-operation, introduced in 2014, tends to reinforce the role of those Parliaments in bringing about and implementing co-operation. Since uniform Acts consist of two or more identical Acts, adopted after a specific procedure, but do not consist of one single joint or unified Act, they do not actually constitute a new form of legislation. Nevertheless, should the Constitutional Court find all or part of an uniform Act in breach of the Constitution, all the other uniform Acts fall to the same extent as the one *sub judice* (Article 8 Special Majority Act on the Constitutional Court);

(vi) the principle of the creation of a 'Brussels Metropolitan Community' (Article 92*bis* §7 Special Majority Act on Institutional Reform) was set out in 2012. This form of co-operation (with an infelicitously chosen and confusing name of 'community') is intended to foster co-operation of the Regions and the local authorities of Brussels and its surroundings. For the moment, however, this instrument of co-operation has not been set up.

339. Admittedly, this area is not without any legal shortcomings and loopholes, such as the lack of any defined relationship between co-operation agreements and the legal orders of the contracting parties, or the imprecision of the various co-operation procedures.[213] The dangers of 'over-regulation' and 'oligarchical federalism' are also ever-present in view of the fact that co-operation is chiefly organised at the executive level. In addition to a substantially increased degree of Community and Region autonomy, however, particularly the 1988–89 Third and the 2014 Sixth State Reforms rightly paid particular attention to the forms of co-operation which might help attenuate future conflicts and centrifugal tendencies. More particularly, since 2014 the composition of the Senate has reflected its role as a 'Second Chamber of States', although its jurisdiction has been greatly reduced.[214]

340. An adequate constitutional functioning of the federal State clearly depends on the element of 'cohesion' outweighing the element of 'autonomy'. This means that, alongside the diversity of the constituent entities, there must also be a feeling of belonging to one nation, 'a national spirit which alone is capable of binding together the whole'.[215] Whether this national spirit still exists in Belgium is an open question.

Moreover, the federal authority and the constituent entities must each have regard for the other's interests. This is the *Bundestreue* obligation, or the principle of federal loyalty. *Bundestreue* is not a concept in itself, but rather the expression of general principles of law which underlie a federal legal system. As a matter of fact, both the Constitutional Court and the Council of State apply the principle of proportionality to their review of the division of powers and the federal Legislative Branch concurred with the opinion of the Constitutional Court regarding the economic and monetary union. These two legal concepts are applications of the principle of federal loyalty, aimed at preventing and resolving conflicts over jurisdiction.[216]

The 1993 Constitution, however, chose to characterise the concept of federal loyalty as a means to avoid conflicts of interest (Article 143 §1 Constitution), namely a purely political rule of conduct that cannot be enforced in a court of law. Nevertheless the Constitutional Court has held the concept of federal loyalty – albeit in combination with the proportionality principle – to imply that every legislature ought to be vigilant when exercising its own powers so as to ensure that its own acts do not unduly interfere with the ability of the other legislatures to exercise their powers.[217] The 2014 Sixth State Reform followed this caselaw by confirming the jurisdiction of the Constitutional Court to review Acts for conformity with the principle of federal loyalty (Articles 1 & 26 Special Majority Act on the Constitutional Court).

213. See Y. Peeters, *De plaats van samenwerkingsakkoorden in het constitutioneel kader* (die Keure, 2016).
214. See Pt. II. Ch. 3. §1. & §3.
215. G. Burdeau, *Traité de Science Politique*, Tome II (LGDJ, 1949) No. 294.
216. See above §3 I D & G.
217. Cons., Judgment No. 119/2004, 30 Jun. 2004 (and see the case comment of W. Pas, *T.B.P.*, 2005, 147–164).

II. The Prevention and Settlement of Conflicts

A. *Conflicts of Interest*

1. The Concept

341. The concept 'conflict of interest' may have a broad and a narrow meaning. Broadly speaking, a conflict of interest may arise within a given Parliament from the exercise of the legislative function. The 'alarm-bell procedure' was introduced in order to prevent possible conflicts between the two language groups within the federal Parliament, and within the Parliament of the Brussels-Capital Region. There also exists an 'alarm-bell procedure' to prevent ideological or philosophical discrimination within the Community Parliaments. In the narrow sense of the term, conflicts of interest arise whenever the federal State, the Communities, or the Regions might be hindering the interests of another entity. In this way, conflicts of interest may arise at both the legislative and the executive levels through the detrimental effect of a legislative or a government initiative, or by the omission of a government initiative, or from the disregard of co-operation procedures by an executive body (Articles 32–33*bis* Act on Institutional Reform of 9 August 1980).

342. Conflicts of interest are characterised in Belgian public law as being of a purely political nature. They are settled through political solutions. The initiation of a procedure involving a conflict over jurisdiction automatically entails the suspension of any procedure involving the settlement of a conflict of interest on the same matter.

When requested to do so, the Legislation Division of the Council of State renders advice on whether or not a conflict of interest might also imply a conflict over jurisdiction (Article 32 §§5–7 Act on Institutional Reform of 9 August 1980).

2. Preventing and Settling Conflicts of Interest

343. Article 143 §§2 and 3 of the Constitution provide that a Special Majority Act lays down the procedure to prevent and to address conflicts of interest. The existing provisions in the Act on Institutional Reform of 9 August 1980 remain applicable, if not altered by a Special Majority Act. At the same time Article 143 §2 gives the Senate a central role in case of conflicts of interest between legislative assemblies.

To help prevent and to settle conflicts of interest, Article 31 of the Act on Institutional Reform of 9 August 1980 has set up the 'Intergovernmental Consultation Committee'. According to Article 31/1 of this Act, this Committee constitutes the centrepoint for consultation, co-operation, and co-ordination among the federal

State, the Communities, and the Regions. This Committee is based on a double parity. It comprises an equal number of members of each language group and is composed of the Prime Minister, acting as Chairman of the Committee, of five members of the federal government, and of six members of the governments of the Communities and the Regions.[218]

Conflicts stemming from executive decisions of the federal State, the Communities, and the Regions are submitted to the Committee by the Prime Minister (for the federal government) or by the Minister-President of a Community or a Region government, as the case may be. In such cases, implementation of the impugned decision is immediately suspended for a period of sixty days, within which the Committee has to reach a decision according to a consensus process. The suspension is lifted after the sixty days or within this period if a solution by consensus has been reached.

A Parliament can, with a three-quarters majority of votes cast, suspend a draft Bill of another Parliament. If the consultations following between the Parliaments involved do not lead to a solution within sixty days, the Senate will then give its reasoned opinion within thirty days. Subsequently the Intergovernmental Consultation Committee has to reach a decision according to the consensus procedure within thirty days.

The specific composition of the Intergovernmental Consultation Committee and the requirement for decisions to be reached by consensus do not make it easier to settle conflicts of interest. One might wonder whether such conflicts – as in other federal States – could not better be settled by more informal means, all the more so because the decisions of the Committee cannot be enforced through the courts.

B. *Conflicts over Jurisdiction*

1. The Concept of Conflicts over Jurisdiction

344. Conflicts over jurisdiction are not political conflicts, but result from the system of distributing legislative powers among the federal State, the Communities, and the Regions, allocating exclusive powers to the Communities and the Regions and reserving the residuary powers for the federal Legislature.

2. Preventing Conflicts over Jurisdiction

345. The task of preventing conflicts over jurisdiction is entrusted to the Legislation Division of the Council of State (legislative implementation of Article 141 Constitution).[219] This advisory body provides the required preliminary opinions on

218. In particular, the Minister-President and a member of the Flemish government, the Minister-Presidents of the French Community government and of the Walloon government, the Minister-President and a member of the government of the Brussels-Capital Region. The Minister-President of the German Community government has a seat when that Community is involved.
219. Pt. II. Ch. 6. §1. II 'The Legislation Division of the Council of State'.

the compliance with higher legal rules of most draft federal government Bills or draft Community and Region government Bills. Draft regulations of the federal government and of the governments of the Communities and the Regions must also be submitted for such a preliminary opinion. One particular aspect, which will be dealt with in the advice of the Council of State, is the question of whether the draft law in issue has been made in compliance with the rules regarding the division of powers laid down in the Constitution and its enacting legislation.

Although the advice of the Legislation Division of the Council of State is not binding, it carries great authority. The role of the Council of State in preventing conflicts over jurisdiction should therefore not be underestimated. Its detailed advice provides the legislative and executive organs of the federal State, the Communities and the Regions with valuable information on the allocation of powers among them.

3. Settling Conflicts over Jurisdiction

346. The question of whether an Act complies with the division of powers among the federal State, the Communities and the Regions is settled finally by the Constitutional Court (Article 142 paragraph 2 1° Constitution).[220]

§5. The Financial Position and Relation Between the Federation and the Federated Entities

347. The financing of the Communities and the Regions has always been a political stumbling block in Belgium. Prior to 1980, they were entirely financed through endowments (appropriations from the national budget) allocated to them on a fixed scale, the spending of which could be decided freely by the Communities and the Regions autonomously. This system was clearly not an adequate model for proper financial responsibility.

348. The desire for greater financial autonomy was an increasingly pressing demand, particularly on the part of Flanders, which rightly felt disadvantaged by the fixed-scale allocation of financial resources. While the population of the Flemish Region (not taking into account the Flemish inhabitants of Brussels) went up from 56.38% (in 1975) to 57.57% (in 1987) of the national population, the Flemish Community was allocated only 55% of Community budget appropriations and the Flemish Region only 51.14% (in 1975) upwards to 52.94% (in 1987) of Region budget appropriations. In 1980, this aspiration was partially met. The Communities and the Regions were included in the Constitution as being authorities with a general taxing power (Articles 170 §2, 171 and 173 Constitution). This power, which has remained unchanged to the present day, should not, however, be overestimated. This is partly so because it is the only 'complete concurrent power', meaning that the Communities and the Regions cannot levy taxes on matters already taxed by the federal

220. See above Pt. III. Ch. 5. §2. II 'The Constitutional Court'.

State and that any Community or Region tax may be repealed by an ordinary federal statute if the national authority were to levy taxes on the same matter, and partly because the Constitutional Court has held that the exercise of taxing power by a Community or a Region must not exceed the limits inherent in the broader view of the State as an economic and monetary union in which all internal customs duties and taxes of equivalent effect are prohibited.

349. An entirely new system of financing public expenditure was introduced in 1988. The Constituent Assembly, seeking greater stability in the matter, provided that the system of financing the Communities and the Regions had to be fixed by a Special Majority Act (Articles 175 and 177 Constitution). That statute – the Special Majority Act on Community and Region Finance of 16 January 1989 – sets out a complicated system. Only the German Community is not governed by this Special Majority Act (Article 176 Constitution) and depends on a special revenue system largely based on endowments out of the national budget.

350. According to the 1989 Special Majority Act on Community and Region Finance, the greater part of the revenue of the Communities and the Regions derives from 'transfers from national taxation revenue', no longer allocated by fixed-scale criteria as was the case for endowments, but on criteria of location or the 'fair return' principle. The Regions are entitled to levy surcharges or to grant tax refunds or rebates, but only within strict confines, in order to preserve the economic and monetary union. In addition to the taxing powers vested in the Communities and the Regions by the Constitution – subject to the restrictions already referred to – the Regions enjoy a limited additional taxing power. Finally, the public finance system also includes the element of solidarity, an essential feature of any federal State: for the Communities, in educational matters, by taking account of the ratio of students, and for the Regions, by providing a federal solidarity contribution where a Region's per capita personal income tax revenue is lower than the national average. Social security also falls exclusively under the ambit of the federal government.

Reforms were continued in 2001, entailing the transfer of substantial additional public finance resources from the federal level to the Communities. The fiscal autonomy of the three Regions was also extended, but at the same time Region tax autonomy was subjected to new limitations.

Finally, the 2014 Sixth State Reform substantially enlarges the fiscal autonomy of the Regions. The Regions can henceforth levy unlimited surcharges on federal personal income tax. This fiscal autonomy replaces the previous dotation out of the revenues from personal income tax. In addition, the Regions can now also increase or decrease taxes, as well as introduce deductions concerning matters falling within their jurisdiction. The collection of surcharges, tax increases and decreases, and deductions, is referred to as 'regional personal income tax'.

The financial resources of the Communities and the Regions will be dealt with in more detail in Pt. V.

351. It may therefore be concluded that the Communities and the Regions have substantial resources with which to finance the jurisdiction allocated to them. From the point of view of comparative federal law, the Belgian Communities and Regions cannot be considered inferior to other federated entities, such as the states of US and Australia, the German *Länder*, the Canadian provinces, or the Swiss cantons. Not only are their powers of revenue allocation broad enough. After the 2014 Sixth State Reform their powers to raise tax revenue have also been substantially enlarged.

§6. The Internal Structure of the Federated Entities

I. General

352. Each Community and Region has its own legislative assembly ('Parliament') and executive body ('government'). The judiciary is organised at the federal level.

The legislative authority of the Communities and the Regions is exercised collectively by their respective Parliament and government: the Parliament adopts a Community or Region Act (*'decreet'* / *'décret'* or for the Brussels-Capital Region, *'ordonnantie'* / *'ordonnance'*) and the government assents to it. The executive authority of the Communities and the Regions is exercised by the government issuing those regulations and orders, which are necessary for the implementation of the Acts of the relevant Parliament, without ever being able to suspend them. The government has no other powers than those formally vested in it by the Constitution and by Acts passed in accordance with the Constitution itself (Articles 20 and 78 Special Majority Act on Institutional Reform).

The Flemish Community and the Flemish Region are governed as one entity, their powers being exercised by a single Parliament (the Flemish Parliament) and government. The specific status of the Brussels-Capital Region will be discussed in §7 of this chapter.

353. The composition and functioning of these Parliaments and governments are basically fixed by the Constitution and Special Majority Acts. With regard to the German Community, ordinary Acts have so provided. Contrary to the general rule in most federal states, the Belgian federated entities have no constitutions of their own. Their institutions are set out in the Constitution and relevant statutes.

The Communities and Regions have only a rather limited institutional autonomy, referred to as 'constitutive autonomy'.[221] The Constitution (Articles 118 §2 and 123 §2) enables the transfer of powers in matters relating to the election of their parliaments and to the composition and functioning of those parliaments and their governments. Following the devolutionary logic of Belgian federalism, these

221. W. Pas, 'A Dynamic Federalism Built on Static Principles: The Case of Belgium' in *Federalism, Subnational Constitutions, and Minority Rights* 168–170 (A. Tarr, R. Williams & J. Marko eds, Praeger 2004); P. Popelier, 'The Need for Sub-national Constitutions in Federal Theory and Practice. The Belgian Case', *Perspectives on Federalism* (2016) 4:36–58.

institutional powers are granted by the federal legislator. As required by the Constitution to specify these matters, a Special Majority Act[222] recognised some institutional autonomy in such areas as the fixing of electoral constituencies, creating incompatibilities of office for Members of the Parliaments and government, and regulating the composition and functioning of the respective parliaments and governments. These powers must be exercised through a Special Majority Community or Region Act, passed by a two-thirds majority in the parliament concerned.[223] For the Brussels-Capital Region, moreover, a majority of votes cast within each language group is required.[224]

Some of the powers that fall within the scope of institutional autonomy are of minor importance (like the power to regulate the Registrar of Parliament), while others pertain to the balance of powers between Parliament and government (like the power to regulate motions of support or non-confidence). The institutional autonomy thus conferred remains rather limited and does not provide a legal basis for the Communities and the Regions to adopt their own constitution.[225]

As a consequence of the lack of real institutional autonomy, the subnational governmental structure is very similar to the federal structure. There are, however, some differences. For example, the Community and Region Parliaments are elected for a fixed term of five years. An earlier dissolution, unlike the case for the federal Parliament, is excluded. The mechanism for determining the members of the government, unlike the federal level where the King plays an important role, follows a different route giving a greater government-making power to that Parliament.

II. The Community and Region Parliaments

A. *The Composition of the Parliaments*

354. Until 1995 the Flemish Parliament, the French Community Parliament and the Walloon Parliament[226] were composed of the directly elected members of the federal Parliament, according to the language group to which they belonged.

The constitutional amendments of 1993, in effect as of the 1995 elections, abolished this system of 'double mandates' and introduced direct elections to these Parliaments, following the example of the Parliament of the German Community (from 1986 on) and the Parliament of the Brussels-Capital Region (from 1989 onwards). This Reform at the same time reshaped the federal bicameral system. Partly because the reforms intended to avoid an excessive proliferation of parliamentary mandates, some forms of 'double mandate' were nevertheless maintained, especially with regard to the Community Parliaments.

---

222. By way of an ordinary Act for the German Community.
223. See in particular Arts 35 and 49 of the Special Majority Act on Institutional Reform.
224. Article 28 of the Special Majority Act on Brussels Institutional Reform.
225. The Flemish Parliament grouped all regulations in the field of institutional autonomy into a Special Act on Flemish Institutions (7 Jul. 2006), creating this way the 'embryo' of a future constitution.
226. Until the constitutional amendment of 25 Feb. 2005, the Community and Region Parliaments were called 'Councils'.

With the exception of the Parliament of the German Community, all Parliaments, even the Community Parliaments, are constituted on a Regional basis. Since the Parliament of the German Community is also elected within its own language region, all Parliaments have a strictly territorial basis. Both voters and candidates must have their residence in the respective language region. Parliaments are elected for a five-year term and without the possibility of early dissolution (Article 117 Constitution), with voting held on the same day as the elections for the European Parliament.[227]

As is the case with federal elections, voting in elections at the subnational level is obligatory and secret, and the electoral system is based on proportional representation.[228]

355. The Flemish Parliament, which is the Parliament of the Flemish Community, is composed of 124 members, 118 of which are elected directly within the Dutch language region and six of which are elected directly within the bilingual Brussels-Capital region. The number of seats may be altered by Special Majority Community Act as long as the proportion between members elected in the Brussels-Capital and the Dutch language regions is respected (Article 24 §1 Special Majority Act on Institutional Reform).

The Walloon Parliament consists of seventy-five members directly elected within the Walloon Region. A Special Majority Region Act may alter this number (Article 24 §§2, 4 Special Majority Act on Institutional Reform).

The French Community Parliament is composed in principle of ninety-four members, that is, the seventy-five members of the Walloon Parliament and nineteen members elected by and out of the French language group of the Brussels-Capital Region Parliament. Those members of the Walloon Parliament who live in the German language region and take the prescribed oath in German cannot, however, take a seat as member of the French Community Parliament.[229] Under certain conditions, a Special Majority Community Act may alter the numbers of seats of this Parliament, as long as the proportion between members elected in the Brussels-Capital and the French language regions is respected (Article 24 §§3, 4 Special Majority Act on Institutional Reform).

The German Community Parliament consists of twenty-five members directly elected in the German language region. To this Parliament members may be added or are associated ex officio without having the right to vote (Article 8 Act on German Community Institutional Reform). This is the case for members of some other Parliaments who have their residence in the German language region. The composition of the Brussels-Capital Region Parliament is addressed below.

---

227. In principle on this same date the federal elections are held (Art. 65 Constitution).
228. Articles 26*bis* and 29 Special Majority Act on Institutional Reform.
229. Articles 31*bis* and 24*bis* §4 Special Majority Act on Institutional Reform. See also Art. 50 of the same Act.

B. Workings of the Community and Region Parliaments

356. The Parliaments operate along the same lines as both federal Houses of Parliament. Accordingly, the rules as to the public character of sittings, the voting procedures and majority requirements, the immunities of members with regard to the opinions and votes expressed in the exercise of their function (Article 120 Constitution), and the prohibition on personally presenting petitions all apply to these Parliaments. Yet two exceptions should be mentioned.

As a bicameral system does not exist at the level of the Communities and the Regions, a 'second reading' procedure was introduced. Each member of the government has the right to request a second reading of a draft Community or Region Act adopted by Parliament. Each Member of Parliament may call for a second reading if the draft has been amended (Article 38 Special Majority Act on Institutional Reform).

A special voting rule is applied in the Parliaments exercising legislative authority in Community as well as in Region matters. The members of the Flemish Parliament elected and domiciled in the bilingual Brussels-Capital region are not entitled to vote in the Flemish Parliament on Region matters. The members of the Walloon Parliament who took the oath in German are not entitled to vote in the Walloon Parliament on matters that are transferred to this Parliament by the French Community (Article 50 Special Majority Act on Institutional Reform).

III. The Governments

A. Composition of the Governments

357. The members of the government are elected by majority vote of their Parliament (Article 122 Constitution). Community and Region Parliaments therefore have stronger government-making powers than the federal House of Representatives. As no single political party usually obtains a majority of the seats within Parliament, a coalition is required. Each government appoints a president among its members, the appointment of whom is ratified by the King who administers the oath of office to the president (Article 60 §4 Special Majority Act on Institutional Reform).

The Flemish government consists of up to eleven members with at least one member belonging to the bilingual Brussels-Capital region (who is not entitled to vote on Region matters). The government of the French Community comprises up to eight members with at least one member from the bilingual Brussels-Capital region. The Walloon government comprises up to nine members, while the government of the German Community consists of at least three, and no more than five, members.[230] The composition of the Brussels-Capital government is dealt with below.

230. These Parliaments can change the maximum number of government members. The French Community and Walloon Parliaments have made use of this power to increase the number from four to eight, and from seven to nine, respectively.

Article 11*bis* of the Constitution obliges the governments to include persons of both genders.

B. The Workings of the Governments

358. The government itself lays down its procedural rules in compliance with Articles 68 and 69 of the Special Majority Act on Institutional Reform, imposing two basic principles as to the decision-making process.

(i) *the principle of collegial deliberation.* This principle means that all decisions emanating from the government must be taken by the government as a whole, by all the members present. When a specific 'portfolio' is attributed to a member of the government, this only implies that he is entrusted with the preparation and the implementation of the decisions taken by the government as a whole, within the scope of his powers. However, the concrete impact of this principle is somewhat tempered by the possibility of delegating decision-making power to individual members. This delegation should be granted by a published Executive Order.
(ii) *the principle of consensus.* This principle, which also applies to the federal government, implies that decisions are reached by consensus. When no consensus can be reached, a member of the government should concede or resign.

IV. The Relationship Between the Parliament and the Government

359. As Belgium is a parliamentary democracy, the federal government is accountable to the federal House of Representatives. This principle of accountability also applies to the Community and Region governments and to every member of them, all who are answerable to their respective Parliaments. (Article 70 Special Majority Act on Institutional Reform). Yet in contrast to the federal government and the King, the Community and Region governments do not have the power to dissolve their respective Parliaments.

The Community and Region Parliaments do have various means of control at their disposal, like the right to hold enquiries. The ultimate means of control are the motion of non-confidence and the motion of support which have to be adopted or rejected respectively by a majority of the members of that Parliament. When a Community or Region Parliament passes a motion of non-confidence in its government or one of its members and at the same time proposes a successor, the government or Minister automatically resigns and a successor is appointed.[231] A motion of non-confidence has to be 'constructive', else it remains without legal effect, in contrast to the federal level where, in case of a 'non-constructive' motion of non-confidence, the federal government does not have to resign, but can instead decide to dissolve

231. Article 71 Special Majority Act on Institutional Reform.

the House of Representatives. When a motion of support, introduced by the government, is rejected, the government is automatically taken to resign.[232] This is different from the federal level, in which rejection of such a motion must be followed by the designation of a new Prime Minister – otherwise there is no forced resignation and the King can decide to dissolve the House. In case of resignation, the government or the Minister must be replaced as soon as possible. As long as the government is not replaced, it may exercise only the 'restricted transitional powers'.[233]

§7. Brussels Institutions

I. The Federal Level: Characterised by Provisions Aimed at Protecting the Minority

360. The coexistence of two major communities within one State constitutes a potential breeding ground for tension. In order to meet Walloon fears of ending up in a permanent minority position, important safeguards were provided in the federal decision process.

As these techniques are discussed in detail elsewhere, we will confine ourselves here to a brief enumeration of the existing safeguards: Special Majority Acts, the 'alarm-bell procedure' in the federal legislature, equal language representation in the Cabinet, and parity in other central State organs. The higher courts – the Constitutional Court, the Court of Cassation and the Administrative Tribunal Division of the Council of State – have equal numbers of Dutch-speaking and French-speaking judges on the bench.

Most of these techniques protect the French-speaking community, which is a demographic minority federally. They are also built into the Brussels institutional framework in order to protect the Dutch-speaking minority that was created by the formation of a separate Brussels-Capital Region.

II. Brussels Institutions: Protection of the Minority Parallel Safeguards at the Federal Level

A. *General*

361. Three specific features of the Brussels-Capital Region determine its complex and specific institutional framework.

First, the Brussels-Capital Region, encompassing the nineteen municipalities of the bilingual Brussels-Capital region, has become a predominantly French-speaking area. French is the main language: according to surveys held between 2001 and 2013, French is spoken and understood by 88% to 95% of the population, while

232. Article 72 Special Majority Act on Institutional Reform.
233. Article 73 Special Majority Act on Institutional Reform.

Dutch is spoken and understood by 23% to 33% of the population.[234] A 2006 survey indicated French as the language at home for 57% of the families, Dutch as the language at home for 7% of the families, and 9% of the families being bilingual French-Dutch.[235] Up to 40% of the Region's households are multilingual, implying that languages other than French and Dutch are spoken at home.[236] In Region elections (1989–2019) between 11% and 15% of the valid votes were cast for Dutch-speaking political parties. Since 1970, the protection of the Dutch-speaking minority in Brussels institutions has developed in a way similar to the safeguards provided for the French-speaking minority at the federal level. Another issue giving rise to extra controversy as to the status of Brussels is the immigration of French-speaking people into six Dutch-speaking residential municipalities bordering Brussels (the 'Brussels periphery municipalities'), a phenomenon which has entailed a growing 'Frenchification' of this area. In these municipalities belonging to the Dutch language region, constitutionally enshrined language facilities have been granted to the French-speaking inhabitants.

Second, the status of Brussels also has a symbolic value, the city of Brussels being the capital of Belgium and the seat of the federal government (Article 194 Constitution). The Flemish Community and Region as well as the French Community have also chosen Brussels as their seat of government.

Third, since the late 1960s, Brussels has become increasingly internationalised. It has become the de facto capital of the EU and houses the headquarters of many international organisations, such as NATO. In 2018 up to 35% of the Brussels population were not Belgian nationals. When the number of Belgian citizens of foreign origin is added, the figure rises to 50% of the population who have non-Belgian origins.[237]

362. These specific distinguishing features of Brussels are the reason why it was such a laborious process to reach an agreement on the status of the Brussels-Capital Region. The Flemish political parties were opposed to the creation of a third – Brussels – Region, since it would create a Flemish minority within this Region, and would become the – mainly French-speaking – arbitrator in a three-region federal structure, thus reducing a Flemish demographic majority into a minority within the federal structure. The French-speaking political parties have always wanted the full recognition of Brussels as a third Region. Consequently, the status of Brussels is the result of a very complex compromise, as laid down in the Special Majority Act on Brussels Institutional Reform.

---

234. R. Janssens, 'BRIO-taalbarometer 3: diversiteit als norm' (2013) (https://www.briobrussel.be/node/14488?language=nl); see also R. Janssens, *Meertaligheid als opdracht. Een analyse van de Brusselse taalsituatie op basis van taalbarometer* (BRIO, VUBPress 2018).
235. R. Janssens, *Language Use in Brussels and the Position of Dutch. Some Recent Findings*, Brussels Stud. (no. 13) (2008) (www.brusselsstudies.be).
236. J.L. Genard, E. Corijn, B. Francq & C. Schaut, *Citizens' forum of Brussels. Brussels and culture*, Brussels Stud. (no. 8) (2009).
237. E. Corijn, C. Vandermotten, J.M. Decroly & E. Swyngedouw, *Brussels as an international city*, Brussels Stud. (no. 13) (2009).

363. This Special Majority Act, implementing in the first place Articles 39 and 134 of the Constitution, grants the Brussels-Capital Region a status which to a large extent is similar to that of both the other Regions, but with differences on certain important points. This Special Majority Act also regulates the Brussels Conurbation (implementing Article 166 §2 of the Constitution), as well as the three Community Commissions (implementing Articles 135, 136 and 166 §3 of the Constitution). These organs, with status as legal persons, have their own deliberative and executive institutions, of which the members are the same as the members of the Brussels-Capital Region institutions.

The nineteen municipalities of the administrative district 'Brussels-Capital' constitute the bilingual Brussels-Capital region, the Brussels Conurbation, and the Brussels-Capital Region.

The organs of the Brussels-Capital Region exercise not only Region powers but also some Community ones as well. And the Flemish Community and the French Community also have jurisdiction in Community matters regarding institutions in the bilingual Brussels-Capital region which, because of their subject matter (cultural and educational matters) or their organisation (person-related matters), must be regarded as belonging exclusively to their respective Community. The institutions of the Brussels-Capital Region also exercise the powers of the Brussels Conurbation. Complicated though the system may be, it is not exceptional from the point of view of comparative law.

B. *The Brussels-Capital Region*

1. Powers

364. The Brussels-Capital Region is vested with the same powers *ratione materiae* as both the other Regions.[238] Nevertheless, those powers are not exercised through legislation called '*decreten*' / '*décrets*', but rather through '*ordonnanties*' / '*ordonnances*' (called 'Brussels-Capital Region Acts' in this work).

These Brussels-Capital Region Acts – like the Acts of the other Regions and Communities – may repeal, extend, amend, or replace existing legislative provisions (Article 7 Special Majority Act on Brussels Institutional Reform), and are likewise subject to review by the Constitutional Court (Article 9 Special Majority Act on Brussels Institutional Reform). In addition, however, Brussels-Capital Region Acts – unlike the Acts of the other Regions or Communities – are also subject to limited judicial review by the other courts, similar to the review of administrative

238. However, the Brussels-Capital Region does not have an 'institutional autonomy' identical to the other Regions because the specific safeguards for both language groups are excepted from this autonomy. That said, the Brussels-Capital Region does have some additional powers. Brussels is the only part of the country that does not belong to a province. Hence the institutions of the Region, as well as the three Community Commissions, execute some of the powers of the former province of Brabant (Art. 163 Constitution). And the Region has some minor powers in the field of certain bilingual cultural matters (sports, professional training, regional cultural patrimony and institutions (Art. 135*bis* Constitution and Art. 4*bis* Special Majority Act on Brussels Institutional Reform).

acts pursuant to Article 159 Constitution. This second facet of judicial review differs in two ways from the general rules governing judicial review of administrative action. First, the reference standards are limited to the provisions of the Constitution and of the Special Majority Act on Brussels Institutional Reform, with the exception of those reference standards for which the Constitutional Court has exclusive jurisdiction. Second, the Administrative Tribunal Division of the Council of State is not entitled to annul a Brussels-Capital Region Act and may only refuse to apply such Act in the case submitted to it. In certain cases, the federal authorities may exercise a limited administrative supervision 'in order to protect the international role of Brussels and its function as the country's capital'. A Royal Decree in Council may thus suspend Brussels-Capital Region Acts, regulations, and orders in matters of municipal planning and regional land use and management, and in matters of public works and transport. Thereafter, the matter is submitted to a co-operation committee comprising an equal number of members of the federal government and of the government of the Brussels-Capital Region. If no consensus can be reached, the suspension may be extended for a specified period within which the House of Representatives, by majority vote of both language groups, may decide to annul the Brussels-Capital Region Act, regulation, or order in issue. If the House does not take such action, the suspension is lifted automatically (Article 45 Special Majority Act on Brussels Institutional Reform).

2. Internal Structure

a. The Brussels-Capital Region Parliament

365. The Brussels-Capital Region Parliament consists of eighty-nine members directly elected on the basis of proportional representation, for a five-year term. The members are divided into two language groups and are elected on the basis of unilingual lists.

From 2004 onwards, the number of seats available for each language group is fixed by the Special Majority Act on Brussels Institutional Reform: seventy-two seats are reserved for the French-speaking group, while seventeen seats go to the Dutch-speaking group.[239]

In the Region's elections, political parties of the same language group can opt for combining their respective lists to form electoral alliances. This way, all the votes cast for all the lists of the same language group can be taken effectively into consideration in distributing the available seats.[240]

366. Decisions within the Brussels-Capital Region Parliament require an overall majority, or a two-thirds majority for matters falling under institutional autonomy, but do not legally require a majority within each language group except for some

---

239. On the evaluation of this fixed representation in Art. 20 §2 of that Act by the Constitutional Court (Cons., Judgment No. 35/2003, 25 Mar. 2003), see W. Pas, 'Minority Issues in Belgium: A Brief Overview of Recent Developments', *European Y.B. Minority Issues* (2005–2006) 5: 511–520.

240. This measure is aimed to isolate extreme-right-wing political parties. See P. Peeters, 'The Fifth Belgian State Reform ('Lambermont'): A General Overview', *Eur. Pub. L.* (2003) 9: 10–11.

matters such as issues related to institutional autonomy, legislation on municipalities, or parliamentary standing orders. Regarding those latter two categories, however, from 2004 onwards a majority in each language group is only required in a first vote. If that majority is not reached, the approval of one-third in each language group is sufficient.[241]

As is the case at the federal level, an 'alarm-bell procedure' may be initiated by motion signed by three quarters of the members of a language group within the Parliament (Article 31 Special Majority Act on Brussels Institutional Reform). The president and the vice president of Parliament belong to a different language group. At least one-third of the members of the steering committee must be chosen from the smaller language group.

b. The Government

367. The government of the Brussels-Capital Region consists of five members, including its President. All members are elected by the Parliament of the Region. At least two members of the government belong to the French-speaking group and at least two to the Dutch-speaking group.

All are chosen by an overall majority in the entire Parliament, and a majority in every language group. If this turns out to be impossible, the President is elected by the entire Parliament, and the other members are elected by majority of the Parliament and a majority in their respective language group (Article 35 Special Majority Act on Brussels Institutional Reform).

Three Region 'Secretaries of State' are elected in the same way. One of them should belong to the smaller language group in Parliament. The Region Secretaries of State do not belong to the government but may attend its meetings. Each Region Secretary of State is attached to a member of the government belonging to his language group who determines the Secretary's powers (Article 41 Special Majority Act on Brussels Institutional Reform).

368. As is the case at the federal level, the government consists of an equal number of French-speaking and Dutch-speaking members, apart from the President. Other safeguards for the Dutch-speaking minority are the principle of collegial deliberation, the principle of decision-making by consensus, a system of guaranteed powers for each member of the government (Article 37 Special Majority Act on Brussels Institutional Reform), and the special system of a 'constructive motion of non-confidence'. When a motion of non-confidence is introduced against the government as a whole, a majority is required within each language group of the Parliament for the motion to be adopted. When the motion aims only at substituting a single member of the government other than the President, a majority is needed within the language group of the member against whom the motion is brought (Article 36 Special Majority Act on Brussels Institutional Reform).

241. Article 28 Special Majority Act on Brussels Institutional Reform.

c. Other Institutions

369. A co-operation committee has been created to deliberate on the initiatives, which the federal State and the Brussels-Capital Region may take jointly 'to improve and to promote the international role of Brussels and its function as the country's capital' (Articles 43–46 Special Majority Act on Brussels Institutional Reform).

370. The Brussels-Capital Region is represented within the Intergovernmental Consultation Committee by its President and by a second member of the government belonging to the other language group. Where both members of the Brussels government reject a proposed solution under the prescribed consensus procedure, the Committee is barred from adopting that 'consensus solution' (Articles 31 §1 and 33*bis* Act on Institutional Reform of 9 August 1980).

3. Other Functions of the Brussels Institutions

a. The Brussels Conurbation

371. In 1970 a third level of local government was introduced. The federal legislature was granted the authority to establish associations of various municipalities, called 'conurbations' and 'federations of municipalities', the powers and the organisation of which had to be determined by Act of Parliament (Article 165 Constitution). These 'territorially decentralized institutions' were set up to enable the municipalities and cities to tackle problems that extend beyond purely municipal matters and to promote co-operation and co-ordination in certain specific fields. In practice, this constitutional provision has been implemented only in the Brussels Conurbation, which comprises the nineteen municipalities making up the administrative district of 'Brussels-Capital'. The powers of the Brussels Conurbation are exercised by the Parliament and by the government of the Brussels-Capital Region, taking into account the above-mentioned safeguards (e.g., the 'alarm-bell procedure' within Parliament and decisions taken by consensus within the government) (Article 166 §2 Constitution and Book II Special Majority Act on Brussels Institutional Reform). To that effect, regulations and orders are issued in exhaustively enumerated matters, such as public security, fire protection, urgent medical aid, urban transport, and data processing for municipalities. These administrative acts are subject to the general rules of administrative supervision and judicial review.

b. The Community Commissions

372. The language groups in Parliament and government of the Brussels-Capital Region make up the French and the Flemish Community Commissions, institutions with a distinct legal personality (Article 136 Constitution). They exercise two kinds of powers by means of regulations and orders. Firstly, they may, each for its own Community, create, manage, and subsidise institutions in cultural, educational, and person-related matters. Secondly, they exercise, each for its own Community, the powers delegated to them by the Parliament of the French Community or the Flemish Parliament (Article 166 §3 Constitution and Book III Special Majority Act on Brussels Institutional Reform).

Their regulations and orders are subject to administrative supervision by the French Community or the Flemish Community, as the case may be, who also provide the Commissions with financial resources.

Their powers illustrate the fact that these Community Commissions are conceived as decentralised authorities of the French and Flemish Community. Where the French Community Commission is concerned, however, important legislative powers have been transferred to it by the French Community on the basis of Article 138 of the Constitution. The French Community Commission has the power to enact legislation for the French-speaking institutions in the bilingual Brussels-Capital region concerning those matters, which include professional training, sports facilities, tourism, school transport, and certain other matters relating to social assistance.

373. The two Community Commissions together constitute the Joint Community Commission, an institution with a distinct legal personality.

The institutions of the Joint Community Commission are constituted out of the deliberative and executive bodies of the Community Commissions.[242] Through legislative acts, called '*ordonnanties*' / '*ordonnances*', the Joint Community Commission exercises jurisdiction over those person-related matters regarding individual persons and bilingual institutions in the bilingual Brussels-Capital region which come neither under the jurisdiction of the French Community nor under the jurisdiction of the Flemish Community (Article 135 Constitution). With regard to the policy of family benefits, the Joint Community Commission has exclusive jurisdiction, excluding the jurisdiction of the two Communities (Article 63 Special Majority Act on Brussels Institutional Reform). These '*ordonnanties*' / '*ordonnances*' carry legal force as statutes in the same way as Brussels-Capital Region Acts do for Region matters, but they are not subject to any form of administrative supervision (Article 69 Special Majority Act on Brussels Institutional Reform). In principle, they must be passed by a majority vote in both language groups in the Council of the Joint Community Commission. After 2001, if this required majority is not reached, then legislation may yet pass if an overall majority and a one-third majority in each language group are attained in a second round of voting (Article 72 Special Majority Act on Brussels Institutional Reform).

242. In order to guarantee real parity in the composition of the Joint Community Commission government, the Region Secretaries of States who are members of the Community Commissions are not members of the Joint Community Commission government, while the Minister-President of the Brussels-Capital Region government has only an advisory vote (Arts 60 and 77 Special Majority Act on Brussels Institutional Reform).

§8. CONCLUSIONS

374. For constitutional lawyers, federalism is the legal form, reflected in the institutions of the State, of a balanced relationship between the power of the central order of government and the autonomy of the federated entities. The characteristics peculiar to each State are decisive in this regard and each federal State is sui generis. As regards the 'Belgian construction', the bipolar and centrifugal aspects to the structure, which deviate from general federal practice, have already been emphasised.

In the past, and particularly following the 1970 constitutional amendments, the question in Belgium was whether the new State structure was or was not a 'federal system'. It may be said that following the 1988–1989 Third State Reform no reasonable doubt remains in that respect. Even the Constitution itself confirmed and expressed the federal character of the Belgian State in 1993, stating in Article 1: 'Belgium is a federal State composed of Communities and Regions'.

The essential elements of a federal system are indeed present in the Belgian State structure.

(1) *the element of autonomy*: The Communities and the Regions both have their own legislative and executive bodies, as well as legislative power and financial autonomy.
(2) *the element of participation*: In general, the element of participation implies that the federated entities have an effective say in the framing of the federal constitution and other laws through their representation in the legislative body of the union, the 'Second Chamber of States'. Since 2014 the Senate is composed almost entirely of senators appointed by the Parliaments of the Communities and the Regions. And the jurisdiction of the Senate is limited to the main constitutional and institutional rules. Through the language groups in the House of Representatives, the 'major' communities have a decisive say in federal decision-making by the federal Parliament. Because of the 'alarm-bell procedure' and in view of the qualified majorities necessary to adopt constitutional revisions and Special Majority Acts, it is unlikely that the House might pass an Act against the interests of one of the major communities.
(3) *the element of co-operation*: We have stressed how Belgium transformed 'dual federalism' into 'co-operative federalism'.

375. In any overall assessment of the Belgian State reforms, it is all too easy to emphasise the more negative aspects: its complexity, notably due to the fact that the three Communities do not entirely coincide with the three Regions; the proliferation of institutions in Brussels-Capital; the language issue; and the bipolar and centrifugal character that allegedly would make any federal State system impossible. But things may be seen in another light, as the following list shows: the emphasis put on the international role of Brussels and its function as the country's capital, in which any form of 'sub-nationality' is excluded; the concept of an economic and monetary union; the solidarity manifested in a federal social security scheme; the various avenues of co-operation; and the control of linguistic problems through a 'pacification law' (namely, the Local Official Language Proficiency Act of 8 August 1988).

As explained earlier, any federal system is sui generis. Federal structures cannot be dissociated from their underlying geographical, economic, historical, and even ideological factors. All these factors are manifest in Belgian federalism. It is self-evident that in a federal State made up of two large communities, it is more difficult to maintain a balance between the requirements of the autonomy of the federated entities on the one hand and an efficient central policy on the other. This explains why the Belgian institutional system, which at first sight seems immensely complex, is based on a set of interlocking balances. The mere fact that national consensus has been reached on this system may be called a remarkable achievement in itself. Whether this national consensus will hold in the future, is an open question.

Chapter 3. Decentralised Authorities

§1. Territorial Decentralisation

I. General

A. *Historical Outline of the Evolution of the Local Government Level*

376. In the General Introduction we stressed the importance in the Middle Ages of local communities, namely counties, cities, prince-bishoprics, and the municipalities comprising the Seventeen Provinces. The emergence of the modern State necessarily implied a transfer of power to central State organs. This was clearly the case under the French regime. In the French period, the former duchies and counties were transformed into French 'Departments' (the present provinces of Belgium). Administrative organisation was integrated into the French unitary and Jacobin system. This was considered to be a means of ensuring national unity and the equality of all citizens before the law. The Departments were reduced to merely territorial subdivisions.

377. In the United Kingdom of the Netherlands, the concept of a centralised unitary State was abandoned. The Departments were renamed 'Provinces' and each could exercise their respective jurisdiction more or less autonomously. The Belgian National Congress adopted the same concept. Although the starting point in the organisation of the Belgian State is that all powers issue from one authority, the Nation, the Constitution explicitly enshrines a delegation of power to local institutions, provinces and municipalities. In seeking to break with Jacobin centralism, the Belgian Constituent Assembly did not restrict the provinces and municipalities to merely territorial subdivisions, as may be deduced from their inclusion in Heading III of the Constitution after the enumeration of central State authorities. In this respect, decentralisation was viewed as a means of increasing the direct democratic involvement of local citizens in their locally elected bodies and as a means of attuning the State administration to local needs. This goal was later reinforced with powers granted to the decentralised authorities to organise local advisory referenda about matters of local interest (Article 41 paragraph 5 Constitution).

378. Provinces and municipalities are nonetheless viewed as subordinate governments. The delegation of power to the local government level is indeed limited by the fact that it should on no account endanger the unity of the State. As entities having legal personality, the decentralised authorities are granted jurisdiction over 'all matters of provincial and of municipal interest' (Articles 41 and 162 paragraph 2 2° Constitution). This general and undetailed power is clearly not unlimited, since the federal legislature on the basis of its residual powers has provided – directly or indirectly – whether any given matter is of provincial or of municipal interest. Consequently, the range of municipal – and even more so provincial – interests has been considerably reduced by the national authorities, with local autonomy being increasingly ousted in favour of 'co-management' (the involvement of higher tiers of government pursuing policy at a local level). The provinces have increasingly been allotted the task of ensuring the co-ordination between central and local authorities (the latter being the municipalities).

The autonomy of the provinces and municipalities is further limited by the power given to the Regions to appoint representatives within provincial and municipal institutions. The institutions of Belgian local governments are characterised by a threefold structure. There are democratically elected deliberative bodies (Provincial Councils and Municipal Councils). A majority within each respective body elects the executive organ (the Provincial Executive and the Municipal Executive). The head of the particular local executive organ (the Provincial Governor and the Mayor) is a representative appointed by the Region government. Moreover, the appointment of the Provincial Governor by the Region government requires prior approval by the federal Cabinet.

Provincial and municipal by-laws are also subject to administrative review by higher authorities who may either, on the one hand and where prescribed, refuse approval or authorisation of, or advise against, a proposed local measure, or on the other hand annul the measure, all on the grounds of preventing a breach of the law or harm to the public interest (Article 162 paragraph 2 6° Constitution). As is the case for all administrative acts, the acts of the subordinate governments are subject to the judicial review by the courts and tribunals.

The taxing powers of the representative bodies of local government must be exercised within the limits set by the federal Legislative Branch.

The boundaries of the provinces and municipalities may be changed or rectified by or by authority of a Region Act. Yet inasmuch as a change of boundaries would affect the boundaries of the language regions, a Special Majority Act of the federal legislature is required.

379. The Belgian federalisation process has not entailed the elimination of the local government level. It has, however, led to the federated entities being attributed significant powers with regard to the provinces and municipalities. From 2002 onwards, the Regions have acquired powers over the composition, organisation, competences, functioning of, and elections in, the representative bodies of the provinces and municipalities. Since the 2014 Sixth State Reform, the Regions even have the power to abolish the provinces. This attribution of powers highlights the importance of the federated entities, whose powers already included *inter alia* administrative supervision.

B. *Constitutional Principles Regarding Local Government*

1. 'Territorial Decentralization'

380. 'Territorial decentralization' is used to describe the level of local government in Belgium, being the provinces and municipalities. This concept refers to a form of government according to which the Constitution and the legislation implementing its provisions attribute decision-making power over those matters generally and vaguely described as 'of provincial and of municipal interest' to autonomous public authorities having a distinct legal personality. It is thereby held to be essential that such decision-making bodies be directly elected and have received democratic legitimacy.

The leading distinctive feature of the decentralised authorities is the autonomy in their respective decision-making powers. This autonomy is clearly reflected in their legal personality, their various institutions and territory, and their fiscal means. It should not be forgotten, however, that all their actions are subject to a limited – but effective – administrative supervision.

2. Territorial Decentralisation Constitutionally Enshrined

381. The National Congress delegated to the Legislature the authority to determine the jurisdiction and functioning of decentralised institutions (Article 162 Constitution).

The Constituent Assembly sought, however, to guarantee in the Constitution the autonomy of the decentralised authorities by prescribing certain essential principles to which the legislation organising provincial and municipal institutions should adhere. Such Acts must ensure the application of the following six principles (Article 162 paragraph 2 Constitution): (1) the direct election of the members of the Provincial and Municipal Councils, (2) the jurisdiction of the Provincial and Municipal Councils over all matters of provincial or municipal interest, without prejudice to approvals of their acts in the cases and in the manner prescribed by Act, (3) the decentralisation of power to provincial and municipal institutions, (4) public meetings of the Provincial and Municipal Councils within the limits prescribed by Act, (5) the public accessibility of budgets and accounts, and (6) intervention by a supervisory authority or the legislature to prevent a breach of law or harm to the public interest.

II. The Decentralised Authorities

A. The Provinces

1. Introduction

382. The territory of Belgium is divided into ten provinces. The Flemish Region comprises the Provinces of Antwerp, Limburg, West Flanders, East Flanders, and Flemish Brabant. The Walloon Region comprises the Provinces of Hainaut, Liège, Luxembourg, Namur, and Walloon Brabant (Article 5 Constitution).

The territory of the Brussels-Capital Region does not belong to any of the ten provinces. The powers of the elected provincial bodies are wielded by the Flemish and French Communities, the Community Commissions, and the Brussels-Capital Region, each according to its own powers (Article 163 Constitution). Before the

2014 Sixth State Reform, the territory of the Brussels-Capital Region did have its own Governor and even a Vice-Governor. In 2014 the function of the Governor of Brussels-Capital was abolished. His powers have now been conferred on the Minister-President of the Brussels-Capital government and to a high officer nominated by the same government. They are in charge of safety co-ordination in the Brussels-Capital Region. The function of Vice-Governor has been retained and is in charge of supervising the implementation of statutes and regulations concerning the use of languages in administrative matters in Brussels-Capital.

The Province of Flemish Brabant also has a Vice-Governor of its own, who is in charge of supervising the implementation of the language laws and regulations regarding administrative matters in the six Brussels periphery municipalities (with special language arrangements).

383. Since the evolution of Belgium into a federal State, the abolition of the provinces as intermediate subordinate governments has repeatedly been considered. This intermediate level between the regional and the municipal level would be too expensive, too detached from the local community, and above all redundant. A decrease in their number or an abolition of the provinces as a whole was, however, considered to be impossible without amending the Constitution itself.

Those constitutional amendments have been made by the 2014 Sixth State Reform. The Regions have been granted the power to abolish the provinces by Special Majority Region Act (Article 41 Constitution). In that case, the Regions can replace the provinces with supra-municipal authorities which – like the provinces and the municipalities – enjoy local autonomy (Article 162 paragraph 3 Constitution), with their Councils acting in all matters of supra-municipal interest. This power to abolish provinces has not yet been used.

384. A Special Majority Act can remove certain territory (the boundaries of which it defines) from division into provinces and confer a special status on it by placing it under the direct authority of the federal government (Article 5 paragraph 2 Constitution). This constitutional provision, which has never been applied, was introduced in order to assuage concerns over the Voeren/Fourons municipalities. In 1962–1963, upon drawing the language boundary, those municipalities were detached from the Province of Liège and attached to the Province of Limburg. This meant that they came under the Dutch-language regime, although special language arrangements were established for administrative and educational matters. After their transfer to the Province of Limburg, the language status of those municipalities was a matter of some dispute between the two linguistic communities. Consequently, the problems surrounding those municipalities developed into a highly symbolic issue. In order to appease the tensions between the two communities, the possibility of forming an autonomous district under federal government authority was thus written in the Constitution.

B. Provincial Jurisdiction Ratione Materiae

385. The scope of provincial jurisdiction has already been described in general terms: a province is allowed to act in all matters which it considers to be of provincial interest on condition that it does not infringe on the jurisdiction of municipal authorities and provided that a higher authority (the State, the Community, or the Region) has not yet legislated on the matter concerned.

The autonomy of the provinces has gradually declined to such an extent that their abolition has been made possible under the Constitution. The jurisdiction of the provinces (and the municipalities) is more and more restricted to acts of 'co-management', whereby provincial bodies are called upon to apply the federal, Community, and Region legislation and also to act as an executive and advisory instrument of those higher authorities.

C. Provincial Institutions

1. The Provincial Council

386. The Provincial Council is the deliberative body of the province, composed of directly elected members, the number of which depends on the number of inhabitants of the province. Their term of office is six years.

As a deliberative body, the Provincial Council decides on all matters of a provincial interest (decisions related to, for example, provincial assets, provincial finances and budget). It may issue standing orders (such as rules governing the use of the cultural infrastructure of the province) and rules on province subsidies. It may also issue police regulations.

2. The Provincial Executive

387. The Provincial Executive is composed of members elected by the Provincial Council from among its members and is presided over by the Provincial Governor appointed by the Region government with the prior approval of the federal Cabinet.

The Provincial Executive is the provincial executive organ in charge of all matters concerning the day-to-day administration of the province. Hence the Provincial Executive *inter alia* prepares those matters of provincial interest which will be submitted to the Provincial Council, and implements the decisions taken by the Provincial Council.

3. The Provincial Governor

388. The Provincial Governor is appointed and dismissed by the Region government with the prior approval by the federal Cabinet.

The Provincial Governor acts in a dual capacity. On the one hand, he is the representative of the province, being the president of the Provincial Executive, and authorised to attend the meetings of the Provincial Council and to submit to this Council all matters for deliberation. On the other hand, he serves as the representative of the higher authorities, entrusted with implementing federal, Community, and Region statutes and regulations (unless this power has been conferred on another provincial organ), with maintaining peace and public order within the province, and with administrative supervision over municipal acts.

In order to safeguard this second task, a Provincial Governor will remain in function should the province be abolished. In that case he will take on the status and capacity of a commissioner of the government of the federal State, the Community, or the Region within its territorial department (Article 6 §1 VIII 1° paragraph 4 Special Majority Act on Institutional Reform).

III. The Municipalities

A. *Introduction*

389. Belgians have always been particularly attached to their local institutions. The experiment during the French regime of breaking with the autonomy of municipalities proved to be a complete failure. Eventually, a balance was sought between an excessive degree of local autonomy, as was the case in the Middle Ages, and a much too centralised institutional structure. The municipalities play a much more important role as instruments of local democracy than do the provinces. The police force, for instance, is partly organised at the municipal level. Public Centers for Social Welfare too are organised at this level. Despite their far-reaching integration in the municipal structure, they do remain a separate legal entity.

Up until 1976, Belgium consisted of 2,359 municipalities. Then the number of municipalities was reduced to 589 by a number of Royal Decrees in Council and later ratified by Act of Parliament. As of 1 January 2019, this number has been further reduced to 581, following the fusion of 15 Flemish municipalities into 7 new municipalities. These fusions were actively supported by the Flemish Region which provided a financial bonus to these municipalities in the form of debt assumption.

B. *Municipal Jurisdiction* Ratione Materiae

390. As explained above, municipal interests are primarily stipulated by the various legislatures. This may be done in a direct or in an indirect way. Federal, Community, and Region Acts may assign certain matters to municipal powers or may withdraw other matters from their jurisdiction, assigning them to another authority. Indirectly done, Acts regulate the matter itself or empower the Executive Branch to regulate the matter in its entirety. The Constitutional Court protects municipal and provincial autonomy against legislative incursion by applying the principle of proportionality. Legislation will be in breach of that principle when its effects would result in municipalities (or provinces) being deprived fully, or of the essence, of their powers or when restrictions on their jurisdiction cannot be justified by its better being exercised at another level.[243] There is one instance in which the Constitution itself entrusts a specific matter to the municipal authorities: the drawing up birth, marriage, and death certificates and the keeping of those registers belong exclusively to the jurisdiction of the municipal authorities (Article 164 Constitution).

C. Municipal Institutions

1. The Municipal Council

391. The Municipal Council is the deliberative body of the municipality, composed of directly elected members, the number of which depends on the number of inhabitants in the municipality. Their term of office is a fixed period of six years.

The Municipal Council in principle decides on everything that is of municipal interest, such as municipal assets, municipal finances and budget, and rules governing the appointment, the promotion, and the financial status of its civil servants. It may issue standing orders (namely the Council's rules of procedure) and internal regulations governing the organisation and use of municipal services. It may also issue by-laws. These must be consistent with any legislation issued by higher authorities.

Within the framework of co-management, the Municipal Council deliberates on every matter submitted to it by higher authorities.

As of 1 January 2019, in the Flemish Region the members of the Municipal Council also constitute the Council of Public Centre for Social Welfare.

2. The Municipal Executive

392. The Municipal Executive consists of the Mayor and a number of Municipal Councillors, the number of which depends on the number of inhabitants in the municipality. The Municipal Councillors are elected for a fixed period of six years by the Municipal Council from among its sitting members.

It is the executive body of the municipality, having assigned powers. It is in charge of the day-to-day administration of the municipality, involving the administration of municipal assets, the conduct of cases involving the municipality, the supervision of municipal civil servants, the maintaining of the civic status registries, and so on. It is entrusted with the implementation of the decisions taken by the Municipal Council, with the exception of police regulations coming exclusively under the executive competence of the Mayor.

Within the framework of co-management the Municipal Executive may be charged with the implementation of rules laid down by higher authorities.

243. Cons., Judgments No. 95/2005, 25 May 2005; No. 89/2010, 29 Jul. 2010; No. 109/2011, 16 Jun. 2011; No. 16/2015, 12 Feb. 2015; No. 100/2015, 2 Jul. 2015.

As of 1 January 2019, in the Flemish Region the members of the Municipal Executive also constitute the executive body of Public Centre for Social Welfare.

3. The Mayor

393. The Mayor is appointed by the Region government. Usually the Mayor is already a member of the Municipal Council figuring on a list signed by a majority of Council-members. The Region government, however, has the right to appoint a person who is not a member of the Municipal Council. But it will exercise this right only in exceptional circumstances. The term of office of Mayor is six years. A Mayor, however, may be suspended or dismissed by the Region government.

394. Like the Provincial Governor, the Mayor serves in a dual capacity. He is both head of the municipality, as president of the Municipal Executive, and the representative of the higher authorities entrusted with the implementation of federal, Community, and Region Acts and rules (unless expressly delegated to another municipal body). As head of the municipal police force, the Mayor also has particular policing powers, having to implement the various police statutes and regulations. In case of an emergency, riots for example, he is authorised to enact police regulations which must be confirmed afterwards by the Municipal Council.

As of 1 January 2019, in the Flemish Region the Mayor is also the president of the executive body of the Council of Public Centre for Social Welfare.

4. Special Arrangements

395. In the six Brussels periphery municipalities and in the municipalities of Comines-Warneton / Komen-Waasten and Fourons / Voeren, the councillors and the members of the Councils and executive bodies of the Public Centers for Social Welfare are elected directly by the population.

Furthermore, there is a specific procedure for the appointment of the Mayors in the six Brussels periphery municipalities. This specific procedure was introduced in the 2014 Sixth State Reform in order to end repeated disputes in some of these municipalities regarding a refusal by the Flemish government to appoint the candidate nominated by a majority of the councillors on grounds of infringements of language legislation. According to this new procedure, the refusal can be challenged before the general assembly of the Administrative Tribunal Division of the Council of State. This guarantees a decision by a bench having an equal number of Dutch-speaking and of French-speaking judges. Where the Council of State quashes the decision to refuse, the candidate nominated becomes automatically appointed. On the other hand, an upholding of the refusal means that it is definitive and the Municipal Council must then propose another candidate.

396. In the bilingual Brussels-Capital region (composed of nineteen municipalities), some guarantees were built into the rules governing municipal institutions to ensure the presence of the smaller language (Flemish) community in Brussels municipal institutions.

§2. Functional Decentralisation

397. The concept of State which the 1831 National Congress laid down in Article 33 of the Constitution is based on a unified, integrated structure of government. The King was vested with the authority to organise the Executive Branch by setting up and organising ministerial departments. Parliament exercised its prerogatives through financial supervision and by calling Ministers to account for the way in which they managed their department, and it created by Act decentralised authorities. In 1831, there were only a limited number of Ministries and a few decentralised authorities with limited financial means. Belgium's evolution into a welfare State has entailed that the State has to fulfil a much broader range of tasks. Consequently, there has been – as in other European countries – an important and steady increase in the number of public autonomous bodies that are neither part of a ministerial department nor of any local (territorially decentralised) authority.

This development has led to a fragmentation of decision-making. Belgian commentators have characterised this phenomenon as 'functional decentralization'. This refers to a form of government according to which decision-making in well-defined tasks of general interest is entrusted to an autonomous public authority having legal personality and enjoying a relative degree of independence. Unlike territorial decentralisation which is enshrined in the Constitution, functional decentralisation is not provided for under the Constitution, and has in fact a very weak constitutional basis. According to Article 33 of the Constitution, the exercise of State powers may indeed be delegated only to 'constitutional authorities'. Furthermore, functional decentralisation entails a weakening of parliamentary control, which has been limited in certain areas to verifying whether a Minister has appropriately exercised administrative supervision over the relevant functionally decentralised institution. For these reasons, functionally decentralised institutions are invariably set up by legislative action, which may delegate authority to the relevant branch of the Executive.

398. A distinctive feature of functionally decentralised institutions is that they are no longer subject to a hierarchy of control under the relevant Minister, unlike the operations of the Ministry itself. The degree of autonomy, however, varies greatly from institution to institution, and depends on the statute (federal, Community, or Region as the case may be) setting up the functionally decentralised institution and granting it legal personality. That autonomy may be limited in various ways.

(i) As the existence of the functionally decentralised institutions is not mentioned in the Constitution, they may be abolished by an ordinary statute, in contrast to territorially decentralised institutions, the abolition of which is only possible through a revision of the Constitution, or for the provinces, through a Special Majority Act.

(ii) The statute determines the composition of the various executive committees and/or deliberative assemblies, the government (federal, Community, or Region) retaining a right of appointment of key positions. In the socio-economic sphere the relevant government sometimes has to make a choice from among candidates submitted by interest groups. The Belgian collective bargaining economy often implies more or less formalised procedures of consultation with various interest groups within consultative bodies, often organised as a functionally decentralised institution.

(iii) The Executive Branch (federal, Community, or Region) generally retains a right of control through administrative supervision or by way of the right to appoint a government commissioner monitoring the legality and the financial impact of the decisions taken by the organs of the functionally decentralised institutions.

(iv) Each statute also organises the financial means of the functionally decentralised institution: some institutions (mainly in the financial sphere) are largely self-supporting because of the financial charges imposed on the beneficiaries of the services they provide (e.g., the Commission for Banking and Finance, which to some extent may be compared to the Securities and Exchange Commission in the US); others are (entirely) State-subsidised. This may affect to a large extent the autonomy of functionally decentralised institutions. Because of budgetary restraints, financial control has gradually been increased by imposing on them a duty to inform the relevant Minister of Finance of any decision which might have an important financial impact, and by making any projected addition to staff subject to the prior approval of the government.

In conclusion, the lack of coherence in the status of the various functionally decentralised institutions – which greatly depends on the relevant constitutive statute – should be stressed. A first (rather limited) attempt at co-ordination was undertaken by the Act regarding Controls on Certain Public Institutions of 16 March 1954, organising the administrative and financial control over various specifically listed institutions.

399. The Act Restructuring Certain State-owned Enterprises of 21 March 1991 has endowed some State-owned companies, such as Bpost, the Belgian National Railway Corporation, Infrabel, Belgocontrol (now 'Skeyes' – air-traffic control), and Proximus (a telecoms company), with a great deal of autonomy by conferring on them the status of 'autonomous public companies'. Moreover, the Act draws up a framework making it possible to grant such status to other institutions which are already in existence or which are yet to be established. These public companies enjoy autonomy from the supervising Minister in their management. The Minister is to negotiate a management contract with the company's management committee and Board of Directors. This management contract lays down the public service tasks to be performed and the rules to be applied as to the setting of rates. Besides such public service tasks, autonomous public companies may also trade on a standard competitive basis just like any other private company. In that respect, they may enter into partnerships with private companies by jointly setting up subsidiaries or by enabling private investors to acquire a minority stake in its capital.

400. Functionally decentralised institutions may have either limited or very broad powers. Some of them are primarily advisory, consultative bodies. This mostly involves institutions with socio-economic powers, the National Labour Council (*Nationale Arbeidsraad / Conseil National du Travail*), by way of example. Others have a more executive function, such as deciding in individual cases whether to grant loans, or particular social security benefits. Still other institutions have been assigned regulatory powers.

401. To sum up, the resulting fragmentation of the decision process should be stressed. Very often, new services have been set up to suit a particular need without considering whether already existing institutions could handle the matter. As a result, various institutions have overlapping jurisdiction, a phenomenon which sometimes entails uncoordinated policies. It is sometimes also forgotten to abolish those institutions which no longer meet a particular need. The segmentation of decision-making is further enhanced by the federalisation process which has led in many cases to the splitting up of various, previously nationally organised, institutions resulting in an increased number of institutions. Moreover, the Communities and the Regions may establish new decentralised services, establishments and enterprises (Article 9 Special Majority Act on Institutional Reform). It should also be noted that functionally decentralised institutions do not have the same democratic legitimacy as the territorially decentralised ones, the office holders of which do periodically have to stand for election.

SELECTED FURTHER READING

Alen, A., B. Dalle, K. Muylle, W. Pas, J. Van Nieuwenhove & W. Verrijdt (eds) *Het federale België na de Zesde Staatshervorming* (die Keure, 2014).

Jadoul, P., B. Lombaert & F. Tulkens (eds). *Le paraétatisme. Nouveaux regards sur la décentralisation fonctionelle en Belgique et dans les institutions européennes* (La Charte, 2010).

Mast, A., J. Dujardin, M. Van Damme & J. Vande Lanotte. *Overzicht van het Belgisch Administratief Recht* (21st) (Wolters Kluwer, 2017).

Uyttendaele, M. (ed.). *Regards sur la démocratie locale en Wallonie. Les nouvelles règles applicables aux communes, aux CPAS et aux provinces* (Bruylant, 2006).

Part IV. Nationality and the Administration of Justice

Chapter 1. Belgian Nationality

§1. Constitutional Provisions Concerning Nationality

402. According to Article 8 of the Constitution, the status of Belgian nationality is acquired, kept, and lost according to the rules established by civil law. The Constitution and other legislation concerning political rights determine what requirements are to be fulfilled – apart from Belgian nationality – in order to exercise these rights.

The Constitution states that naturalisation is conferred by the federal Legislature (Article 9), which power is exercised in this case by the King and by the House of Representatives (Article 74). The Constitution requires the Legislature – and not the Executive – to decide who shall possess Belgian nationality, the Legislature laying down the general rules and granting Belgian nationality through naturalisation in individual cases.

403. Article 8 paragraph 2 of the Constitution implies that Belgian citizens exercise political rights. On 9 July 1998, the ECJ held that Belgium had failed to fulfil its obligations under Council Directive 94/80/EC of 19 December 1994 which set down detailed arrangements for citizens of the EU residing in a Member State of which they are not nationals to exercise a right to vote and to stand as a candidate in municipal elections there.[244] The third and fourth paragraphs of Article 8 of the Constitution, added on 11 December 1998, now allow the federal Legislature to provide the right to vote in municipal elections for residents who are not Belgian nationals. However, such legislation can only grant those rights to citizens of the EU (non-Belgian) 'in compliance with the international and supranational obligations of Belgium'. And this voting right may be expanded by federal statute to those residents of Belgium who are not citizens of a Member State of the EU only under the conditions and in the manner specified by such Act.[245]

244. ECJ, Case C-323/97 (*Commission v Belgium*), 9 Jul. 1998.
245. See further below, Ch. 5 §1 II.

404. Article 10 paragraph 2 of the Constitution provides that 'all Belgians are equal before the law; they alone may be appointed to civil and military posts, barring such exceptions as may be established by Act in specific cases'. This implies that non-Belgians may not be appointed to civil service or military functions, save for such general and express exceptions as set by federal, Community, or Region Act. This provision, of course, is not applicable to ecclesiastical functions, or to employment in the private sector.

The concept 'civil and military posts' must be defined narrowly when applying it to the citizens of the EU pursuant to Articles 26 §2 and 45 TFEU on securing the freedom of movement for workers within the Union, and prohibiting any discrimination on grounds of nationality as to this right. According to Article 45 §4 of this treaty, the provisions of that Article shall not apply to 'employment in the public service'. This exception must be strictly interpreted as covering the exercise of public authority. In certain judgments involving Belgium, the ECJ has ruled that this exception refers to 'a series of posts which involve direct or indirect participation in the exercise of powers conferred by public law and duties designed to safeguard the general interests of the State or of other public authorities. Such posts in fact presume on the part of those occupying them the existence of a special relationship of allegiance to the State and reciprocity of rights and duties which form the foundation of the bond of nationality'.[246]

On the other hand, the exception contained in Article 45 §4 does not apply to posts which, while falling under the purview of the State or other organisations governed by public law, nevertheless do not involve any association with tasks belonging to the 'public service' properly so called.[247] EU citizens must have equal access to them, under the same conditions of employment, and may not be disqualified from them simply on grounds of nationality.

As EU law prevails over national law, it has been proposed to revise Article 10 paragraph 2 of the Constitution in order to reconcile it to the caselaw of the ECJ.

It should be noted that, apart from federal legislation, the legislation of the Communities and Regions may also establish exceptions to the requirement of Belgian nationality for appointments to civil and military posts.

§2. The Belgian Nationality Act

405. The attribution, acquisition, loss, or recovery of Belgian nationality are currently governed by the much amended Belgian Nationality Act of 28 June 1984 (the most recent amendment thereto being enacted on 18 June 2018).

246. See, e.g., ECJ, Case C-149/79 (*Commission v Belgium*), 26 May 1982.
247. For example, public bodies responsible for the distribution of water, gas, and electricity: see ECJ, Case C-173/94 (*Commission v Belgium*), 2 Jul. 1996.

I. Obtaining Belgian Nationality

406. Belgian nationality may be obtained by attribution or by acquisition. While children, under certain conditions, will automatically be attributed Belgian nationality, adults can acquire Belgian nationality either by a simple declaration or – exceptionally – by applying for naturalisation.

A. *Attribution of Belgian Nationality*

407. The automatic attribution of Belgian nationality was initially restricted to the children of Belgian (natural or adoptive) parents. Since 1991, Belgian nationality is also automatically attributed to children born in Belgium of foreign (natural or adoptive) parents who were born in Belgium and whose grandparents had immigrated to Belgium (termed 'third-generation immigrants'). Attributing Belgian nationality on the basis of *ius soli* rather than *ius sanguinis* (which as a rule is the basis of the Belgian Nationality Act) must be seen from the perspective of government policy to enhance the integration of immigrants into Belgian society. Similarly, the attribution of Belgian nationality to children born in Belgium of foreign parents born abroad (termed 'second-generation immigrants') has become less formalised.

408. Belgium nationality is automatically attributed to the following children:

(i) a child who, on the date of birth, has a Belgian national for a father or mother (Article 8 Belgian Nationality Act). If the child is born outside Belgium, the parents must in principle make a claim of Belgian nationality for their child within five years after the birth;
(ii) a child adopted by a Belgian parent provided that, at the date on which the adoption becomes effective, the child has not reached the age of 18 years or is emancipated in law (Article 9 Belgian Nationality Act). In the case where the child is born outside Belgium, the adoptive parents must in principle make a claim of Belgian nationality for their (adopted) child within five years after the adoption becomes effective;
(iii) a child born or found in Belgium who, at any moment before the age of 18 years or prior to emancipation in law, would be stateless if the child did not acquire Belgian nationality (Article 10 Belgian Nationality Act). This rule does not apply where the child can obtain another nationality provided his legal guardian(s) undertake that act before the diplomatic or consular authorities of the country of the parents or of one of them;
(iv) a child born in Belgium whose (adoptive) parent has been born in Belgium, provided that the latter has had his main residence in Belgium during at least five out of the last ten years preceding the birth of the child or the date on which the adoption becomes effective (Article 11 Belgian Nationality Act);
(v) a child born in Belgium whose (adoptive) parents have made a claim of Belgian nationality for their (adopted) child under 12 years, provided that the child has had its main residence in Belgium since birth, that the (adoptive)

parents have had their main residence in Belgium during the ten years preceding the claim, and that at the moment of the claim, at least one of the parents is allowed to reside in Belgium for an indefinite period (Article 11*bis* Belgian Nationality Act);

(vi) a child not having reached the age of 18 years or not having been emancipated in law before this age, in the case of the acquisition or the recovery of Belgian nationality by a parent (adoptive or natural) who exercises authority over the child, provided that Belgium is the principal residence of the child (Article 12 Belgian Nationality Act).

B. *Acquisition of Belgian Nationality*

409. Adults may acquire Belgian nationality by simple declaration or by application for naturalisation. In the case of a simple declaration, the person who fulfils the legal requirements is in principle entitled to acquire Belgian nationality. Naturalisation, on the other hand, is considered to be a privilege granted by the federal legislator. Hence the House of Representatives has considerable discretion to grant or refuse naturalisation, even when the legal requirements are fulfilled.

410. The requirements to acquire Belgian nationality were liberalised significantly with the amendments of 1 March 2000 to the Belgian Nationality Act. These amendments, amongst others, deleted all references in the Act to the applicant's will to integrate into Belgian society and knowledge of one of the official languages. By Act of 4 December 2012, this liberalisation has been reversed. Pursuant to these last amendments, foreigners who want to acquire Belgian nationality must have a permanent right of residence in Belgium; know one of the official languages, and be integrated into society. Moreover, naturalisation has been restricted to exceptional cases and the possibility to revoke Belgian nationality has been broadened. Finally, declarations or applications to acquire Belgian nationality can no longer be filed from abroad.

411. Some people may acquire Belgian nationality by making a declaration to that effect before the Civil Status Registrar for the place where they officially reside. Only the Public Prosecutors Office may object to such declaration, for example on the grounds of serious impediments of a personal nature (e.g., a criminal record). In that case, the matter can be brought before the Family Court, with appeals from its judgments coming before the Court of Appeal (Article 15 Belgian Nationality Act).

The following persons may, generally speaking, acquire Belgian nationality by declaration when they have reached the age of 18 and enjoy a permanent right of residence in Belgium (Article 12*bis* Belgian Nationality Act):

(i) 'second-generation immigrants' (born in Belgium of foreign parents who were born abroad) legally in Belgium and whose principal residence since birth has been Belgium;

(ii) foreigners legally in Belgium whose principal residence for at least five years has been Belgium and who can prove knowledge of one of the official languages, their social integration, and participation in the economy;
(iii) foreigners legally in Belgium whose principal residence for at least five years has been Belgium, whose spouse or (adoptive) child have Belgian nationality, and who can prove knowledge of one of the official languages and their social integration;
(iv) foreigners legally in Belgium whose principal residence for at least five years has been Belgium, and who can prove that they cannot participate in the economy because of illness, invalidity, or age, and
(v) foreigners legally in Belgium whose principal residence has been Belgium for at least ten years and who can prove knowledge of one of the official languages and their participation in community life.

In addition, where a person's Belgian nationality, conferred initially in error but yet held in good faith thereafter for an uninterrupted period of ten years, is then revoked, that person can make a declaration before the Civil Status Registrar for the place where he officially resides in order to regain Belgian nationality (Article 17 Belgian Nationality Act).

412. The persons who may not acquire Belgian nationality by simple declaration, or whose declaration has been rejected, can apply for Belgian nationality through naturalisation.

Before the amendments of 4 December 2012 to the Belgian Nationality Act, any person having attained the age of 18 years could apply for naturalisation after they had established their main legal residence in Belgium for at least three years, being reduced to two years if their status as a refugee or statelessness had been recognised in Belgium.

Since those December 2012 amendments, the acquisition of Belgian nationality by application for naturalisation is restricted to exceptional cases. It is necessary for applicants (Article 19 Belgian Nationality Act):

(i) to have attained the age of 18 years or be emancipated in law;
(ii) to have a right of permanent residence in Belgium;
(iii) to provide reasons why it is almost impossible to acquire Belgian nationality by declaration, and
(iv) to be able to prove exceptional merit to Belgium in the field of sciences, sports, or sociocultural activities, and in this way be an exceptional contribution to Belgium's international standing. This exceptional merit can be proven:
 (a) in the field of sciences, by a doctoral degree;
 (b) in the field of sports, by achieving international or Belgian selection criteria for a European Championship, a World Championship, or the Olympic Games, or by having a sports federation advise that the person concerned can be of added value for Belgium in these tournaments, or

(c) in the field of sociocultural activities, reaching the final selection of an international cultural competition or being internationally recognised for merit in the cultural field or for social engagement.

In addition, the legislator has retained the possibility to apply for naturalisation for those persons whose statelessness has been recognised in Belgium, if their legal residence has been in Belgium for at least two years and they have a permanent right of residence.

413. The application for naturalisation is addressed to the Civil Status Registrar in the municipality where the applicant resides or the House of Representatives, and is filed with the Public Prosecutors Office in the judicial district of the applicant's residence, with the Immigration Services, and with the State Security Service. These officials will investigate whether serious impediments to the application exist or not. It will then be forwarded to the House of Representatives for a final decision. The House has a wide margin of appreciation in granting or refusing naturalisation. Integration and knowledge of one of the official languages are considered to be important elements in this decision. The deed of naturalisation is approved by the House of Representatives, assented to and promulgated by the King as an ordinary statute, and is published in the *Gazette*. It takes effect on the day of publication (Article 12 Belgian Nationality Act).

II. Loss of Belgian Nationality

414. The Belgian Nationality Act prescribes several ways to lose Belgian nationality. In principle, Belgian nationality can only be lost in case the person concerned would not become stateless as a result.

The loss of Belgian nationality occurs, generally speaking, in the following situations (Article 22 Belgian Nationality Act):

(i) anyone who has reached the age of 18 years may make a declaration renouncing Belgian nationality before the appropriate Civil Status Registrar;
(ii) non-emancipated children not having reached the age of 18 years may, in some cases, lose Belgian nationality when they are adopted by foreigners or when their parents (adoptive or natural) lose their Belgian nationality, or
(iii) Belgians who were born abroad, who from the age of 18 to 28 years continuously had their main residence abroad, and who are not employed abroad by the Belgian government or by a Belgian company will lose their Belgian nationality if they did not obtain nationality between the ages of 18 and 28 years or if they have not made before the age of 28 years a declaration to retain nationality.

Furthermore, persons can lose their Belgian nationality through revocation. This measure can only be pronounced by a judge. Hence, the Court of Appeal can revoke the Belgian nationality of those who, at their date of birth, do not hold their nationality through descent from a Belgian parent (natural or adoptive), and those to whom their Belgian nationality was not attributed under Article 11 or 11*bis* of the Belgian Nationality Act (Article 23 Belgian Nationality Act):

(i) if they acquired their Belgian nationality on the basis of a deception through providing false information, committing forgery, relying on false or falsified documents, committing identity fraud or fraud in acquiring a right of residence, or
(ii) if they are seriously remiss in their duties as Belgian citizens.

Furthermore, a criminal court judge can revoke the Belgian nationality of those who, at their date of birth, do not hold their nationality through descent from a Belgian parent, and those to whom Belgian nationality was not attributed under Articles 11 of the Belgian Nationality Act (Article 23 §1, §2 Belgian Nationality Act):

(i) if they are sentenced to a term of imprisonment of at least five years for serious crimes (such as attacks on the King, violations of international human rights, human trafficking) or for crimes which were facilitated by the possession of Belgian nationality, the crimes being committed within ten years and five years after the day they obtained Belgian nationality, respectively, or
(ii) if they are sentenced to a term of imprisonment of at least five years for a crime of terrorism;
(iii) if they have acquired Belgian nationality on the grounds of a marriage of convenience.

A person losing his Belgian nationality through revocation may only recover it through naturalisation (Articles 23 §9, 23/1 §4 & 23/2 §4 Belgian Nationality Act). Anyone who has lost Belgian nationality in any way other than through revocation may recover it under certain conditions by the application procedure (Article 24 Belgian Nationality Act).

Selected Further Reading

Closset, Ch.-L. & B. Renauld. *Traité de la nationalité en droit belge* (Larcier, 2004).
Van de Putte, M. & J. Clement. *Nationaliteit* (Story-Scientia, 2001).
Wautelet, P. & F. Collienne. *Droit de l'immigration et de la nationalité: fondamentaux et actualités* (Larcier, 2014).

Chapter 2. Fundamental Rights and Liberties

§1. General

I. Introduction

415. No field of law is influenced more by the Europeanisation of the Belgian legal order than human rights law. Although the Belgian Constitution has always contained a vast catalogue of human rights, the European and international human rights treaties currently play a much more important role, which even extends to the interpretation of the constitutional rights. Nevertheless, the latter remain important insofar as they guarantee specific rights not enshrined in the European and international treaties, or insofar as some constitutional rights offer a further-reaching protection than the corresponding human rights laid down in these treaties.

II. Sources

416. The main sources of the rights and liberties in Belgian law are as follows.

(i) *the Constitution.* The main reason why the Belgian Constitution was called 'a model of constitutionalism'[248] and why it influenced many later constitutions is its catalogue of human rights. Most previous written constitutions did not contain a human rights catalogue because the human rights were laid down in a separate Bill of Rights. Conversely, the constitutional rights and liberties in Belgium were laid down in Title II of the Constitution (Articles 8–32), entitled 'Belgians and Their Rights', and in some other constitutional provisions (Articles 148–150, 170, 172 and 191). Typically for that period, the 1831 Constitution was confined to listing classic civil and political rights, the only arguable exception being the freedom of education, which can be considered to be a social and cultural right. That particular freedom is indicative of the constitutional rights' reactionary nature. The constitutional human rights catalogue indeed focuses on the rights the Dutch King Willem I particularly tampered with and imposes formal criteria requiring legislative involvement in order to limit human rights. The breakthrough of economic, social and cultural rights in the Belgian Constitution only happened in 1994, when its current Article 23 was inserted.

(ii) *the EConvHR.* Articles 2–18, and the First, Fourth, Sixth, Seventh[249], and Thirteenth Protocols to the Convention guarantee certain additional rights. Belgium has, until now, not ratified the Twelfth Protocol to the Convention, guaranteeing a general prohibition on discrimination.[250]

248. Recently, it has been called 'the first lasting document of European constitutionalism': ECtHR (GC), *Delfi AS v Estonia* (16 Jun. 2015) (dissenting opinion of Judges Sajó and Tsotsoria).

249. Belgium only ratified this Protocol on 13 April 2012, and it entered into force in Belgium on 1 July 2012.

250. The other Protocols relate to the procedure before the ECtHR.

(iii) *the ICCPR* (Articles 2–27). This plays a far less important role in the daily Belgian human rights practice than the EConvHR.
(iv) *the Charter of Fundamental Rights of the European Union ('EU Charter of Rights').* The Charter entered into force on 1 December 2009. Even before that date, the Belgian Constitutional Court relied on the Charter as a source of inspiration when interpreting constitutional rights.[251] It should nevertheless be kept in mind that the EU Charter of Rights only applies within the substantive scope of EU law, as defined in its Article 51.1 and in the ECJ's jurisprudence.[252]

In principle these international conventions are self-executing in Belgium.

417. There are in addition a number of other international human rights conventions to which Belgium has acceded. Some of these treaties are self-executing in Belgian law, such as the International Convention on the Elimination of All Forms of Racial Discrimination, the Convention on the Elimination of All Forms of Discrimination against Women, the Convention against Torture and other Cruel, Inhuman or Degrading Treatment and the Convention on the Rights of the Child. Other treaties are not self-executing, such as the Revised European Social Charter and the ICESCR. The relevance of the distinction between self-executing treaties and other human rights treaties has diminished for two reasons. First, it is currently generally accepted that the classic civil and political rights also entail positive obligations for State organs. Second, the Constitutional Court reviews legislation through the prism of Articles 10 and 11 and Title II of the Constitution in respect of all international treaties, whether or not they are self-executing.[253]

418. Fundamental rights may also be recognised in ordinary legislation, such as the right to (social) assistance under the framework statute governing Public Centers for Social Welfare at the municipal level, the conditional right to abortion, the conditional right to euthanasia, and the right to same-sex marriage. Criminal law also penalises infringements of fundamental rights, a notable recent example being the Act of 22 May 2014 criminalising sexism under the conditions specified therein.

Finally, the caselaw often protects fundamental rights through general principles of law, for example the requirement for an independent and impartial judge and the right to a fair trial.

251. Cons., Judgments No. 167/2005, 23 Nov. 2005 (concerning academic freedom); No. 81/2007, 7 Jun. 2007 (concerning the proportionality of criminal penalties).
252. Cons., Judgment No. 145/2012, 6 Dec. 2012 (the Court only applied Art. 19 Constitution and Art. 9 EConvHR, but not Art. 10 EU Charter of Rights, because the petitioners did not succeed in linking their case to the substantive scope of EU law).
253. Cons., Judgments No. 41/2002, 20 Feb. 2002 and No. 136/2004, 22 Jul. 2004.

III. Historical Outline

419. The concept of fundamental rights protecting a citizen against the authorities goes back to the Middle Ages. As explained above in the General Introduction, Belgium was divided into several autonomous entities until the era in which the Dukes of Burgundy successfully pursued a 'centralization policy'. The main entities were the County of Flanders, the Duchy of Brabant, and the Prince-Bishopric of Liège. During the Middle Ages, these entities were characterised by an ever-varying balance of power among the Head of State, the Church, the nobility, and in particular the rising bourgeois class in the cities. This balance of power was often formally laid down in a written pact concluded between the Head of State and his subjects. Those texts, which can be considered the first 'constitutions' in the provinces making up the present Belgium, guaranteed protection of certain fundamental rights enjoyed by the inhabitants.

As early as the thirteenth century, 'Land Charters' were imposed upon the Dukes of Brabant who had to pledge to observe the rights of the people. The most notable early example was the Charter of Kortenberg, adopted on 27 September 1312. On 3 January 1356, the 'Inauguration Charter' (*Blijde Inkomst*) was adopted, reasserting all rights laid down in the Land Charters, such as free trade, due process, and protection from criminal offences by royal servants. Later on other rights were added, including the prohibition against arbitrary searches, the protection of property rights against seizure, the right to personal freedom, and the right of citizens to be treated 'in accordance with the law and with judicial decisions'. If the Charter was violated, the people could exercise the traditional right of resistance to the King. When Joseph II tried to rescind a part of the Inauguration Charter, the result was the Revolution of Brabant in 1789.

As for the Prince-Bishopric of Liège, the 'Peace of Fexhe' (*Paix de Fexhe*) signed on 18 June 1316, enshrined similar principles. The 1831 Constitution shows some striking similarities with this medieval pact. In fact, except for the principle of equality, all fundamental rights in the first Belgian Constitution have their origins in medieval public law.

420. The French *Déclaration des droits de l'Homme et du Citoyen* of 26 August 1789 constituted an important step towards the further development of fundamental rights. Nevertheless, in spite of the annexation of the Belgian Provinces by France from 1795 to 1814, the text of the Belgian Constitution was influenced by the Anglo-Saxon system of effective, concrete, and pragmatic guarantees rather than by the theoretical declarations of principles produced by the French Revolution.

421. In 1830, the Belgian Revolution reacted against the enlightened despotism of King Willem I. One of the factors which brought about the Belgian Revolution was extreme dissatisfaction with the King's tampering with fundamental rights. The Catholics were upset because of the King's interventionism in religious matters and in the freedom of education. The Liberals, the vast majority of which were French-speaking, did not accept the King's language policy and the censorship of the press.

The so-called 'monster coalition' between these ideological camps having produced a recipe for a successful revolution, the current Constitution still guarantees these fundamental rights.

422. As a consequence of the adoption of the Universal Declaration of Human Rights on 10 December 1948, the classical civil and political liberties received a new boost, leading to the adoption of the EConvHR and the ICCPR. Furthermore, the emergence of the welfare state led to the adoption of treaties guaranteeing economic, social, and cultural rights, in particular the Revised European Social Charter and the ICESCR.

IV. General Rules

A. *Those Entitled to Rights and Liberties*

423. Although Title II of the Constitution is entitled 'Belgians and Their Rights', these rights are not granted to Belgian citizens exclusively. Under Article 191 of the Constitution, every foreigner who is within the territory of Belgium benefits from the protection of person and property, save for the exceptions prescribed by Act. But this does not mean that the legislator is granted an unlimited discretion to distinguish between Belgians and foreigners. The Constitutional Court requires such Acts to meet three conditions: (i) the distinction between Belgians and foreigners must be clearly and unambiguously defined in said Act; (ii) it may not violate international treaties to which Belgium is a party, and (iii) any arbitrary distinction between Belgians and foreigners is forbidden because Article 191 of the Constitution must be combined with the principle of equality and non-discrimination guaranteed by its Articles 10 and 11.[254]

424. The only rights the Constitution reserves for Belgian citizens are election rights and appointments to the civil service and the military, although even these reservations have been significantly qualified by EU law.

425. Until 1998, only Belgian citizens could vote and stand for election – as far as the legislative bodies and the municipal and provincial councils were concerned (Article 8 Constitution). This prohibition never included elections of the (at present twenty-one) Belgian representatives in the European Parliament.[255] Implementing a European directive, the constitutional amendment of 11 December 1998 added a third and a fourth paragraph to Article 8, allowing the federal Legislature to confer the right to vote on non-Belgian EU nationals 'in compliance with the international and supranational obligations of Belgium'. The fourth paragraph of Article 8 allows

254. Cons., Judgments No. 61/94, 14 Jul. 1994; No. 4/96, 9 Jan. 1996; No. 92/2004, 19 May 2004, and No. 68/2005, 13 Apr. 2005.
255. See also Pt. IV. Ch. 1. §1 'Constitutional Provisions Concerning Nationality'.

the federal Legislature to grant to non-EU nationals residing in Belgium the right to vote, provided that these rights are not broader than the election rights of EU nationals.

Since these European obligations only pertain to municipal councils, the Act of 27 January 1999 allows all EU nationals residing in Belgium to be candidates in and to vote in those municipal elections if, excepting Belgian nationality, they meet all electoral criteria otherwise applicable to Belgian nationals. While these EU nationals may be elected as members of the Municipal Council or even as Municipal Councillors, the function of mayor is still reserved to Belgian nationals. The Act of 19 March 2004 grants a more limited voting right to non-EU nationals residing in Belgium: these have only the right to vote, and not the right to be elected, in municipal elections; they have to have resided in Belgium for at least five consecutive years, and they have to declare in writing that they will obey the Constitution, Belgian law, and the EConvHR.

426. The right to be appointed to public or military functions is reserved to Belgian nationals, except for those 'special cases' established by federal, Community, or Region Act (Article 10 Constitution). That legislation may not adopt a general exception for the nationality requirement: it must always set out the precise categories to which the exception applies.

For EU nationals, Article 10 of the Constitution must be read together with Article 45 TFEU which guarantees the free movement of workers and forbids discrimination based on nationality within the scope of this freedom of movement. Although its Article 45 §4 states that this provision is not applicable to employment in the public service, the ECJ has read this exemption in a very restrictive way. The free movement of workers is not applicable when the posts concerned are those 'which involve direct or indirect participation in the exercise of powers conferred by public law and duties designed to safeguard the general interests of the State or of other public authorities'. Such posts presume, according to the Court of Justice, 'on the part of those occupying them the existence of a special relationship of allegiance to the State and reciprocity of rights and duties which form the foundation of the bond of nationality'.[256] The functions concerned are the armed forces, the police, the judiciary, the tax authorities, and the Foreign Service. For other functions (such as education, health services, postal services, public transport, and so on) EU nationals and Belgian citizens must be treated on an equal footing.

427. Article 1 EConvHR requires Contracting States to secure for everyone within their jurisdiction the rights and freedoms defined in the EConvHR and in its Additional Protocols. Under Article 2 ICCPR, each State Party undertakes to respect and to ensure for all individuals within its territory and subject to its jurisdiction the rights recognised therein. Neither the EConvHR nor the ICCPR contains any limitations relating to nationality. The provisions of the EU Charter of Rights are addressed to the institutions and bodies of the EU and to the Member States only when they are implementing EU law (Article 51 §1). Certain rights connected to

256. ECJ, Case C-149/79 (*Commission v Belgium*) 26 May 1982.

citizenship (Articles 39–46 EU Charter of Rights) are reserved for citizens of the EU and those persons residing in the EU.

B. Conditions for Restrictions on Rights and Liberties

428. The Belgian Constitution allows fundamental rights to be limited under two, cumulative, formal conditions: (1) the restriction should be established by an Act of Parliament, and (2) it should not be a 'preventive' measure. Both conditions can be explained as reactions against the Dutch King Willem I's 'decree government' which led to distrust in the Executive and confidence in the Legislature.[257]

The requirement that restrictions be laid down in an Act of Parliament guarantees that they are discussed and adopted by a democratically elected organ, avoiding the possibility that the Executive Branch might disregard human rights without the prior consent of the Legislative Branch. This requirement always went hand in hand with judicial power not to apply general, provincial, and local rules and regulations if they violated higher norms. While that jurisdiction has always been enshrined in Article 159 of the Constitution, Acts of Parliament were considered immune until 1971 as far as self-executing treaties were concerned, and even until 1985 as far as the Constitution was concerned. Hence, the requirement that restrictions be laid down in an Act of Parliament at the same time deprived citizens of remedies against most human rights violations for a very long time.

The prohibition against 'preventive measures' means that human rights may only be restricted through regulatory or repressive measures. Regulatory measures concern the orderly exercise of rights and liberties, provided that the latter are not deprived of their essence. A typical example is the local authorities' ability to set out the route a demonstration may take. Repressive measures concern the punishment of unlawful acts committed while exercising rights and liberties, either with criminal penalties or administrative fines. A typical example is the criminal liability of an author for slander and libel. Conversely, forbidding the publication of a book said to contain defamatory statements is not possible, since this would be a preventive measure.

The only exception to the prohibition against preventive measures is the freedom of assembly in open air (Article 26 paragraph 2 Constitution), which can be restricted preventively and by relevant law. This exception was nevertheless interpreted by the Court of Cassation as a general principle to be applied to all rights and liberties when exercised in public, in which case preventive measures, such as the requirement of any prior authorisations and consents, may be imposed.[258] The Council of State does not subscribe to that point of view, strictly limiting the admissibility of preventive measures to open-air meetings.[259]

---

257. See General Introduction §1 'An Outline of Belgian Constitutional History'.
258. Cass., 23 Jan. 1879, *Pas.*, 1879, I, 75.
259. Council of State, Administrative Tribunal Division, Judgment No. 80.282, 18 May 1999 (*Van der Vinck et al.*).

429. Under applicable international human rights conventions, any limitations on fundamental rights and liberties are examined according to substantive, rather than formal, criteria. Both the EConvHR and the ICCPR specify that, with the exception of certain fundamental rights which allow no derogations at all, not even in time of war or other public emergency (Article 15 EConvHR; Article 4 ICCPR), restrictions may be imposed on the exercise of the rights guaranteed under the provisions of those Conventions, provided that three substantive criteria are met.

(i) Any restriction must be in accordance with 'the law'. This criterion does not, however, require an Act of Parliament. The ECtHR only requires the rule containing the restriction to be sufficiently accessible to the citizen and sufficiently precise in order to enable an adjustment of behaviour.
(ii) It must also be in the interest of one of the goals enumerated in the Convention, such as national security, public safety, health, morals, or the rights and freedoms of others.
(iii) The restriction, finally, must be necessary in a democratic society. According to the caselaw of the ECtHR, this means that any limitation of rights should meet a pressing social need and that it should be proportionate to the relevant, legitimate aims it would pursue.

430. Article 52(1) of the EU Charter of Rights imposes similar substantive criteria. Any limitation on the exercise of the rights and freedoms recognised by the Charter must be provided for by law and respect the essence of those rights and freedoms. Subject to the principle of proportionality, limitations are permissible only if they are necessary and genuinely meet objectives of general interest recognised by the EU or the need to protect the rights and freedoms of others.

431. National courts are to ensure that these conditions are met when examining any limitation of a human right set out in the human rights conventions. Accordingly, when the Belgian Constitutional Court reviews an Act for conformity with constitutional provisions, which also find counterparts in those conventions, the Court, will examine whether the statute complies both with the two formal criteria laid down in the Constitution and with the three substantive criteria laid down in these conventions.[260]

C. *Remedies for Violations of Rights and Liberties under the Belgian Constitution*

432. Ensuring observance of rights and liberties is entrusted to the Judicial Branch. Which court and which judge has jurisdiction depends on which authorities are alleged to have violated a fundamental right.

260. Cons., Judgments No. 136/2004, 22 Jul. 2004; No. 202/2004, 21 Dec. 2004.

433. The rights and freedoms guaranteed under the Belgian Constitution were above all intended as a protection against the excesses of the Executive Branch. Belgian judges may not apply an administrative rule or regulation which is incompatible with one of the fundamental rights guaranteed under Title II of the Constitution or with a fundamental right recognised as such by an Act (Article 159 Constitution).

Moreover, such a rule or regulation may, on application by everyone having standing (i.e., with the necessary capacity and interest), be declared null and void by the Council of State's Administrative Tribunal Division. Insofar as such a rule or regulation causes damage to an individual, the latter may start a tort action in the ordinary courts, or since 2014, the Administrative Tribunal Division of the Council of State itself, as an accessory action to a petition for annulment.

Finally, criminal sanctions may be imposed on anyone who violates a right or liberty, insofar as this violation is made punishable by or by authority of an Act. No prior authorisation by the administrative authorities is necessary to bring an action against civil servants with regard to their administrative acts (Article 31 Constitution).

434. Since Belgian courts and tribunals have always ruled that they do not possess the power to declare Acts of Parliament unconstitutional, there was until recently no effective remedy against violations of constitutional rights and liberties by the Legislative Branch. In 1988, the predecessor to the Constitutional Court, the Court of Arbitration, was empowered to review the compliance of legislation with three expressly enumerated fundamental rights, being the principle of equality (Article 10 Constitution), the principle of non-discrimination (Article 11 Constitution), and the freedom of education (Article 24 Constitution).[261] The Court held early on that, when examining an Act's compliance with the principle of equality and non-discrimination, it could also examine whether other provisions of the Constitution[262], provisions of international treaties[263], or general principles of law[264] have been infringed in a discriminatory way. Since the amendments on 9 March 2003 to its constitutive Special Majority Act, the Constitutional Court may also review the conformity of all Acts of Parliament with the fundamental rights guaranteed in Title II of the Constitution and with Articles 170, 172, and 191 of the Constitution without the need to establish a link with Articles 10 and 11. The Court still does not possess the jurisdiction to review directly an Act's compliance with all constitutional provisions. For those articles of the Constitution which are not a part of the division of powers nor the specified rights, review via Articles 10 and 11 remains necessary. Moreover, since the Constitutional Court still possesses no jurisdiction to examine an Act's conformity with treaty provisions, it has developed its own jurisprudence of taking into account analogous human rights provisions in international treaties when dealing with a fundamental right in the Constitution.[265]

261. See further above Pt. II. Ch. 5. §2 'Judicial Review'.
262. Cons., Judgment No. 23/89, 13 Oct. 1989.
263. Cons., Judgment No. 18/90, 23 May 1990.
264. Cons., Judgment No. 72/92, 18 Nov. 1992.
265. Cons., Judgment No. 136/2004, 22 Jul. 2004.

435. Protection of rights and liberties against decisions of the courts is provided by those legal remedies available against judgments, such as appeals on the law and the facts and 'cassation' appeals (i.e. final appeal only on questions of law).

436. Under Articles 1382 and 1383 of the Civil Code, anyone causing injury to another through a wrongful act or negligence is liable to pay (compensatory) damages to the victim. These general tort provisions also apply to damages for injury caused by the violation of constitutional rights or rights protected by international treaties, regardless of whether the party liable for the injury is a private person or a public authority.

Moreover, anyone who violates the human rights of others is liable to punishment if the infringement of the fundamental right is punishable by, or by authority of, an Act. Furthermore, it is widely accepted in Belgium that human rights possess '*Drittwirkung*' (horizontal effect among individual parties).

437. According to the Court of Cassation's reading of Article 17 of the Civil Procedure Code, lawsuits before civil judges could only be initiated by those persons who were directly and adversely affected by the challenged act or negligence.[266] Following this caselaw, human rights violations could only be challenged in court by the victims, but not by a non-profit organisation ('NPO'). In 2013, the Constitutional Court ruled that an NPO's lack of access to a court to challenge human rights violations was discriminatory.[267] In order to implement that judgment, the federal legislator has amended Article 17 of the Civil Procedure Code by Act of 21 December 2018.[268] NPOs are now able to challenge human rights violations in court if their mission statement, as laid down in their by-laws, concerns human rights protection and if it allows them to initiate legal proceedings in order to fulfil that mission statement. This new access to court is subject to four conditions. First, the NPO's mission statement should be phrased in more specific terms than 'defending the general interest', for an *actio popularis* is not allowed. Second, they are only allowed access to court in order to defend a 'collective interest', namely an interest distinct from the individual interests of their members. Third, the object of their lawsuit must fall within the ambit of their mission statement. And fourth, the NPO must prove that it systematically pursues that mission.

D. *Remedies for Violations of Rights and Liberties under International Conventions*

438. Most constitutional and treaty-based human rights provisions may be invoked not only against public authorities, but also against individuals, groups, and organisations. For example, both participants in a telephone conversation are

266. Cass., 19 Nov. 1982, *Arr. Cass.*, 1982–1983, No. 172.
267. Cons., Judgment No. 133/2013, 10 Oct. 2013.
268. *Gazette*, 31 Dec. 2018.

allowed to record it for their own use, but judges must examine whether other unauthorised uses of that audio recording constitute a breach of the right to privacy, taking into account the aim of the use and the reasonable expectation of the other party that the recording would remain private.[269] The horizontal effect of the right to privacy, the right to a reputation, and the freedom of speech is also apparent in cases concerning the dismissal of employees for defamatory posts on social media.[270] By contrast, in a heavily criticised judgment, the Court of Cassation has stated that Articles 10 and 11 of the Constitution only hold obligations for official bodies, and not for citizens.[271] The Constitutional Court disagrees, imposing the principle of equality and non-discrimination upon all legal actors as soon as they are in a (legal or factual) dominant position empowering them to harm the rights of others in a discriminatory manner.[272]

In addition to judicial recognition of the horizontal effect of human rights, legislation itself is increasingly being enacted with the aim of strengthening horizontal effect. For example, the three Anti-Discrimination Acts of 10 May 2007 aim to enhance the horizontal effect of the principle of equality and non-discrimination, laid down in Articles 10 and 11 of the Constitution. Likewise, a recent Act concerning squatting rights aims at reconciling the squatter's right to housing and his right to respect for private and family life on the one hand, with the owner's right to peaceful enjoyment of property on the other.

The remedies sought by individuals in cases of human rights violations typically consist of damages, criminal liability, and the nullification of contracts.

439. More generally, the remedies which may be had in Belgium in cases where the rights and liberties guaranteed under international conventions are violated by State organs are determined by their position in the hierarchy of the legal system. Belgian jurisprudence holds the EConvHR, the Protocols thereto, the ICCPR, and the EU Charter of Rights as self-executing. Since the Court of Cassation's ruling in 1971 that 'when the conflict is one between a rule of domestic law and a rule of international law having direct effect in the domestic legal order, the rule established by the treaty must prevail'[273], the aforesaid instruments are given primacy over conflicting national legislation, irrespective of the latter's date of promulgation. Therefore, no Belgian judge may apply legislation conflicting with self-executing treaties binding Belgium. The sanctions set out in the paragraphs above apply to those government regulations and orders infringing upon those treaty provisions.

440. Under the EConvHR, the ECtHR's judgments carry a great deal of weight in the Belgian legal system, affecting Belgian caselaw which has often adapted its views in line with the caselaw of the Strasbourg Court. In several cases in which

269. Cass., 8 Sep. 2008, *Arr.Cass.*, 2008, No. 458; Cass., 1 June 2016, *R.W.*, 2017–2018, 380.
270. E.g., Labour Court Brussels, 4 Mar. 2010, *Soc. Kron.* 2011, 396.
271. Cass., 29 Mar. 2010, *J.T.T.*, 2010, 241.
272. Cons., Judgments No. 17/2009, 12 Feb. 2009; No. 64/2009, 2 Apr. 2009.
273. Cass., 27 May 1971 (*Fromagerie Franco–Suisse Le Ski*), *J.T.*, 1971, 460. See above Pt. I. Ch. 1. §2 'Treaties. Hierarchy'.

the Court has found a violation, Belgian authorities have been prepared to make the appropriate legislative and administrative amendments in order to comply with the Court's findings.

Since December 2007, criminal cases can be reopened even after final judgment upon a condemnation of the Belgian State by the ECtHR (Articles 442*bis*–442*octies*, Criminal Procedure Code). The reopening of a case can also be applied for by those convicted in similar cases other than the one in which that Court has ruled. The application for reopening can be made by the person convicted, his relatives, or by the Prosecutor-General for the Court of Cassation. If such reopening is sought within the first six months after the ECtHR's judgment has become final, the Court of Cassation examines whether the judgment *a quo* was contrary to the EConvHR, taking into account the ECtHR's judgment against the Belgian State.

441. International enforcement of the ICCPR is much less developed than that of the EConvHR. Belgium has ratified the First Optional Protocol to the ICCPR on 17 August 1994. Nevertheless the Human Rights Committee only possesses the competence to address its non-binding conclusions to the applicant and to the respondent State, which it cannot condemn.

These limited remedial powers explain why, in the Belgian caselaw, the ICCPR plays a less important role. The parties rather make use of the European human rights treaties, which usually benefit from a more detailed supranational caselaw and which offer stronger remedial powers.

E. *Rules Having Precedence When Differences Between Domestic and International Provisions Exist*

442. In accordance with Article 53 EConvHR and Article 5 §2 ICCPR, the most far-reaching protection takes precedence. Although the Belgian Constitution goes back as far as 1831, the protection it provides may sometimes be broader than the one offered by international treaties. This is the case, for instance, for the protection against expropriation (Article 16 Constitution) and the free use of languages (Article 30 Constitution). In most cases, however, these Conventions offer protections broader than that of the Belgian Constitution. This is the case, for example, with the provisions prohibiting retroactive legislation in criminal law (Article 7 EConvHR and Article 15 ICCPR).[274]

The principle of the most far-reaching protection is also enshrined in Articles 52 §3 and 53 of the EU Charter of Rights, the text of which seems to mirror the content of Article 53 EConvHR. Nevertheless, the ECJ has ruled that where an EU legal act calls for national implementation measures, the national authorities and the courts remain free to apply national standards of protection of fundamental rights,

274. Nevertheless, the Constitutional Court currently combines these treaty provisions with Arts 12 and 14 of the Constitution, thus reading the further-reaching guarantees concerning retroactive legislation in criminal law into said constitutional provisions (e.g. Cons., Judgment No. 54/2017, 11 May 2017).

provided that the level of protection established in the Charter (as interpreted by the Court) and the primacy, unity, and effectiveness of EU law are not thereby compromised.[275] The Belgian Constitutional Court recognises the primacy of EU law insofar as there is no infringement of national identity or of the basic values protected by the Constitution.[276]

When comparing the Belgian Constitution to the above-mentioned international conventions, it should be pointed out that the latter employ 'autonomous' concepts which may differ from like concepts used in the domestic legal order. For example, this is the case with 'civil rights', as addressed below.

V. Equality

443. Before the 1988 extension of the Constitutional Court's jurisdiction, judicial attention to the principle of equality and non-discrimination was focused on the conformity of government rules with Article 10 of the Constitution. The question whether Royal Decrees concerning unemployment benefits violated the principle of equal rights for men and women, for example, led to a difference of opinion between the Court of Cassation and the Council of State. The question of equal treatment of men and women as regards access to employment, vocational training, promotion and working conditions is addressed in the section on Belgium in the *International Encyclopaedia for Labour Law and Industrial Relations*.

Since that extension of the Constitutional Court's jurisdiction, the principle of equality and non-discrimination has become in daily practice the most important constitutional right. First of all, it is relied on in some 80% of the Constitutional Court's caselaw, as a reference provision protecting citizens from interference by federal and federated legislation. Second, it underpins the Constitutional Court's jurisdiction to review indirectly legislation as against constitutional provisions falling outside its direct reference provisions, as against European and international treaties, and as against general principles of law. Belgian lawyers, meanwhile, have become accustomed to addressing human rights violations through the prism of equality. Third, ordinary legislation adds to the protection of the principle of equality and non-discrimination, for example, through the three federal Anti-Discrimination Acts of 10 May 2007. Hence, the Constitutional Court is right to call the principle of equality and non-discrimination 'one of the foundations of a democratic State respecting the rule of law'.[277]

444. Today, all three Belgian superior courts (the Constitutional Court, the Court of Cassation, and the Council of State) interpret the principle of equality and non-discrimination in a similar way. The review based on Articles 10 and 11 of the Constitution starts with assessing whether the law under scrutiny creates a distinction between two categories: (1) equal situations treated equally (thus no discrimination) and (2) unequal situations treated unequally. The Constitutional Court possesses a

275. ECJ (GC), Case C-399/11 (*Stefano Melloni*), 26 Feb. 2013, para. 60.
276. Cons., Judgment No. 62/2016, 28 Apr. 2016. See above Pt. I. Ch. 1. §2. 'Treaties. Hierarchy'.
277. Cons., Judgment No. 17/2009, 12 Feb. 2009.

wide margin of appreciation to establish whether certain differences are commensurable or not.[278] However, if equal situations are treated unequally, or unequal situations are treated equally, this does not suffice to establish a discrimination: a distinction can be justified if three cumulative conditions – conditions that are strongly influenced by the caselaw of the ECtHR[279] – are met.

(i) The distinction has to pursue a legitimate aim. This aim is in most cases found in the parliamentary documents. Only in very rare cases, especially where the legislature is seen as trying to influence a pending lawsuit, is the aim found to be illegitimate.[280]

(ii) The criteria on which the distinction between the two categories is based, have to be objective and relevant. The criteria are objective if they are sufficiently clear as to which persons belong to which category. They are relevant if they represent a means to attain the aim pursued. In the vast majority of cases, the criteria meet both requirements. In a notable case, the Court decided that being married, as opposed to living together under a cohabitation agreement, is not a relevant criterion in granting a tax-free sum for fixed household costs.[281]

(iii) The last and most important test is the proportionality test which requires the law's consequences to be in a fair balance with the aim pursued. Since the border between law and politics is thin, the Court here grants the legislature a large margin of appreciation because it does not have the same scope for appraisal as does a democratically elected legislature. Hence it is unable to examine whether a measure taken by the legislator is opportune and desirable.[282] Nevertheless, the proportionality test proves to be more stringent when human rights are at stake.[283] Since 2004 the Court considers itself able to examine whether the legitimate aim could have been pursued with less disadvantageous means than set by the Act concerned.[284] The proportionality principle is the main tool for balancing the private interests at stake with the public interest. The Constitutional Court's scrutiny is strict when the private sphere of individuals or gender equality is at stake, while it is more lenient when dealing with delicate political compromises and with socio-economic policy choices.

445. The principle of equality and non-discrimination does not only apply when unequal treatment results from a distinction made by existing legal provisions. It also applies when persons under one of either category (equals treated equally / non-equals treated differently) are covered by existing legislation, whereas persons in the

278. Cons., Judgments No. 23/2003, 12 Feb. 2003; No. 36/2007, 7 Mar. 2007.
279. ECtHR, *Belgian Linguistic Case* (23 Jul. 1968).
280. Cons., Judgment No. 138/2002, 2 Oct. 2002.
281. Cons., Judgment No. 140/2001, 6 Nov. 2001.
282. Cons., Judgment No. 23/89, 13 Oct. 1989.
283. Cons., Judgment No. 74/92, 18 Nov. 1992.
284. Cons., Judgment No. 162/2004, 20 Oct. 2004.

other category are disadvantaged by an absence of legislation regulating their situation. In such cases, the Constitutional Court claims jurisdiction to declare a 'legislative lacuna'. The legislator is then expected to fill this gap by enacting new legislation regulating the situation of persons in the second category. Additionally, the Constitutional Court increasingly allows judicial and administrative judges to correct that lacuna themselves – before the legislator has enacted new legislation – thereby extending the scope of existing legislation to a category of persons not falling under its ambit.

446. According to both the Constitutional Court and the Council of State's Legislation Division, 'positive action' (i.e. measures aiming at improving the situation of a category of persons who have historically been disadvantaged) can only be allowed insofar as these measures are themselves compliant with the principle of equality and non-discrimination. The Constitutional Court subjects measures of positive action to a four-step test: (i) they are only allowed if the existing disadvantage of the protected group is significant; (ii) the disadvantage's elimination must be an important policy goal; (iii) the measures must be of a temporary nature, and must cease as soon as their goal has been reached, and (iv) they may not lead to disproportionate restrictions on the rights of others.[285]

447. In certain, specific circumstances, the Constitutional Court holds that the principle of equality and non-discrimination does not apply to unequal treatment *ratione loci* or *ratione temporis*.

Ratione loci, that principle may not lead to questioning the basic tenets of Belgian federalism, such as the legislative autonomy of the Communities and the Regions. Parties before the Constitutional Court sometimes argue that the principle of equality and non-discrimination is violated because of different legislative choices in two Communities or in two Regions, leading to an unequal treatment of Belgian citizens based on the territorially competent legislator. The Constitutional Court, however, always refuses to review such a situation as against the principle of equality and non-discrimination, explaining that the federated legislators are allowed to make different policy choices: their autonomy would become meaningless if different treatment between the inhabitants of the different Communities or Regions could in itself be said to violate Articles 10 and 11 of the Constitution.[286]

Ratione temporis, the principle of equality and non-discrimination may not preclude legislative change. Thus the Court takes the position that it will not review subsequent versions of the same legislation against Articles 10 and 11 of the Constitution, because legislative change always distinguishes between those subject to the previous version of an Act and those now subject to the amended version.[287]

448. The principle of equality is reiterated in constitutional provisions other than Article 10.

---

285. See, e.g., Cons., Judgments No. 9/94, 27 Jan. 1994; No. 17/2009, 12 Feb. 2009.
286. Cons., Judgments No. 44/93, 10 Jun. 1993; No. 63/2011, 5 May 2011; No. 36/2015, 19 Mar. 2015; No. 115/2018, 20 Sep. 2018.
287. Cons., Judgments No. 168/2003, 17 Dec. 2003; No. 91/2017, 6 Jul. 2017.

(i) The 1970 Constituent Assembly deemed it necessary to insert a new Article 11, stating that the rights and freedoms conferred on Belgians must be assured without discrimination. To that end, federal, Community, and Region Acts should guarantee the rights and liberties of ideological and philosophical minorities. The Constitutional Court always refers to Articles 10 and 11 together, since the principles of equality and non-discrimination are two sides of the same coin.
(ii) The absence of privileges in gaining access to the courts (Articles 13, 31 and 146).
(iii) The absence of privileges in the freedom of education (Article 24 §4).
(iv) Prohibiting privileges in tax matters (Article 172).
(v) Forbidding the King from granting privileges when conferring titles of nobility (Article 113).
(vi) In 2002 two constitutional amendments regarding the equality of men and women were added. First, Article 10 of the Constitution now expressly guarantees equality among women and men. This amendment implements Article 2 of the Convention on the Elimination of All Forms of Discrimination against Women. Second, a new Article, Article 11*bis*, was added and states that federal, Community, and Region legislations should guarantee for women and men equal exercise of their rights and freedoms, and in particular, promote their equal access to elected office and positions in the public service. The latter provision also requires that the federal Cabinet, the governments of the Communities and the Regions, and local governments include persons of both genders.

A. *The 2007 Anti-Discrimination Acts*

449. The three federal Anti-Discrimination Acts of 10 May 2007, the General Anti-Discrimination Act, the Anti-Racism Act, and the Gender Equality Act, further implement Articles 10 and 11 of the Constitution and the relevant EU Directives. These Acts apply both to the government and to private parties, in matters falling under federal jurisdiction. Their scope is limited, however, to the supply of goods and services, social protection, social benefits, social security, labour relations, terms in official documents, membership of professional organisations, and the exercise of economic, social, cultural and political activities.

These Acts prohibit direct and indirect discrimination. Direct discrimination occurs when someone is treated disadvantageously without proper justification. Indirect discrimination occurs when a seemingly neutral treatment nevertheless disadvantages a specific group of persons protected by the Acts. Unequal treatment, either direct or indirect, only amounts to discrimination if it cannot be justified. In some circumstances, any justification is possible; but in other circumstances, the Acts restrictively list the possible justifications.

450. The Anti-Discrimination Acts do not contain a general prohibition of discrimination: the forbidden grounds of discrimination are exhaustively listed. The General Anti-Discrimination Act forbids direct and indirect discrimination based on age, sexual orientation, civil status, birth, wealth, religion, political preference, language, current or future health, handicap, physical or genetic features, or social background. The Constitutional Court opposes such an exhaustive list because the principle of equality and non-discrimination applies to all persons in all situations. It therefore found that this list violates Articles 10 and 11 of the Constitution insofar as it does not mention trade union membership.[288] The Anti-Racism Act forbids direct and indirect discrimination based on nationality, race, skin colour, origin, and national or ethnic ancestry. The Gender Equality Act prohibits direct and indirect discrimination based on gender.

451. The Acts contain both civil and criminal sanctions. The civil sanctions include damages, nullity of contracts, lump sum compensation, and interlocutory proceedings for urgent matters (allowing for an interim injunction against the discriminatory treatment). The criminal sanctions concern the crimes of incitement to discrimination, segregation, hatred, or violence based on one of the exhaustively listed criteria. The Acts also subject public officers and civil servants to criminal liability for discriminating in their official capacity against protected persons or groups. The Anti-Racism Act establishes specific criminal acts covering *inter alia* discrimination based on the listed criteria in labour relations and the dissemination of ideas based on racial superiority and racial hatred.

452. The application of these three Acts is monitored by public bodies established by certain Acts. An Act of 15 February 1993 established the Centre for Equality of Opportunities and the Combat of Racism (since 2016 called 'Unia'), whose task is to combat all forms of discrimination based on the General Anti-Discrimination Act and the Anti-Racism Act, with the exception of discrimination based on language. It may initiate lawsuits in all cases concerning the application of these two Acts, although it may proceed only after the victim's consent. Unia has no competence regarding the Gender Equality Act, which is monitored by a specific body: the Institute for the Equality of Women and Men established by Act of 16 December 2002. The Institute oversees the application of all federal gender legislation and combats all gender-based discrimination.

453. Most Communities and Regions have enacted their own specific anti-discrimination legislation for those matters falling under Community and Region jurisdictions. Unia being an inter-federal body, it also oversees the application of these federated Acts.[289]

288. Cons., Judgment No. 64/2009, 2 Apr. 2009.
289. See the Co-operation Agreement of 3 April 2014, *Gazette,* 11 Apr. 2014 (2nd ed).

§2. CIVIL AND POLITICAL RIGHTS

I. Sources

454. In Belgium, civil and political rights are guaranteed under Title II of the Constitution, the EConvHR and the Protocols thereto, the ICCPR, and under the EU Charter of Rights. As a detailed study of the EConvHR, the ICCPR, and the EU Charter falls outside the scope of the present work, this section will focus on the Belgian Constitution and on Belgian cases brought before the ECtHR. Political rights, guaranteed under Articles 8 and 10 of the Constitution for which the Belgian nationality is required, are discussed above.[290]

Civil rights guaranteed under Articles 12–32 of the Constitution (except Article 23 guaranteeing economic, social, and cultural rights) protect Belgian citizens as well as foreigners, save for the exceptions prescribed by Act (Article 191 Constitution).

II. Individual Integrity, Liberty and Security

A. *The Right to Life and Individual Integrity*

455. In the eyes of the Constituent Assembly, the right to life was so self-evident that it was not deemed necessary to guarantee it explicitly in the text of the Constitution. Nevertheless, the Constitutional Court has held that, while the Constitution does not expressly mention the right to life, the exercise of the fundamental rights in the Constitution presupposes a respect for the right to life as guaranteed by Article 2 EConvHR.[291]

The last execution took place in 1950. Since then, the King has always exercised his prerogative of pardon (Article 110 Constitution) when the death penalty was pronounced, commuting these sentences to life imprisonment. In 1996 legislation abolished the death penalty in times of peace and in war. This abolition was enshrined in the Constitution in 2005 by Article 14*bis*. In 2003 Belgium ratified Protocol No. 13 to the EConvHR concerning the abolition of the death penalty in all circumstances.

B. *The Prohibition of Torture and of Inhuman or Degrading Treatment*

456. The Constitution does not guarantee a prohibition of torture or a prohibition on inhuman or degrading treatment or punishment. The only constitutional guarantee relevant in this regard is the abolition of 'civil death' (Article 18 Constitution), a criminal sanction entailing a person losing his entire legal existence and

290. See Pt. IV. Ch. 1. §1 'Constitutional Provisions Concerning Nationality'; Pt. IV. Ch. 2. §1. IV. A 'General Rules. Those Entitled to Rights and Liberties'.
291. Cons., Judgment No. 91/2006, 7 Jun. 2006.

capacity leading to the inability to own property, to have legally recognised family ties, or more generally, to do anything that would carry any legal effect.

457. Belgium is nevertheless bound by Article 3 EConvHR and it has ratified the European Convention for the Prevention of Torture and Inhuman or Degrading Treatment or Punishment. The Constitutional Court has jurisdiction to review legislation against these norms through the prism of the Articles 10 and 11 of the Constitution. It thus annulled a legal provision subjecting all prisoners to 'naked body searches' after each visit because such a general obligation fails to distinguish between those presenting a risk of smuggling dangerous items into prison and others.[292]

In recent years, the ECtHR has repeatedly held Belgium to be in breach for inhuman and degrading treatment of psychiatric detainees. A lack of specialised centres for their treatment leads to their prolonged incarceration in ordinary prisons, where they do not receive adequate psychiatric treatment.[293] In 2016 the Court noted that these cases originate from the systemic dysfunction of the psychiatric detainee system. It therefore pronounced a pilot judgment ordering Belgium to take structural measures within a two-year period and suspending some fifty similar pending cases until that date.[294] The Constitutional Court mentioned this landmark judgment in a case in which it annulled several reforms of Belgian legislation on detention. In its judgment, the Court also reminded the courts to apply that legislation taking into account the ECtHR caselaw.[295]

458. The living conditions inside Belgian prisons have also given rise to violations of Article 3 of the EConvHR. In 2014, the ECtHR observed that the problems arising from prison overcrowding in Belgium and the problems of unhygienic and dilapidated prison institutions were systemic in nature and did not concern the applicant's situation alone. It therefore recommended that Belgium consider adopting general measures guaranteeing prisoners' conditions of detention compatible with Article 3 EConvHR and affording them an effective remedy by which to remedy an alleged violation or allow them to obtain an improvement of their conditions of detention.[296]

292. Cons., Judgment No. 20/2014, 29 Jan. 2014.
293. See, e.g., the judgments of the ECtHR in *Aerts v Belgium* (30 Jul. 1998); *De Clippel and De Donder v Belgium* (6 Dec. 2011); *L.B. v Belgium* (2 Oct. 2012); *Claes v Belgium* (10 Jan. 2013); *Swennen v Belgium* (10 Jan. 2013); *Dufoort v Belgium* (10 Jan. 2013); *Caryn v Belgium* (9 Jan. 2014); *Oukili v Belgium* (9 Jan. 2014); *Van Meroye v Belgium* (9 Jan. 2014); *Plaisier v Belgium* (9 Jan. 2014); *Gelaude v Belgium* (9 Jan. 2014); *Saadouni v Belgium* (9 Jan. 2014); *Lankester v Belgium* (9 Jan. 2014); *Moreels v Belgium* (9 Jan. 2014); *Smits v Belgium* (3 Feb. 2015); and *Vander Velde and Soussi v Belgium* (3 Feb. 2015).
294. ECtHR, *W.D. v Belgium* (6 Sep. 2016).
295. Cons., Judgment No. 80/2018, 28 June 2018.
296. ECtHR, *Vasilescu v Belgium* (25 Nov. 2014).

459. Belgium has also been held in breach of Article 3 EConvHR for extraditing an Iraqi national convicted in absentia for membership in a terrorist organisation. According to the Court, Belgium should have obtained diplomatic assurances that the petitioner would not be subjected to any treatment contrary to Article 3 of the Convention upon return to Iraq.[297]

460. In an important Grand Chamber case, the ECtHR decided that Article 3 of the Convention would be violated if a Georgian national, having committed severe crimes in Belgium, would be deported to Georgia, since he was a leukaemia patient in need of a donor transplant and this procedure was not available in Georgia.[298]

C. *The Right to Liberty and Security of Person*

461. In general terms, this right may be defined as the freedom to live and to act according to one's will, within the limits necessary for the smooth functioning of a democratic society. In that sense, the right is the source of other civil rights. Article 12 of the Constitution refers to the British concept of habeas corpus: the right not to be placed under arbitrary arrest or detention. It provides that, apart from the case of arrest *in flagrante delicto*, no one may be arrested other than on the authority of a court order, supported by reasons, served at the time of arrest or within forty-eight hours at the latest.[299] It should be noted that, even in the case of arrest *in flagrante delicto*, an arrest warrant must nevertheless be served within forty-eight hours.

462. After a condemnation of Belgium by the ECtHR[300], amendments on 6 August 1971 to the Act Outlawing Begging and Vagrancy of 27 November 1891 provided a judicial remedy against the detention of vagrants. The Act on Protections for those with Mental Illness of 26 June 1990 was amended on 18 July 1991 to provide that persons of unsound mind may be deprived of their liberty only after judicial proceedings. Pursuant to a judgment of the ECtHR against Belgium[301], the amendments on 17 July 1990 to the Act Protecting Society against Serious Offenders and Recidivists of 1 July 1964 guarantee periodic judicial review of the continuing legality of internment ordered by the Minister of Justice for offenders placed under a restriction order.

In 1989, Belgium was held in breach of Article 5 §4 EConvHR because of the inability of the applicant's counsel to access case records during the first thirty days of detention thus denying any effective challenge of the statements and opinions advanced by the Public Prosecutors Office on the basis of these records.[302] The Court of Cassation immediately concurred with this judgment of the ECtHR. Belgian legislation was adjusted in line with the Convention by Act of 20 July 1990,

297. ECtHR, *M.S. v Belgium* (31 Jan. 2012).
298. ECtHR (GC), *Paposhvili v Belgium* (13 Dec. 2016).
299. Prior to the constitutional amendment of 24 Oct. 2017, *Gazette,* 29 Nov. 2017, the period was twenty-four hours.
300. ECtHR, *De Wilde, Ooms and Versyp v Belgium* (18 Jun. 1971).
301. ECtHR, *Van Drooghenbroeck v Belgium* (24 Jun. 1982).
302. ECtHR, *Lamy v Belgium* (30 Mar. 1989).

resulting in a procedure guaranteeing greater due process (more 'equality of arms') to a person arrested on suspicion of having committed a criminal offence.

Belgium has been condemned on several occasions by the ECtHR under Article 5 §1 EConvHR concerning the deportation of foreigners who were denied a residence permit. For instance, a 2002 judgment found Belgium to be in breach having lured several Roma families to police stations under false pretences, only to arrest and deport them.[303] In a 2006 judgment, the victim was a 5-year-old unaccompanied Congolese girl detained in a closed refugee centre in conditions not adapted to her extreme vulnerability.[304] In a 2008 judgment, Belgium was condemned for detaining two Palestinian refugees denied refugee status in an airport transit zone for over two weeks, despite this zone having no separate bedrooms or beds.[305] In a 2011 judgment, the victim was an HIV patient detained because she had ignored several orders to leave the territory. The ECtHR took into account that she had a stable place of residence known to the authorities, that she had always attended when the authorities contacted her, that her health deteriorated while being detained, and that she did not present a risk of going off radar given that she was dependent on urgent medical help.[306] In a 2012 judgment, Belgium was condemned for the continued detention of an Iraqi national convicted for terrorist offences, while it was clear that his detention could no longer serve the interest of extraditing him to Iraq, as the asylum bodies had concluded that he would face a real risk of torture or inhuman or degrading treatment on Iraqi soil.[307]

463. Article 5 EConvHR falls under the Constitutional Court's review competences, either through the prism of the Articles 10 and 11 of the Constitution or combined with the analogous Article 12 of the Constitution. According to the Court, the habeas corpus is such an essential aspect of a citizen's freedom that all persons on Belgian soil have standing before it to challenge the constitutionality of legislation concerning arrest and detainment. Likewise, all exceptions to the habeas corpus must always be interpreted restrictively.[308] In 2018 the Court annulled a legislative provision stipulating that a suspect must not necessarily be released if the investigating magistrate has omitted to sign the arrest warrant or to give reasons for the arrest.[309]

---

303. ECtHR, *Conka v Belgium* (5 Feb. 2002).
304. ECtHR, *Mubilanzila Mayeka and Kaniki Mitunga v Belgium* (12 Oct. 2006). See also ECtHR, *Mushkadzhiyeva et al. v Belgium* (19 Jan. 2010) and ECtHR, *Kanagaratnam et al. v Belgium* (13 Dec. 2011) concerning, respectively, Chechen and Sri Lankan mothers and their children, in which the Court specified that the mere fact that the children were accompanied by their mothers does not suffice to cure a violation of Art. 5 EConvHR.
305. ECtHR, *Riad and Idiab v Belgium* (24 Jan. 2008).
306. ECtHR, *Yoh-Ekale Mwanje v Belgium* (20 Dec. 2011).
307. ECtHR, *M.S. v Belgium* (31 Jan. 2012).
308. Cons., Judgment No. 201/2011, 22 Dec. 2011.
309. Cons., Judgment No. 91/2018, 5 Jul. 2018.

III. Intellectual Freedoms

464. Willem I's policy of intervention in religious matters and his language policy explain why the National Congress attached such great importance to intellectual freedoms, such as the free use of languages and the freedom of religion. These two specific intellectual freedoms, having particular importance for Belgium, are discussed in Chapter 3 below and in Pt. V. Ch. 4.

A. *Freedom of Expression*

465. Freedom of expression (Article 19 Constitution) is the freedom to express personal opinions in every possible way and 'to seek, receive and impart information and ideas of all kinds regardless of frontiers, either orally, in writing or in print, in the form of art, or through any other media' (Article 19 §2 ICCPR). The Belgian Constitution guarantees the freedom of expression but not the freedom of opinion, which was considered too evident to even mention. The protection of the freedom of expression provided under the Belgian Constitution differs in two ways from the protection guaranteed under international conventions, such as the EConvHR, the ICCPR and the EU Charter of Rights.

First, the Belgian Constitution contains separate regulation for the freedom of the press. Paragraph 2 of Article 25 of the Constitution establishes a specific system for the prosecution of press offences, known as 'serial liability': if the identity of the author is known and if he has a place of residence in Belgium, the publisher, the printer, or the distributor cannot be prosecuted. This provision aims at avoiding 'private censorship' by publishers afraid of the legal consequences of publishing controversial texts.

Article 150 provides that a jury (and thus the Criminal Assizes) adjudges press offences. The Constituent Assembly has amended Article 150 of the Constitution in 1999. Press offences motivated by racism or xenophobia are excepted from the trial by jury requirement and are brought before judges alone in the ordinary criminal courts. In this way the fight against racism is intended to become more effective. In conduct of press offence cases, only a unanimous court may order a hearing *in camera* (Article 148 Constitution).

Second, the Belgian Constitution forbids all preventive measures, even if such restrictions would seem necessary in a democratic society to preserve a legitimate aim. Paragraph 1 of Article 25 of the Constitution states that no form of censorship of the press may ever be established and that no security may be required of authors, publishers, or printers. A judge banning a publication before it has been significantly distributed would violate this provision. Only after the public has had the opportunity to take notice of the publication's content would restricting further distribution be allowed, since it then constitutes only a repressive measure.[310]

466. The Court of Cassation has defined press misdemeanours as 'criminal offences violating the rights of society or of citizens by abusing the expression of

310. Cass., 29 Jun. 2000, *R. Cass.*, 2001, 35; Cons., Judgment No. 157/2004, 6 Oct. 2004.

an opinion through several printed and published writings'.[311] Established caselaw of that Court held that when the offence was committed not in the print media but in other media such as radio, television, or the internet, that constitutional provision (Article 25) which dated back to 1831 and used the concept 'press' could not be read as encompassing such modern technologies.[312] As a result of this very restrictive definition and to avoid trial by the Criminal Assizes bestowing more undue publicity on the author's writings, press offences were not prosecuted. The system of compensatory damages granted by the ordinary courts (Article 1382 Civil Code) functioned as an alternative remedy against abuses of the freedom of the press.[313]

Only recently has the Court of Cassation accepted that offences committed via the internet constitute press criminal misdemeanours if they concern written texts, implying the requirement to bring these cases before a jury if they do not concern racism or xenophobia.[314] By contrast, spreading images, audio recordings, or videos over the internet does not amount to a press criminal misdemeanour, implying the ordinary criminal courts' jurisdiction if this spreading constitutes a misdemeanour.

467. Though the public office of civil servants does not deprive them of the freedom of expression, current caselaw assumes that it does involve certain restraints, in particular the obligation to observe confidentiality in the exercise of their functions.

468. According to the ECtHR, a journalist's right to keep his sources secret is an essential part of the freedom of the press: this right may not be infringed solely because of possible unlawfulness surrounding these sources. Hence, when a journalist accuses a European civil servant of fraud based on confidential documents belonging to the European anti-fraud agency, a search of his home carried out by the Belgian authorities aimed at finding the leak within that agency breaches Article 10 EConvHR.[315] By the Act of 7 April 2005 regarding Protecting a Journalist's Sources[316], the Belgian legislator has incorporated the principles of the Strasbourg caselaw: disclosure of a journalist's sources may only be ordered by a judge when it is absolutely necessary in order to avoid a criminal act endangering a person's physical integrity and if the information required cannot be obtained in any other way.

469. Apart from the aforementioned *De Haes and Gijsels* and *Tillack* cases, the ECtHR has condemned Belgium for violation of the freedom of expression in two other press-related cases.

311. Cass., 7 Dec. 1971, *Arr. Cass.*, 1972, No. 345; Cass., 7 Feb. 1995, *A.J.T.*, 1995–1996, 248.
312. Cass., 9 Dec. 1981, *Arr. Cass.*, 1981–82, No. 491; Cass., 2 Jun. 2006, *J.L.M.B.*, 2006, 1402.
313. See however ECtHR, *De Haes and Gijsels v Belgium* (24 Feb. 1997) in which Belgium was held in breach because two journalists having heavily criticised four judges were obliged to pay damages to those judges.
314. Cass., 6 Mar. 2012, *J.T.*, 2012, 505; Cass., 29 Jan. 2013, *Arr. Cass.*, 2013, No. 71; Cass., 8 Nov. 2016, P.16.0958.N.
315. ECtHR, *Tillack v Belgium* (27 Nov. 2007).
316. *Gazette*, 27 Apr. 2005.

The 2003 *Ernst* judgment concerned a search of the premises of three newspapers and one public TV broadcasting company resulting in the seizure of several documents. None of the journalists or editorial offices were suspected of having committed any criminal act. Rather, these measures were only intended to discover which members of the Public Prosecutors Office systematically leaked to the press secret information concerning ongoing criminal investigations. The respondent Belgian government failed to prove that this objective could not be attained by less far-reaching methods, such as an internal inquiry within the Public Prosecutors Office. In any event, the investigators' access to all journalistic sources during these searches was a disproportionate breach of the secrecy of journalistic sources.[317]

The 2011 *RTBF* judgment concerned an order by the interlocutory proceedings (urgent basis) judge prohibiting the broadcasting of a documentary about malpractices by a certain doctor. That restriction to the freedom of expression lacked a sufficiently clear legal basis, founded as it was on the general provision concerning interlocutory proceedings for urgent matters (Article 584 Code of Civil Procedure). Moreover there was divergent jurisprudence as to whether that judge could order preventive measures.[318]

470. According to the Constitutional Court, the freedom of expression being a cornerstone of the democratic States governed by the rule of law, all restrictions to this freedom must be interpreted restrictively. These restrictions must also be necessary in a democratic society, respond to a pressing social need and be proportionate to the legitimate aim they pursue.

In an important judgment on the public funding of political parties represented in Parliament, the Court explained that a democratic society must protect the values and principles underlying the EConvHR against persons or groups aiming at destroying them. Therefore, a legal provision stipulating that a political parties' public funding may be put on hold if that political party shows hostility towards the rights and freedoms protected by the EConvHR does not violate the freedom of expression. The Court did, however, specify that 'hostility' in this context can only mean the political party's inciting others to violating fundamental rules.[319]

In 2010 the Constitutional Court annulled a French Community Act forbidding all commercials by political parties, because it also applied outside election periods and because it prevented smaller political parties from making their views public.[320]

In 2016, the Constitutional Court validated an Act criminalising sexist expressions. This Act aims at improving the equality between women and men, which is of fundamental importance in a democratic society and which is protected by Articles 10 and 11*bis* of the Constitution. The Court did, however, specify that this

317. ECtHR, *Ernst et al. v Belgium* (15 Jul. 2003).
318. ECtHR, *RTBF v Belgium* (29 Mar. 2011).
319. Cons., Judgment No. 195/2009, 3 Dec. 2009.
320. Cons., Judgment No. 161/2010, 22 Dec. 2010.

Act only complies with the freedom of expression insofar as it is proven that the offender had the intention to express inferiority and that his actions have indeed affected another person's dignity.[321]

The legislator is allowed to criminalise the spreading of messages with the aim of incitement to terrorist acts, but only insofar as the very nature of such messages involves a genuine risk of actually inciting others to commit terrorist acts.[322]

The legislator is also allowed to impose upon those applying for an asylum status or another residence permit the obligation to sign a declaration in which they accept the fundamental values and norms of the Belgian society.[323]

B. Freedom of Education

471. Ever since the creation of the Belgian State, freedom of education has been a contentious issue. The original text of Article 24 of the Constitution read as follows:

> Education is free; all preventive measures are forbidden; punishment of offences is regulated only by Act. Public education provided at the expense of the State is also regulated by statute.

This provision permitted the setting up of free – and in particular, Catholic – educational institutions, in addition to the official education system established by the State. And it has been very well used, so that, to this day, education, especially in Flanders, is organised to a large degree by free (Catholic) initiative. This was possible after several political confrontations (the 'School Issues' of 1878–1879 and of 1954–1959) had taken place, resulting in measures of 'pacification' under which the State agreed to subsidise free (Catholic) educational institutions, while itself retaining the right to set up its own education network. This pacification was laid down in the 'School Pact' and in the School Pact Act of 29 May 1959, which implemented the principle of putting the official networks (State, provinces, and municipalities) and the free-school networks on an equal footing with regard to subsidising their operations, staff salaries, and the building of schools, as well as the principle of neutrality of State-organised education. Only in this way could all parents enjoy the constitutionally guaranteed right to choose freely the education they wanted for their children.

472. When, in 1988, powers over education were almost entirely transferred to the Communities, fears of ending up in a minority position arose on both sides of

321. Cons., Judgment No. 72/2016, 25 May 2016.
322. Cons., Judgments No. 9/2015, 28 Jan. 2015; No. 31/2018, 15 Mar. 2018.
323. Cons., Judgment No. 126/2018, 4 Oct. 2018.

the language border. In Flanders, state schools were outnumbered, while in Wallonia, free schools formed the minority. To remove those fears, the essential principles of the School Pact were set out in Article 24 of the Constitution. Besides the freedom of organising education, Article 24 provides since 1 January 1989, *inter alia*:

> §1. …
> The Community guarantees a freedom of choice to parents.
> The Community organizes non-denominational education. Non-denominational includes, among other things, respect for the philosophical, ideological, or religious beliefs of parents and pupils.
> Schools set up by public authorities offer, until the end of compulsory education, a choice between instruction in one of the recognized religions and instruction in non-denominational ethics.
> §3. Everyone has the right to education, with respect for fundamental rights and freedoms. Access to education is free until the end of compulsory education.
> All pupils subject to compulsory education have the right at the Community's expense to moral or religious instruction.
> §4. All pupils or students, parents, staff and educational institutions are equal before federal or Community Acts. Federal Acts and Community Acts take account of objective differences, including the particular characteristics of each organizing jurisdiction, that justify any specially adapted treatment.

Moreover, the Constitutional Court was empowered to review compliance of legislation with Article 24 of the Constitution.

473. Although the Community must subsidise the free schools, freedom of education does not impede it from imposing minimum quality requirements and even making subsidies dependent on meeting these requirements.

In order to guarantee the quality of home education, the Flemish Community could therefore rightfully oblige the pupils receiving such education to take State exams, and force them into the ordinary schooling system if by the age of 15 they had not passed any of these exams.[324]

474. Furthermore, it should be pointed out that there is an essential difference between private and public educational institutions. While a private institution may be set up with a particular religious or philosophical orientation, public authorities must comply with principles governing the public service, in particular the principle of equality and the freedom of opinion.

According to the text of the Constitution, public schools can fulfil their obligations by offering until the end of the compulsory education period a choice between instruction in one of the recognised religions or in non-denominational ethics. The

324. Cons., Judgments No. 80/2014, 8 May 2014; No. 60/2015, 21 May 2015.

Constitutional Court, however, has held that this does not suffice to guarantee all philosophical points of view. It found that parents should also have the choice to exempt their children from receiving any religious or philosophical education at all.[325]

C. Freedom of Assembly and of Association

475. Article 26 of the Constitution guarantees the right to assemble, unarmed and peacefully. A prerequisite for this right, however, is that one must comply with the applicable, substantive laws in force regulating the exercise of this right. Nevertheless, these regulations may not subject the exercise of this right to prior authorisation. The guarantees apply only to meetings held in an enclosed space which is freely accessible by all. When assemblies are held in an enclosed space not able to be attended freely by everyone and which are of a private nature, a more robust protection applies: the inviolable privacy of one's home (Article 15 Constitution). Open-air meetings, on the other hand, remain fully subject to police regulations. For those gatherings, such as public demonstrations, not only regulatory, but also preventive measures may be imposed.

476. Article 27 of the Constitution guarantees the right of association which also implies the right of non-association[326] and the right to freely choose the association's internal organisation.[327] This right may not be subject to any preventive measures, but repressive and regulatory measures may be imposed. In Belgium, associations are numerous and play important roles. Commercial companies and philanthropic not-for-profit associations, both of which are legal persons, as well as political parties and trade unions without legal personality, all come under the purview of the right of association. Article 27 of the Constitution guarantees a typical civil right, and therefore possesses no standstill effect, not even when the right to collective negotiations by trade unions is concerned.[328] As Article 27 of the Constitution aims at promoting the establishment of private associations and the participation in its activities, its scope does not comprise municipalities and cities.[329]

477. The ECtHR has found the Belgian policy of state consultations with only a particular and limited number of employee organisations not incompatible with trade union freedoms.[330] It has also ruled that Article 11 EConvHR was not violated by the obligation imposed on all doctors to join the medical association which was

325. Cons., Judgments No. 34/2015, 12 Mar. 2015; No. 66/2016, 11 May 2016.
326. Cons., Judgment No. 130/2016, 13 Oct. 2016.
327. Cons., Judgment No. 151/2017, 21 Dec. 2017.
328. Cons., Judgment No. 107/2017, 28 Sep. 2017.
329. Cons., Judgment No. 73/2014, 8 May 2014.
330. ECtHR, *National Union of Belgian Police v Belgium* (27 Oct. 1975).

established by statute to exercise control over the practice of medicine, provided that medical practitioners were not prevented from establishing or from joining other professional associations.[331]

Seeing as trade union freedoms are discussed at length in the Belgium contribution to the *International Encyclopaedia for Labour Law and Industrial Relations*, we will confine ourselves here to the following two issues. First, trade union premiums, namely those contributions which, in the private as well as in the public sectors, are paid by employers to members of their staff affiliated with (certain) trade unions, are constitutionally permissible. The jurisprudence has held this practice to be constitutional insofar as there exist objective and reasonable grounds for granting those advantages (e.g., in order to maintain social peace), and if the advantages in question do not take on such dimensions that they would invade the free choice of the other workers.[332] Second, under international conventions (e.g., Article 8 ICESCR; Part II, Article 6 §4, and Part V, Article G Revised European Social Charter), national law may impose restrictions or limitations on the exercise of the right to strike for some categories of workers and employees, such as members of the armed forces or of the police, insofar as the restrictions are necessary in a democratic society for the protection of certain interests, such as the public interest and national security. Belgian legislation denies the army the right to strike and also imposes some restrictions on the right of the police to strike.

According to the Belgian Constitutional Court, an Act temporarily suspending the automatic indexation of wages for State budget reasons does not violate the right to collective negotiation over wages.[333]

Apart from the freedom to form trade unions, the freedom of association does not play an important role in the current constitutional caselaw. Recently, the Constitutional Court validated a Flemish Community Act forbidding the association of more than two local radio broadcasting stations, because such associations would impair the very concept of local radio.[334] It also accepted a Walloon Region Act requiring the management boards of retirement homes to contain at most a 2/3 – 1/3 gender balance.[335]

D. The Right to Address Petitions

478. The right to address petitions played an important role in the opposition to Willem I. Consequently, it was self-evident for the right to address petitions to public authorities, signed by one or more persons, to be recognised explicitly in the Belgian Constitution (Article 28). This right, however, has been restricted in two ways. Only 'prescribed authorities'[336] have the right to file petitions under a collective name (Article 28 paragraph 2). It is also forbidden to submit petitions in person to

331. ECtHR, *Le Compte, Van Leuven and De Meyere v Belgium* (23 Jun. 1981).
332. Cass., 27 Apr. 1981, *Pas*., 1981, I, 964.
333. Cons., Judgment No. 152/2016, 1 Dec. 2016.
334. Cons., Judgment No. 151/2017, 21 Dec. 2017.
335. Cons., Judgment No. 145/2015, 22 Oct. 2015.
336. Prescribed, that is, by the Constitution or by appropriate legislation.

the Houses of Parliament (Article 57 paragraph 1 Constitution). The House of Representatives has the right to refer the petitions addressed to it to the relevant Ministers, who must provide explanations as to the contents, whenever the House so requires (Article 57 paragraph 2).[337] Analogous provisions apply to the Parliaments of the Communities and the Regions.

IV. The Right to Respect for Private and Family Life

479. The Belgian Constitution did not contain a general provision on the right to respect for private and family life before 1994. Its 1831 version only guaranteed specific aspects of this right, such as the inviolability of private residence and the secrecy of the post. By constitutional amendment of 31 January 1994, a new Article 22 was inserted into the Constitution guaranteeing that 'everyone has the right to respect for his private life and family life, excepting the cases and under the conditions prescribed by Act'. The parliamentary *travaux* indicate that the aim of this provision was to provide the same content and interpretation as Article 8 EConvHR. Therefore, this constitutional provision allows the Constitutional Court to review all legislation against that convention provision, taking into account the relevant jurisprudence of the ECtHR. In recent years this right's importance has grown significantly in the Constitutional Court's caselaw.

There is, however, one important difference between Article 22 of the Constitution and Article 8 EConvHR: restricting this constitutional right requires a basis in formal legislation. A delegation to another organ is only allowed insofar as its phrasing is sufficiently clear and it concerns only the execution of measures whose essential elements have been regulated by Act. The Act itself must determine the hypotheses in which a restriction of the right to respect for private and family life is allowed.[338]

As far as the division of powers is concerned, Article 22 of the Constitution characterises guaranteeing the right to respect for private and family life as a parallel power. By contrast, restricting that right seems to be reserved to the federal legislator by the text of Article 22. Yet the Constitutional Court has qualified restricting that particular right as a limited concurrent power. That is, the federal legislator has jurisdiction to impose general restrictions on the right to respect for private and family life, whereas the Communities and the Regions may impose specific restrictions while respecting that federal framework.[339]

337. See also the Act of 2 May 2019, *Gazette,* 6 Jun. 2019. This Act provides for a right to be heard when such an address has sufficient support.
338. Cons., Judgment No. 77/2018, 21 Jun. 2018.
339. Cons., Judgment Nos 50 and 51/2003, 30 Apr. 2003.

A. The Right to Respect for Private Life

480. The right to respect for private life secures for the individual a sphere within which he can freely pursue the development and fulfilment of his personality. The elements making up the concept of 'private life' are developing and are highly personal. The scope of the private life of a politician or of a sports star, for instance, is not as extensive as an ordinary citizen's private life. In the broadest sense, the right to privacy comprises not only protections against acts such as being put under surveillance, monitoring operations, pestering, or against the disclosure of information subject to professional secrecy, but also against infringements of 'personality rights', such as the right to physical, psychological, and moral integrity of the body, and the protection of reputation and honour.

481. Article 22 of the Constitution grants every individual the right not to have his private life interfered with by the government, and imposes an obligation on all legislators to take sufficient measures to protect the private and family life from intrusions by others. According to the Constitutional Court, Article 22 of the Constitution and Article 8 EConvHR do not preclude investigative measures by the Public Prosecutors Office or by the intelligence services, if a clear and unambiguous legal basis delineating such measures is in place and if full judicial review of both the orders allowing the measures and their execution is guaranteed to the persons subjected to them.[340] The same conditions apply to access by the police to databases containing personal data, provided that, additionally, the legislator takes sufficient measures in order to avoid abuses of access.[341] Under these conditions, the Court has also allowed the exchange of personal data between certain Flemish civil servants in order to avoid domicile fraud.[342] Likewise, it has accepted that certain civil servants designated by the Minister may have access to criminal records in order to decide on licensing applications for private detectives[343], and that the tax administration may access banking information in cases of strongly suspected tax fraud.[344]

The Constitutional Court has condemned a systematic publication of every doping offence by professional athletes on a publicly accessible website, because such a measure overreaches any interest in effectively combatting doping. The data can be used by others for unrelated purposes long after the athlete's suspension has expired.[345]

Article 22 of the Constitution also applies to a person's decision whether or not to smoke cigarettes. But given the legislator's ample margin of appreciation, legislation is allowed to prohibit smoking inside prison walls, considering that inmates are allowed to smoke when walking in the prison's outdoor spaces.[346]

---

340. See, e.g., Cons., Judgments No. 202/2004, 21 Dec. 2004; No. 145/2011, 22 Sep. 2011; No. 174/2018, 6 Dec. 2018.
341. See, e.g., Cons., Judgments No. 108/2016, 14 Jul. 2016; No. 153/2018, 8 Nov. 2018.
342. See, e.g., Cons., Judgment No. 104/2018, 19 Jul. 2018.
343. See, e.g., Cons., Judgment No. 106/2011, 16 Jun. 2011.
344. See, e.g., Cons., Judgment No. 39/2013, 14 Mar. 2013.
345. See, e.g., Cons., Judgment No. 16/2005, 19 Jan. 2005.
346. See, e.g., Cons., Judgment No. 32/2015, 12 Mar. 2015.

482. Two more specific guarantees encompassed by Article 8 EConvHR were already protected by the Constitution since 1831. Article 15 of the Constitution stipulates that a private residence is inviolable. No search of a private residence may take place other than in the cases legislation stipulates and in the manner it prescribes. This means that a search warrant issued by a judge is needed to enter a private residence, unless the occupant agrees, or during the commission of an offence, or in case of an emergency. Like the European Court's caselaw concerning the 'home' in Article 8 EConvHR,[347] the term 'private residence' is interpreted very broadly. It includes each actual residence, as well as all garages, stables, gardens, and delimited property surrounding it. It can also involve company premises insofar as the activities there have a private character or inasmuch as private letters are being kept there.[348]

The right to inviolability of the residence being civil in nature, the procedural rights guaranteed by Article 6 §1 EConvHR must be respected in all cases involving an intrusion into one's premises. Any court order allowing a search of premises must therefore fall under the subsequent scrutiny of a judge. This does not mean, however, that the court order must be served in advance, as this might impair the very goal of the search.[349]

Article 15 of the Constitution does not preclude 'fiscal visitation' (an on-site tax audit): the tax administration's powers to access corporate premises and to review accounts, provided that formal legislation limits the visitation's goals, that the visitation takes place during office hours, that it is proportionate to the aim pursued, and that judicial review is subsequently available to the company concerned.[350]

483. The second specific guarantee already encompassed by the 1831 Constitution is the secrecy of the post, protected by Article 29. Although the text of this provision seems to exclude any limitation to that right, the Constitutional Court has ruled that limitations are possible if they are necessary in order to guarantee other fundamental rights, such as to punish crimes effectively, and if there is a proportional relationship between those limitations and the objective pursued.[351]

B. The Right to Respect for Family Life

484. Apart from private life, Article 22 of the Constitution and Article 8 EConvHR also mention family life. The ECtHR has ruled that Article 8 EConvHR applies to the 'family life' of an 'illegitimate' family as much as to that of a 'legitimate' family. In the Court's opinion, this implies the right to recognition of a legal relationship between members of a family and it includes at least the ties among near relatives, such as, for instance, those between grandparents and grandchildren, since

347. See, e.g., ECtHR, *Niemietz v Germany* (16 Dec. 1992); the trio of ECtHR, *Funke v France, Crémieux v France,* and *Miailhe v France* (No. 1) (25 Feb. 1993); and ECtHR, *Ernst v Belgium* (15 Jul. 2003).
348. Cass., 19 Feb. 2002, *P&B*, 2002, 210. See also Cons., Judgment No. 154/2007, 19 Dec. 2007.
349. Cons., Judgments No. 171/2008, 3 Dec. 2008; No. 132/2015, 1 Oct. 2015.
350. Cons., Judgment No. 116/2017, 12 Oct. 2017.
351. Cons., Judgment No. 202/2004, 21 Dec. 2004.

such relatives may play a considerable part in family life. In the Court's view, Article 8 EConvHR does not merely compel the State to abstain from interference in the exercise of the right to respect for family life. In addition to this primarily negative duty, there may be positive obligations inherent in an effective 'respect' for family life. According to the Court, this means that, when the State determines the regime applicable to certain family ties in its domestic legal system, such as those between an unmarried mother and her child, it must allow those concerned to lead a normal family life. The ECtHR found Belgian legislation in breach of Article 8 EConvHR inasmuch as the Act, in addition to the production of the birth certificate of an illegitimate child, set other conditions on the creation of a legal relationship between mother and child, such as formal recognition by the mother or a procedure for legitimising the child. And it was likewise held with respect to denying an illegitimate child 'adopted' by the mother a legal relationship with the mother's parents, as well as denying an illegitimate child rights equal to those of a legitimate child.[352]

485. This judgment of the ECtHR has had a great impact on Belgium, especially because it has sparked a discussion on the legal effect of the judgments of the European Court. Various Belgian courts have invoked the judgment rejecting any discrimination between children born in wedlock and those born out of wedlock, notably in the cases dealing with lineage, adoption, and the right of inheritance. The Court of Cassation, however, has held that Article 8 EConvHR was too vague to be self-executing as far as positive obligations on the part of the authorities were concerned. In the opinion of the Court of Cassation, any legislative initiative remained the discretion of Parliament.[353] Eventually change was effected by legislation on 31 March 1987, granting in principle equal rights to all children. The ECtHR and the Constitutional Court had rejected the opinion of the Court of Cassation, and had accepted the direct effect of Article 8 in the period between the judgments of the ECtHR and the 1987 Act.[354]

486. As the ECtHR has confirmed in a ruling against Belgium[355], public authorities must measure, when deciding on the deportation or expulsion of a foreign non-national whose family is settled in Belgium, the proportionality between the reasons for removal from the territory and the disruption to the family this may cause. Article 8 EConvHR would be violated if a seriously ill Georgian national, dependent on the care of his family members who are validly permanent residents, would be deported to Georgia without due consideration of his health by the Belgian authorities.[356]

On the other hand, Article 8 EConvHR does not comprise a right to be granted permission to reside permanently in the country, not even for minors in vulnerable

352. ECtHR, *Marckx v Belgium* (13 Jun. 1979).
353. Cass., 10 May 1985, *Pas.*, 1985, I, 1122.
354. ECtHR, *Vermeire v Belgium* (29 Nov. 1991), and Cons., Judgment No. 18/91, 4 Jul. 1991.
355. ECtHR, *Moustaquim v Belgium* (18 Feb. 1991).
356. ECtHR (GC), *Paposhvili v Belgium* (13 Dec. 2016).

positions. The Contracting States indeed remain free to control the access to and the stay in their territory of foreign nationals.[357]

487. According to the Constitutional Court, the legislator may set criteria for reuniting families within the framework determined by EU law providing the criteria are sufficiently clear and proportionate to the aim pursued. Setting a 'willingness to integrate' as a criterion is allowed, but a condition phrased as 'the applicant's criminal history' is insufficiently determined because it allows immigration officials to take into account all criminal convictions, regardless of their nature, impact, and punishment.[358]

C. The Rights of the Child

488. Belgium has ratified the UN Convention on the Rights of the Child adopted on 20 November 1989. On 23 March 2000, Article 22*bis* was inserted into the Constitution and stipulates, 'Every child has the right to respect for his moral, physical, mental and sexual integrity.' Its second paragraph, amended on 22 December 2008, provides, 'Every child has the right to express his opinion on all matters which concern him; this opinion is taken into account in accordance with his age and capacities.' It also provides that every child has the right to measures and services which advance his development, and that in every decision concerning the child, the child's interests should be the prime consideration. Federal, Community, and Region Acts guarantee the protection of these rights.

489. Prior to this last revision, the added value of Article 22*bis* was limited since it only provided rights which were already protected by other constitutional rights. The primacy of the child's interests has, however, rapidly become a key provision in the Constitutional Court's caselaw.

This provision has led the Constitutional Court to declare significant parts of the legislation on lineage unconstitutional. This legislation, reformed in 2006 in order to take into account previous judgments by the ECtHR and the Constitutional Court, often bars the search for the biological truth because of a child's living with its legal father, or because of rather short statutes of limitation. According to the Court, however, the interest of the child requiring an *in concreto* examination, such absolute limitations to lawsuits challenging legal fatherhood or vesting lineage from the biological father cannot be accepted.[359]

---

357. ECtHR, *Chbihi Loudoudi et al. v Belgium* (16 Dec. 2014).
358. Cons., Judgment No. 126/2018, 4 Oct. 2018.
359. See, e.g., Cons., Judgments No. 144/2010, 16 Dec. 2010; No. 20/2011, 3 Feb. 2011; No. 54/2011, 6 Apr. 2011; No. 96/2011, 31 May 2011; No. 122/2011, 7 Jul. 2011; No. 29/2013, 7 Mar. 2013; No. 96/2013, 9 Jul. 2013; No. 165/2013, 5 Dec. 2013; No. 118/2014, 17 Jul. 2014; No. 35/2015, 12 Mar. 2015; No. 102/2015, 2 Jul. 2015; No. 168/2015, 26 Nov. 2015; No. 18/2016, 3 Feb. 2016, and No. 3/2018, 18 Jan. 2018.

V. The Right to a Fair Trial

A. Sources

490. The Constitution contains a number of general guarantees concerning due process and the administration of justice. Pursuant to Article 13, no person may be denied appearing before a judge assigned to him by statute. According to Article 146, no tribunal or court may be established save by authority of an Act, and no extraordinary courts or commissions may be created. No prior authorisation is necessary to bring proceedings against civil servants with regard to their administrative actions (Article 31). Articles 144 and 145 guarantee access to a judge with a view to protecting civil rights and political rights. Public hearings (Article 148), the making public of judgments (Article 149), the reasoning of judgments (Article 149), and the appointment of judges for life (Article 152) are also guaranteed by the Constitution.

Article 6 EConvHR, which will be discussed below, also guarantees the due administration of justice but in a more exhaustive way. This article has become the EConvHR provision most invoked in Belgian courts. The Constitutional Court reads the substantive guarantees offered by Article 6 EConvHR into Article 13 of the Constitution, explaining that the right of access to a judge would be deprived of any use if that judge would not meet the due process standards.[360]

491. The Constitution also contains a number of specific guarantees as to the administration of criminal justice. Articles 12 and 14 entrench the principle *nullum crimen, nulla poena, sine lege*. As well, the Belgian Constitution expressly forbids two penalties dating back to the *ancien régime*: the general confiscation of property (Article 17) and 'civil death', by which someone was deemed deceased so as to impose the loss of legal recognition of status and capacity (Article 18). The death penalty was formally abolished in 2005 (Article 14*bis*).

The prohibition on the retroactive application of criminal law to the detriment of the accused is only provided for in Article 2 of the Criminal Code, but since Article 7 EConvHR, Article 15 ICCPR, and Article 49 EU Charter of Rights contain the same principle, every judge should refuse to apply any statutory provision violating this principle. The general principle that everyone charged with a criminal offence shall be presumed innocent until proven guilty according to law is guaranteed in Article 6 §2 EConvHR, Article 14 §2 ICCPR, and Article 48 §1 EU Charter of Rights. Article 6 §3 EConvHR and Article 14 §3 ICCPR provide a number of minimum guarantees for everyone charged with a criminal offence.[361] Belgian jurisprudence has long held that Article 6 §1 EConvHR and Article 14 §1 ICCPR were not applicable to the Committal and Bail Court because this Court only addresses the results of preliminary investigations without determining guilt and imposing sentences. After the ECtHR had ruled that Article 6 §1 may nonetheless play a role in

360. Cons., Judgments No. 195/2009, 3 Dec. 2009; No. 139/2012, 14 Nov. 2012; No. 148/2017, 21 Dec. 2017; No. 62/2018, 31 May 2018.
361. See also Art. 48(2) EU Charter of Rights.

the early stages of a criminal investigation because an initial breach of the guarantees laid down in that provision might in some cases jeopardise the fairness of the entire trial[362], the Constitutional Court and the Court of Cassation have adopted the same reasoning.[363] And this same rationale can be extended to the guarantees in Article 6 §3.

Finally, Articles 2–4 of the Seventh Protocol to the EConvHR and Articles 14 §§5–7 ICCPR contain guarantees for those convicted of a criminal offence, such as the principle of *non bis in idem* ('double jeopardy').

B. *Scope of the Guarantees*

492. The question as to which proceedings are subject to the requirements of a fair trial and due process has raised important controversies in Belgium, particularly as to the scope of the words 'in the determination of his civil rights and obligations' of Article 6 §1 EConvHR. This discussion is now largely outdated because the Constitutional Court firstly aligns its appreciation of the scope of Article 6 §1 EConvHR to ECtHR jurisprudence and, secondly, holds that even outwith the immediate scope of the Article, its substantive guarantees nevertheless apply as general principles of law. Therefore the Constitutional Court often confines itself to stating that it does not need to examine whether Article 6 §1 EConvHR applies, as it can apply the ECtHR's jurisprudence in any event.[364] Although the Court of Cassation used to be of the view that Article 6 §1 EConvHR did not apply to disciplinary proceedings, it now concurs with the view of the European Court.[365]

493. Administrative decisions should also comply with the general principles of law, such as the obligation to render a decision within a reasonable time, the rule of *non bis in idem*, and protections against any reasonable apprehension of bias.

C. *Substance of the Guarantees*

494. Article 6 §1 EConvHR provides a right of access to a court or tribunal which has 'full jurisdiction' to hear both facts and law and which, moreover, must meet certain requirements briefly identified below. By 'full jurisdiction', the ECtHR means that a court must be able to deal with all the questions of fact and of law, including proportionality. According to the Constitutional Court, this also implies that a judge must have the exact same jurisdiction as the administrative body to modulate, lower, or quash administrative fines.[366]

362. ECtHR, *Imbrioscia v Switzerland* (24 Nov. 1993).
363. Cons., Judgment No. 56/2002, 28 Mar. 2002; Cass., 24 Oct. 1997, *Arr. Cass.*, 1997, No. 1028.
364. See, e.g., Cons., Judgments No. 157/2009, 13 Oct. 2009; No. 155/2011, 13 Oct. 2011, and No. 53/2017, 11 May 2017. See also Cass., 23 May 1985, *Pas.*, 1985, I, 1194.
365. Cass., 14 Apr. 1983, *J.T.*, 1983, 607.
366. Established caselaw since Cons., Judgment No. 96/2002, 12 Jun. 2002.

The right of access to a judge implies that procedural rules may not be applied in an excessively formalistic manner. During the last decade, Belgium has been held in violation of the Article on four occasions for excessive formalism. In a 2009 case, the Council of State's Administrative Tribunal Division had declared a petition inadmissible solely because the facts of the case were not summarised in the application form, but in an annex to it.[367] A 2011 judgment criticised the Court of Cassation's finding of inadmissibility, based solely on the failure of applicants to mention in their appeal from an interlocutory order Article 584 Civil Procedure Code on interlocutory proceedings for urgent matters as a provision violated by the appellate court below. The ECtHR noted there that the 'cassation' appeal (i.e. final appeal only on questions of law) concerned the freedom of expression rather than the interlocutory procedure itself.[368] In a 2017 case, the Council of State's Administrative Tribunal Division declared a petition inadmissible solely because the petitioner had invoked the violation of only the specific norm applicable to the case at hand without also referring to the general norm to which the former gave a concrete expression.[369] And in a 2018 case the Council of State's Administrative Tribunal Division declared a petition inadmissible because the applicant had lost his standing in a case challenging the results of a comparative exam for promotion to a higher civil service ranking because the validity of the list of candidates had meanwhile expired. According to the ECtHR, the Council of State failed to take into account that the long duration of the applicant's case before the Tribunal had contributed directly to that situation.[370]

The most notable Constitutional Court case concerning the right of access to a judge involved the Criminal Assizes (trial by jury). Article 150 of the Constitution guarantees the right to be tried by a jury in all 'criminal' cases, meaning cases in which legislation prescribes lengthy terms of imprisonment. The legislator had undercut that right in statutory amendments allowing criminal cases to be tried by criminal court judges without jury where the Committal and Bail Court had established mitigating circumstances. The Constitutional Court noted that the legislator had not even guaranteed that the most severe crimes were to be tried by jury, while the sentences imposed by the judge-alone criminal courts did not differ significantly from those a jury could impose. As a result the Constitutional Court annulled these legislative reforms, which were aimed at reducing the number of costly and time-consuming Assizes cases, for violation of Articles 13 and 150 of the Constitution.[371]

In another case, the Constitutional Court decided that Article 144 of the Constitution and Article 6 §1 EConvHR did not preclude measures taken by a prison governor regarding civil rights (e.g. holding an inmate liable for damages for goods he destroys within the prison precincts) provided that the inmate subsequently has access to a judge with full jurisdiction.[372]

367. ECtHR, *L'Erablière v Belgium* (24 Feb. 2009).
368. ECtHR, *R.T.B.F. v Belgium* (29 Mar. 2011).
369. ECtHR, *Dakir v Belgium* (11 Jul. 2017).
370. ECtHR, *Ronald Vermeulen v Belgium* (17 Jul. 2018).
371. Cons., Judgment No. 148/2017, 21 Dec. 2017.
372. Cons., Judgment No. 20/2014, 29 Jan. 2014.

495. The guarantee of a fair trial notably implies that the litigating parties should enjoy 'equality of arms' (the opportunity for full answer and defence), and a right to full argument. The ECtHR has condemned Belgium for failing to allow a defendant to confront and examine a plaintiff claiming damages on all points of the claim,[373] and for permitting the Public Prosecutors Office to make submissions for rejecting an appeal before the Court of Cassation without the parties themselves being allowed to reply and further to participate in the deliberations of the Court.[374] Like the ECtHR,[375] the Court of Cassation examines whether the case on the whole has been dealt with fairly.

The equality of arms also implies that the legislator should not interfere in pending court cases by retroactively changing the applicable legislation or by retroactively validating an executive act which is claimed to have violated an Act. The Constitutional Court reviews such legislation against the same standard as the ECtHR, requiring 'exceptional circumstances or a pressing social need' in order to justify the interference.[376]

496. The right to full argument implies a right to be heard. According to Article 148 of the Constitution, court hearings are open to the public, unless such public access poses a danger to order or good behaviour, in which case the Court declares so by judgment. Pursuant to Article 149 of the Constitution, each judgment is supported by reasons and is made public in the manner prescribed by Act. For criminal cases, the verdict is pronounced in open court.

In Belgium, the jury used to answer the questions on guilt in criminal cases by a mere 'yes' or 'no'. The ECtHR found that that this did not allow the person convicted to a lengthy prison sentence to understand the reasons for his conviction.[377] The jury now has to provide its 'most important reasons' in support, as required by the Court of Cassation and pursuant to an Act of 21 December 2009[378] implementing that ECtHR decision.

The Constitutional Court has accepted that the President of the Chamber of the Council of State's Administrative Tribunal Division may declare a 'cassation' appeal (i.e. final appeal and only on questions of law) inadmissible without a court hearing, given the specific aims of a cassation appeal, and taking into account that the parties have already benefited from the court hearing before a lower administrative judge.[379]

The Constitutional Court has also accepted that the costs related to representation by counsel in litigation are not reimbursable in full by the losing party, but only a fixed sum calculated mainly according to the value of the claims in the lawsuit.[380]

---

373. ECtHR, *Bricmont v Belgium* (7 Jul. 1989).
374. ECtHR, *Borgers v Belgium* (30 Oct. 1991) overruling *Delcourt v Belgium* (17 Jan. 1970).
375. ECtHR, *Vidal v Belgium* (22 Apr. 1992).
376. Cons., Judgments No. 131/2010, 18 Nov. 2010; No. 114/2013, 31 Jul. 2013; No. 48/2016, 24 Mar. 2016; No. 51/2018, 26 Apr. 2018.
377. ECtHR, *Taxquet v Belgium* (13 Jan. 2009) and confirmed by the Grand Chamber on 16 Nov. 2010. See also ECtHR (GC), *Lhermitte v Belgium* (21 Nov. 2016).
378. *Gazette,* 11 Jan. 2010.
379. Cons., Judgment No. 1/2009, 8 Jan. 2009.
380. Cons., Judgment No. 182/2008, 18 Dec. 2008.

But the obligation to pay such a sum must be reciprocal: if a party has the right to claim fixed costs upon winning a case, it is also liable to pay that when it loses, regardless whether the parties are private or public.[381]

497. The right to be heard also implies the right to have one's case argued by a lawyer. The ECtHR condemned the Belgian State for a violation of this right because the Belgian legislation at the time did not allow a lawyer to plead in criminal cases when the accused was not present.[382] A 2003 statute responded to that judgment by offering the accused the choice to appear in personam or to be represented by a lawyer (Article 185 Criminal Procedure Code). In a subsequent judgment, the ECtHR ruled that, although the accused's presence is important for finding the truth, the right to be heard is met if an accused convicted in absentia is later granted the chance to appear before and be heard by a court. Belgium was nevertheless found to be in breach because the procedures to apply for this rehearing were excessively formalistic.[383] The Constitutional Court now applies this jurisprudence by imposing an obligation to notify both a person placed under legal custody and his guardian of the judgment rendered in absentia against that person.[384]

Belgium has been held in breach by the ECtHR because a murder suspect transferred from France was questioned without first being able to speak with or be assisted by a lawyer and without being informed of his right to remain silent. In those circumstances, he gave investigators substantial information which proved to be contradictory to his later defence and played a significant role in his conviction.[385]

498. Judicial independence, which implies that a court must found its decision on its own opinion as to the facts and the law without any external pressure, is guaranteed for Belgian courts and tribunals by the appointment of judges for life (Article 152 Constitution). The ECtHR has raised no objection to the presence of members of a professional body on disciplinary tribunals, as long as they were not subject to any authority other than having to account only to their own conscience.[386]

499. As to the guarantee of impartiality, the ECtHR does not confine itself to a purely subjective test. It also takes account of considerations relating to the functions exercised, and to internal organisation (the objective approach). In this regard, even appearances may be important, as in the words of the maxim, 'Justice must not only be done, it must also be seen to be done.' If legitimate doubts arise concerning the impartiality, the judge must withdraw from the case. On the basis of this 'objective approach', the ECtHR has ruled that the impartiality requirement is violated if the president of a tribunal had already been involved in an earlier stage of the case as a public prosecutor[387], or if one of the judges had already acted as an

381. Cons., Judgment Nos 68-70/2015, 21 May 2015.
382. ECtHR, *Van Geyseghem v Belgium* (21 Jan. 1999).
383. ECtHR, *Da Luz Domingues Ferreira v Belgium* (24 May 2007).
384. Cons., Judgment No. 134/2018, 11 Oct. 2018.
385. ECtHR (GC), *Beuze v Belgium* (9 Nov. 2018).
386. ECtHR, *Le Compte, Van Leuven and De Meyere v Belgium* (23 Jun. 1981).
387. ECtHR, *Piersack v Belgium* (1 Oct. 1982).

examining magistrate.[388] The Court of Cassation went further in applying the aforementioned principles to the case of a judge who had previously acted as a member of the Committal and Bail Court in the same case.[389] The ECtHR did not object to the presence of former parliamentarians on the Belgian Constitutional Court, finding no grounds to doubt the Court's impartiality in politically sensitive cases.[390]

While the judge's subjective partiality may not be invoked for the first time before the Court of Cassation, objective impartiality's *ordre public* character implies that this part of the impartiality requirement can be invoked for the first time before the Court of Cassation.

When a party before the Constitutional Court seeks to disqualify one of its judges hearing a case, the Court applies the ECtHR's criteria and at the same time takes account of the specific mission of constitutional justice, namely to review legislation as against the Constitution instead of deciding the particular claims of citizens. Hence, the mere fact that a judge works at the same university as one of the lawyers, that his political affiliation is well known, that he is a freemason, or that he has advocated in his academic capacity certain points of view, does not suffice to cast legitimate doubts as to impartiality.[391]

500. Article 6 §1 EConvHR puts the High Contracting Parties under the structural obligation to organise their legal systems in such a manner that the requirement of rendering judgments within a reasonable time is met. Like the ECtHR, the Court of Cassation does not judge 'reasonable time' in the abstract, but takes into account the specific circumstances of the case, such as its nature and complexity, the conduct of the applicant and of the competent authorities, and, in civil cases, the importance of the case for the applicant.[392] In Belgium, complying with the 'reasonable time' requirement is a considerable problem for the Court of Appeal in Brussels[393] and it used to be a problem for the Council of State.[394]

Since its *Kudla* judgment[395], the ECtHR combines the reasonable time requirement with Article 13 EConvHR, obliging the Contracting Parties to provide for effective internal remedies able to compel the speeding up of those proceedings where the reasonable time requirement has been breached and to remedy the damages incurred by the delays. In criminal cases, Article 136*bis* of the Criminal Procedure Code obliges the Public Prosecutors Office to report all cases in which the investigation took more than one year. Since 1998, the suspect and the victim may address a complaint to the Committal and Bail Court if the investigation takes longer than one year. The ECtHR found that this procedure was not sufficiently

388. ECtHR, *De Cubber v Belgium* (26 Oct. 1984).
389. Cass., 29 May 1985, *Pas.*, 1985, I, 1220.
390. ECtHR (dec.), *Vergauwen v Belgium* (10 Apr. 2012).
391. Cons., Judgment No. 157/2009, 13 Oct. 2009.
392. Cass., 4 Oct. 1978, *Pas.*, 1979, I, 153.
393. For example (among many others), ECtHR, *Boca v Belgium* (15 Nov. 2002); *Nelissenne v Belgium* (23 Oct. 2003); *Lenaerts v Belgium* (11 Mar. 2004); *De Staerke v Belgium* (28 Apr. 2005); *Mariën v Belgium* (3 Nov. 2005) and *Hamer v Belgium* (27 Nov. 2007).
394. See, *inter alia*, ECtHR, *Conka v Belgium* (5 Feb. 2002); *Enterprises Robert Delbrassine v Belgium* (1 Jul. 2004) and *Defalque v Belgium* (20 Apr. 2006).
395. ECtHR, *Kudla v Poland* (6 Oct. 2000).

effective, since investigating magistrates refused to apply it in practice.[396] Also in criminal cases, since 2000 Article 21*ter* of the Preliminaries Section of the Criminal Procedure Code offers a court the option to take into account a breach of the reasonable time requirement by imposing a sentence below the legal minimum sentence, or even by a mere declaration of guilt without imposing any sentence. Finally, a claim for damages against the State is possible where the State has failed to organise the legal system in such a manner that the courts render their judgments within a reasonable time.[397] The ECtHR has held that this claim for damages before a Belgian civil judge is an effective remedy to be exhausted in the sense of Article 35 EConvHR.[398] But because the Belgian government could show no demonstrable improvement or correction to the situation, the ECtHR further held that such claims for compensatory damages could no longer be regarded as an effective remedy (*in casu* to complain about the length of the judicial investigation stage in criminal proceedings) such that compensation claims arising out of criminal proceedings need not be initiated before the Belgian courts first before making their way to the ECtHR.[399]

501. Like the Belgian courts, the ECtHR considers publicity as a means of guaranteeing a fair trial. In the above-mentioned *Le Compte* case, the European Court held that publicity may be dispensed with before disciplinary tribunals, but only if it is unequivocally waived by the accused and if the lack of publicity does not conflict with any important public interest.

It should be noted that, as far as the ordinary law courts are concerned, Articles 148 and 149 of the Constitution impose a broader obligation of publicity than does Article 6 §1 EConvHR, and should accordingly be applied whenever this is to the advantage of the interested party.

502. Belgium has also been condemned by the ECtHR because of a violation of the right to be presumed innocent, guaranteed by Article 6 §2 EConvHR. An inspector who had found irregularities in public procurements immediately concluded in his reports they were due to criminal acts committed by the applicant, yet without any subsequent examination of the case from a neutral point of view. The criminal courts did not redress that violation, having merely noted that the applicant's possible criminal liability expired under the statutory limitations period without further assessing his guilt or innocence.[400]

396. ECtHR, *Stratégies et Communications and Dumoulin v Belgium* (15 Jul. 2002); *De Clerck v Belgium* (25 Sep. 2007); *Beheyt v Belgium* (13 May 2008); *Wauters and Schollaert v Belgium* (13 May 2008).
397. Cass., 28 Sep. 2006 (*Ferrara Jung*), *J.T.*, 2006, 594.
398. ECtHR, *Depauw v Belgium* (15 May 2007); *Nagler and Nalimo v Belgium* (17 Jul. 2007); *Jouan v Belgium* (12 Feb. 2008) and *Poncelet v Belgium* (30 Mar. 2010).
399. ECtHR, *Panju v Belgium* (28 Oct. 2014).
400. ECtHR, *Poncelet v Belgium* (30 Mar. 2010).

VI. Peaceful Enjoyment of Property

503. Article 16 of the Constitution reads as follows, 'No one can have his property expropriated other than for the public good, in the cases and in the manner prescribed by legislation and with fair compensation paid in advance.'

The National Congress expressed five guarantees for protecting the citizens against an arbitrary deprivation of property by the public authorities.

(i) Deprivation of property is only possible 'in the public interest', with a view to enlarging or to improving the public domain of the public authorities. Explicit legal authorisation is required for expropriation by private persons. Judges examine whether a compulsory purchase decision meets the requirement of 'public interest'.

(ii) Deprivation of property is only possible 'in the cases laid down by legislation'. The federal Parliament has authorised the King to decide on expropriations under certain conditions. The governments of the Communities and the Regions possess the same power within their jurisdiction (Article 79 Special Majority Act on Institutional Reform) and since the 2014 Sixth State Reform they also have the power to adopt an expropriation procedure of their own. Within the scope of their jurisdiction, they may also empower subordinate authorities, such as municipalities and provinces, to proceed with an expropriation.

(iii) Deprivation of property should take place 'in the manner prescribed by legislation'. Unless there is an amicable settlement, a judge always intervenes.

(iv) There must be 'just compensation' indemnifying the owner completely, allowing him at least to acquire another property of the same value.

(v) That compensation must be made 'in advance'. Only after payment of compensation by the public authorities may they take possession of the property.

504. The Constitution does not encompass a general guarantee of the peaceful enjoyment of property. The scope of Article 16 of the Constitution is limited to expropriations. Moreover, the only constitutional provision on property protection is its Article 17 which forbids the general confiscation of property. Nevertheless, the Constitutional Court's caselaw has extended the scope of the constitutional protections in three regards.

First, following the ECtHR's caselaw[401], the Constitutional Court has accepted that certain measures not amounting to formal expropriations are of such a far-reaching nature that they deprive title to property of its very essence and should therefore be considered de facto expropriations. Article 16 of the Constitution applies to such measures, so that full compensation and an authorisation in formal legislation are required.[402]

401. ECtHR, *Sporrong and Lönnroth v Sweden* (23 Sep. 1982); *Papamichalopoulos et al. v Greece* (24 Jun. 1993).

402. Cons., Judgments No. 9/97, 5 Mar. 1997; No. 115/2004, 30 Jun. 2004; No. 107/2005, 22 Jun. 2005.

Second, the Court has accepted that Article 16 of the Constitution and Article 1 of the First Protocol to the EConvHR are analogous provisions.[403] This does not mean that full compensation is required for measures not amounting to a formal or de facto expropriation.[404] The analogy mainly allows the Constitutional Court to review legislation imposing other restrictions on the peaceful enjoyment of property against the so-called 'third rule' in Article 1 of the First Protocol to the EConvHR without referring to Articles 10 and 11 of the Constitution. This review comes down to a proportionality test, in which the Court examines whether the measures concerned strike a fair balance between the general interest and the right to peaceful enjoyment of property, taking into account the large margin of appreciation allowed the legislator and the terms of compensation offered to the owner. In most cases, the Constitutional Court has accepted restrictions on the right to peaceful enjoyment of property, but in recent years it has found measures to be in breach. For instance it annulled a Flemish Region Act obliging landowners to reserve for social housing up to 20% of housing plots or the houses developed on them. As the owners were not compensated for this burden, the 'third rule' of Article 1 of the First Protocol to the EConvHR was held to have been violated.[405]

Third, in the absence of a written constitutional provision guaranteeing the right to peaceful enjoyment of property, the Constitutional Court and the Court of Cassation refer to the unwritten constitutional principle of equal distribution of public burdens. This principle holds that a government may not impose burdens greater than those which a person ordinarily bears in the public interest without fair compensation. Both Courts explain that the negative consequences of legitimate public policy in excess of its normal social and commercial impact should not be borne by the narrow group of persons caught thereby, but that those burdens should be distributed over the community as a whole. According to the Court of Cassation, police officers carrying out a search warrant in connection with drug-related crimes are allowed to break down apartment doors in order to gain access, but the apartment owner who has nothing to do with that crime should be compensated for the damage thus caused.[406] According to the Constitutional Court, a Flemish Region Act may put in place a legal framework for heritage preservation even if the measures to be taken may involve severe restrictions on certain owners in their free enjoyment of their property. Nevertheless, the Court makes the constitutionality of that legal framework conditional upon a judge having jurisdiction to examine *in concreto* whether the principle of equal distribution of public burdens warrants financial compensation.[407]

403. Cons., Judgments No. 32/2010, 30 Mar. 2010; No. 71/2012, 31 May 2012.
404. Cons., Judgments No. 74/2013, 30 May 2013; No. 98/2015, 25 June 2015.
405. Cons., Judgment No. 145/2013, 7 Nov. 2013.
406. Cass., 24 Jun. 2010, *R.W.* 2010–2011, 1227.
407. Cons., Judgment No. 132/2015, 1 Oct. 2015.

§3. Social, Economic and Cultural Rights

505. Socio-economic fundamental rights, being that set of rights by which each individual may attain complete personal and social development, impose on the authorities a positive obligation to act, and grant citizens the right to demand action from the authorities.

Belgium is party to a number of international human rights conventions which guarantee socio-economic rights, in particular the Revised European Social Charter and the ICESCR. In general, no self-executing effect is attributed to those instruments in Belgian law: they only possess a standstill effect, namely a prohibition on the legislator from enacting legislation which goes significantly below the level of protection offered by the current legislation, without compelling reasons related to the general interest.[408] Hence the Constitutional Court applies the same criteria as for Article 23 of the Constitution.

506. Only in 1994 were socio-economic rights inserted in the Belgian Constitution. Article 23 reads as follows:

> Everyone has the right to lead a life in dignity.
> To that end, federal, Community, and Region Acts guarantee economic, social and cultural rights, taking into account corresponding duties, for which those Acts prescribe the conditions for the their exercise.
> These rights include, in particular:
>
> 1 the right to work and to the free choice of an occupation within the framework of a general employment policy that, among other things, is aimed at guaranteeing a level of employment as high and as stable as possible; the right to fair terms of employment and fair wages, as well as the right to information, consultation, and collective bargaining;
> 2 the right to social security, to health protection, and to social, medical, and legal aid;
> 3 the right to decent accommodation;
> 4 the right to the protection of a healthy environment;
> 5 the right to cultural and social development;
> 6 the right to a child allowance.[409]

It should be noted that the enumeration of some socio-economic rights in the third paragraph of Article 23 should not be read as an exhaustive list.

During the parliamentary debate leading up to its adoption, it was often repeated that Article 23 would not possess any direct effect, but that it did impose a standstill obligation on the relevant governments. The Administrative Tribunal Division of the Council of State followed this, but added that it should not be seen as an absolute

---

408. Cons., Judgment No. 85/2017, 16 Jul. 2017.
409. Added by the 2014 Sixth State Reform.

obligation: 'compelling reasons' may force a legislature to go below the level of protection offered when Article 23 entered into force.[410]

In the past, the Constitutional Court has been reluctant in accepting this standstill effect. Nowadays, its jurisprudence has become more consistent with it. The Court accepts that all rights mentioned in the third paragraph of Article 23, as well as the overarching right to lead a life in dignity mentioned in its first paragraph, possess *standstill* effect.[411] This means that the competent legislator may not significantly reduce the level of protection offered by current legislation without compelling reasons related to the general interest. On the other hand, Article 23 of the Constitution does not intend to induce passivity in citizens: rights holders also have obligations, such as the duty to co-operate in the social and economic advancement of society. The legislator may therefore impose obligations on the beneficiaries of the social rights enshrined in Article 23 of the Constitution, and even make access to these rights conditional upon fulfilment of those obligations.

Given the ample margin of appreciation granted to the legislator, the Constitutional Court usually decides that even a significant reduction in the level of protection meets the standards of Article 23 of the Constitution. For example, a temporary ban on the automatic indexation of all wages in order to improve the general employment rate passes constitutional muster.[412]

Article 23 of the Constitution also encompasses a legality principle, but according to the Constitutional Court, its threshold is low. The legislator is not itself even required to regulate all essential elements of the measure reducing the level of protection: it can confine itself to defining the subject matter of the measures to be taken while delegating their implementation to the Executive Branch.[413]

Selected Further Reading[414]

Alen, A. 'Kanttekeningen bij de samenwerking tussen de hogere rechtscolleges inzake mensenrechten'. In *Liberae Cogitationes. Liber amicorum Marc Bossuyt* edited by A. Alen, V. Joosten, R. Leysen & W. Verrijdt (Intersentia, 2013) 7–32.

Alen, A., S. Lambrecht & W. Verrijdt. 'Belgique'. In *Traité des rapports entre ordres juridiques* edited by B. Bonnet (LGDJ, 2016) 1393–1418.

Alen, A. & W. Verrijdt. 'The Dialogue Between the European Court of Human Rights and Domestic Constitutional Courts – The Belgian Example'. In *Liber Amicorum Paul Lemmens* edited by K. Lemmens, S. Parmentier & L. Reyntjens (Intersentia, 2019) 155–202.

Alen, A. & W. Verrijdt. 'The Influence of the Belgian Constitutional Court on the Case-Law of the European Court of Human Rights and the European Court of Justice'. In *The Role of Constitutional Courts in the Globalised World of the 21st Century* (Constitutional Court of the Republic of Latvia, 2019) 75–116.

410. Council of State, Administrative Tribunal Division, Judgment No. 80.018, 29 Apr. 1999 (*Jacobs*).
411. Cons., Judgment No. 67/2015, 21 May 2015. By contrast, the other human rights provisions in the Belgian Constitution lack standstill effect, seeing as they have direct effect: Cons., Judgments No. 18/2018, 22 Feb. 2018; No. 62/2018, 31 May 2018.
412. Cons., Judgment No. 130/2016, 13 Oct. 2016.
413. Cons., Judgment No. 86/2018, 5 July 2018.
414. See also the Selected Bibliography.

De Schutter, O. & S. Van Drooghenbroeck. *Droit international des droits de l'homme devant le juge national* (Larcier, 1999).

Lambrecht, S. 'The Attitude of Four Supreme Courts towards European Court of Human Rights: Strasbourg has Spoken...'. In *The Judge in International and European Law* edited by S. Besson & A. Ziegler (LGDJ, 2013).

Lambrecht, S. 'Belgium: The EU Charter in a Tradition of Openness'. In *The EU Charter of Fundamental Rights: Ten Years On* edited by M. Bobek & J. Prassl (Hart Publishing, 2020).

Schaiko, G., P. Lemmens & K. Lemmens. 'Belgium'. In *Implementation of the European Convention on Human Rights and of the Judgments of the ECtHR in National Case-Law. A Comparative Analysis* edited by J. Gerards & J. Fleuren (Intersentia, 2014) 95–143.

Vande Lanotte, J. & Y. Haeck (eds). *Handboek EVRM. Algemene beginselen. Artikelsgewijze commentaar* (Intersentia, 2004–2005) 3 vols.

Van Dijk, P., F. Van Hoof, A. Van Rijn & L. Zwaak (eds). *Theory and Practice of the European Convention on Human Rights* (5th) (Intersentia, 2018).

Velu, J. & R. Ergec. *Convention européenne des droits de l'homme* (2nd) (Bruylant, 2014).

Verdussen, M. & N. Bonbled (eds). *Les droits constitutionnels en Belgique* (Bruylant, 2011) 2 vols.

Chapter 3. Constitutional Safeguards for Specific Groups and Minorities

507. The Constitution of 1831 reflected the two divisions in Belgian society. In proclaiming the freedom of language use in Belgium, the Constitution reflected the linguistic heterogeneity of the population, but, as was already pointed out above, the National Congress had no intention of treating the different languages equally. Given the historical struggles between Catholics and secular interests, the original Constitution provided for the freedom of religion, and an obligation to fund out of the State budget the salaries and pensions of clerics.[415]

Throughout Belgian history, protections were established in the fields of language (§1) and of opinion and belief (§2), concerning both procedures for 'conflict resolution' and protective measures *sensu stricto*. More recently, Belgium has implemented legislation on non-discrimination, gender equality, and the elimination of racism (§3).

§1. Language Groups

508. It should be taken into account that throughout Belgium's history, the French-speaking population, while being a numerical minority, have nevertheless held a politically predominant position. Further, it should be noted that although the ratio of Dutch-speaking to French-speaking inhabitants is generally about 60% to 40%, it is the inverse in Brussels being 80% to 20% in favour of the French-speaking group. In Belgium, there is also a real language minority, namely the German-speaking population.

When Belgium was created, the Constitution stipulated – and it still does – that the use of languages spoken in Belgium is free and that it cannot be regulated except by legislation, and only for the acts of public authorities and for judicial matters. Theoretically, conditions did not look bad for Dutch-speaking Belgians. The Constitution guaranteed language freedom and it stipulated that 'all Belgians are equal before the law'. In practice, however, as we have pointed out earlier, the new administrative authority spoke French exclusively. When citizens tried to use Dutch with the administration or before the courts, their claims were countered by the theory that officials and magistrates had the constitutional right to use French exclusively. Thus a constitutional right was in practice used to legitimate a denial of rights to Dutch-speakers.

509. This language issue became the prime objective in the Flemish struggle for equal rights. Notwithstanding a series of unsatisfactory reforms in the 1880s and the 1920s, the foundations of the present language regulation in Belgium go back to a series of Acts in the 1930s. Pursuant to these Acts, the Dutch language acquired a status in law equal to French in matters of education, public service, administration

415. See below Pt. V. Ch. 4.

of justice, and the armed forces. With respect to those matters, the new legal framework as to the use of languages established unilingual regions, by dividing Belgium into three official unilingual regions along the lines of the principle *cuius regio eius lingua*. In these regions the language of the region is used exclusively between citizens and the regional and local authorities, the courts, and the schools of that region. The Brussels-Capital region and the national civil service became bilingual.

This legislation implied the definite failure of complete bilingualism and French unilingualism. But since the social and economic predominance of the Brussels francophone establishment subsisted, the application of the 1930s language-use Acts was put back for another generation. French-speaking supremacy in public life remained virtually unaffected.

The 1960s language-use Acts established the language boundary and adjusted the provincial and municipal boundaries to coincide with it. Belgium now applies regional unilingualism, albeit qualified in certain instances. The legislative creation of a language boundary allowed the Dutch language region to become a linguistically secure area. The Flemish felt they needed this protection because a French-speaking individual spoke a more dominant language and, in general, would not easily integrate into a Dutch-speaking environment, resulting in an ongoing 'Frenchification' of the Flemish region close to Brussels due to the 'urban sprawl' of city-dwellers moving to the periphery (the Brussels 'oil stain').

510. In 1970, the territorial division of Belgium into four language regions was enshrined in Article 4 of the Constitution, thus confirming the principle of territorial linguistic homogeneity laid down in previous legislation. The constitutional recognition of the language regions goes beyond a mere geographical classification. It constitutes a safeguard for the language of the unilingual region giving it precedence over other languages. Article 4 of the Constitution thus limits the free use of languages and constitutes a restraint on the jurisdiction of both federal and Community legislators. For example, a Community Parliament may not regulate the use of languages in administrative matters so as to reinstate bilingualism in its civil service.

The constitutional amendments of 1970 were the result of a sense of discrimination felt by both Walloons and Flemings. Walloons feared the consequences of their demographic inferiority. In the past, French-speakers held power in Belgium, so naturally they tried to maintain the status quo. Flemings wanted to take into their own hands their cultural and educational institutions in the Dutch language region and the bilingual Brussels-Capital region. The 1970 constitutional amendments protected French-speakers from the Flemish majority and was the starting point for the reforms leading to a federal State based on the territoriality principle.

As a result language groups in Belgium are protected by (a) checks and balances in the State organisation, (b) territorial autonomy of the Communities and the Regions, and (c) language legislation.

I. Checks and Balances

511. As already noted, important safeguards were provided in the national decision-making process in order to allay Walloon fears of ending up in a permanent minority position. Article 99, paragraph 2 of the Constitution imposes language parity in the composition of the federal Cabinet. Article 43 of the Constitution prescribes the division of Parliament into Dutch and French language groups, which is required for passing Special Majority Acts. The Constitution requires Special Majority Acts for those issues, which are sensitive to the language groups, such as State reform, and the language-use regimes in certain municipalities. In addition, if a language group considers its interests to be seriously prejudiced by a Bill introduced into Parliament, it may initiate the 'alarm-bell procedure' provided by Article 54 of the Constitution.

512. Article 32 of the Act on Institutional Reform of 9 August 1980 creates a procedure in case conflicts of interest arise out of Bills tabled in the other legislatures. These provisions may obviously be used to protect several kinds of interest, for example interests of a linguistic nature. Pursuant to this procedure, a House of Parliament, or a Parliament of the Communities or the Regions may move for the suspension of the Bill. This motion must be carried by three quarters of the votes cast. In that case, the parliamentary proceedings are immediately suspended for a period of sixty days, during which consultations take place. If no solution is reached during that period, the matter is referred to the Senate which must submit within thirty days its recommendation and reasons therefore to the Intergovernmental Consultation Committee. This body in turn has another thirty days to reach a consensus on a final decision. If the motion is initiated by one of the Houses of Parliament, there will be no further intervention of the Senate. The federal government and the governments of the Communities and the Regions may also submit conflicts of interest to the Intergovernmental Consultation Committee with regard to government decisions.

513. In the bilingual Brussels-Capital region, the balance between the Dutch-speaking and the French-speaking part of the population is the opposite of the nationwide situation. The various safeguards to protect the Dutch-speaking minority in Brussels have been outlined above, namely the division of the Brussels-Capital Region Parliament into language groups, the 'alarm-bell procedure', language parity within the government of the Brussels-Capital Region, and the Community Commissions.[416] Consequently, the protective measures are similar to those granted to the French-speaking minority at the federal level.

In the bilingual Brussels-Capital region, the federal legislature retains the power to regulate the use of languages. Some measures guarantee minimum representation of the Dutch-speaking residents of the bilingual Brussels-Capital region at the municipal level, and encourage the election of at least one Dutch-speaking councillor to every Municipal Executive.

416. See Pt. III. Ch. 2. §7. 'Brussels Institutions'.

There is no German language group in the House of Representatives, but the Parliament of the German Community elects one senator among its members.

II. Territorial Autonomy

514. As a result of the process of reorganising the State begun by the 1970 constitutional amendments, the Flemish, the French, and the German Communities were granted their own parliaments, their own governments, and their own administration, with jurisdiction in such matters as culture and education, in the Dutch, the French, and the German language regions respectively, as well as in the bilingual Brussels-Capital region (for only the Flemish and the French Communities). As Flanders obtained more autonomy for cultural and educational matters, it was able to develop the Dutch language and culture in its own secure area. In the bilingual Brussels-Capital region, the French Community became competent for matters regarding French language schools and cultural institutions, and the Flemish Community, for that regarding Dutch language schools and cultural institutions.

515. Articles 129 and 130 §1 5° of the Constitution have implicitly amended Article 30, granting the Flemish Community, the French Community, and the German Community the power to regulate the use of languages pertaining to education and – as far as the Flemish and the French Communities are concerned – to certain aspects of the civil service and labour relations. In conjunction with Article 30, and in view of the territorial jurisdiction of the Communities, this implies:

(i) that the Flemish Community and the French Community are entitled to regulate the use of languages in administrative matters, in education, and in employment relations within their territory, apart from the municipalities with special language arrangements;
(ii) that the German Community is entitled to regulate the use of languages in education within its territory;
(iii) that the federal legislator retains the power to regulate the use of languages in administrative matters, in education, and in labour relations for the bilingual Brussels-Capital region, and for the municipalities with special language arrangements;
(iv) that the federal legislator retains the power to regulate the use of languages in administrative matters and in labour relations within the German language region, and
(v) that, within constitutional limits, the federal legislator also retains the power to regulate the use of languages for judicial matters and regarding public authorities, which are not of an administrative nature (e.g., the use of languages in legislative proceedings and in the army).

516. The German-speaking minority has been constitutionally recognised as a German language region (Article 4 Constitution) and as a German Community (Article 2 Constitution). The Act on German Community Institutional Reform of 31 December 1983 constituted another step towards putting the German Community on an equal footing with the other two Communities. There are still some differences left, nonetheless. For example, the German Community is denied the right of regulating the use of languages in administrative matters and in labour relations.

III. Official Languages Legislation

A. *Introduction*

517. Outlined below is the legislation governing the use of languages in Belgium. Those Acts have the character of *ordre public*. It should be pointed out that this official language legislation concerns two rights: the right of a citizen to speak his own language and to be assisted in his language – a right generally interpreted on the basis of the territoriality principle, and the right of a language minority to fair access to public services, guaranteed through job quota rules.

518. The ECtHR has ruled that the principle of territoriality, on which Belgian language legislation is based, is an objective factor of general concern, such that any difference in treatment arising out of it is not considered an unlawful discrimination.[417] In connection with the same principle of territoriality, which upholds the general institutional structure of the Belgian State, the Court has also held that the parliamentary election system which entails the need for language minorities to cast their votes for persons capable of and ready to use the language of their region does not necessarily constitute a threat to the interests of those minorities, particularly not where the political and legal system provides multiple guarantees, as is the case in Belgium.[418]

B. *The Use of Languages in Administrative Matters*

519. The legislation governing the use of languages in administrative matters has been consolidated by Royal Decree of 18 July 1966. It embodies the territoriality principle: the official language of the region is the official language in administrative matters. For all public officials dealing with local matters, exclusive use of the official language of the region is compulsory in those dealings and in other matters. This requirement applies both to official documents and to official acts. To be qualified for a job or for a promotion, a civil servant must be proficient in the official language of that language region.

520. This linguistic constraint is mitigated for tourist centres and for certain municipalities with special language arrangements. As all those municipalities belong to a unilingual language region, they have to use the official language of that region in their internal documents and in their dealings with other public services. They are allowed, however, to use the language of the protected minority in their

417. ECtHR, *Belgian Linguistic Case* (23 Jul. 1968).
418. ECtHR, *Mathieu–Mohin and Clerfayt v Belgium* (2 Mar. 1987).

dealings with the public. In those cases, documents may or must be drafted in both the language of the region and in that of the protected minority or, in the case of a tourist centre, in at least three languages. Public authorities must address citizens in the language chosen by the latter. Those citizens have 'language facilities' to that effect, and the municipalities concerned are known as the 'municipalities with special language arrangements'. Those municipalities are the six Dutch-speaking (Bever, Herstappe, Mesen, Ronse, Spiere-Helkijn, Voeren) and four French-speaking municipalities (Comines-Wareneton, Enghien, Flobecq, Mouscron) on the language border, the six 'Brussels periphery municipalities' in the Dutch language region but bordering the bilingual Brussels-Capital region (Drogenbos, Kraainem, Linkebeek, Sint-Genesius-Rode, Wemmel, Wezembeek-Oppem), the nine municipalities in the German language region (Amel, Büllingen, Burg-Reuland, Bütgenbach, Eupen, Kelmis, Lontzen, Raeren, Sankt-Vith), and the two municipalities around Malmédy in the French language region, but bordering the German language region (Malmédy, Weismes).

Regarding these municipalities with special language arrangements, the rules governing the use of official languages in administrative matters, in education, and in labour relations may only be modified by Special Majority Act (Article 129 §2 Constitution).[419] 'Language facilities' are thus guaranteed under the Constitution and may only be changed with the consent of both language groups in Parliament. In spite of said facilities, these municipalities remain nonetheless integral parts of the Flemish Region or the Walloon Region, as the case may be, and hence come under the administrative supervision of the respective governments of these Regions.

Although the German language region is a language region to which unilingualism should apply, 'language facilities' are granted to the French-speaking inhabitants.

521. The facilities for language minorities benefit those administered, and not the administrators. Those administering local services encompass not only civil servants but also municipal organs and individual office holders (at least when acting as administrative authorities). The caselaw of the Council of State and of the Constitutional Court holds that the use of the relevant official language is compulsory for members of municipal institutions. For example, a member of a Municipal Council who refuses to take the oath of office in the official language is presumed to forgo his seat. Knowledge of the language of the region is, however, not a prerequisite for exercising the right to be a candidate in municipal elections and to be elected directly for municipal office. It is only a condition for municipal office holders not directly elected, such as the mayor, as well as for civil servants. It is noteworthy in this context that, since 1988, the members of the Municipal Councils as well as the members of the Councils of the Public Centers for Social Welfare are directly elected in the six Brussels periphery municipalities and in the municipalities of Comines-Warneton and Voeren.

419. See, e.g., Cons. Judgment No. 28/2015, 12 Mar. 2015.

522. The provisions addressing local services in the bilingual Brussels-Capital region are more intricate. In this language region, the rules on which official language is to be used in internal matters or in dealings with other services depend on the location of the acts in question. As a rule, services which cover several municipalities make use of the official language of that region. As it is quite conceivable that such 'regional services' cover municipalities in different language regions, the legislature had to consider all possibilities and determine the language(s) to be used there. Finally, the central civil service is bilingual and, in its dealings with a particular region, it uses the official language of that region. In its dealings with individual citizens, it uses the national language chosen by the citizen.

523. Undoubtedly, the provisions analysed so far protect rather the language majority in a given region. Only in a limited number of municipalities are 'language facilities' granted to the language minority. Some of these provisions reveal the characteristics which the protective measures usually have, notably the regulations requiring both the central civil service and the Brussels administration to employ an equal number of Dutch-speaking and of French-speaking senior civil servants.

For the central civil service and below the level of 'director', the King determines the job quota ratio, taking into account the importance the service in question holds for both communities. Management level positions and that of executive director of a central service are distributed equally among both language groups. For those posts in the civil service of the Brussels-Capital Region below the level of 'director' (namely all positions for which no or only bachelor degrees are required), the government of the Brussels-Capital Region determines the job quota ratio, taking into account the importance each service in question holds for both communities. The positions in the higher categories are also distributed equally among both language groups. One-third of the members of the governing bodies of the 'functionally decentralized institutions' of the Brussels-Capital Region should belong to the smaller language group.

In the nineteen municipalities of the Brussels-Capital Region, at least 50% of the functions must be distributed equally between both language groups, and from a certain level upwards (*chef de division* – the lowest but one in the level for which a university degree is needed), all posts must be filled equally by civil servants from both language groups.

524. An advisory and supervisory body has been created, the 'Official Languages Commission'. This Commission gives advisory opinions on compliance with the official languages legislation, and may apply to the Council of State to annul an administrative act incompatible with legislation governing the use of languages in administrative matters. The Commission may receive complaints and may carry out inspections on its own initiative. Special commissioners supervise the implementation of the legislation in certain municipalities: a 'district commissioner' for Mouscron, a deputy 'district commissioner' for Voeren, a 'Government Commissioner' bearing the title of 'Vice-Governor' for the nineteen municipalities of Brussels-Capital, and a 'Government Commissioner' bearing the title of 'Deputy-Governor' for the six Brussels periphery municipalities.

C. Official Languages Before the Courts

525. The Act on the Use of Languages in Court Proceedings of 15 June 1935 makes a distinction between civil and criminal proceedings. In civil proceedings, the general principle holds that the language to be used in court in the unilingual language regions is the official language of that region. Which official language is to be used in proceedings in the bilingual Brussels-Capital region is the choice of the defendant. Criminal proceedings are guided by broad concerns for the rights of the accused: he may request free translations of any document, and may also request that his case be transferred to a division of the court operating in his own national language. Of course, an accused who does not speak any of the official languages is entitled to an interpreter free of charge, both under this Act and under the EConvHR.

A 1985 Act governing the use of German in judicial matters created a distinct judicial district for the German language region.[420]

D. Official Languages in Legislative Matters

526. The Act governing the Use of Languages in Legislative Proceedings of 31 May 1961[421] provides that Acts of Parliament are adopted, assented to, promulgated and published both in Dutch and in French. Both versions have the same legal force. Similar rules apply to the legislation of the Brussels-Capital Region and the Brussels Joint Community Commission. In principle, Royal and Ministerial Decrees are issued in both languages. Acts of the Flemish Community / Region and of the French Community, and their executive regulations are published with a translation in the other official language. Acts of the Walloon Region and its government regulations are published with a translation in the other two languages. German Community Acts and its government regulations are published in German with a translation in French and in Dutch.

527. Dutch and French are the sole official languages for statutes, Royal and Ministerial Decrees, and since 1991 an authentic German text of the Constitution exists. There is a specific procedure for the translation of federal legislation, Royal and Ministerial Decrees into German. This process was intensified after the Constitutional Court ruled that there was an effective obligation to translate all federal statutes and regulations into German within a reasonable time.[422]

420. Act concerning the Use of German in Court Proceedings and on the Structure of the Courts of 23 September 1985, *Gazette,* 5 Nov. 1985.
421. *Gazette,* 21 Jun. 1961.
422. Cons., Judgment No. 59/94, 14 Jul. 1994.

E. Official Languages in the Armed Forces

528. The Act concerning Use of Languages in the Military of 30 July 1938 set out the principle that soldiers must receive training in their native language, and that military commanders must use the native language of their subordinates in all circumstances. That 'native language' is presumed to be the language of the region of one's residence. Residents of the bilingual area have to opt for one of the two national languages. Nevertheless recruits may choose to serve in a unit coming under a linguistic regime other than that of their mother tongue. Thus, the use of languages in the armed forces does not strictly observe the territoriality principle applied in other matters.

Officers must be bilingual, this being necessary in order to ensure that an officer may serve with a unit coming under either one of the two linguistic regimes. Proficiency in the other national language is tested at various stages in the recruitment and the promotion process. The higher echelons of the military hierarchy require equal job apportionment between Dutch-speaking and French-speaking officers.

F. Official Languages in Education

529. The Act regulating Languages in Education Matters of 30 July 1963[423] established the territorial unilingualism principle in the field of primary and secondary education: the official language of the region being the language of education. Failure to comply with the Act may entail disciplinary action or the withdrawal of subsidies and a refusal to recognise/homologate diplomas.

Children living in the bilingual Brussels-Capital region receive tuition in French or in Dutch, in accordance with the choice of the family. If necessary, public authorities must provide the schools: children of a family living in Brussels should be able to attend a school in their native language within a reasonable distance of their residence.

Special 'minority schools' are provided for families residing in one of the municipalities with special language arrangements. Those 'language facilities' may force the public authorities to organise nursery schools and primary education in that minority (official) language.

530. The ECtHR has ruled on the linguistic homogeneity of education in its 'Belgian Language Case'.[424] There the Court endorsed the territorial solution given by Belgium to its language disputes. The Court held that a measure based on an objective element, namely the language region, cannot be considered to be arbitrary and that this measure (ensuring that teaching in all public schools established in a unilingual region should take place in the language which is essentially that of the region) is based on the public interest. Since private schools are permitted, the measure is not disproportionate either. The one complaint that was accepted as

423. *Gazette*, 22 Aug. 1963.
424. ECtHR, *Belgian Linguistic Case* (23 Jul. 1968).

grounded, concerned the accessibility of minority schools. Minority schools in Belgium are only accessible for children of parents living in one of the municipalities with special language arrangements where such a school is situated. According to the Court, this limited accessibility violated the equality principle in connection with the right to education insofar as the minority schools in the six Brussels periphery municipalities are concerned. In the opinion of the Court, these six Brussels periphery municipalities benefitted from a bilingual status. The Court had no problem with limited accessibility to minority schools in municipalities with a unilingual status. As was explained in a declaration to the Committee of Ministers of the Council of Europe, Belgium remedied in 1970 any violation by explicitly placing the six Brussels periphery municipalities in the Dutch language region in order to make clear that they had no bilingual status. The Committee of Ministers declared itself satisfied with this explanation.

531. By virtue of Articles 129 and 130 §1 5° of the Constitution, the Flemish Community, the French Community, and the German Community are empowered to regulate the use of languages in education. So far, the principles of the 1963 Act have not yet been modified. As to teaching and administrative matters, the Flemish Community Code of Higher Education has stipulated that, in principle, the use of Dutch is compulsory for all Flemish universities and colleges. Given increasing mobility in education, however, Flemish universities and colleges are nevertheless conditionally allowed to organise study programmes, entirely or in part, in other languages.

G. *Official Languages in Employment and Commerce*

532. In relations between employer and employee as well as the corporate instruments and business records prescribed by Act and regulation, the official language of the region in which the business is located must be used. Deeds or documents, which do not meet this requirement, are not void but must be translated or replaced; they are then valid retroactively.

533. The power to regulate the use of languages in employment matters has been conferred on the Flemish and the French Communities, each with respect to its own territory, save for the municipalities with special language arrangements. The Community having jurisdiction is that in which the business is located. The Communities have enacted Acts imposing more rigid obligations. Deeds or documents which do not comply with the requirements set out in these Community Acts are null and void until they are replaced. Under federal law, the only sanction is compulsory replacement. However in 2013 the European Court of Justice (Grand Chamber) ruled that Article 45 TFEU must be interpreted as precluding legislation of a federated entity which requires all employers whose established place of business is located in that entity's territory to draft cross-border employment contracts exclusively in the official language of that federated entity, failing which the contracts are to be declared null and void by the national courts of their own motion.[425] Hence, the Flemish Community has amended its Act[426] to comply with this judgment. It is to be seen whether the amended Flemish Community Act[427] and other Acts regulating the use of languages in employment matters comply with EU law.

§2. International Protection of Language Groups

534. Article 27 ICCPR states that persons belonging to linguistic minorities shall not be denied the right to enjoy, in community with the other members of their group, their own culture or to use their own language. According to a 1998 judgment of the Constitutional Court, that Article does not concern the use of languages in administrative matters.[428] In a further judgment in 2003 the Constitutional Court ruled that a Flemish Community Act limiting subsidies to those public libraries which have at least 75% of their books in Dutch does not constitute a discriminatory limitation on the right of French-speakers in municipalities with special language arrangements in the Dutch language region, to enjoy in community with the other members of their group their own culture pursuant to Article 27 ICCPR.[429]

535. In connection with the protection of language groups in Belgium, the treaty generally receiving the most attention is the Framework Convention for the Protection of National Minorities adopted by the Committee of Ministers of the Council of Europe on 10 November 1994 and entering into force on 1 February 1998. As part of a wider compromise on the reorganisation of the State, the Belgian federal government decided in 2001 to sign the Framework Convention. Its signature was accompanied by a reservation stating in short that, as far as language groups are concerned, the Convention would apply without prejudice to the territoriality principle. Due to a lack of consensus between Dutch- and French-speakers on the identification of language minorities, Belgium has still not ratified the Convention.

In Resolution 1301 of 26 September 2002, the Parliamentary Assembly of the Council of Europe pronounced on the question of the identification of minorities in Belgium. At the request of the Assembly, the European Commission for Democracy through Law (the Venice Commission) analysed this question as follows:

> 39. As regards the Brussels Region, the Commission notes that the Dutch-speaking, although representing only 15% of the population, are granted substantial guarantees and in many respects put on the same level as the French-speaking. Accordingly, they seem to be in a co-dominant position and are not to be considered as a minority within the meaning of the Framework Convention. …

---

425. ECJ (GC), Case C-202/11 (*Las*), 6 Apr. 2013.
426. Act of 19 July 1973, *Gazette,* 6 Sep. 1973.
427. Act of 14 March 2014, *Gazette,* 22 Apr. 2014.
428. Cons., Judgment No. 26/98, 10 Mar. 1998.
429. Cons., Judgment No. 88/2003, 24 Jun. 2003.

> 43. The Commission is of the opinion that in Belgium, in the light of the existing equilibrium of powers between the Dutch-speaking and the French-speaking at the State level, French-speakers are in a position of co-dominance and therefore do not constitute a minority within the meaning of the Framework Convention at this level, despite being numerically inferior to Dutch-speakers …
> 45. At the regional level, having regard to the distribution of competences between the various regions and communities and of the territorial division of the country, the Commission considers that French-speakers in the Dutch-language Region and in the German-language Region may be considered as a minority in the sense of the Framework Convention, as may Dutch-speakers and German-speakers in the French-language Region.[430]

In Belgium there seems only to be a consensus that the German-speakers qualify as a minority. As far as Dutch- and French-speakers are concerned, the aforesaid opinion is much criticised. The main criticism from French-speakers is that it is hard to understand why a minority group would lose its status when it is protected. The Flemish feel a need for protection, even in their own Dutch language region. They argue that all language groups should be protected even if the group is numerically superior to the rest of the population.

§3. Ideological Minorities

I. 'Pillarization'

536. It has already been pointed out earlier that being mindful of the three lines dividing Belgian society is essential for a good understanding of Belgian political history. These are the division between Catholics and secular groups, the cultural-linguistic division and the socio-economic division. These three dividing lines led to the phenomenon known as vertical pluralism or 'pillarization' of which the 'elitist consensus' and the 'pacification policy' are consequences.

Belgian society used to be divided into separate worlds organised along the lines of different ideological and philosophical principles. 'From the cradle to the grave', an individual grew up within the Catholic, the Socialist, or the Liberal 'pillar' which governed all aspects of his life: youth movement, primary, secondary, and university education, trade union membership, health insurance, hospital, bank, sports and leisure, newspaper, library, and so on, and even his electoral allegiance. It is self-evident that these networks of social organisation originally set up for the promotion of their members' well-being within or against a sometimes hostile State, became extremely useful for political parties to mobilise and to maintain their voters.

'Pillarization' also played a role as a method for resolving political conflicts, since the social networks are part of the political system and determine the issues

430. Advice of 8–9 March 2002, Annex I to the Report 'Protection of minorities in Belgium' adopted by the Parliamentary Assembly of the Council of Europe, Doc. 9536 (5 Sep. 2002).

on the political agenda. The networks reach compromises on major and minor political issues. In this respect, it is striking that the State has entrusted certain functions to the 'pillars'. Thus, they became the 'social partners' of the State, involved for example in the payment of unemployment benefits and in medical care. Labour policy and health service policy come about as a result of collective bargaining between the State and the representative organisations of the 'pillars'.

Whereas secularisation, individualism, technological development, and new social ideas, such as a concern for the environment, gain momentum on the one hand, and on the other hand governments, parliaments, political parties and civil society groups are confronted with a legitimacy crisis, so too is the phenomenon of 'pillarization' also changing. The traditional Belgian political scene (based on the three pillars) is collapsing and being restructured beyond the pillars. Networks, notwithstanding their declining traditional role as a channel for political, economic, and social preferences, do continue to subsist, but are less monolithic, less affiliated with political parties and have a lesser impact. People are more and more attracted to one or other network because of the quality of the services offered, and to one or another political discourse because of dissatisfaction and/or populism.

The creation of the new legislative entities, the Communities, raised anxieties among non-Catholics in Flanders and among Catholics in Wallonia. It was feared that the ideological equilibrium between Catholics and non-Catholics in Belgian society might be upset. In return for the necessary votes to amend the Constitution in 1970–1971, the Liberal Party succeeded in obtaining certain constitutional safeguards, in Articles 11 and 131 of the Constitution (and as implemented in statutes). This is a perfect example of the 'pillarization' phenomenon.

II. Constitutional Provisions and Their Statutory Implementation

537. Article 11 of the Constitution provides a general prohibition on discrimination and an obligation for federal and Community legislators to guarantee the rights and freedoms of ideological and philosophical minorities. Article 131 of the Constitution compels the federal legislator to pass statutory provisions to prevent in the Communities all forms of discrimination for ideological or philosophical reasons. The Constitutional Court is entitled to review federal, Community and Region Acts which violate the general prohibition on discrimination provided in Article 11 of the Constitution.

538. An Act of 3 July 1971[431] introduced an 'alarm-bell procedure' to prevent ideological or philosophical discrimination in the Flemish and the French Community Parliaments. The procedure resembles the language 'alarm-bell procedure' provided by Article 54 of the Constitution.[432] If a Bill introduced in the Flemish Parliament or in the Parliament of the French Community is considered discriminatory on the basis of ideology or philosophy, one quarter of the members of that legislature may request the suspension of the Bill. The motion must be introduced

431. *Gazette,* 6 Jul. 1971.
432. See Pt. II. Ch. 3. §4. IV 'The Alarm-Bell Procedure'.

before the final vote on the Bill. If the Presidents of the federal Houses of Parliament and of the Community Parliaments, convened in joint meeting, rule in favour of admissibility, the motion must be reviewed on its merits by the federal Houses of Parliament. The Community Parliament may not consider the Bill further, unless the House of Representatives and the Senate declare that there are no grounds for the motion. The involvement of the federal Parliament in this 'alarm-bell procedure' prevents any risk of certain ideological tendencies at the Community level being reduced to a minority. A similar procedure applies to the Parliament of the German Community, in which case the President of this Parliament takes part in the decision-making of the joint meeting. This procedure has been applied in 1985 to a draft Bill recognising commercial broadcasting companies and most recently in 2020 to a draft Bill recognising sociocultural organisations and granting subsidies, both submitted in the Flemish Parliament. The House and the Senate in both cases declared the motions unfounded.

539. Since the above provisions deal with legislation and have not succeeded in entirely removing all fears of discrimination by the Executive Branch, political parties agreed to a 'Culture Pact' which the federal Parliament subsequently passed as the Cultural Co-operation and Non-discrimination Act of 16 July 1973.[433] Implementing Article 11 of the Constitution, the Act enshrines an individual's right to no discrimination on account of ideological or philosophical opinions. Furthermore, the Act establishes group rights; that is, all ideological and philosophical groups (not only minorities) have a right to participate in the development of cultural policy concerning youth, the fine arts, the media, sports, physical education, and so on.

All public authorities must involve the users of the cultural infrastructure and groups in the development and implementation of cultural policies. To that end, advisory bodies must be set up, in which such users and groups are proportionately represented, but without any particular group having any undue predominance. Furthermore, public authorities must involve end-users and groups in the administration of cultural institutions created by those authorities, ensuring their fair representation on the governing boards. Everyone should have equal access to the cultural infrastructure, without there being any discrimination or intervention on the part of the authorities. All groups have access to public broadcasting and are involved in its administration. Objective standards must be established in law for the granting of subsidies.

Personnel exercising cultural functions are employed and promoted on the basis of the principle of equality. Article 20 of the 1973 Act states that those functions must be spread fairly over all groups, ensuring each group a minimum presence and preventing any one particular group from gaining a monopoly or an unjustified predominance. The Constitutional Court has held that Article 20 violates Article 11 of the Constitution because the system it installs inevitably results in discriminating against officials because of their ideological or philosophical convictions, and furthermore contains the risk of discriminating against those officials who rely on their rights as citizens not to divulge their personal convictions.[434]

433. *Gazette,* 16 Oct. 1973.
434. Cons., Judgments No. 65/93, 15 Jul. 1993; No. 7/94, 20 Jan. 1994 and No. 47/99, 20 Apr. 1999.

Finally, the Act has set up a Commission composed of thirteen Dutch-speaking and thirteen French-speaking members designated by their respective Community Parliaments. This 'Commission for Cultural Co-operation and Non-discrimination' has both advisory and conciliatory powers in case an individual or a group appeals an allegedly discriminatory act by a local authority in cultural matters. This right of appeal need not be exhausted before proceeding in the Administrative Tribunal Division of the Council of State.

540. When assessing the Act, it may be asserted that the pluralism of Belgian society is recognised and enhanced in a dual manner. External pluralism, for example, may be seen in the requirement of objective and legally embodied standards for granting subsidies or for every group to be involved in the development of cultural policy. Internal pluralism, on the other hand, may be found in the rules on participation in the administration of cultural institutions or on job allocation. It is noteworthy that in the latter case, the main beneficiaries are the groups as such, and not merely the individual persons in their capacity as members of a minority.

One positive aspect of the Act may also be highlighted. It has contributed to putting an end to a minor form of 'apartheid' at the level of the local authorities: previously absolute majorities of one group having all too readily disregarded the aspirations of minorities. On the other hand, the weight of the Act, not only providing protection but also enhancing participation, is reduced to the problem of distributing subsidies. Also, the institutionalisation of pluralism in the Belgian State has not only offered protection to minorities, but has also enhanced its politicisation. It is noteworthy that Article 20 of the 1973 Act is still unamended, despite the Constitutional Court having held in 1993 that it violated Article 11 of the Constitution.

§4. Non-discrimination, Gender Equality and the Elimination of Racism

541. The Constitution protects the right to equality and non-discrimination in several of its provisions, most notably Articles 10, 11 and 11*bis*. The constitutional and statutory provisions on non-discrimination are addressed above.[435]

Selected Further Reading

Alen, A. 'Deux rapporteurs suisses sur les minorités nationales belges'. In *Mensch und Staat – L'homme et l'Etat. Festschrift/Mélanges Th. Fleiner* edited by P. Hänni (Eds University Fribourg, 2003) 239–257.

Alen, A. & R. Ergec. 'Le principe de territorialité dans la jurisprudence belge et européenne. Un essai de synthèse'. *J.T.* (1998): 785–790.

Alen, A. & K. Henrard. 'The Relevance for South Africa of Minority Protection in Belgium'. In *Institutional Development in Divided Societies* edited by B. De Villiers, F. Delmartino & A. Alen (HSRC Publishers, 1998) 93.

435. Part IV Ch. 2 §1 V. 'Equality'.

Bayart, C., S. Sottiaux & S. Van Drooghenbroeck (eds). *De nieuwe federale anti-discriminatiewetten / Les nouvelles lois luttant contre la discrimination* (die Keure / La Charte, 2008).

Clement, J. 'The Principle of Equality in Linguistic Matters from a Belgian Perspective'. In *The Principle of Equality. A South African and a Belgian Perspective* edited by J. Vande Lanotte, J. Sarkin & Y. Haeck (Maklu, 2001) 177–196.

Clement, J. *Taalvrijheid, bestuurstaal en minderheidsrechten. Het Belgisch model. Een constitutionele zoektocht naar de oorsprong van het territorialiteitsbeginsel en de minderheidsrechten in de bestuurstaalwetgeving* (Intersentia, 2003).

Clement, J. & X. Delgrange. 'La protection des minorités – De bescherming van de minderheden'. In *Het statuut van Brussel – Bruxelles et son statut* edited by E. Witte, A. Alen, H. Dumont & R. Ergec (Larcier, 1999) 517–555.

De Pelsmaeker, T. & E. Vandenbossche, 'Het decreet van 14 maart 2014 tot wijziging van het zogenaamde "Septemberdecreet": een oplossing met beperkte houdbaarheidsdatum'. *T.B.P.* (2016): 3–15.

Domenichelli, L. *Constitution et régime linguistique en Belgique et au Canada* (Bruylant, 1999).

Dumont, H. *Le pluralisme idéologique et l'autonomie culturelle en droit public belge* (Bruylant, 1996).

Granata-Menghini, S. 'The Application of the Framework Convention for the Protection of National Minorities in Belgium: The Opinion of the European Commission for Democracy Through Law'. *European Yearbook on Minority Issues* 2 (2002–2003): 357.

Huyse, L. *Passiviteit, pacificatie en verzuiling in de Belgische politiek* (Standaard, 1970).

Huyse, L. *De verzuiling voorbij* (Kritak, 1987).

Huyse, L. *Over politiek* (Van Halewyck, 2003)

Huyse, L. *De democratie voorbij* (Van Halewyck, 2014)

McRae, K.D. *Conflict and Compromise in Multilingual Societies, Volume 2, Belgium* (Wilfrid Laurier University Press, 1986).

Muylle, K. 'La représentation de la Communauté germanophone au sein des institutions fédérales: entre la logique de la participation et celle de la protection d'une minorité'. In *La Communauté germanophone de Belgique – Die Deutschsprachige Gemeinschaft Belgiens* edited by K. Stangherlin (La Charte, 2005) 246–286.

Verstichel, A., A. Alen, B. De Witte & P. Lemmens (eds). *The Framework Convention for the Protection of National Minorities: a Useful Pan-European Instrument?* (Intersentia, 2008).

Chapter 4. Judicial Control of Administrative Action

§1. Mechanisms of Preventive Legal Protection

I. Introduction: The Rule of Law

542. Belgium is a *rechtsstaat / état de droit*, a State based on the rule of law.[436] This means first of all that all State action is subject to the law. The rule of law also entails that the legality of State action can be challenged: public authorities and officers must be sanctioned if they are in breach of the law, and a remedy for their unlawful acts must be available. To this end, an elaborate system of judicial review has been set up. Though petitioning a court undoubtedly constitutes a real guarantee against possible arbitrary decisions, this safeguard has proved to be incomplete and not effective enough. Whereas administrative acts can be immediately enforceable, judicial review only takes place *a posteriori*, thus sometimes leaving irreparable the effects of the administrative act in question. Moreover, not all people have sufficient financial means to bring a case to court. It is therefore imperative that various checks and balances are provided for in the administrative decision process itself. Belgium does not have a systematic 'Administrative Law Code' nor does it have a general system of preventive legal protection. Over the last three decades, however, initiatives have been undertaken to improve the remedies available.

II. Public Access to Official Documents

543. The widespread trend in the West towards greater government openness has also reached Belgium. On 18 June 1993 the Constitution was amended, following the example of municipal by-laws and the Acts of the Communities and Regions, with the addition of Article 32. This Article safeguards a right of access to, and to a copy of, documents held or produced by government institutions and administrative authorities, under the conditions and subject to the exceptions provided for by federal, Community, or Region Act. Public access to official documents is based on two pillars, an 'active' one and a 'passive' one. For the 'active' component of the right on access to official documents, administrative authorities are obliged actively to inform citizens on policy, legislation, regulations, and individual decisions. For the 'passive' component, natural and legal persons also have the right to obtain copies of acts and decisions which are of interest to them.

436. See also General Introduction §2 I 'Rechtsstaat, Constitutionalism and the Rule of Law'. And see A. Alen & W. Verrijdt, 'The Rule of Law in the Case Law of the Belgian Constitutional Court: History and Challenges' in *International Conference of the Constitutional Court of the Republic of Slovenia – 25 Years* 91–120 (J. Sovdat ed., Bled 2016).

Article 32 of the Constitution also entails the obligation for federal, Community, and Region Acts to determine the conditions and exceptions applicable to public access to official documents. For every entity of the federal state, such legislation has been passed.[437]

The different levels of the federal State, moreover, have adopted specific legislation regarding public access to official documents, for instance regarding environmental documents.[438]

It should also be noted that public access to official documents is also governed by international treaties, which have direct effect in Belgian internal law. This is the case, for instance, with the Convention of 25 June 1998 on Access to Information, Public Participation in Decision-Making and Access to Justice in Environmental Matters (the 'Aarhus Convention').

III. Giving Reasons for Individual Administrative Decisions

544. By virtue of the Act on Giving Reasons for Administrative Decisions of 29 July 1991[439], administrative authorities must give reasons for every individual and unilateral administrative decision affecting an individual or a legal person. They have to state the factual circumstances and the legal grounds underlying the administrative decision. Well-reasoned decisions are not only vital for the purpose of showing citizens that the law has been complied with; they also impose a kind of restraint on public servants. The formal requirements must be observed in order to avoid rendering the administrative decision null and void. The reasoning must also be adequate: it must substantiate the decision. The Administrative Tribunal Division of the Council of State, the highest federal administrative court in Belgium, may examine whether the administrative decision is based on factually and legally relevant considerations or whether non-relevant considerations invalidate it. When there are grounds that cast doubt on the existence of proper reasons, the Council of State may order the administrative authority concerned to provide all administrative documents that underpin the decision concerned and its reasons. If the administrative authority refuses to do so, the Council of State will hold the administrative decision concerned not to be based on valid reasons, and accordingly will annul it.

545. The Constitutional Court has recognised that the Communities and the Regions are empowered to implement further and specify the federal Act of 29 July 1991 regarding matters coming within their jurisdiction, but they must respect the minimum provisions set by the federal legislator.[440]

---

437. See, for instance, at the federal level, the Act of 11 April 1994 on the Public Access to Official Documents, *Gazette,* 30 Jun. 1994 (2nd ed.).
438. See, for instance, at the federal level, the Act of 5 August 2006 on Public Access to Environmental Information, *Gazette,* 28 Aug. 2006.
439. *Gazette,* 12 Sep. 1991.
440. Cons., Judgments No. 55/2001, 8 May 2001; No. 128/2001, 18 Oct. 2001; No. 91/2013, 13 June 2013; No. 74/2014, 8 May 2014.

IV. Ombudsmen

546. The independent Ombudsmen also have an important role in encouraging administrative authorities to act properly. Each level of government in Belgium has appointed an Ombudsman, charged with assessing governmental acts, both on own initiative or upon request of a citizen.[441] Moreover, ombudsmen are also appointed to deal with specific issues (e.g., the Flemish Children's Rights Commissioner, or the ombudsmen for telecom services). Above all, the Ombudsman must act as a mediator between citizen and government.

The role of the Ombudsmen as a preventive remedy has been emphasised by the federal Act of 20 January 2014, which amended Article 19 paragraph 3 of the Consolidated Council of State Act. The maximum time period of sixty days to start proceedings before the Council of State to challenge an administrative decision is suspended when a complaint has also been filed with the Ombudsman, provided it was also filed within sixty days.

V. 'Administrative Loop'

547. The concept of the 'administrative loop' (*'bestuurlijke lus'*) has its origin in Dutch legislation. It seeks to remedy actionable, reviewable improprieties as soon as possible within the decision-making process itself and without having to wait for the conclusion of that decision procedure.

In Belgium, the concept has been introduced, for instance, in Article 13 of the Flemish Region Act of 25 April 2014 on the Single Permit.[442] Both the administrative authorities in first instance and those handling an administrative appeal can remedy wrongs, for instance, relating to the organisation of the public inquiry, or by seeking the advisory opinion erroneously not requested.

The procedure avoids having to restart the whole decision process *ab initio*, and its only effect on the pending procedure is that the period within which a permit decision must be taken, will be extended.

This concept of the 'administrative loop' has also been introduced into judicial review proceedings, where a tribunal, pending the annulment proceedings, can repair the deficiency of the administrative acts. The system, however, led to criticism from the Constitutional Court (see below §2 III H 'Remedies. Administrative Loop').

441. See, e.g., the federal Act of 22 March 1995 establishing the Federal Ombudsman, *Gazette,* 7 Apr. 1995, and the Flemish Community and Region Act establishing the Flemish Ombudsman Office of 7 July 1998, *Gazette*, 25 Aug. 1998.

442. *Gazette,* 23 Oct. 2014.

§2. JUDICIAL REVIEW

I. Introduction

548. While the review of administrative acts in Belgium is exercised primarily by the courts, there are also various other ways of challenging administrative decisions. Before seeking judicial review, an aggrieved party may request the administrative authority concerned to reconsider the decision, or the party can appeal to a higher-level administrative authority or to a supervising organ, as the case may be. In some instances, this right of administrative appeal is formally prescribed by federal, Community, or Region legislation. In that case, this right of appeal must be exhausted before filing an action with the Administrative Tribunal Division of the Council of State. When hearing an appeal, the administrative authorities will reconsider the decision under appeal with respect to both the merits and the law.

549. Judicial review in Belgium is exercised by both the ordinary courts and the administrative courts – primarily the Administrative Tribunal Division of the Council of State. It differs significantly from the system of administrative appeal because in principle the courts must confine themselves strictly to the question of legality.

The grounds of the judicial review (§2 II) will first be outlined, and then the types of remedies available in judicial review proceedings will be discussed (§2 III).

II. Grounds for Judicial Review

550. Generally speaking, judicial review aims at reviewing whether administrative authorities have acted *ultra vires*. The simple proposition that an administrative authority may not exceed its power covers various forms of 'illegality'. Continental administrative law has generally distinguished between two forms of illegality: (1) 'external illegality', meaning the absence of a power on the part of the authority adopting the measure concerned, and any infringement of essential procedural requirements, and (2) 'internal illegality', meaning an infringement of the law and abuse of power. When a court is called upon to review the 'legality' of an administrative act, it will quite naturally first consider external illegality, since this is easier to determine. The court will then proceed to consider any internal illegality. At this stage, the court will review not only whether the legal requirements regarding the proper exercise of its powers have been met, but also whether the administrative authority has exercised its powers in a lawful way.

551. The expansion of government activities after the Second World War has given the Executive Branch more and more extensive, discretionary powers subject to little effective control by Parliament. The courts have thus developed general doctrines in their caselaw regarding the exercise of executive power with proper restraint, in terms of both substantive and procedure. They have refused to endorse broad discretionary powers exercisable by administrative authorities. Rather, they have required executive power to be exercised reasonably and in good faith, for proper purposes only, and in accordance with both the spirit and the letter of the empowering Act. Accordingly, the courts have also developed stringent procedural requirements.

Since modern legislation usually only defines the scope of the powers attributed to public authorities in a very general way, it was left to the courts to develop criteria to restrict arbitrary administrative action. The Council of State has taken the lead by establishing a set of general principles of administrative law: the 'general principles of good governance'. These general principles are comparable to the principles of natural justice in English administrative law. The general principles of good governance include, among others, the right of due process (including *audi alteram partem* and the right to counsel), the principle of impartiality (rule against bias, *nemo judex in causa sua*), the principle of due care, the principle of legal certainty (including non-retroactivity and protecting legitimate expectations), the principle of non-discrimination (*patere legem*), the principle of reasonableness, the principle of proportionality, and the obligation to observe due standards of financial responsibility to taxpayers.

552. Generally, as noted above, the courts review administrative law issues on their legal aspects; the principle of the separation of powers does not entitle them to review the merits of a decision. Nevertheless, because courts assess administrative decisions by a standard of reasonableness, the borderline between judicial review on the merits and on the legality of an administrative act has become blurred. Without having the right to substitute their own judgment for administrative decisions (adopted under discretionary power), the courts may yet conclude that administrative authority has been exercised in an unreasonable way: that the administrative authority has come to a conclusion 'so unreasonable that no reasonable authority acting under the same circumstances could ever have come to it'. This 'margin of appreciation' test (*appréciation marginale*) was inspired by the work of Dutch legal scholars.

Although the judicial review exercised by ordinary courts and that by the Administrative Tribunal Division of the Council of State have a similar scope, two differences should be noted. Firstly, whereas proceedings before the ordinary courts are accusatorial in style, proceedings before the Council of State are inquisitorial. That explains why, in general, the Administrative Tribunal Division reviews the legality of administrative acts with greater scrutiny. Secondly, the judgments of the Administrative Tribunal Division annulling decisions operate *erga omnes*, whereas the judgments of the ordinary courts operate only *inter partes*.

III. Available Remedies

553. With those general principles governing the review of administrative acts by the courts in mind, this section will examine the remedies available for administrative decisions held to be unlawful.

A. Defence of Illegality

554. Administrative decisions can be reviewed indirectly in the course of a prosecution or other judicial proceedings. The defendant may plead in his defence that the regulation or order sought to be enforced does not accord with higher legal norms. If the defendant does not invoke the defence of illegality himself, courts are compelled to do so ex officio. Article 159 of the Constitution obliges courts not to apply any regulation or order unless it complies with the law. Judgments refusing to enforce administrative acts only operate *inter partes*. The act challenged remains generally effective, and is merely not applied in that specific case before the court. In other cases, courts may even rule the challenged administrative act to be lawful, despite previous judgments to the contrary.

The defence of illegality set forth in Article 159 of the Constitution is available in proceedings before all courts, including the administrative courts. It is particularly important in criminal proceedings. Another important feature of the defence is that it is not subject to any limitation periods.

555. The defence of illegality is primarily invoked as a shield, but it has also come to be used as a sword – a direct challenge to remedy the wrongs caused by the regulation or order. If enforcing the regulation or order, held to be illegal, will cause damage to a citizen, a judge can order the administrative authority (if necessary, by way interlocutory proceedings in cases of urgency) to take all necessary action to minimise or avoid any damage. Thus the result is effectively to prohibit the government from enforcing the regulation or order.

B. Damages in Tort Claims

556. Ordinary courts may order administrative authorities to pay compensation for any loss or injury suffered by a citizen. This claim for damages may be founded on tort liability, which would arise from the breach of law by the administrative authorities.

557. The basic rules governing tort liability under Belgian law are set forth in Articles 1382 et seq. of the Civil Code. In order to establish a prima facie case for liability in tort, generally the plaintiff must prove the following:

(i) wrongdoing by the administrative authority in the nature of an act or omission violating a constitutional or a legislative rule prohibiting or compelling an administrative authority's action or violating the general duty of due care;[443]
(ii) that the breach of those rules and/or duty of due care by the administrative authority is the actual direct cause of the plaintiff's injury, and[444]

---

443. Cass., 13 May 1982, *J.T.*, 1982, 772.
444. The link between an act or omission and the damage is established when the damage would not have occurred in the absence of that act or omission.

(iii) damage to the plaintiff's person or property.

In principle, under Belgian law, administrative authorities are subject to the same tort liability rules as those applied to natural and legal persons. There is no separate law of (administrative) liability for the wrongful acts of administrative authorities.

558. In practice, however, administrative authorities have enjoyed for a long time a virtual immunity from tort liability. Until 1920, the Belgian ordinary courts systematically declared themselves without jurisdiction regarding tort claims against the government for acts committed in its capacity as a public authority. They only asserted jurisdiction in disputes between citizens and the government if the latter acted as a private person. This reluctance of the courts to interfere in disputes where the public administration was involved, was based on a far too strict conception of the separation of powers implying that '*juger l'administration, c'est encore administrer*'. Since no other judicial instance – besides the ordinary courts – could grant financial redress for wrongful or negligent acts or omissions by administrative authorities, it left citizens without any remedy. It was the opposite of what the National Congress had intended, that all administrative acts had to be subject to judicial review by either the ordinary courts or by the administrative courts.

559. Proposals to create a Council of State in order to secure an effective remedy against abuses by public authorities induced the judiciary to reconsider its approach. In 1920, the Court of Cassation ruled that every civil right is entitled to judicial protection, even when infringed upon by an administrative authority. It also recognised the exclusive jurisdiction of the ordinary courts to grant compensatory damages for any tort committed by an administrative authority interfering with a 'civil' right.[445] And from the 1960s onwards, judicial protection of citizens against the wrongful or negligent acts or omissions of administrative authorities gradually improved. Consequently, the Court of Cassation held that the government is bound by the general duty of due care when executing its statutory obligations[446], when performing regulatory activity[447], and when supplying information.[448] The government bears responsibility for its orders[449] and for its regulations,[450] for its acts and for its omissions[451], for infringements of civil rights[452], political rights[453], and of legitimate expectations.[454]

At present, as the caselaw of the Court of Cassation now stands[455], any administrative authority in breach of an internal norm (the Constitution, a legal norm, or

445. Cass., 5 Nov. 1920 *(Flandria), Pas.*, 1920, I, 193.
446. Cass., 7 Mar. 1963, *Pas.*, 1963, I, 744 (obligation to ensure safety on public roads).
447. Cass., 26 Apr. 1963, *Pas.*, 1963, I, 306.
448. Cass., 4 Nov. 1982, *Pas.*, 1983, I, 297.
449. Cass., 9 Jan. 1997, *Pas.*, 1997, I, 44.
450. Cass., 26 Apr. 1963, *Pas.*, 1963, I, 306.
451. Cass., 23 Apr. 1971, *J.T.*, 1972, 689.
452. Cass., 5 Nov. 1920 *(Flandria), Pas.*, 1920, I, 193.
453. Cass., 16 Dec. 1965, *Pas.*, 1966, I, 513.
454. Cass., 13 May 1982, *J.T.*, 1982, 772.
455. See e.g., Cass. 21 Dec. 2007, C.06.0457.F.

a principle of good governance) or an international treaty with direct effect[456], either of which obliges the authority to act or refrain from acting in a specific way, is subject to an 'obligation of result'. This means that whenever the conditions to establish a tort claim are met, the authority will be held liable unless it can invoke force majeure[457] or another ground of justification.[458]

When no specific legal norm applies, the administrative authority will only be subject to an 'obligation of means': it will bear liability in tort only where it has failed to comply with the general duty of due care.

560. The State, being a legal person, inevitably acts through public servants. Pursuant to the Act of 10 February 2003[459], public servants are personally liable only in exceptional occasions, such as for fraud or deception, serious offences, or frequently recurring error. Tort claims for damages arising out such actions may be filed against the State. Public servants are, under the Act of 10 February 2003, no longer responsible for an occasionally recurring light error. This, however, does not prevent an aggrieved party holding the State responsible for that error.

In practice, most tort actions brought against the State relate to traffic accidents caused by a public servant exercising his official function. In those cases, the injured party may start an action against the State's insurance company, based on the Compulsory Automobile Insurance Act, or against the State itself if the State acts as its own insurer.

Similar principles as set out here also apply to administrative authorities other than the State.

561. A torts claim against a public authority may be filed in normal proceedings, and also in preliminary proceedings.

The limitations period for such claims before the civil courts is in principle five years, provided that the injured party knew, or was aware, of the fault that caused the injury, and of the identity of the tortfeasor (Article 2262*bis* Civil Code, to be read in conjunction with Article 113 Budgetary Provisions and State Finances Act of 22 May 2003).

C. No-Fault Liability for Interference with Property Rights

562. Citizens may also claim compensation before the ordinary courts against administrative authorities for breach of the law imposed on owners or occupiers of property. An administrative authority must substantially interfere with an individual's use or enjoyment of property (e.g., undertaking public works affecting private property rights). To be considered 'substantial' the interference must be of a sort that may be reasonably viewed as inconvenient to an average person in the community.

456. Cass., 14 Jan. 2000, *Arr. Cass.* 2000, No. 104.
457. Cass., 8 Feb. 2008, *J.T.* 2008, 569.
458. Cass. 8 Nov. 2002, *R.A.B.G.*, 2003, 851; Cass. 10 Apr. 2014, C.11.0796.N.
459. *Gazette,* 27 Feb. 2003.

Liability here does not originate in tort law but in property rights and the inconvenience which residents of a neighbourhood have to endure. Hence this relies on Article 544 of the Civil Code and Article 16 of the Constitution. Because every person is entitled to use his/her own property in a reasonable way, the argument is that both the principle of fairness and Article 16 of the Constitution entitle the owner to fair compensation for any unreasonable interference with this right by a third party.

Recently, the general principle of equal distribution of public burdens has found broader application in the caselaw of the Court of Cassation[460] and the Constitutional Court.[461] Under this principle, citizens are entitled to claim fair compensation when the burdens imposed by public authorities are not equally distributed and exceed the ones a citizen is reasonably expected to bear in the public interest.[462]

D. *Special Damages Before the Council of State*

563. Only in those cases where the ordinary courts do not have jurisdiction is the Administrative Tribunal Division of the Council of State allowed to award special damages (moral or material) for injury caused by an administrative authority.[463] In such cases the action is not founded on tort law, nor is it based on inconvenience endured by residents of a neighbourhood. Instead the remedy is an equitable one and only available when the ordinary courts have no jurisdiction. Because these very restrictive conditions are rarely met, few such claims have been (successfully) brought before the Council of State.

E. *Appeal for Annulment and Request for Suspension*

564. The Administrative Tribunal Division of the Council of State was established in 1946 as a response to deficiencies in the legal protection of individuals against abuses by the public administration. Up to that point, individuals did not have any remedy in order to challenge directly the legality of an administrative act. Furthermore, the judgment of a court not to apply illegal regulations or orders pursuant to Article 159 of the Constitution only operated *inter partes*. Hence the establishment of the Administrative Tribunal Division, authorised to suspend and annul administrative decisions.[464]

565. The Council of State's jurisdiction to annul covers unilateral, binding administrative regulations and orders. Recommendations or agreements do not come within the scope of its jurisdiction. The regulatory act challenged must be that of a Belgian administrative authority, namely a public (or even a private) institution

460. Cass., 24 Jun. 2010, *R.W.*, 2010–2011, 1217.
461. Cons., Judgment No. 55/2012, 19 Apr. 2012.
462. See also Pt. IV. Ch. 2. §2. VI 'Peaceful Enjoyment of Property'.
463. Article 11 Consolidated Council of State Act.
464. Articles 14 and 17 Consolidated Council of State Act.

acting in the general, public interest, and empowered to impose unilateral obligations in accordance with its statutory purposes (e.g., the examining board of a private university). As a consequence of a 1996 Constitutional Court judgment[465], Article 14 §1 of the Consolidated Council of State Act has been amended[466] in order to extend the jurisdiction of the Administrative Tribunal Division to cover disputes concerning orders and regulations adopted by the Legislative and Judicial Branches regarding public contracts or public servants.

Annulment proceedings are also available if an administrative authority refrained from taking a decision. In that case, the interested party may notify the authority and ask for an express decision. A failure to take a decision by way of adopting a regulation or an order within four months after notification implies that an authority has rendered an implicit negative decision, and that this decision can be challenged (Article 14 §3 Consolidated Council of State Act).

566. Annulment proceedings before the Administrative Tribunal Division of the Council of State are initiated by a petition filed within sixty days following either the publication of the regulation or notification of the administrative act, or the day on which the party took notice of the act concerned if no publication or notification was required. After the expiration of the sixty-day period, the Council of State no longer has jurisdiction to annul an administrative act, but it may still refuse to apply a regulation in a specific case dealing with another administrative act, on the basis of Article 159 of the Constitution.

567. The petitioner must have the required legal capacity and a sufficient interest for standing. Specifically, the claimant must show a direct, personal, and legal interest in the remedy sought. The interest requirement must be met at all times during the proceedings, from the filing of the petition to the final judgment. Associations without legal personality may also have standing before the Council of State. Their standing may be grounded in an explicit authorisation to that effect by law (e.g., trade unions) or in their articles of association (explicit inclusion of public interest goals). It may also result from the public goal they are pursuing and which is set forth in their articles of association.

568. In the 1990s, judicial backlog before the Administrative Tribunal Division of the Council of State became an increasing problem, leading to annulment proceedings that easily lasted for several years. In order to allow citizens a more efficient and legal remedy, the Act of 19 July 1991 granted the Council of State the power to suspend the execution of regulations or orders.[467] A claimant could include accordingly a request to suspend the decision in his/her annulment request following that 1991 Act. The claimant had to establish that serious grounds justified the suspension and that an immediate execution of the regulation or order would cause irreparable damages.

465. Cons., Judgment No. 31/96, 15 May 1996.

466. Act of 25 May 1999, *Gazette,* 22 Jun. 1999; Act of 15 May 2007, *Gazette,* 8 Jun. 2007, and Act of 20 January 2014, *Gazette,* 3 Feb. 2014.

467. Article 17 Consolidated Council of State Act.

Since the entry into force of the Act of 20 January 2014, the combined request to annul and suspend has been abolished.[468] A request to suspend the execution of a regulation or order can now be filed at any stage of the proceedings, provided that this is justified by urgent circumstances.

In extremely urgent circumstances, separate proceedings can be started to suspend the regulation or order. These proceedings can lead to a judgment within very little time when the circumstances require it (for instance, when a demonstration is prohibited), but such proceedings are only used in a restrictive way.

569. Similar to an annulment judgment of the Constitutional Court, an annulment judgment of the Administrative Tribunal Division of the Council of State is stated to be *erga omnes*. Hence that judgment is binding on all public authorities and powers.

Legislators too should comply with judgments of the Council of State in order to respect the principle of the separation of powers. According to the caselaw of the Constitutional Court, a retroactive confirmation of administrative acts annulled by the Administrative Tribunal Division is incompatible with the constitutional principle of equality: a retroactive Act must not infringe on peremptory judicial decisions.[469]

570. The judgments of the Council of State do have retroactive effect: annulled decisions are considered never to have been adopted. This may give rise to some problems, such as when the challenged decision is annulled but only many years after the annulment proceedings were initiated.

The sanction of annulment implies that the administrative authority must readopt the administrative decision, and restart the adoption procedure at the point where the illegality took place. In order to avoid 'unwilling' administrative authorities adopting once again the administrative acts with the same illegalities, the legislator has added some additional mechanisms to prevent such an occurrence. The claimant before the Council of State can request that the Council of State gives further explanation in the judgment to clarify for the parties how the illegality which led to the annulment can be remedied.[470]

Moreover, when the judgment has the result that the administrative authority must adopt a new decision, the claimant can also request the Council of State to issue a mandamus order requiring the new decision to be taken within a certain period of time. Such a request can be filed during the annulment proceedings, or in separate proceedings provided that the claimant has sent a formal letter of notice and the request for mandamus is filed not later than three months after notification of the judgment. When the decision to be adopted after annulment judgment leaves no discretionary power to the administrative authority, the judgment itself takes the place of that decision. When the judgment implies that the administrative authority must refrain from certain acts, the Council of State may impose these explicitly.[471]

468. *Gazette,* 3 Feb. 2014.
469. See Pt. II. Ch. 3. §5. II 'Legislation Having Retroactive Effect'.
470. Article 35/1 Consolidated Council of State Act, as inserted by Act of 20 January 2014.
471. Article 36 §1 Consolidated Council of State Act, as inserted by Act of 20 January 2014.

571. The judgments of the Administrative Tribunal Division are final. Appealable only before the Court of Cassation, they may be quashed only on very specific grounds, namely an infringement of the division of jurisdiction between the different administrative courts and the ordinary courts (Article 158 Constitution).[472]

F. Interactions Between Appeals for Annulment and Damage Claims

572. Given the *erga omnes* nature of a judgment of the Council of State, a decision on the illegality of an administrative act is binding for the ordinary courts when these courts have to adjudge claims for compensation due to loss or damage arising from the annulled act. More particularly, the annulment of an administrative decision establishes the fault of the administrative authority. And as discussed above, for a plaintiff to make out successfully the tortious liability of an administrative authority, the plaintiff must also prove damages and a causal link between the fault (the annulled act) and the damage suffered.

Proceedings before the Council of State were completely separate from the tort claims before the ordinary courts. In order to succeed in a damage claim, a plaintiff would first have to file an annulment action with the Council of State, and then only afterwards file a tort claim with the ordinary court. Recently, however, two mechanisms have been introduced which depart from this strict distinction.

573. First, according to Article 2244 §1 paragraph 3 of the Civil Code, as amended by Act of 25 July 2008[473], the filing of an annulment appeal before the Council of State suspends the running of the limitation period for the tort claim to the extent that the decision grounding the claim is annulled. This Article seeks to prevent the tort action for damages being out of time at the moment the Council of State annulled the administrative act concerned (something which could take several years). The Constitutional Court has held that even judgments rejecting annulment should have a suspensory effect on limitation period for the tort proceedings. A rejection could arise from many different causes, and could still be relevant for initiating tort proceedings even if the petition for annulment had been rejected.[474]

574. Second, before 2014, except for claims for special damages (see above D), the Council of State could only suspend and/or annul the decisions of administrative authorities. And, in general, plaintiffs could only claim damages afterwards by launching a torts claim before the ordinary courts on the basis of the error, the infringement of a 'civil' right, leading to annulling the administrative decision at issue. Indeed, according to Article 144 of the Constitution, disputes regarding such 'civil' rights fall exclusively under the jurisdiction of the ordinary courts. The 2014

472. See also Arts 33–34 Consolidated Council of State Act, and above Pt. II. Ch. 5. §1. I. C 'The Court of Cassation'.
473. *Gazette*, 22 Aug. 2008.
474. Cons., Judgment No. 148/2018, 8 Nov. 2018.

Sixth State Reform created the possibility of empowering the Council of State by way of an Act to determine in its judgment the effects on such 'civil' rights (Article 144 paragraph 2 Constitution).

Implementing the Constitution, the federal legislator has made it possible since 1 July 2014 for a complainant before the Council of State not only to seek the annulment of an administrative act, but also claim damages (at the latest within sixty days after notification of the annulment judgment).[475] Hence the legislator aimed at centralising the two different proceedings. The complainant, however, can still choose to file annulment proceedings before the Council of State and then afterwards claim damages before the ordinary courts. The principle '*una via electa*' applies: damages can either be claimed before the Council of State, excluding any recourse to the ordinary courts, and vice versa. It should also be noted that the calculation of damages is slightly different. Whereas the Council of State will use a 'balance of interest' test, the ordinary courts will refer to the traditional tort claim rules of Article 1382 of the Civil Code.

G. *Other Administrative Tribunals: Specialised Federal Administrative Tribunals and Community/Region Administrative Tribunals*

575. At the end of the last century and the beginning of the new one, the Council of State faced an increasing number of asylum cases, which increased the already existing judicial backlog even more. Additionally opinion was gaining momentum that for certain matters, more specialised administrative tribunals needed to be established. Together this led to the creation of the Immigration and Asylum Tribunal at the federal level. Moreover, since the 1993 Fourth State Reform, Belgium is a federal State (Article 1 Constitution), and the Flemish Region in particular wanted to exercise its autonomy by establishing its own administrative tribunals.

576. At the federal level, the Immigration and Asylum Tribunal was established by the Act of 15 September 2006.[476] The Tribunal is authorised to deal with all individual decisions regarding access to Belgian territory, the right to reside and settle there, and removal from it. The Tribunal is also exclusively authorised to hear appeals from decisions taken by the Commissioner-General for Refugees and Stateless Persons in which the status of refugee is conferred, refused, or withdrawn in accordance with the Geneva Treaty of 28 July 1951.[477]

577. At the Community and Region level, in particular the Flemish Region, a considerable number of new administrative tribunals were set up.

First, the Permit Disputes Tribunal (*Raad voor Vergunningsbetwistingen*) was created by Flemish Region Act of 27 March 2009, and has been sitting since 1 September 2009. This Tribunal was originally authorised to hear all disputes regarding registration decisions, building permits, and allotment permits. By Flemish Region

475. Article 11*bis* Consolidated Council of State Act.
476. *Gazette,* 6 Oct. 2006.
477. Articles 39/1 & 39/2 of the Act of 15 December 1980, *Gazette,* 31 Dec. 1980.

Act of 25 April 2014, which entered into force on 23 February 2017, building permits, allotment permits, and environmental permits are centralised into one single permit, hence also broadening the jurisdiction of the Tribunal. Additionally, disputes regarding expropriation, which also became a regional matter[478], have been allocated to this Tribunal from 1 January 2018 onwards.

The Permit Disputes Tribunal was the first important Region administrative tribunal, in line with Region jurisdiction over municipal planning law. Its creation was highly contested, and the Flemish Region was said to be in breach of the Constitution which empowers the federal legislator in matters of judicial organisation and more particularly under Article 161 of the Constitution, the establishment of administrative tribunals. The Constitutional Court, however, upheld the Flemish Region Act.[479] Although it stated that the Region legislator did not have the express authority to establish administrative tribunals, it could still do so on the basis of the 'implied powers' theory.[480] For the Constitutional Court, the conditions for the exercise of implied powers were fulfilled: (i) the matter at stake was necessary for the exercise of Region jurisdiction; (ii) the matter could be exercised in a differentiated way, and (iii) the impact at the federal level was only marginal because the jurisdiction of the Tribunal was limited to individual decisions and a further appeal (on questions of law) to the Council of State was possible. The Constitutional Court hence paved the way for the establishment of other Region and Community administrative tribunals.

578. Second, the Environmental Management Commission was created by Flemish Region Act of 21 December 2007. This administrative tribunal was authorised to annul decisions by the Region administration which imposed specified 'exclusive administrative penalties' or 'alternative administrative penalties' (i.e., penalties of a financial nature) for breach of environmental laws. In general, environmental law is more and more enforced by imposing administrative sanctions rather than criminal penalties. By Flemish Region Act of 25 April 2014, in force on 1 March 2018, new enforcement rules were adopted regarding the new single permit. From then on, the Environmental Management Commission was rebaptised the 'Enforcement Commission' and was authorised to hear appeals against financial penalties imposed for breach of the Acts and regulations involving the single permit.

579. Third, the Election Disputes Tribunal is regulated by the Flemish Act of 4 April 2014. It authorised to hear all disputes arising out of local elections.

580. Fourth, the Commission for Study Programmes and Student Disciplinary Disputes (*De Raad voor betwistingen inzake studievoortgangsbeslissingen*) was established pursuant to Article II.285 of the 2013 Codex of Higher Education. This Commission hears appeals from a whole range of decisions taken by universities or by other post-secondary colleges.

478. Flemish Act of 24 February 2017 on Expropriation for the General Interest, *Gazette*, 25 Apr. 2017.
479. Cons., Judgment No. 8/2011, 27 Jan. 2011.
480. See above Pt. III. Ch. 2. §3. I. F 'Communities and Regions also having Implied Powers'.

581. In order to ensure a minimum of uniformity, the Flemish legislator has created the Administrative Tribunals Service which provides operational support and acts as an umbrella support service for the above-mentioned administrative tribunals, except the Commission for Study Programmes and Student Disciplinary Disputes. Procedural unity, to a certain extent, is created by one Act applicable to all those administrative tribunals.[481] On a procedural level, all judgments of those administrative tribunals discussed above can still be appealed to the Council of State, acting as a 'court of cassation'.[482] That is, the Council of State can only hear questions of law, reviewing whether the relevant rules have been correctly applied, and may not enter into the merits of the case.

H. 'Administrative Loop'

582. According to the 'administrative loop' (*bestuurlijke lus*) doctrine, pending the annulment proceedings an administrative tribunal can repair the deficiency of the administrative act.

The system was introduced into the Council of State by the federal Act of 20 January 2014, which added a new Article 38 to the Consolidated Council of State Act. Certain conditions had to be met. First, the deficiency had to be reparable within three months or within a reasonable period of time. Second, the administrative authority did not explicitly refuse these proceedings. Third, the deficiency should lead to a final outcome of the proceedings pending. Fourth, the reparation of the deficiency had to lead to the outcome that the decision challenged was no longer unlawful, and also that the content of the decision itself remained unchanged. The Constitutional Court, however, has annulled this new type of proceeding.[483] The Court held that the Council of State, by proposing to start administrative loop proceedings, would disclose its view on the merits of the administrative question underpinning the dispute, thus violating the principle of judicial independence and impartiality. Moreover, no guarantees existed that the newly adopted decision, after the administrative loop had been proposed by the Council of State, would not unreasonably affect interested parties, irrespective of whether they were involved in the actual proceedings before the Council of State or not. The newly adopted decision also was in breach of the Act on Giving Reasons for Administrative Decisions of 29 July 1991, considering that it would become possible to comply with this Act only after the administrative loop had been proposed, whereas a natural or legal person is entitled to know immediately the reasons underlying the decision of an administrative authority concerning them.

The 'administrative loop' was also introduced in the Region legislation for administrative tribunals, in particular Article 34 of the Flemish Act of 4 April 2014 concerning the Organization and Proceedings of Certain Flemish Administrative Tribunals. The Constitutional Court also annulled this Article on grounds similar to

481. See the Flemish Act of 4 April 2014 concerning the Organisation and Proceedings of Certain Flemish Administrative Tribunals, *Gazette,* 1 Oct. 2014.
482. Article 14 §2 of the Consolidated Council of State Act.
483. Cons., Judgment No. 103/2015, 16 Jul. 2015.

those in its judgment regarding the Consolidated Council of State Act.[484] In order to comply with the Constitutional Court's case law, the Flemish legislator replaced Article 34 with another regulation.[485] The Constitutional Court has rejected an annulment appeal against this new regulation.[486]

I. Restoration in Kind

583. In 1980, the evolution in holding administrative authorities accountable was affirmed in a judgment by the Court of Cassation.[487] The Court held that ordinary courts may not only award damages in tort to natural persons or legal persons for injury caused by administrative authorities, but also that the courts were further entitled to order restoration in kind from the administrative authority, without violating the separation of powers.

J. Monetary Compliance Penalties

584. In order to ensure compliance with judgments not involving a monetary claim, a plaintiff may request of the ordinary courts[488] and some administrative tribunals[489] the imposition of a monetary penalty which will become due if and when the judgment is not adequately complied with. The monetary penalty may be imposed as a lump sum or as a periodic amount per violation or per time unit. In its judgment, the court or tribunal will set an ultimate time frame within which the administrative authority has to comply, failing which the penalty will be due and payable until the judgment has been complied with.

There are, however, some differences between a monetary penalty imposed by the ordinary courts and one imposed by the Council of State. First, if the remedy is sought from the ordinary courts, the entire penalty amount is payable to the petitioning party. For penalties set by the Council of State, only one-half is payable to the petitioning party. The other half goes into a special fund aimed at modernising and organising administrative courts. Second, a monetary penalty can be sought at the initial stage of proceedings before the ordinary courts (before judgment is rendered). In proceedings before the Council of State, the remedy may only be sought after judgment is rendered against the administrative authority, and after specific and separate proceedings have been commenced. Third, the ordinary courts can impose payment of the penalty directly on a public servant, whereas the Council of State will impose it on the administrative authority itself.

---

484. Cons., Judgment No. 152/2015, 29 Oct. 2015.
485. Article 5 of the Flemish Act of 3 July 2015, *Gazette,* 16 Jul. 2015.
486. Cons., Judgment No. 153/2016, 1 Dec. 2016.
487. Cass., 26 Jun. 1980, *Pas.*, 1980, I, 1341.
488. Articles 1385*bis* et seq. Civil Procedure Code.
489. See, e.g., Art. 36 Consolidated Council of State Act.

K. Enforceability and Execution of Judgments Against Administrative Authorities

585. Until the 1990s, the impact of judgments ordering compensation was limited since Belgian courts held that such judgments could not be enforced seeing as administrative authorities were in principle immune from enforcement. This immunity was based on the principle of continuity, namely that the public service must function without interruption and in a regular way.

Both the caselaw and legislation have increasingly diluted the force of this principle. In a case against Belgium, the ECommHR considered the principle of immunity, which delayed the enforcement of judgments or even prevented it, to interfere unduly with an individual's right to peaceful enjoyment of property, as guaranteed under Article 1 of the First Protocol to the EConvHR.[490] The ECtHR, for its part, held that the enforcement of a judgment of any court must be regarded as an integral part of the right to a fair trial as guaranteed by Article 6 EConvHR. The right of access to the courts would be illusory if a legal system permitted a final, binding judicial decision to remain inoperative.[491] In 1994, Article 1412*bis* was added to the Civil Procedure Code indicating which property of an administrative authority can be subject to execution if the authority were held liable.

Selected Further Reading

Leroy, M. *Contentieux administratif* (5th) (Anthemis, 2011).

Lewalle, P. & L. Donnay. *Contentieux administratif* (3rd) (Larcier, 2008).

Mast, A., J. Dujardin, M. Van Damme & J. Vande Lanotte. *Overzicht van het Belgisch Administratief Recht* (21st) (Kluwer, 2017).

Pâques, M. *Principes de contentieux administratif.* (Larcier, 2017).

Salmon, J., J. Jaumotte & E. Thibaut. *Le Conseil d'Etat de Belgique* (Bruylant, 2012) 2 vols.

Theunis, J. *De exceptie van onwettigheid* (Die Keure, 2011).

---

490. ECommHR, Report, 6 Mar. 1990, *Dierckx v Belgium*, No. 11966/86.

491. ECtHR, *Hornsby v Greece* (19 Mar. 1997).

Chapter 5. Rights and Status of Foreigners

§1. Constitutional Rights and Protections

I. Equal Protection

586. One of the cornerstones of a State under the rule of law is the principle that public authorities must offer equal protection in law to all citizens. In German-speaking countries, this principle has been the subject of much discussion and is called the '*Gleichheitssatz*'. In the Belgian Constitution, this is laid down under Title II, 'Belgians and their Rights', providing in Article 10 that all Belgians are equal before the law. From the wording of Article 10 and Heading II, it might be (wrongly) deduced that only Belgian citizens are entitled to benefit from equal protection. Article 10 should be read, however, in conjunction with Article 191 of the Constitution providing that every foreigner who is within the territory of Belgium benefits from the same protection of person and property, with the exception of specific cases established by an explicit and unequivocal Act of Parliament. Moreover, any such restrictions must comply with the international conventions to which Belgium has acceded. Article 1 of the EConvHR may be mentioned in this respect. Pursuant thereto, Belgium has undertaken to secure the rights and freedoms granted under the EConvHR to everyone within its jurisdiction, including foreigners, howsoever short their stay on Belgian territory may be.

II. Restrictions

587. The Constitution contains a number of provisions which distinguish between nationals and non-nationals. As mentioned previously[492], the Constitution restricts in principle the exercise of political rights, namely the right to vote and the right to be elected, to Belgian citizens. However, the Constitution authorises the federal Parliament to derogate from this rule both for EU citizens who do not have Belgian nationality and for residents of Belgium who are not citizens of a Member State of the European Union (Article 8 Constitution).

588. Since legislation in 1999, EU citizens duly registered with the municipal authorities have had the right to vote and stand as candidates in municipal elections.[493] In order to be included on the list of registered voters, European citizens must submit a written application to the municipality where they reside, recording their nationality and address. If they meet all other requirements (e.g., having attained the age of 18), and the Municipal Executive decides to add their names to the list of registered voters, they will be allowed to vote and be elected. A denial by

492. See Pt. IV. Ch. 1. §1 'Constitutional Provisions Concerning Nationality'.
493. Implementation of Directive 94/80/EC of 19 December 1994 by Act of 27 January 1999, *Gazette*, 30 Jan. 1999.

the municipality may be challenged before the Court of Appeal. Non-Belgian candidates may be elected to the Municipal Council, and may become only Municipal Councillors but not Mayor.

589. After a vociferous political debate[494], persons who are not citizens of an EU Member State have been granted the right to vote in municipal elections by the Act of 19 March 2004.[495] They too must submit a written application to the municipality where they reside. In addition to recording their nationality and address, applicants from outside the EU must also declare that they will respect the Constitution, the laws of Belgium and the EConvHR. They must also have been in Belgium legally and without interruption for five years. And in contrast to EU citizens, persons who are not citizens of an EU Member State do not have the right to stand as candidates (the passive voting right).

590. Regarding elections for municipal district governments, citizens of EU Member States and persons who are not citizens of an EU Member State both have like voting rights for those elections.[496]

591. As covered earlier[497], the appointment to civil service and military functions is also restricted to Belgians, but legislation may establish exceptions in specific cases (Article 10 paragraph 2 Constitution). This provision relates *inter alia* to the particular status of EU citizens, deriving from the caselaw of the ECJ on Article 45 §4 TFEU. It has been proposed to revise Article 10 paragraph 2 of the Constitution in order to reconcile it to the caselaw of the ECJ. According to this caselaw the restriction to Belgians only applies for those functions which involve direct or indirect participation in the exercise of powers conferred by public law and duties designed to safeguard the general interests of the State or of other public authorities and which therefore require a special relationship of allegiance to the State.

592. As for civil rights, the distinction between Belgians and foreigners is of only minor importance, the exercise of civil rights being irrespective of Belgian citizenship (Article 3 Civil Code). Aliens authorised to become established in Belgium and duly recorded in the municipal register of inhabitants, enjoy all the civil rights granted to Belgians for as long as they continue to reside in Belgium (Article 5 Civil Code). Everywhere in Belgium, real and personal property may be inherited, disposed of and held by aliens in the same manner as by Belgian citizens (Article 726 Civil Code). A differential treatment of foreign non-nationals as to the exercise of civil rights can be found in the field of civil procedure.[498]

494. Unlike the voting rights for citizens of a Member State of the European Union, granting voting rights to residents who are not citizens of an EU Member State does not stem from European or international obligations.

495. *Gazette,* 23 Apr. 2004.

496. At present, municipal district governments only exist in Antwerp.

497. See Pt. IV. Ch. 1. §1.

498. The most important example of such different treatment is the obligation imposed on some foreign plaintiffs to provide security for costs and damages, the *cautio judicatum solvi*: Article 851 Civil Procedure Code. Within the scope of EU law, however, the ECJ has considered this obligation as

593. Foreigners are subject to a number of restrictions in the socio-economic field. The restrictions applying to foreign workers in their access to the Belgian labour market are quite rigorous. Foreign workers who are not citizens of an EU Member State must obtain permission to work. In order to be allowed to work in Belgium as a self-employed person, they must have a professional card. On the other hand, foreigners must also pay taxes and are in principle entitled to social security benefits.

§2. Immigration, Expulsion, and Extradition of Foreigners

I. Immigration and Deportation

594. The following sketches the general legislative principles governing permission to enter to, and deportation from, Belgian territory.[499] Specific rules concerning certain privileged categories of foreign non-nationals, such as recognised asylum seekers[500], students, and cross-border workers are not dealt with. Since March 2008, there is a specialised Minister of Immigration and Asylum Policy, administering the executive powers under the Immigration and Asylum Act. This Minister is also responsible for the relevant government department.

A. *Entry into Belgian Territory*

595. As a preliminary remark, it may be observed that entry into Belgian territory automatically entails a right of entry to the territory of the Schengen countries, the Schengen Agreements having eliminated internal border controls. It also implies that a visa is issued for the whole of the Schengen territory (with some restrictions possible).

596. In order to enter Belgian territory, a person must meet the following general conditions of: (1) bearing the required documents, (2) disposing of adequate means of support, (3) not being reported as an undesirable person in Belgium or in the other Schengen countries (e.g., as a result of a conviction for a criminal offence

a prohibited discrimination when the same requirement may not be imposed on home state nationals: see, e.g., ECJ, Case C-323/95 (*Hayes*), 20 Mar. 1997.

499. Pursuant to, in general, the Act of 15 December 1980 regarding Permission to Enter Belgium, Period of Stay, Settlement and Deportation of Foreigners, *Gazette,* 31 Dec. 1980 (the 'Immigration and Asylum Act').

500. Foreign non-nationals may be recognised as refugees, if they meet the conditions required by Art. 48/3 of the Immigration and Asylum Act which implements the 1951 Geneva Convention Relating to the Status of Refugees. Alternatively, an asylum seeker may be granted subsidiary protection if he meets the conditions of Art. 48/4 of the Act. The Belgian Commissioner-General for Refugees and Stateless Persons is responsible for decisions concerning both refugee status and subsidiary protection. Both an asylum seeker and the Minister responsible, or his representative, may lodge an appeal against the Commissioner's decision with the Immigration and Asylum Tribunal (an administrative court). An asylum seeker recognised as a refugee or granted subsidiary protection cannot be sent back to the country from which he has fled.

punishable by extradition), (4) not being considered by the responsible Minister as potentially prejudicial to public peace, order, national security, or international relations, and (5) not having been subject to an entry ban.

A foreign non-national who enters Belgian territory in compliance with the above-mentioned conditions is not allowed to remain more than three months in Belgium unless otherwise provided, such as where his travel documents stipulate another period of time ('short stay'). Unless exempted, a foreigner not staying in hotel accommodation must register within three working days of arrival with the municipal authorities of the place where he is staying.

597. In order to be allowed to stay in Belgium for a period beyond three months, a person must have obtained residence permit from the Minister or his representative. In principle, an application for this authorisation must be made in the Belgian embassy or with the consular representative in the country of residence of the applicant. In some cases, the application may occur in Belgium. For instance, in 'exceptional circumstances' which make it impossible for the applicant to return to his country of origin, the application may be submitted in Belgium. In this case, applicants may obtain a residence authorisation from the Minister providing specific elements support their remaining in Belgium.[501] This may be the case, for example, with applicants who have a family with Belgian children. The same is true for those foreigners who, suffering from severe illness, demonstrate that there are no adequate medical means for treatment in their country of origin.[502]

598. Some categories of persons are legally entitled to establish themselves in Belgium either on the basis of an international treaty (e.g., TFEU) or on the basis of an Act (e.g., foreigners fulfilling the conditions (other than those pertaining to residence) for acquiring or reacquiring Belgian nationality). Others may apply for an authorisation of establishment in Belgium. In principle, this authorisation may only be granted to those who are already permitted or authorised to reside in Belgium. A request for an establishment authorisation must be addressed to the municipal authorities who then transmit the file to the Foreigner's Affairs Office. Unless there are objections based on reasons of public order or national security, an establishment authorisation may be granted to a foreign non-national who proves that he has lived legally and without interruption in Belgium for five years. The establishment authorisation is valid for an indefinite period. Foreigners authorised to become established in Belgium are recorded in the municipal register of inhabitants for the municipality where they reside.

Since 2008, foreign non-nationals who are not citizens of an EU Member State and who are permitted or authorised to reside in Belgium may also apply for the status of 'long-term resident'.[503]

---

501. This possibility for a 'regularization' is based on Art. 9*bis* of the Immigration and Asylum Act.
502. This possibility for a 'medical regularization' is based on Art. 9*ter* of the Immigration and Asylum Act.
503. In accordance with Directive 2003/109/EC of 25 Nov. 2003 concerning the status of third-country nationals who are long-term residents.

599. A foreign non-national permitted or authorised to stay more than three months in Belgium is recorded in the foreigners register by the municipality of his place of residence. A residence permit is granted for an indefinite period, unless a time limit is otherwise expressly set on account of the applicant's particular circumstances.

600. Some categories of persons are, however, exempted from the obligation to apply for a residence permit and are legally entitled to reside in Belgium for more than three months. A foreigner's right of residence may, for example, be recognised by an international treaty. This is the case, for instance, for citizens of an EU Member State and their family members (spouses, dependents, and parents). They enjoy the right of entry and of residence by virtue of the TFEU. Other categories of persons legally entitled to reside in Belgium for over three months are family members (spouses, non-dependent children) of foreigners authorised to reside in Belgium, or certain foreign non-nationals fulfilling the conditions (other than those pertaining to residence) for acquiring or reacquiring Belgian nationality.

B. *Exclusion from Belgian Territory*

601. The Immigration and Asylum Act provides for various kinds of exclusion measures. First, Belgian border control authorities may refuse entry into Belgian territory to those foreign non-nationals who do not fulfil the prerequisite port-of-entry conditions, in effect turning them back.

602. Second, in some cases (e.g., when the port-of-entry conditions are not, or are no longer, fulfilled) the Minister or his representative may order a foreigner, who is neither authorised nor permitted to remain for over three months on Belgian territory or to become established in Belgium, to leave the territory. Such order may, for example, be issued for tourists or businessmen who have legally gained access to Belgian territory, but who then remain beyond the normally permitted three month period. In this case, the foreign non-national may, if it is judged necessary, be immediately taken to the border. He may then be detained during the period strictly necessary to carry out the order.

603. Third, the Minister or his representative may order a foreign non-national, who is otherwise authorised or permitted to remain in Belgium for more than three months or to become permanently established in Belgium, to leave Belgian territory for (serious) reasons of public order or national security.

II. Extradition

604. This section covers the main principles of Belgian extradition law. A distinction must be drawn between extradition to a Member State of the EU and extradition to those States which are not part of the EU. Regarding the latter, extradition is restricted to foreign non-nationals: Belgium does not extradite Belgian nationals to non-EU States. This matter is governed by the 1833 and 1874 Extradition Acts[504] and various bilateral and multilateral treaties to which Belgium has acceded. Article 1 of the 1874 Extradition Act stipulates that Belgium may only extradite if there is an extradition treaty between Belgium and the requesting State providing for reciprocity in the extradition of offenders.

605. Belgium will only extradite if the requesting State has charged a person with or convicted him of a criminal offence constituting an extradition offence. Two conditions must be fulfilled before a criminal offence may be considered an 'extradition offence'. First, the offence alleged in the extradition request must be a criminal offence under both the legislation of the requesting State and of Belgium (the dual criminality principle). The extradition of an accused may be allowed for offences which, under the legislation of both the requesting State and of Belgium, are punishable by imprisonment for a maximum term of at least one year. The extradition of a convict to serve a prison sentence may be granted if a period of at least one year's incarceration was imposed. Extradition is also possible for the enforcement of security measures imposed for an indefinite period of time or for a period of at least four months' confinement. Second, the criminal offence for which extradition is requested must not be excluded under the extradition treaty concluded between Belgium and the requesting State. A person shall not be extradited for an offence punishable by death in the requesting State, unless the requesting State guarantees explicitly not to carry out the death penalty. Except in special cases, only offences of a non-political character may be considered extradition offences (political offence exception). Nor will extradition be allowed when there are serious grounds for assuming that the request is made in order to prosecute or punish a person on the grounds of race, religion, nationality, or political opinion, or when there is a risk that the accused's situation will be aggravated because of these grounds. Finally, extradition is not allowed when there is a serious risk that the person to be extradited will be subject to flagrant or clear abuse of due process, to torture or to inhuman and degrading treatment in the State requesting the extradition.

606. Extradition proceedings in Belgium regarding States not members of the EU involves two phases. The first takes place in the Committal and Bail Court (Appeal Division) for the judicial district where the person was arrested. This Court renders a non-binding opinion on the legality of the extradition request. The second stage involves the federal government deciding whether or not to grant extradition. An appeal against the Ministerial Decree granting extradition may be filed with the Administrative Tribunal Division of the Council of State.

607. The 'European arrest warrant' has replaced the above-mentioned extradition procedure in respect of extraditions to Member States of the EU.[505] In Belgium, the European arrest warrant procedure has been implemented by a 2003

504. *Gazette,* 4 Oct. 1833 and *Gazette,* 17 Mar. 1874.
505. Council Framework Decision of 13 June 2002 on the European arrest warrant and the surrender procedures between Member States.

Act.[506] A European arrest warrant is valid throughout the EU and may be issued by a national judicial authority for persons accused of an offence for which the minimum penalty is at least a year in prison, or for persons sentenced to a prison term of at least four months. The European arrest warrant has created faster and simpler surrender procedures, and means that Belgium cannot refuse to surrender Belgian citizens to another Member State of the EU on the grounds of being nationals. Moreover, the dual criminality principle is abolished for thirty-two categories of serious offences, such as terrorism, trafficking in human beings or illicit trafficking in arms.[507] Unlike the standard extradition proceedings, there is here no involvement of the Belgian government or the Minister of Justice. In the case where the person concerned so consents, the Public Prosecutor will decide on the implementation of the European arrest warrant. In cases where no consent is forthcoming, the Committal and Bail Court (Trial Division) decides whether or not to extradite.

III. Substantive and Procedural Rights in Expulsion and Extradition Cases

A. *The Immigration and Asylum Act*

608. All administrative decisions must be well reasoned: they have to set out the facts justifying the decision, except if matters of national security prevent their disclosure. The decisions must be communicated to the persons concerned. Notice of the decision must also indicate the possible next steps, and their respective limitation periods.

609. Appeals against administrative decisions concerning foreign non-nationals are brought before the Immigration and Asylum Tribunal.[508] In asylum cases (concerning refugee status and subsidiary protection), the Tribunal has the authority both to annul decisions and to substitute a decision of its own. During these proceedings, the asylum seeker cannot be removed from Belgian territory (with restrictions in case of multiple asylum applications). In other cases (e.g., concerning visas, reuniting families, orders to leave the territory, etc.) the Tribunal has only the authority to annul or suspend the administrative decision in issue. Moreover, in general, the fact that proceedings are still ongoing does not suspend the possibility of removing the foreign non-national from Belgian territory. In urgent cases, an interlocutory procedure is available.

610. In a limited number of cases, a 'cassation' appeal (i.e. final appeal only on questions of law) may be brought before the Administrative Tribunal Division of the Council of State against decisions of the Immigration and Asylum Tribunal. The

506. Act of 19 December 2003, *Gazette,* 22 Dec. 2003.
507. The Constitutional Court has rejected a petition for annulment criticising this list: Cons., Judgment No. 128/2007, 10 Oct. 2007 (after having submitted a preliminary question to the ECJ: ECJ (GC), Case C-303/05, 3 May 2007).
508. Established in 2006 pursuant to the Act of 15 September 2006, *Gazette,* 6 Oct. 2006 and coming into force on 1 Jun. 2007.

Administrative Tribunal Division of the Council of State deals with questions of law only, and does not examine the merits of the case.

611. A foreigner who is subject to a measure depriving him of his liberty may challenge the legality of that measure by appeal before the relevant ordinary courts, in particular, the Committal and Bail Court.

B. *Human Rights Conventions*

612. Neither the EConvHR nor the ICCPR expressly provide a right not to be extradited or expelled. These treaties do, however, impose an obligation on the High Contracting Parties to comply with certain procedural guarantees. Article 13 ICCPR provides:

> … an alien lawfully in the territory of a State Party to the (aforesaid) Covenant may be expelled therefrom only in pursuance of a decision reached in accordance with law and shall, except where compelling reasons of national security otherwise require, be allowed to submit the reasons against his expulsion and to have his case reviewed by, and be represented for the purpose before the competent authority or a person or persons especially designated by the competent authority.

The Immigration and Asylum Act may be considered to have been adopted in compliance with Article 13 ICCPR. A similar procedural guarantee is laid down in Article 1 of the Seventh Protocol to the EConvHR.

613. On the other hand, Belgium has acceded to the Fourth Protocol to the EConvHR prohibiting collective expulsion of foreign non-nationals in its Article 4.

In the *Conka* case, the ECtHR held Belgium to be in breach of the Fourth Protocol because of its collective expulsion of four Slovakian nationals of Roma origin.[509] In the same case, the Court stressed that Articles 5 and 13 EConvHR provide additional fundamental rights for foreign non-nationals facing expulsion. The Court held that the applicants did not have a remedy available that satisfied the requirements of Article 13 to air their complaint under Article 4 of the Fourth Protocol. Moreover, the Court found that there had been a violation of Article 5 due to the absence of effective remedies against the detention of the four foreigners.

The Fourth Protocol – as well as Article 12 §§1–3 ICCPR – contains two other rights on the exercise of which some restrictions may be imposed: 'the right for everyone lawfully within the territory of a State to liberty of movement within that territory and freedom to choose his residence' (Article 2 §1) as well as 'the freedom to leave any country, including his own' (Article 2 §2).

614. A decision to extradite or to expel a person may also give rise to an issue under Article 3 EConvHR, if substantial grounds are shown for believing that the

509. ECtHR, *Conka v Belgium* (5 Feb. 2002).

person concerned faces a real risk of being subjected to torture, or to inhuman or degrading treatment or punishment in the receiving State.[510]

The ECtHR has found Belgium liable for its practice of 'liberating' foreign non-nationals in the in-transit zone of the Brussels Airport (instead of detaining them pending refoulement after denial of their asylum claim).[511] The Court held that this practice resulted in an illegal deprivation of liberty, and that this practice constituted inhuman or degrading treatment. Hence, the Court concluded that Belgium had violated Articles 3 and 5 of the EConvHR. As a result of this judgment, Belgium is no longer authorised to 'liberate' foreigners in the in-transit zone. The ECtHR has found Belgium in breach of these Articles in other cases as well.[512]

Belgium has been found in violation of Article 3 EConvHR when it extradited an Iraqi national, convicted in absentia for membership of a terrorist organisation.[513] The Court held that Belgium should have acquired diplomatic assurances that the petitioner would not be subjected to any treatment contrary to Article 3 EConvHR after his return to Iraq.

In an important Grand Chamber case, the ECtHR decided that Article 3 of the EConvHR would be violated if a Georgian national who had committed serious crimes in Belgium would be deported to Georgia, because he was a leukaemia patient in need of a donor transplant and this procedure was not available in Georgia.[514]

Another important Grand Chamber case is *M.S.S. v Belgium and Greece*.[515] It concerned the expulsion of an asylum seeker to Greece by the Belgian authorities pursuant to the EU Dublin II Regulation. Despite applying the Regulation, Belgium was nonetheless found to have violated Article 3 EConvHR because of having exposed the asylum seeker both to the risks linked to the deficiencies in the asylum procedure in Greece and to detention and living conditions in Greece which themselves were in breach of Article 3.

615. Article 8 EConvHR grants everyone the right of respect for his family life. It implies that a foreigner lawfully settled in Belgium may argue that he is being deprived of the companionship of his family, and, according to the particular circumstances of the case, may oblige the State to admit members of his family on its territory.[516] Article 8 EConvHR also entails that a foreign non-national at risk of deportation may object to deportation on the basis of an interference with his family life in violation of the conditions set out in Article 8 §2 EConvHR, namely, that the order for deportation or expulsion was not given 'in accordance with the law' or

510. ECtHR, *Soering v UK* (7 Jul. 1989) (extradition); *Cruz Varas v Sweden* (20 Mar. 1991) (expulsion).
511. ECtHR, *Riad and Idiab v Belgium* (24 Jan. 2008).
512. ECtHR, *Mubilanzila Mayeka and Kaniki Mitunga v Belgium* (12 Oct. 2006) (detention of an unaccompanied 5-year-old Congolese girl in a closed refugee centre); *Muskhadzhiyeva et al. v Belgium* (19 Jan. 2010) (detention of mother and children in a closed refugee centre not adapted for children); *Kanagaratnam et al. v Belgium* (13 Dec. 2011).
513. ECtHR, *M.S. v Belgium* (31 Jan. 2012).
514. ECtHR (GC), *Paposhvili v Belgium* (13 Dec. 2016).
515. ECtHR (GC), *M.S.S v Belgium and Greece* (21 Jan. 2011). For a critical comment, see M. Bossuyt, *Eur. Human Rights Law Rev.* (2011) 581–596.
516. ECtHR, *Abdulaziz, Cabales and Balkandali v UK* (28 May 1985).

cannot be considered to be 'necessary in a democratic society' within one or more of the legitimate goals explicitly listed there. For example, an expulsion order against a serious juvenile offender, 22-years-old and a second-generation immigrant, was held to constitute a violation of his right of respect for his family life.[517]

On the other hand, Article 8 EConvHR does not include a right to be granted a permanent residence permit in a Contracting State, not even for minors in vulnerable circumstances. The Contracting States remain indeed free to control the access to and stay periods in their territory by foreign non-nationals.[518]

SELECTED FURTHER READING

Bossuyt, M. *Strasbourg et les demandeurs d'asile: des juges sur un terrain glissant* (Bruylant, 2010).

Carlier, J.-Y. & S. Saroléa. *Droit des étrangers* (Larcier, 2016).

Denys, L. *Overzicht van het vreemdelingenrecht* (4th) (INNI, 2019).

Foblets, M. & D. Vanheule (eds). *Legal Remedies in European Migration Law* (Intersentia, 2012).

517. ECtHR, *Moustaquim v Belgium* (18 Feb. 1991).
518. ECtHR, *Chbihi Loudoudi et al. v Belgium* (16 Dec. 2014).

Part V. Specific Issues

Chapter 1. War, Treaty and Foreign Affairs Powers

§1. National Defence and the Police Services

616. In matters of national defence, the Executive Branch plays a predominant role. The power of the King relating to national defence stems from several constitutional provisions: (i) Article 107 paragraph 1 conferring on the King the power to bestow military rank; (ii) Article 91 paragraph 2 having the King take the oath ' … to maintain this country's independence, and preserve its territorial integrity', and most importantly (iii) Article 167 granting the King the power to command the armed forces, to declare a state of war or cessation of hostilities, and to conclude treaties falling within the federal jurisdiction.

617. It is now widely assumed – though the opposite view was once held – that the King's exercise of command over the armed forces occurs under Ministerial responsibility, as is the case for all his powers. Parliament has thus the power of supervision *a posteriori*, through the ordinary processes of political supervision over government policy.

Some matters nonetheless require a prior decision of the House of Representatives. An Act determines in which way the army is recruited, and regulates promotions, and the rights and duties of military personnel (Article 182 Constitution). Military personnel cannot be deprived of rank, honours and pensions other than in the manner prescribed by Act (Article 186 Constitution). It determines by annual Act the number of military personnel on active duty (Article 183 Constitution). Finally, foreign troops may not be admitted in service of the State, nor occupy the territory or traverse it other than by authority of an Act (Article 185 Constitution). Thus, a 1962 Act provides that armies of countries which, like Belgium, are part of the North Atlantic Treaty Organization (NATO), may be stationed on Belgian territory or may pass through it.[519] In the 1980s, the question whether this statute authorised the Belgian government to enter agreements permitting the stationing on Belgian territory of cruise missiles under foreign supervision, caused much controversy in Belgium.

519. Act of 11 April 1962, *Gazette,* 20 Apr. 1962.

618. Apart from the provisions on the military, Title VI of the Constitution 'The Armed Forces' also addresses in Article 184 the integrated police service, structured on two levels, which provides that its organisation and powers are regulated by federal Act.[520] Those two levels are federal and local. The essential elements to the status of police services personnel are regulated by federal Act.[521]

619. A 1991 Act details the circumstances in which an export or transit license for weapons, for ammunition, and for equipment which may be used for military purposes or law enforcement, as well as for related technology is to be denied.[522] This is the case, for example, if the export or transit would seriously jeopardise the international objectives Belgium has set and, in particular, if it would entail a manifest violation of human rights. The 2003 amendments to Article 6 §1 VI of the Special Majority Act on Institutional Reform made the Regions competent for the import, export, and transit of weapons, ammunition, and equipment specifically intended for military use or law enforcement, as well as for related technology products and dual-use technologies, without prejudice to federal jurisdiction over imports and exports concerning the Belgian army and police, and in compliance with the criteria defined by the European Union Code of Conduct on arms exports. On 17 July 2007 a co-operation agreement was concluded between the federal State and the Regions concerning these matters.[523]

§2. Foreign Relations and the Impact of Restructuring the State

I. Introduction

620. The way in which the conduct of international relations is organised in federal Belgium has produced decentralisation to a degree virtually without precedent in comparative federal law. Prior to the 1993 Fourth State Reform, the division of powers in international matters between the federal authorities and the constituent entities had been the source of much controversy. The new system put in place by the 1993 amendments centres around two essential principles: (i) extending the internal autonomy of the federated entities as widely as possible into the international arena without sacrificing the coherence of Belgian foreign policy, and (ii) strengthening the jurisdiction of the federal authorities over the implementation of international and supranational law by the federated entities.

520. Act of 7 December 1998, *Gazette,* 5 Jan. 1999.

521. Essential Elements to the Status of Members of the Police Services and Related Provisions Act of 26 April 2002, *Gazette,* 30 Apr. 2002.

522. Import, Export and Transit of and Combatting the Illegal Trade in Weapons, Munitions and Related Materials and Technologies Act of 5 August 1991, *Gazette,* 10 Sep. 1991.

523. *Gazette,* 20 Dec. 2007.

II. The Treaty-Making Power

621. In foreign relations, an ever-increasing number of agreements are being concluded among States under public international law. The formal process of making treaties is rather cumbersome. We will not address the legal force of treaties in Belgium[524], but rather will discuss here the way Belgium enters treaties, as well as the effects of the State restructuring on this process.

A. *General Principles*

622. According to Article 167 §1 of the Constitution, the King, as the head of the federal executive power, 'directs international relations'. However, a qualification immediately follows: 'without limiting the powers of Communities and Regions to regulate international co-operation, including the concluding of treaties, for those matters for which they have jurisdiction pursuant to or by authority of the Constitution'. The King concludes treaties concerning other matters (Article 167 §2 Constitution). Hence, the internal, national system of the division of (exclusive) powers *ratione materiae* between the federal State, the Communities, and the Regions has been transposed to the international level.

The fact that the King 'directs international relations' cannot be considered as a jurisdictional rule, nor considered as a rule of interpretation for resolving jurisdictional disputes. No implied authority can be deduced from this to ground overseeing the exercise of Community and Region powers in the domain of international co-operation. The powers in foreign affairs can and should be exercised by the King only according to the legally prescribed mechanisms of federal supervision.

623. The Community and Region governments have the exclusive powers to enter treaties that relate exclusively to matters falling within their jurisdiction. Treaties that relate exclusively to federal matters are entered into by the King under the general rules of ministerial responsibility. Federal, Community, and Region treaties take effect only after they have been approved by the relevant Legislature (Article 167 §§2–3 Constitution). At the federal level, since the 2014 Sixth State Reform only the House of Representatives has jurisdiction over Acts approving treaties (Article 167 §2 Constitution).

624. The exclusive treaty-making powers of each government is also reflected in their exclusive powers to terminate a treaty (Article 167 §5 Constitution). Treaties concluded after 18 May 1993 that relate exclusively to the jurisdiction of the Communities and Regions are terminated by the Community or Region government concerned. Treaties before 18 May 1993 that relate exclusively to the jurisdiction of the Communities and Regions are terminated by the King at the request of the Community or Region government concerned. Where the governments of all the Communities and Regions concerned all agree, the King is obliged to terminate a treaty at their request. Where agreement cannot be reached among them, the issue

524. See Pt. I. Ch. 1. §2. 'Treaties. Hierarchy'.

may be referred to the Inter-ministerial Conference on Foreign Policy. If no consensus can be reached by the Inter-ministerial Conference, the King will negotiate with the other treaty party about a possible partial termination of the treaty.

B. Treaties and 'Mixed Jurisdiction'

625. The introduction of a parallelism between the internal division of powers and the foreign relations powers immediately raises the question as to what happens with treaties on matters where jurisdiction is 'mixed'. The international community cannot be expected to adapt the making of treaties to the internal Belgian division of powers. On the other hand, the division of powers in Belgium in practice shows that complete separation among them is impossible. On the contrary, they prove to be essentially interwoven.

According to Article 167 §4 of the Constitution, a Special Majority Act is to specify the rules for concluding 'mixed jurisdiction treaties'. But no Act as yet has specified these rules. Instead, and pursuant to Article 92*bis* §4*ter* of the Special Majority Act on Institutional Reform, the federal State, the Communities, and the Regions may do so by way of a 'co-operation agreement'. The 8 March 1994 Co-operation Agreement was adopted pursuant to the latter provision.[525]

It should be made clear that the term 'mixed jurisdiction treaties' refers only to those treaties invoking simultaneously the powers of the federal authorities and those of the Communities and/or the Regions. The term does not refer to treaties pertaining exclusively to matters under mixed Community and/or Region jurisdiction, without involving any matter of federal jurisdiction. No specific rules are provided for this type of mixed jurisdiction treaty. The 8 March 1994 Co-operation Agreement is not applicable to this latter case. For treaties that pertain exclusively to either Community or Region matters, the Community or Region has exclusive jurisdiction (see also below section D). For treaties relating to both Community and Region matters, co-ordinated action is necessary since it is improbable that the international community would accept separate action by a Community or a Region. The Communities and Regions would then be obliged to conclude a co-operation agreement to co-ordinate their actions.

C. The Co-operation Agreement of 8 March 1994

1. Negotiating and Concluding Mixed Jurisdiction Treaties

626. Whenever the federal government intends to start negotiations regarding a mixed jurisdiction treaty, it immediately informs the Inter-ministerial Conference on Foreign Policy. Likewise, when a Community or a Region government intends to start negotiations, it too advises the Inter-ministerial Conference so that the federal government may take steps towards concluding the treaty. The Inter-ministerial

525. *Gazette*, 17 Dec. 1996.

Conference on Foreign Policy is to establish within sixty days the character of the intended mixed jurisdiction treaty, as well as the composition of the Belgian delegation and its negotiating position. There is no hierarchy as between the delegates of the different governments. The negotiations take place under the co-ordinating leadership of the federal Department of Foreign Affairs.

Mixed jurisdiction treaties are signed by the federal Minister of Foreign Affairs or his representative, and by the designated ministers of the Community and/or Region governments concerned or their representatives.

627. A Community or Region government may inform the Inter-ministerial Conference on Foreign Policy that it does not wish to participate in negotiations for the proposed mixed jurisdiction treaty. If the Inter-ministerial Conference nevertheless decides by consensus to conclude the treaty without all the responsible authorities in Belgium taking part, the federal Minister of Foreign Affairs must inform the other treaty parties that the treaty will not have effect throughout Belgium. If no objection is raised and the treaty is duly signed, Belgium must make a reservation on the application of the treaty in its territory. Only then can the King ratify the treaty without the approval of all the federal, Community, and/or Region legislative bodies.

Already during the preparatory discussions to the 8 March 1994 Co-operation Agreement, the Legislative Division of the Council of State had indicated a growing resistance at the international level to any limitation of a treaty to certain parts of a country (the 'federal clauses'). Such a limitation is considered to be incompatible with the principles of legal security and of reciprocity of treaty obligations. In any case, in multilateral treaties, the negotiating power of any one party is very restricted because of the large number of participant parties. As for EU treaties, no such reservations are admitted.

2. Approving and Ratifying Mixed Jurisdiction Treaties

628. Mixed jurisdiction treaties can take effect only after they have been approved by the House of Representatives and by the relevant Community or Region Parliaments. The various governments have to inform one another of the approval of their respective legislatures.

Ratification is done by the King, but only after approval of the treaty by all the legislatures involved. In some cases this may mean that eight of Belgium's nine legislative assemblies have to debate a treaty. The withholding of approval by any one of them makes ratification impossible unless a reservation has been accepted.

3. Implementing and Terminating Mixed Jurisdiction Treaties

629. Each level of government and legislature concerned is charged with the implementation of a treaty in the internal legal order, insofar as the matters in the treaty come within its jurisdiction.

Mixed jurisdiction treaties are terminated by the King, but only after approval by the relevant governments within the framework of the Inter-ministerial Conference on Foreign Policy. Every government level concerned can take the initiative for termination.

D. Mechanisms Ensuring the Coherence of Foreign Policy

630. In order to ensure the coherence of Belgian foreign policy, the King can resist some treaty initiatives of the Communities and Regions. The mechanism for this is contained in Article 81 §§1–5 of the Special Majority Act on Institutional Reform implementing Article 167 §4 of the Constitution. Several steps have to be followed. The Community and Region governments must inform the federal government whenever they intend to start negotiating a treaty; and this obligation to inform applies to each subsequent act in the process towards the conclusion of the treaty (such as initialling, signatures, ratification). If the federal government objects to the intended treaty, it must communicate its objection within thirty days to the Community or Region government concerned and to the president of the Inter-ministerial Conference on Foreign Policy. The treaty-making procedure is then suspended and the Inter-ministerial Conference is required to meet in a bid to find a solution. It does so within thirty days of the date of notification of objections and, if by consensus it meets the objection, the temporary suspension is lifted. The treaty procedure can then be continued.

631. If there is no consensus within the thirty-day period, the temporary suspension will be extended to sixty days (after communication of the objection) unless the King (i.e., the federal government) confirms the suspension before that time. The Community or Region government concerned will then have to end the treaty procedure. Confirmation of the suspension by the federal government can take place only by means of a Royal Decree in Council supported by reasons, and then only on the grounds of one of the following objective criteria:

(i) the other party to the treaty is a State not recognised by Belgium;
(ii) Belgium has no diplomatic relations with the other party;
(iii) a decision or act of the State shows that relations between Belgium and the other party are broken off, suspended, or seriously jeopardised, or
(iv) the intended treaty is contrary to the international or supranational obligations of Belgium.

In the two last circumstances, the federal government can, in accordance with the same procedure, even suspend execution of treaties which have already been concluded by a Community or Region and which are exclusively related to Community or Region jurisdiction.

632. A Royal Decree by which the treaty procedure or the execution of a treaty is definitively suspended may be challenged by an appeal for annulment before the Administrative Tribunal Division of the Council of State. The Council of State has to decide the appeal within six months.

For its part, the federal government has to inform Community and Region governments regularly about its foreign policy, either voluntarily or at the request of a government, at the Inter-ministerial Conference on Foreign Policy.

III. Diplomatic Representation and Representation in International and Supranational Organisations

A. Diplomatic Representation of Belgium

633. Given the principle that the King directs international relations, he decides which States are recognised by Belgium and with which States it has diplomatic relations. Pursuant to Article 107 paragraph 2 of the Constitution, the King also makes appointments to the Foreign Service (e.g., ambassadors, consuls, other diplomats).

634. The Communities and Regions cannot grant diplomatic status to representatives they send abroad. They can, however, through voluntary co-operation agreements with the federal authorities designate 'community attachés' or 'economic and commercial regional attachés'. These attachés are then placed on the diplomatic or consular lists of Belgian embassies, consulates general, or other permanent missions as compiled by the federal Minister of Foreign Affairs. Accordingly, they fall under the diplomatic authority of the head of mission as appointed by the federal authorities.[526] The Communities and Regions may of course appoint representatives abroad or with international institutions. But these agents do not have diplomatic or consular status.

B. Representation of Belgium in International and Supranational Organisations

635. According to Article 92*bis* §4*bis* of the Special Majority Act on Institutional Reform, the federal, Community, and Region authorities must conclude one or more co-operation agreements concerning the representation of Belgium in international and supranational organisations and the procedures to determine the unified policy positions taken there (avoiding any conflicts of interest).

526. See also Cons., Judgment No. 80/2015, 28 May 2015.

1. The European Union

636. The 8 March 1994 Co-operation Agreement (as amended in 2003 and 2004) arranges the representation of Belgium in the Council of Ministers of the EU.[527] Presided by the federal Minister of Foreign Affairs, preparatory meetings are held with the Communities and the Regions. In case of disagreement, the dispute is brought before the Inter-ministerial Conference for Foreign Policy. If the disagreement is not resolved there, the Belgium representative in the European Council of Ministers may, exceptionally, abstain from voting. In that case or in urgent cases, the representative may adopt *ad referendum* the point of view closest to the general interest. Following further internal consultations, Belgium's definitive point of view must then be communicated within three days to the European Presidency.

637. The Community and Region governments are empowered to commit Belgium in the European Council of Ministers (Article 81 §6 Special Majority Act on Institutional Reform). The 8 March 1994 Co-operation Agreement divides the European Councils of Ministers into six categories. In Category I, Belgium is represented exclusively by a federal Minister (general affairs, economic and financial affairs, budgetary affairs, justice, telecommunications, consumer affairs, development co-operation and protection of the citizen portfolios). In Category II, the federal Minister is assisted by a Community or Region Minister (internal market, public health, energy, transport and social affairs portfolios). In Category III, Belgium is represented by a Community or Region Minister assisted by a federal Minister (industry and research, environment). In Category IV, Belgium is represented exclusively by a Community or Region Minister (culture, education, youth, tourism, housing and municipal planning). In Category V, Belgium is represented exclusively by the relevant Minister of the Flemish Region (fishing). In Category VI, the federal Minister is assisted by the relevant Ministers of the Flemish and the Walloon Regions (agriculture), and the former must abstain from voting in case of a disagreement between the Regions. For Categories II, III and IV, a rotation system is agreed among the Communities and the Regions so that Belgium is always represented by only one Minister with voting power in each category of the European Council of Ministers. This Minister is assisted in the European Council of Ministers of Categories II, III and VI by one or more minister-assessors.

2. Other Organisations

638. Pursuant to Article 92*bis* §4*bis* of the Special Majority Act on Institutional Reform, a co-operation agreement was concluded on 30 June 1994 concerning the representation of Belgium on issues of 'mixed jurisdiction' in other international organisations.[528] The most important of them are the United Nations and its specialised agencies, the WTO, the OECD, the Council of Europe, and the Benelux. To

527. Co-operation Agreement of 8 March 1994, *Gazette,* 17 Nov. 1994, amended on 13 Feb. 2003, *Gazette,* 25 Feb. 2003 and 7 Jun. 2004, *Gazette,* 4 Mar. 2010.
528. *Gazette,* 19 Nov. 1994.

determine the Belgian point of view at the ministerial conferences of these organisations, preparatory meetings are held with the Communities and the Regions presided by the federal Minister of Foreign Affairs. These consultations also deal with the composition of the Belgian delegation. For organisations where regular intergovernmental conferences take place, the delegation is headed by the authority principally concerned. Finally, the Communities and the Regions each appoint a representative to Belgium's permanent missions in international organisations.

639. In case of disagreement among the governments as to the approach to be taken at an international conference, an ad hoc working group or, as a last resort, the Inter-ministerial Conference on Foreign Policy will try to resolve the issue and determine a common standpoint. In the case of continued disagreement, no one government can impose its position on another. Hence the Belgian delegation will not have an agreed position and it may be therefore obliged to abstain from voting. If the delegation is asked to change its viewpoint during negotiations, the head of delegation must consult with the governments involved. If there is no sufficient time to obtain the opinions of each of them, the head of delegation has the right to adopt a standpoint *ad referendum*. Where the international organisation does not allow for such positions, or if there is continued disagreement, the delegation must register an abstention.

640. Separate co-operation agreements can make the general rules of the 30 June 1994 Co-operation Agreement also applicable to Belgian representation in international organisations, the activities of which relate to the exclusive powers of the Communities and Regions. These co-operation agreements must be preceded by consultations among the federal government and the Community and Region governments concerned.

IV. Proceedings Before International and Supranational Tribunals; Substitution Mechanism; Specific Substitution Mechanism Concerning Climate Change

641. Article 81 §7 of the Special Majority Act on Institutional Reform provides the rules for commencing actions before international and supranational tribunals. Here too a distinction has to be made according to the subject matter of the dispute. If it concerns only a federal matter, the federal authorities have exclusive jurisdiction to appear before the international or supranational tribunal. Where the dispute relates solely to matters within the jurisdiction of the Communities or Regions, the federal State will begin an action, at the request of the Community or Region government involved, against the international party concerned. Such a request must be filed with the Inter-ministerial Conference on Foreign Policy. The Conference will decide by consensus among the governmental authorities concerned whether it is necessary to issue process. If no consensus can be reached there, the King is obliged to file the necessary claim immediately. When the dispute concerns matters of mixed federal and Community and/or Region powers, the federal State acts according to the procedures provided for in a co-operation agreement concluded pursuant to Article 92*bis* §4*ter* of the Special Majority Act on Institutional Reform. Pursuant to the 11 July 1994 Co-operation Agreement, the Inter-ministerial Conference on Foreign Policy will decide by consensus on the necessity to launch proceedings.[529]

642. Until the 1993 Fourth State Reform, whereas federal authorities could be held responsible where the Communities or Regions did not observe international or supranational law, those authorities had neither the necessary instruments for supervision nor for imposing sanctions to meet the problem. In 1993 the 'substitution mechanism' was introduced into Article 169 of the Constitution and Article 16 §3 of the Special Majority Act on Institutional Reform. This mechanism enables the federal Legislative and Executive Branches temporarily to take the place of the Community or Region legislatures or governments respectively, when, through the acts or omissions of any of them, an international or supranational obligation is breached. The substitution mechanism is effected by federal Act or by Royal Decree, depending on whether a Community or Region Act or an executive measure is involved.

643. The substitution mechanism can be used *a posteriori* only, after the Belgium has been held liable by an international or supranational tribunal for breach of an international or supranational obligation by a Community or Region. It follows, for example, that a preliminary ruling of the ECJ based on Article 256 §3 of the TFEU cannot trigger the substitution mechanism. Only a condemnation *erga omnes* can. In addition to the condition of a prior judgment of an international or supranational tribunal, three other conditions have to be fulfilled to trigger the substitution mechanism. First, the federal authorities must involve the other level of government concerned in the entire dispute resolution procedure, including the proceedings before the international or supranational tribunal. Second, the 11 July 1994 Co-operation Agreement concerning proceedings in mixed jurisdiction matters must be observed. Third, the federal authorities must give notice to the other level of government concerned at least three months before the substitution measure is to be taken, by Royal Decree in Council. The term of three months may, in case of urgency, be shortened by the Royal Decree giving notice.

If these conditions are fulfilled, the federal State takes the place of the Community or Region concerned to implement the decision of the international or supranational tribunal. The measures taken in applying the substitution mechanism cease to have effect as soon as the Community or Region itself implements the decision. The federal authorities have the right to recover damages from the Community or Region involved, regarding, for instance, the cost of proceedings, indemnities in respect of the condemnation, and the costs of the substitution measures. The quantum of damages can be recouped by deduction from (federal) financial allocations to the Communities or the Regions. The conditions for applying the substitution mechanism are extremely severe, and they can be seen as a symbolic deterrent. The mechanism has not yet been applied.

529. *Gazette,* 1 Dec. 1994.

644. An additional substitution mechanism was introduced by 2014 Sixth State Reform to enable the federal State to take measures if a Community or Region was not meeting its international and European obligations to reduce emissions of greenhouse gasses (Article 16 §4 Special Majority Act on Institutional Reform). This specific substitution mechanism is preventive and does not require a ruling by an international or supranational tribunal. It can be triggered when the body founded by (authority of) the United Nations Framework Convention on Climate Change or one of its Protocols determines that the Belgian State does not comply with its obligations. It is also triggered when the Community or Region does not respond to a reasoned opinion by the European Commission regarding a failure to fulfil an EU obligation aimed at reducing greenhouse gas emissions pursuant to the Climate Change Convention or one of its Protocols, even if the EU obligation is stricter.

When those general conditions for the substitution mechanism are fulfilled, and the decision or opinion concerned has been the subject of discussions in the Intergovernmental Consultation Committee, the federal State can take the place of the concerned Community or Region in order to take the necessary steps to end the violation of those international obligations or to execute the operative part of the European Commission's reasoned opinion. These measures stop taking effect as soon as the Community or Region concerned complies with the decision or opinion or when the decision or opinion has been annulled. Similarly, the federal State can recover the costs involved by setting them off against (federal) financial allocations to the Community or Region concerned.

V. Parliamentary Involvement in Developing European Law

645. In order to remedy the 'democratic deficit' so characteristic to the framing of EU law, the Constitution and the Special Majority Act on Institutional Reform provide for certain involvement of the parliamentary assemblies in Belgium in the process of creating this law. From the start of negotiations on every amendment to the treaties establishing the EU, and the treaties and instruments whereby those treaties are modified or supplemented, the federal Houses of Parliament and the Community and the Region Parliaments are kept informed about them. They see the draft treaty before the signing of it (Article 168 Constitution and Article 16 §2 Special Majority Act on Institutional Reform). Draft European secondary legislation, such as regulations and directives, must also be communicated to the various parliamentary assemblies at the same time as they are transmitted to the Council of the European Union. The Parliaments can give their opinion on these drafts to their respective governments (Article 92*quater* Special Majority Act on Institutional Reform).

Moreover, in addition to the above internal provisions, the Treaty on the European Union has strengthened parliamentary supervision of the subsidiarity principle.[530]

SELECTED FURTHER READING

Alen, A. & R. Ergec. *Federal Belgium after the Fourth State Reform of 1993, Texts and Documents* (2nd) (Ministry of Foreign Affairs, External Trade and Development Co-operation, 1998).

Alen, A. & P. Peeters. 'Federal Belgium within the International Legal Order: Theory and Practice'. In *International Law: Theory and Practice. Essays in Honour of Eric Suy* (Martinus Nijhoff, 1998) 123–143.

Belleflamme, F., M. Belmessieri, P.O. de Broux, et. al. 'Les relations internationales de l'Etat belge: entre statu quo et fausse simplification'. In *La sixième réforme de l'Etat: l'art de ne pas choisir ou l'art du compromis?* edited by H. Dumont, M. El Berhoumi & I. Hachez (Larcier, 2015) 185–197.

Ganshof van der Meersch, W.J. 'Le commandement de l'armée et la responsabilité ministérielle en droit constitutionnel belge'. *Rev. Univ. Br.* (1948–1949): 256–321.

Ganshof van der Meersch, W.J. 'Défense nationale et souveraineté'. *Rev. Univ. Br.* (1950–1951): 215–253.

Leroy, M. 'Fédéralisme et relations internationales. Les communautés et régions belges et l'union européenne'. *Administration Publique* (2004): 1–14.

Pas, W. 'The Belgian "National Parliament" from the Perspective of the EU Constitutional Treaty'. In *National and Regional Parliaments in the European Constitutional Order* edited by P. Kiiver (Europa Law, 2006) 55–76.

Pas, W. 'The Role of the Belgian Regions and Communities in International and European Law'. In *Regioni e Autonomie Territoriali nel Diritto Internazionale ed Europeo* edited by L. Daniele (Editoriale Scientifica, 2006) 313–337.

Peeters, P. 'Subnational Government and Foreign Relations – the Belgian Case'. In *Institutional Development in Divided Societies* edited by B. De Villiers et al. (HSRC Publishers, 1998) 345–375.

Vandenbruwaene, W., P. Popelier & C. Janssens. 'Article 260 TFEU Sanctions in Multi-tiered Member States'. *Perspectives on Federalism* (2015): 133–162.

Verrijdt, W. 'Belgium'. In *Member States' Constitutions and EU Integration* edited by S. Griller, M. Claes, L. Papadopoulou & R. Puff (Bloomsbury, forthcoming).

Wouters, J. & L. De Smet. 'The Legal Position of Federal States and Their Federated Entities in International Relations – the Case of Belgium'. In *Ambiguity in the Rule of Law. The Interface Between National and International Legal Systems* edited by T.A.J.A. Vandamme & J.-H. Reestman (Europa Law, 2001) 121–162.

530. According to Declaration No. 51 of Belgium on national parliaments (C83/355, OJ 30 Mar. 2010), not only the Houses of the federal Parliament but also the parliamentary assemblies of the Communities and Regions act, in terms of the competences exercised by the Union, as components of the national parliamentary system or chambers of the national Parliament.

Chapter 2. Taxing and Spending Power

646. No public authority can exist without raising or spending money. In Belgium, the public authorities which have taxing powers are exhaustively enumerated in Article 170 of the Constitution, being the (§1) federal State, (§2) the Communities and the Regions, and the local authorities, namely, the (§3) provinces, and (§4) municipalities, conurbations, and federations of municipalities.

§1. The Federal State

I. Taxing Power

647. A government acquires its revenues mainly from taxes, user fees, social security contributions, loans, and non-fiscal revenues. As the levying of taxes is governed by specific constitutional rules, it is important to have a precise definition of what is considered to be a tax under Belgian law. A 'tax' may be defined as a compulsory financial contribution aimed at covering public spending. A decisive feature of a tax, which distinguishes it from a user fee, is that a tax is not imposed in return for any specific service performed by public authorities. Further, a tax must not be confused with (social security) contributions paid by employers and employees. These 'para-fiscal contributions' – in large measure earnings related – are governed by social security legislation.

In practice, it is often hard to make a clear distinction between taxes (Article 170 Constitution) and user fees (Article 173 Constitution). The relevant caselaw has taken the following elements into account: (*a*) whether the financial contribution has been imposed in return for a specific service performed by public authorities and (*b*) the real cost of that service. Nevertheless, the distinction is important because, for taxes, the principle of legality requires that their essential elements be regulated by the relevant legislature; whereas for user fees, the legislature may limit itself to determining the cases in which they may be levied and may delegate the regulation of the other elements to the executive. Unlike taxes, however, user fees are not subject to the principle of annual terms.

A. *Constitutional Principles*

1. The Principle of Legality

648. The imposition of taxes for the benefit of the State is a matter for the Legislative Branch (Article 170 §1 Constitution). The requirement for the government to have legislative authorisation before it may impose any fiscal burden on the citizen is a fundamental legal principle, which protects the citizen against unauthorised financial charges. It is a confirmation of a long-standing tradition holding that taxes cannot be established unless approved by the elected representatives of taxpayers ('No taxation without representation.'). The principle that no such charge may be imposed except by statute, implies that the Act should regulate the essential elements of a tax, namely the tax base, the taxpayers, the rate and any exemptions. It has aptly been observed that for an authority to have 'a basis in law' is not the same thing as to be completely regulated by statute. Consequently, the King may be authorised by the legislature to regulate the administrative measures leading to a tax assessment as well as the procedures for the collection of taxes, since these aspects do not explicitly affect the tax rate or the defining of taxable income. Nevertheless, the principle of legality has not always been strictly complied with. In cases of urgency, and in order to frustrate attempts by citizens to anticipate new tax legislation before their promulgation, the Legislative Branch has sometimes conferred on the King regulatory powers over the essential elements of a tax. In order to temper criticism that such a delegation is not compatible with Article 170 of the Constitution, it has in most cases made the exercise of those powers subject to confirmation *a posteriori* by Parliament. The Constitutional Court has consistently held that this confirmation by the Legislature within a short period of time is an essential prerequisite for the constitutionality of the delegation statute. Two further, cumulative conditions are the existence of exceptional circumstances and explicit prior authorisation by the Legislature.[531]

2. The Principle of Annual Terms

649. Taxes for the benefit of the State are voted annually. The legislation establishing them is in force for only one year, unless they are renewed (Article 171 Constitution). Tax laws remain in force until they are repealed, just like any other statute, but every year the legislature must renew the government's authority for collecting taxes. In most cases, this authorisation is given in the Ways and Means Budget. The principle of annual terms is intended as a means of ensuring the supervisory role of Parliament.

3. The Principle of Equality

650. Article 172 paragraph 1 of the Constitution applies the general principle of equality before the law (Article 10 Constitution) to taxation, providing that no privileges with regard to taxes may be introduced. Legal equality in taxation entails that all citizens who find themselves in identical situations should be taxed identically on the basis of general, objective and impersonal tax laws. It also implies that any differentiated contributions which may be required of citizens individually as sharing in the burdens of the State should be based on objective and reasonable grounds. As a consequence, the caselaw has consistently held that tax regulations are unconstitutional if the obligation to pay tax depends on a condition that clearly bears no

531. See, e.g., Cons., Judgments No. 88/2004, 19 May 2004; No. 195/2004, 1 Dec. 2004.

relation to either the nature of the tax or its purpose. The Constitutional Court, as well as the Court of Cassation and the Council of State, apply the conventional criteria of principle of equality.

The principle of the legality of taxation also implies that no exemption from or reduction of tax can be introduced other than by Act. This principle is made explicit in Article 172 paragraph 2 of the Constitution. The principle of equality in taxation entails that such exemptions or rebates must be established in a general, objective and collective manner. The taxation authorities have no discretion as to enforcing the payment of taxes.

II. Spending Power

651. The fundamental rules governing the spending power of the federal State are laid down in Articles 174 and 180 of the Constitution. They have been worked out in the Budgetary Provisions and State Finances Act of 22 May 2003.[532] Similar principles apply for the Communities and the Regions[533] and for the subordinate, local authorities.

A. The Principle of Legality

652. Each year, the House of Representatives approves the budget as well as the final accounts (Article 174 paragraph 1 Constitution). Moreover the House and the Senate, each for itself, stipulate each year the appropriations for their respective operating budgets (Article 174 paragraph 1 Constitution). This constitutional provision implies an annual ways and means budget, an annual expenditure budget and a set of annual accounts.

First, the 'budget' may be defined as a list of receipts and expenditures for the next fiscal year. It empowers the government to levy taxes. In addition, the government is granted budgetary authority: the authority to contract and the authority to borrow over the next fiscal year within the limits set under the Budget Act.

The Budget Act consists of the Ways and Means Budget and the General Budget of Expenditures. The Ways and Means Budget provides an estimate of all the receipts of the State and empowers the government to levy taxes during the relevant fiscal year as well as to raise non-fiscal revenues. It authorises the government to borrow within the limits and the conditions set out in the Budget Act. The General Budget of Expenditures contains both an estimate of the various items of expenditure, and an authorisation to proceed with the expenditures listed, by programme, for every department of the central administration.

Second, an essential aspect of parliamentary supervision is that Parliament should be able to ensure that public money is being used for the purposes for which it was intended. This is done through annual approval by the House of Representatives of

532. *Gazette,* 3 Jul. 2003.
533. Articles 50 and 71 of the Special Majority Act on Community and Region Finance of 16 January 1989, *Gazette,* 17 Jan. 1989.

a 'Final Accounts Act' for a given fiscal year. Such Act provides the numerical result of the budget and justifies the use made of the authorisation granted by the House of Representatives in the Budget Act. It is a technique enabling the House to compare the estimates in the Budget Act with the actual receipts and expenditures.

653. The powers over finance are among the more important powers of Parliament. They provide a means of supervising not only the programme of receipts and expenditures and the way this programme is implemented, but also, by the same token, government policy in general. Under the current state of the law, one exception to the general powers of the federal Legislature seems to be accepted. In urgent cases caused by exceptional or unforeseen circumstances, Cabinet may authorise certain financial obligations not funded by any or by sufficient appropriations. This authorisation of Cabinet must be immediately submitted to the House of Representatives and to the Office of the Auditor General. The expenditures thus authorised must eventually be confirmed by statute.[534]

654. The Budget Act and the Final Accounts Act are 'Acts in the formal sense'.[535] That is, they are not subject to prior review by the Legislation Division of the Council of State. They cannot constitute legal grounds for appeal up to the Court of Cassation, nor a legal basis for administrative regulations. They cannot be considered as legislation that confers the required approval of international treaties. However, on a number of occasions, there has been resort to the infelicitous practice of inserting other general provisions into the Budget Act, the so-called *cavaliers budgétaires*. Their validity is limited to the fiscal year in which they have been adopted.

655. Finally, it should be pointed out that the Constitution contains rules whereby the (precise) amount of certain expenditures must be determined by statute. Article 179 of the Constitution states that no pension or gratuity on account of the public treasury can be conferred other than by authority of an Act. Other cases include the salaries of judges (Article 154 Constitution), the salaries of the army (Article 182 Constitution), and the salaries and pensions of religious functionaries and of the representatives of (secular) organisations recognised as providing moral guidance and assistance (Article 181 Constitution). A specific provision concerns the 'civil list' which is established for the duration of the King's reign (Article 89 Constitution).

B. The Principle of Annual Terms

656. The annual character of the budget and the final accounts is laid down in Article 174 paragraph 1 of the Constitution. The annual cycle of revenues and expenditures is intended to ensure that the House of Representatives regularly approve the government's financial proposals. It implies that the budget and the final

534. Article 70 Budgetary Provisions and State Finances Act.
535. See Pt. I. Ch. 3. §1. I 'Ordinary Statutes'.

accounts must be approved each fiscal year. The fiscal year coincides with the calendar year.[536] The Budget Act and the Final Accounts Act only include those receipts and expenditures, which relate to the fiscal year in question.

657. The budgetary procedure starts with the submission of the government's Budget Bills to the House of Representatives. These Bills should be filed with the House of Representatives on no later than 15 October of the year preceding the fiscal year addressed in the proposed Budget. The fiscal, economic and social policy of the government is explained in a 'General Budget Statement', the vote on the budget itself being preceded by a general review of economic and government policy. The Budget must be approved by the House of Representatives no later than 31 December of the year preceding the fiscal year. During the first quarter of every fiscal year, the federal government is held to carry out budgetary review in order to assess whether any adjustments are needed in the Ways and Means Budget and the General Budget of Expenditures. Any amendments ensuing must be approved by the House of Representatives before 30 June of the fiscal year in question.

The deadlines, which apply to the budget procedure, outlined above result from the Budgetary Provisions and State Finances Act. In general the Ways and Means Budget is approved before the start of the relevant fiscal year. As a government has no spending power without prior parliamentary authorisation, it has to seek parliamentary approval for provisional appropriations under the General Budget of Expenditures which is not yet approved before the start of the fiscal year. Provisional appropriations (as authorisation for the disbursement of public money) are advanced out of the General Budget. The use of provisional appropriations is subjected to very strict conditions.

The budget cycle ends with parliamentary approval of the Final Accounts Act. The Constitution requires parliamentary approval not only of the proposed Budget but also of the financial reports set out in the Final Accounts Act. To that end, a Bill must be introduced before the House of Representatives before 30 November of the year following the end of the fiscal year. The vote on the Final Accounts Act was originally intended as a means for Parliament to assess the government's policy. In reality, since the approval of the Final Accounts Act often lags several years behind, it has become a mere formality seeking to release the government from any liability.

C. The Principle of Universality

658. The Budget and the accounts must include all State receipts and expenditures of the State (Article 174 paragraph 2 Constitution), thus excluding the possibility of covert budgets and accounts. The principle of universality implies that the Budget and final accounts must be 'analytic', thus excluding any set-off between receipts and expenditures. This principle also entails that, as a rule, receipts may not

536. There is one exception to this rule, which is laid down in Art. 89 of the Constitution: the income for the King is established for the duration of his reign. See Pt. II Ch. 2. §1. 'Head of State. Designation'.

be earmarked by legislation for a specific item of expenditure and that all receipts and expenditures are centralised in the Treasury Administration within the Finance Department. The Budgetary Provisions and State Finances Act provides that budgetary funds dedicating specific receipts for specific expenditures may be established exceptionally by Act.

Only the receipts and expenditures of the federal State are included in the Budget. The Communities and the Regions, and the subordinate (local) authorities have their own budgets distinct from the federal budget. There is no rule of 'universality of the budget' requiring a consolidation of the budgets of those bodies. Any such rule would be contrary to the principle of financial autonomy.

D. *The Principle of Non-transferability*

659. Another fundamental principle laid down in Article 180 paragraph 2 of the Constitution is that a payment may only be made for the purpose, which the Budget Act has authorised for the expenditure. The Office of the Auditor General ensures that no item of expenditure in the Budget is exceeded and that no transfer takes place from one budget item to another.

E. *The Public Nature of the Budget and Its Accounts*

660. As the Budget and its accounts are approved by Act, they have passed through all the stages of legislative proceedings in the House of Representatives, including publication in the *Gazette*. Their public nature reinforces and facilitates supervision of government financial policy.

§2. The Communities and the Regions

661. The taxing and spending powers of the federated entities are laid down in the Constitution. The Constituent Assembly of 1988 prescribed that the financing system of the Communities and the Regions (except for the German Community) should be determined by a Special Majority Act (Articles 175 and 177 Constitution). This, in turn, was accomplished by the Special Majority Act on Community and Region Finance of 16 January 1989. And as has been outlined above, the financing system of the federated entities is based on two principles: financial autonomy, and solidarity between the entities.

I. Autonomous or General Taxing Power

A. *Main Features*

662. The general taxing power of the Communities and the Regions stems directly from the Constitution: Article 170 §2. It is a 'complete concurrent power', unlike the other powers that are in general exclusive.[537] And it is an autonomous power. The taxing power being in the first place a means for implementing policy, it is not limited to Community or Region matters (regarding the tax base).

B. *Restrictions*

663. An ordinary federal Act may set the exceptions to the taxing power of the Communities and the Regions, which 'prove to be necessary' (Article 170 §2 Constitution). The Constitutional Court has jurisdiction to determine whether this condition of necessity is met.[538] As a consequence, a federal Act may determine which taxes cannot be levied by the Communities or the Regions; the federal statute may also repeal or limit a tax levied by a Community or a Region. A 1989 Act implementing Article 170 §2 of the Constitution prohibits the federated entities from levying taxes and surcharges or from granting rebates in those matters where a federal tax has already been levied.[539] Personal income tax is an exception to this rule: pursuant to Article 6 §2 of the Special Majority Act on Community and Region Finance, the Regions can levy additional regional taxes in respect of personal income tax. On the other hand, Article 2 of the 1989 Act (as amended in 1993) prohibits the federal State and the Communities from levying taxes and surcharges, or granting rebates, on the matters regarding water and waste.

664. The tax legislation of a Community or Region must respect the limits of their application *ratione loci*. This raises specific problems for the application of such Flemish or French Community Acts in Brussels-Capital, since there is no constitutional or statutory rule indicating how and to whom these tax statutes apply in Brussels, there being no 'sub-nationality'. As a consequence, the taxing power of the Flemish and French Communities remains purely theoretical. No such problem exists, however, for taxation by the German Community that applies in the German language region, or for Region taxation.

665. Taxes levied by the Communities and the Regions must not exceed the limits inherent in the broader view of the State as an economic and monetary union, one which prohibits internal customs duties and charges having an equivalent effect.[540] Moreover, the Communities and Regions may not encroach on the taxing powers of the subordinate authorities.

666. When the taxing power is used as a policy instrument, the Constitutional Court has the jurisdiction to verify whether or not the non-fiscal effects of the tax

537. See Pt. III. Ch. 2. §3. I. D 'An Allocation of Powers Based upon Mutual Exclusiveness'.
538. See, e.g., Cons., Judgments No. 66/2001, 17 May 2001; No. 124/2001, 16 Oct. 2001; No. 85/2002, 8 May 2002 and No. 113/2005, 30 Jun. 2005.
539. Act of 23 January 1989, *Gazette,* 24 Jan. 1989, amended by Act of 16 July 1993, *Gazette,* 20 Jul. 1993.
540. See Pt. III. Ch. 2. §3. I. G.

are the primary objectives of the tax and, if so, if there is any disproportionate impact on the division of legislative powers.[541]

C. *Other Conditions*

667. The constitutional provisions on the principles of legality, annual terms and equality also apply to the Communities and the Regions. Article 173 of the Constitution empowers the Communities and the Regions to impose within their jurisdiction by relevant Act user fees, and to delegate this power to other authorities or institutions.

II. Additional Region Taxing Powers: Regional Taxes

668. In addition to the above-mentioned general taxing powers, the Regions – but not the Communities – also have certain additional taxing powers. Pursuant to Articles 3–5 of the Special Majority Act on Community and Region Finance, the Regions may levy the following 'Region taxes':

(1) duties on betting and gambling;
(2) slot machine tax;
(3) tax on opening off-licences/liquor stores;
(4) succession duties;
(5) assessed value tax on property;
(6) registration fees on transfers of real estate;
(7) registration fees on mortgages and on the subdivision of real estate;
(8) registration fees on gifts;
(9) radio and television tax;
(10) annual road-use charge on motor vehicles, and
(11) motor vehicle purchase tax.

The Regions have the power to determine the tax rate, the tax base, any exemptions, and to collect these taxes. In some minor instances, they may first have to conclude a co-operation agreement with the federal State or with the other Regions. The total revenue of the regional taxes is granted to the Regions dependent on the location of the tax revenue.

III. Additional Region Taxing Powers: Additional Regional Personal Income Tax

669. One of the main objectives of the 2014 Sixth State Reform has been to allow the Regions greater room and more direct control over personal income

541. See, e.g., Cons., Judgment No. 31/92, 23 Apr. 1992.

taxation. The fiscal measures of this State Reform were brought into legislation by the Special Majority Act of 6 January 2014 amending the 1988 Special Majority Act on Community and Region Finance.[542] Matters concerning the Regions' powers over personal income tax applied as of the 2015 taxation year. In effect, the federal government has withdrawn a portion of its tax coverage and allowed the Regions to be substituted in its place in order to levy personal income tax in the form of surcharges. Thus the proportion by which the federal intake of personal income tax revenue is reduced, is equivalent to the taxable proportion now open to the Regions. The portions were capped at 25.990% ('autonomy factor') up to the 2018 tax year. As of that tax year, the percentage would be determined on the basis of federal and Region consultation and co-ordination under prescribed formulas.

670. The regional surcharges must be proportional. Flat surcharges are not allowed. The Regions can also allow reductions on their regional surcharges and apply tax decreases and tax increases. The sum of the surcharges, reductions, tax increases and decreases is called the 'regional personal income tax'.

671. The Regions have also acquired exclusive powers for tax reductions and tax credits for expenses in relation to their powers regarding monuments and land use, city renovation, housing, and moderating energy consumption. The same goes for their newly acquired powers with respect to employment and urban policy.

672. The net result of the fiscal changes wrought by the 2014 Sixth State Reform has been calculated to raise the fiscal autonomy (self-financing aspect, revenue sources) of the Flemish Region from 43.5% to 77%. For the Walloon Region, this represented an increase from 38.5% to 71%, and for the Brussels-Capital Region, from 51% to 71%. This increase in fiscal capacity is matched, however, in the State Reform by a corresponding and increasing burden on the federated entities now to contribute to the financing of the entire federal State, including pensions, in addition to the financing their new institutional powers.

IV. Co-operative Principles and Mechanisms Governing the Additional Regional Taxing Powers

673. The 2014 Sixth State Reform has introduced into the Special Majority Act a new Article 1*ter* which lists and restates the co-operative principles applicable to taxing powers. Thus it makes clear the application of the principle of federal loyalty and the prohibition of disloyal fiscal competition. Likewise, the Regions are barred from creating a taxation situation which impairs the overall progressivity of the income tax system. It also reiterates the need to avoid double taxation, the economic and monetary union being the encompassing framework for all legislation, and the principle of free movement of persons, goods, services, and capital within the federation.

542. *Gazette,* 31 Jan. 2014.

674. That 2014 State Reform also carries forward the general theme of co-operative federalism by reiterating the need for co-operation among the various taxing authorities. Thus co-operation agreements continue to be required concerning mandatory notification of the other federal and federated bodies by a Region intending to apply its taxation power, or amend existing tax rules, and requesting their advice on the technical implementation of those measures. In addition, co-operation agreements exist, for instance, on the reduction of double taxation, for arranging the collection of tax revenues, for co-ordinating taxes on commercial vehicles and use of roadways, and to settle the rules regarding the designation of the principal residence and the application of particular Region rules to non-residents (the federal level having principal jurisdiction here).

V. Transfers from Federal Tax Revenue

675. Transfer payments from federal taxation revenue remain an important part of the financial resources of the federated entities (Articles 6–47/11 Special Majority Act on Community and Region Finance). For the Communities these federal transfer payments even continue to be their only tax revenue.

A portion of federal personal income tax returns and of VAT revenue are allocated to the Communities. These taxes are called 'shared taxes'. This notion of 'shared' taxes, however, is misleading since these taxes are levied in a uniform way all over the State without the Communities being allowed to levy surcharges or to grant rebates on those taxes.

676. As in most federal systems, the Special Majority Act on Community and Region Finance combines two different criteria for transferring and distributing federal tax income between the federated entities: 'merit' and 'need'. When applying the 'merit' criterion, the economic performance of the federated entities is taken into account. Financial means are allocated on the basis of personal income tax, namely that portion of the Region in the total of personal income tax revenue. Application of this criterion rewards an increase in regional tax capacity and punishes a decrease in regional tax capacity, thus promoting the accountability of the Region authorities. The merit criterion is used for the financing of Region powers. The 'need' criterion, on the other hand, looks at actual needs, and therefore financial means are allocated according to population numbers, student numbers, and such like. This criterion is typically used for the financing of Community matters (education, family policy, healthcare).

VI. Non-fiscal Revenues

677. Non-fiscal revenues related to areas of Community or Region jurisdiction (e.g., pilotage charges) are allocated to the Communities and the Regions (Article 2 Special Majority Act on Community and Region Finance).

VII. Loans

678. The Communities and the Regions may finance their budgets through loans subject to the conditions set in Article 49 of the Special Majority Act on Community and Region Finance. In order to preserve the economic and monetary union, the King is empowered to restrict, by Decree in Council, the borrowing powers of a Community or Region for a maximum period of two years, during which time each loan entered by the Community or the Region is subject to the approval of the federal Minister of Finance. The obligations of the Communities or the Regions are not guaranteed by the federal State unless otherwise provided for by a Special Majority Act. Communities and Regions are therefore liable for their own borrowings.

VIII. Solidarity Mechanisms

679. When there is too great a divergence between the levels of prosperity in the federated entities, some kind of solidarity is required, either through a redistribution of wealth among those entities (e.g., the *Finanz-Ausgleich* in Germany) or through a transfer of resources from the federal authority to the less prosperous entities.

Under Article 48 of the Special Majority Act on Community and Region Finance, a federal solidarity contribution is paid to the Regions where its personal income tax revenue *per capita* is below the federal average. This rule has favoured the Walloon Region since the entry into force of the solidarity mechanism under that Special Majority Act in 1989, and, since 1997, also the Brussels-Capital Region. Before the 2014 Sixth State Reform, this federal solidarity contribution system could result in 'perverse effects', such as the 'development trap'. A development trap exists when the solidarity mechanism would result in less financial means for a poorer Region in spite of increased tax revenue from economic growth in that Region. The solidarity mechanism would then have the perverse effect that the reduction of the national solidarity contribution would be more sizeable than the increase in tax revenue. The federal solidarity contribution system would thus discourage the poorer Region catching up with the other Regions.

680. The criterion by which VAT revenues are shared with the Communities is the ratio of school pupils per Community, rather than the location of the tax revenue (Article 39 Special Majority Act on Community and Region Finance).

681. With the exception of family benefits, social security policy remains within the scope of federal government powers, and thus constitute a form of 'interpersonal solidarity'.

IX. Tax Administration

682. Within certain limits, the Regions have the power to collect regional taxes and surcharges. But only the federal government retains jurisdiction for the collection of personal income tax, without cost to the Regions (Article 5/1 §5 Special Majority Act on Community and Region Finance). The Regions can, however, leave collection of their taxes to the central tax administration, which will collect them without additional cost (Article 5 §3 Special Majority Act on Community and Region Finance). Autonomous taxes based on Article 170 §2 of the Constitution are collected by the Regions themselves.

X. Spending Powers

683. All the principles outlined above and applicable to the spending powers of the federal State also apply to the federated entities (Article 50 Special Majority Act on Community and Region Finance). The Act of 16 May 2003[543] prescribes the 'general principles' applicable to the budgets, supervision of subsidies, and to the budget accounts of the Communities and Regions. The Communities and Regions may only adhere to and reinforce these minimal requirements, but not alter them. The Communities and Regions may organise, within certain limits, their own Treasury and budgetary controls (Articles 51–52 Special Majority Act on Community and Region Finance).

684. The federated entities are free to decide their own budgetary allocations. Moreover, the Flemish Parliament may use all the resources at its disposal in order to finance either (Flemish) Community or (Flemish) Region matters (Article 1 §3 Special Majority Act on Community and Region Finance).

§3. The Decentralised Authorities

685. The aforementioned principles governing the taxing and spending powers also apply to the local government level, the 'decentralized authorities', on the basis of various constitutional and legislative provisions. The Office of the Auditor General exercises control only on the provinces, however. We restrict ourselves to the following observations.

No tax may be established other than by a decision of the relevant Provincial or Municipal Council. The federal legislature may determine exceptions to this rule which 'prove to be necessary'; may allow other bodies to levy tax; or may repeal a tax (Article 170 §§3–4 Constitution). Furthermore, the taxing power of the provinces may be abolished, in whole or in part, by ordinary Act (Article 170 §3 Constitution).

543. *Gazette,* 25 Jun. 2003.

The public nature of the meetings of the Provincial and Municipal Councils and of the provincial and municipal budgets and accounts is explicitly guaranteed under Article 162 of the Constitution.

Unlike the provinces and municipalities, the Brussels Conurbation enjoys but a very limited fiscal autonomy.

686. The revenues of the provinces, municipalities, and the Brussels Conurbation derive from surcharges on certain taxes levied by the federal State or the Region, such as personal income tax and property tax. Other revenues result from their autonomous taxing powers over a wide range of items (e.g., dogs, neon-light advertisement boards, second homes) and from user fees (e.g., for the use of municipal parking lots). Such taxes are subject to administrative supervision by the Region governments, which will withhold approval for taxes that are illegal or contrary to government policy (Article 162 Constitution).

Surcharges are collected by the federal tax administration; other taxes are collected by the province or municipality that has levied them.

Taxes and user fees represent only a small part of the income of the municipalities and provinces. The larger share of their income derives from funds created by the Regions which have jurisdiction for their general financing (Article 6 §1 VIII 9° Special Majority Act on Institutional Reform).

Selected Further Reading

See also the Selected Further Reading mentioned in Pt. III. Ch. 1 'The Structure of the State: A Federal State Sui Generis' (especially the works on the 2014 Sixth State Reform).

Beckers, J. *Overzicht van het begrotingsrecht in Belgie* (Story-Scientia, 1991).

Matthijs, H. *Overheidsbegrotingen – I. Federale Staat, gemeenschappen en gewesten en bijzondere begrotingsstelsels* (6th) (die Keure, 2015).

Pagano, G. *Le financement des regions et des communautés 1970–2002* (CRISP, 2002).

Peeters, P. 'Fiscale autonomie van de deelstaten in België na de Zesde Staatshervorming'. In *Het federale België na de Zesde Staatshervorming* edited by A. Alen, B. Dalle, K. Muylle, W. Pas, J. Van Nieuwenhove & W. Verrijdt (die Keure, 2014) 557–589.

Tiberghien, A. *Handboek voor Fiscaal Recht 2019–2020* (Kluwer, 2020).

Tiberghien, A. *Manuel de droit fiscal 2019–2020* (Kluwer, 2020).

Van de Voorde, A. & G. Stienlet. *Le budget de l'Etat en Belgique fédérale* (Cepess, 1990).

Willemart, E. *Les limites constitutionnelles du pouvoir fiscal* (Bruylant, 1999).

Chapter 3. Emergency Laws

687. The Belgian Constitution does not contain any provisions regarding emergency laws. The possibility of deviating from constitutional provisions, for example in a crisis situation, is explicitly prohibited by the Constitution. According to Article 187, the Constitution can be neither wholly nor partially suspended. Belgium has nonetheless already found itself in situations during which the constitutional provisions regarding the exercise of powers could not be fully respected.

688. During the First World War, legislative authority was exercised by the King together with his Ministers, and, during the Second World War, by the Ministers alone.[544] The Court of Cassation has ruled that these so-called wartime decrees have the same force of law as normal ordinary Acts. For similar reasons and under like characterisation, the Constitutional Court also considers that its constitutional review jurisdiction extends over wartime decrees.[545]

689. In time of war or other public emergency threatening the life of the nation, any High Contracting Party to the EConvHR may, under certain conditions, take measures derogating from its obligations under that Convention (Article 15 EConvHR). As already pointed out, a similar provision does not exist in the Belgian Constitution. The existence of a state of emergency can thus not be invoked to permit a suspension of rights and freedoms protected by the Belgian Constitution.

690. Force majeure can, however, lead to a de facto suspension of certain constitutional provisions regarding the exercise of powers. If the institutions are in reality completely unable to exercise their powers in full accordance with the Constitution, the principle of continuity can demand the continuation of the exercise of state functions. Moreover, the Legislation Division of the Council of State has held that state of emergency legislation which derogates from the Constitution is permissible when the state of emergency is of such a serious nature that the independence of the country is at risk. Such legislation is only permissible if four conditions have been met. First, the derogation needs to be necessary. Second, such a necessity can only relate to the specific aim of securing the preservation of the Belgian State. Third, the derogation needs to be temporary. Fourth, only the Legislative Branch is allowed to take such measures, which cannot be delegated. The conditions for state of emergency legislation are thus stricter than those stipulated in Article 15 EConvHR.[546]

691. In time of war, Belgian legislation renders it possible to impose serious restrictions on some of the rights and liberties guaranteed under the Constitution. A state of war or martial law must be proclaimed by Royal Decree in Council. A principal consequence is the delegation to military authorities of the responsibility for

544. See Pt. I. Ch. 3. §1. III 'Wartime Decrees'.
545. Cons., Judgments No. 115/99, 10 Nov. 1999; No. 101/2000, 11 Oct. 2000.
546. Council of State, Legislation Division, Opinion of 9 Jun. 1952, *Parliamentary Documents (House of Representatives)* 1952–53, No. 172, 11–14.

keeping the peace. The time of war begins on the day the mobilisation of the army is proclaimed by Royal Decree, and ends on the day the army is once again put on a peace footing by Royal Decree.[547] Under the Wartime Decree of 11 October 1916, the King may, in times of war, exercise all police powers which would normally fall under provincial and municipal authority. During this period, civil and military authorities may, with a view to ensuring the defence of the realm and the security of the army, remove any persons of suspicion from places where they might do damage. Pursuant to the Decree, those authorities may order a search of homes, day or night; search individuals; ban meetings which could result in unrest, and check, retain, or seize mail. In times of war, the publication or dissemination of information which may aid the enemy or may have a damaging effect on the morale of the population and of the troops is forbidden. Contrary to Articles 19 and 25 of the Constitution, the government is also authorised to take all preventive measures to stop the dissemination of such information. A Wartime Decree of 12 October 1918 authorises the Minister of Justice to intern all persons who have acquired their Belgian nationality by naturalisation and who are suspected of maintaining close relations with the enemy. The Minister having jurisdiction over border controls, asylum and immigration, and the establishment and removal of foreigners can do likewise regarding foreigners within the territory. However, the constitutionality of these decrees is rather questionable.

692. In 1968, Article 196 was inserted in the Constitution. It states, 'No amending of the Constitution may be commenced or pursued during time of war, or when the Houses of Parliament are hindered from meeting freely on the federation's territory.'

693. In 2002, Article 157 paragraph 1 was amended to limit the active jurisdiction of the Courts Martial to when the King has declared a state of war. During peacetime, the Criminal Courts have jurisdiction to try offences committed by military personnel.

SELECTED FURTHER READING

Ergec, R. *Les droits de l'homme à l'épreuve des circonstances exceptionnelles* (Bruylant, 1987).

Ergec, R. 'L'état de nécessité en droit constitutionnel belge'. In *Le nouveau droit constitutionnel* (Bruylant, 1987) 143–171.

Ganshof van der Meersch, W.J. & Diderich, M. 'Les états d'exception et la Constitution belge'. *Ann. Dr. Sc. Pol* (1953): 49–124.

Van Haegenborgh, G. & W. Verrijdt. 'De noodtoestand in het Belgische publiekrecht'. In *Preadviezen 2016,* Vereniging voor de vergelijkende studie van het recht van België en Nederland (Boom Juridisch, 2016) 11–85.

547. See also Art. 167 §1 Constitution.

Chapter 4. The Constitutional Relationship Between Church and State

§1. Introduction

694. The historic compromise between Catholics and Liberals in 1831 has shaped the constitutional position of the Catholic Church. Under the slogan 'Freedom in everything and for everybody', the National Congress adopted a particular 'separation' of Church and State, which was envied by all Catholics across the Continent. The Liberal (anticlerical) group in the Constituent Assembly abandoned its attempt to subject the Church to absolute governmental supervision of its activities, whereas the Catholic group no longer upheld the once privileged position of the Church of Rome.

§2. Freedom of Religion

695. Generally, constitutional rights and liberties also apply to religious matters, as regards, for example, freedom of education (Article 24 Constitution) or freedom of the press (Article 25 Constitution), but the Constitution also expressly provides for the freedom of religion as such. Freedom of worship and its open practice in public are guaranteed under Article 19 of the Constitution, with the exception of punishing criminal offences committed during the exercise of this freedom. No one can be forced in any way to participate in the rites and ceremonies of any religion or to observe its days of rest (Article 20 Constitution).

696. The Constitution also provides for a freedom of ecclesiastical organisation in Article 21, precluding the State from intervening in the appointment of or in the inauguration of ministers of any religion or forbidding them from corresponding with their superiors and from publishing documents from these superiors, but without limiting, in this latter case, any general liability relating to publication and the press. Thus, the State may not supervise the Church and the latter is free to choose its own internal structure. Article 21 of the Constitution also provides that a civil wedding ceremony must always precede its religious consecration, with the exception of specific cases established by Act.

Each religious group is therefore free to establish a new church or administrative unit, like a diocese, without any need for permission by the secular authorities.[548] But this decision will have a secular effect, such as regarding the budget, only after those civil authorities decide themselves to give it effect. Religious functionaries are not civil servants.[549] The courts only have jurisdiction to examine who is entitled to the salaries and pensions, by establishing for example whether a minister has been duly appointed or dismissed by the competent religious authority according to its

548. Council of State, Administrative Tribunal Division, Judgment No. 78.465, 1 Feb. 1999 (*Van Reusel*).

549. Cass., 4 Mar. 1847, *Pas.*, 1847, I, 315; Cass., 23 Nov. 1957, *Arr. Cass.*, 1958, No. 172.

rules, but the courts may not review the reasons for dismissal.[550] This caselaw has come under criticism in light of certain ECtHR judgments.[551]

697. Article 9 EConvHR holds a less restrictive and a more modern view of the freedom of religion, including not only the outward aspects of manifesting one's religion or belief in worship, but also in its teaching, practice, and observance, either alone or in community with others as well as in public or private. Article 18 §1 of the ICCPR and Article 10 §1 of the EU Charter of Rights are worded in similar terms. The EU Charter of Rights also recognises the right to conscientious objection (Article 10 §2) and respect of religious diversity (Article 22).

Up to now, two complaints against Belgium for breach of Article 9 have been significant. The first case concerned a banning burqas, where the federal legislator had penalised the wearing of full head and face covering (in public). The Belgian Constitutional Court had accepted that such legislative provisions were directed at three legitimate aims protected under Article 9 §2 EConvHR: (1) public safety; (2) a particular vision on living together in a society, and (3) the protection of women from undue pressure by family members or their community to hide their faces when in public.[552] The ECtHR has adopted this approach and reasoning in judgments against France[553] and Belgium.[554]

The second instance concerned Article 759 of the Civil Procedure Code which provides that parties in a courtroom may not wear any headgear.[555] The ECtHR held Belgium to be in breach of Article 9 EConvHR where a witness in a criminal trial was ordered to quit the courtroom because she refused for religious reasons to remove her headscarf. Removing an ordinary citizen, a civilian not representing the State, on that basis even though she was not behaving in a disorderly way constituted a disproportionate restriction on her freedom of religion. The Belgian Constitutional Court had previously declared in other proceedings involving an analogous situation the case to be inadmissible because it did not involve religious reasons and thus any answer to would not provide a solution for the referring judge.[556]

698. All religions benefit from the guarantees in Articles 19–21 of the Constitution. They are equal before the law and are equally protected. Some offences against the freedom of worship in public are punishable under the Criminal Code. For example, no one may disturb religious ceremonies or defame the ministers of any religion. On the other hand, religious ministers who criticise the government are punishable if they do so in the exercise of their function ('*délit de chaire*').

---

550. Cass., 20 Oct. 1994, *R.W.*, 1994–95, 1082; Cass., 3 Jun. 1999, *Arr. Cass.*, 1999, No. 767.
551. See, e.g., ECtHR, *Pellegrini v Italy* (20 Jul. 2001).
552. Cons., Judgment No. 145/2012, 6 Dec. 2012 (but the wearing of a burqua within a place of worship may never be the subject of criminal penalty).
553. ECtHR (GC), *S.A. S. v France* (1 Jul. 2014), but rejecting the public safety argument on the grounds that such a significant limitation on women's religious rights can only be justified by clear and present danger.
554. ECtHR, *Belkacemi and Oussar v Belgium* (11 Jul. 2017). The final Belgian judgment was that of the Constitutional Court (No. 145/2012) noted above.
555. ECtHR, *Lachiri v Belgium* (18 Sep. 2018).
556. Cons., Judgment No. 8/2008, 17 Jan. 2008.

699. As early as 1834, the Court of Cassation ruled that no subjective values should be applied in determining what is to be seen as a religion. In deciding whether a certain group may be considered to profess a religion, the following elements may be taken into account: the number of members, the originality of the doctrine, and the worship of one or more divine beings.[557] For example, denominations, which have satisfied these juridical criteria, include the Salvation Army, the Baha'i and the Jehovah's Witnesses.

§3. Official Recognition of a Religion and Its Effects

700. A number of religions have been officially recognised by or by authority of a federal statute, the criterion being the religion's social value as a service to the population.[558] Currently, six denominations enjoy this status: Catholicism (Act of 18 Germinal of year X, being 8 April 1802), Protestantism (Act of 18 Germinal of year X, being 8 April 1802), Judaism (Decree of 17 March 1808), Anglicanism (Act of 4 March 1870 on the organisation of the temporal needs of the religions), Islam (Act of 19 July 1974 amending the 1870 Act) and the joint Orthodox Churches (Act of 17 April 1985 amending the 1870 Act).

701. The most important consequence of such recognition is that these religions, and they alone, come under Article 181 §1 of the Constitution. According to this provision, 'the salaries and pensions of religious functionaries are borne by the State' and 'the amounts required therefor are drawn annually from the budget'. Nonetheless, as noted above, religious functionaries are not civil servants.

It was not before the 5 May 1993 revision of the Constitution that a similar regulation applied to the salaries and pensions of representatives of organisations recognised by federal Act as providing moral assistance according to a non-denominational philosophy (Article 181 §2 Constitution).

702. Apart from the salaries for religious functionaries provided for in the federal budget, recognition entails several other benefits for the religions concerned. Legal personality is attributed to the ecclesiastical administration responsible for the property and other temporal needs of the religious group,[559] and any deficit incurred by it must be paid for by the municipalities or the provinces. A recognised religion may request subsidies for the construction or renovation of its buildings. Ministers of a recognised religion must be given appropriate housing, and any expenditures for this purpose are chargeable to the municipalities or to the provinces. Recognised religions may appoint army and prison chaplains, whose salaries are paid by the federal State.

557. Cass., 27 Nov. 1834, *Pas.*, 1834, I, 330.
558. Council of State, Administrative Tribunal Division, Judgment No. 45.652, 12 Jan. 1994 (*Ibrahim*).
559. By contrast, neither the Catholic Church itself, nor its parishes and dioceses, enjoy legal personality: Council of State, Administrative Tribunal Division, Judgment No. 78.465, 1 Feb. 1999 (*Van Reusel*).

On the other hand, the recognition of a religion also thereby implies a minimal form of organisational structure in order to guarantee an effective communication with public authorities. The obligations that are imposed on the religious organisations should be, however, proportionate to this specific goal and may not interfere unnecessarily with the (internal) organisational autonomy of religions.[560]

703. Since 1 January 2002, the ecclesiastical administration responsible for the property and other temporal needs of a recognised religion falls within the jurisdiction of the Regions (Article 6 §1 VIII 6° Special Majority Act on Institutional Reform). This jurisdiction is limited to the administration of property and revenues and expenses of those recognised religions. The recognition of religions, and salaries and pensions, remain federal matters, as well as any legislation concerning non-recognised religions.[561]

704. Another consequence of recognition is the fact that only recognised religions are entitled to provide religious instruction in schools organised by public authorities until the end of the period of compulsory education (Article 24 §1 Constitution). Teachers of religion in these schools are appointed or dismissed by the public authorities upon the formal request of a church's administration. The freedom of internal organisation of the churches prevents the courts from exercising a full, fulsome review of any dismissal. Nevertheless, the rights to equal treatment and to due process presuppose that the courts can at very least control the grounds relied on by the religious authorities in those instances.[562]

In Belgium, teaching has been one of the areas in which the Catholic Church has been particularly active, by developing and maintaining a nationwide network of primary, secondary, and higher schools. This private school network was set up before the public school system organised at the State (now, the Community), provincial, and municipal levels. Nowadays, both school networks enjoy almost equal financial treatment. Subsidies for working expenses and for salaries are granted to the private school network, provided the curricula are drafted along the lines of a minimum standard programme, and provided qualified teachers are appointed and an inspection of the criteria is allowed.

Selected Further Reading

De Pooter, P. *De rechtspositie van erkende erediensten en levensbeschouwingen in Staat en maatschappij* (Larcier, 2003).

Mertens, K. & F. Judo (eds). *Handboek erediensten. Bestuur en organisatie* (Larcier, 2011).

Sägesser, C. & J.-Ph. Schreiber (eds). *Le financement public des religions et de la laïcité en Belgique* (Eds Academia, 2010).

Somers, W. & J. Dujardin, B. Houbrechts, T. Loose. *Bestuur van de erediensten* (3rd) (die Keure, 2014).

560. Cons., Judgments No. 148/2005, 28 Sep. 2005 and No. 203/2019, 19 Dec. 2019.
561. Cons., Judgment No. 203/2019, 19 Dec. 2019.
562. Cons., Judgment No. 45/2017, 27 Apr. 2017.

Theunis, J. 'The Case Law of the Belgian Constitutional Court'. In *Legal Aspects of Religious Freedom: International Conference 15–18 September 2008* (Office of the Government of the Republic of Slovenia for Religious Communities, 2008) 25–40.

Torfs, R. 'Church Autonomy in Belgium'. In *Church Autonomy. A Comparative Survey* edited by G. Robbers (Peter Lang, 2001) 607–631.

Selected Bibliography

§1. Before the 2014 State Restructuring

Alen, A. *Algemene beginselen en grondslagen van het Belgisch publiek recht* (Story-Scientia, 1988).

Alen, A. *Rechter en bestuur in het Belgische publiekrecht. De grondslagen van de rechterlijke wettigheidskontrole* (Kluwer, 1984) 2 vols.

Alen, A. with the assistance of J. Clement, G. Van Haegendoren & J. Van Nieuwenhove, *Handboek van het Belgisch Staatsrecht* (Kluwer, 1995).

Alen, A. & K. Muylle. *Compendium van het Belgisch Staatsrecht* (4th) (Kluwer, 2014) 2 vols.

Alen, A. & K. Muylle. *Handboek van het Belgisch Staatsrecht* (Kluwer, 2011).

Delpérée, F. *Droit constitutionnel* (Larcier, 1986–1989) 4 vols.

Delpérée, F. *Le droit constitutionnel de la Belgique* (Bruylant, 2000).

De Meyer, J. *Staatsrecht* (11th) (Wouters, 1985) 2 vols.

Ergec, R. *Introduction au droit public* (2nd) (Kluwer, 1994 & 2003).

Errera, P. *Traité de droit public belge* (Giard & Brière, 1909).

Huyse, L. *De gewapende vrede. Politiek in België na 1945* (Kritak, 1980).

Lambert, P. *La Belgique devant la Cour européenne des droits de l'homme* (Nemesis, 2002).

Mast, A. *Overzicht van het Belgisch Grondwettelijk Recht* (9th) (updated by J. Dujardin) (Story-Scientia, 1987).

Orban, O. *Le droit constitutionnel de la Belgique* (Dessain/Giard & Brière, 1906–1911) 3 vols.

Pâques, M. *Droit public élémentaire en quinze leçons* (Larcier, 2005).

Perin, F. *Cours de Droit Constitutionnel* (Liège UP, 1973) 2 vols.

Perin, F. *Introduction au Droit Public. Théorie générale de l'État* (Liège UP, 1981) 2 vols.

Rimanque, K. *De grondwet toegelicht, gewikt en gewogen* (Intersentia, 2004).

Senelle, R. *Commentaar op de Belgische Grondwet* (Ministry of Foreign Affairs, Texts and Documents No. 301, 1974).

Thonissen, J.J. *La Constitution belge annotée* (3rd) (Bruylant, 1879).

Uyttendaele, M. *Précis de droit constitutionnel belge. Regards sur un sytème institutionnel paradoxal* (2nd) (Bruylant, 2005).

Velaers, J. *De Grondwet en de Raad van State, afdeling Wetgeving* (Maklu, 1999).

Velu, J. *Notes de droit public* (2nd) (Brussels UP, 1977–1978) 3 vols.

Velu, J. with the assistance of Ph. Quertainmont and M. Leroy, *Droit Public. Tôme Ier – Le statut des gouvernants* (Bruylant, 1986).
Verdussen, M. & N. Bonbled (eds). *Les droits constitutionnels en Belgique* (Bruylant, 2011) 2 vols.

§2. After the 2014 State Restructuring

Behrendt, C. & F. Bouhon *Introduction à la Théorie générale de l'État* (3rd) (Larcier, 2014) 2 vols.
Behrendt, C. & M. Vrancken. *Beginselen van het Belgisch staatsrecht* (die Keure, 2020).
Behrendt, C. & M. Vrancken. *Principes de droit constitutionnel belge* (La Charte, 2019).
Ergec, R. *Protection européenne et internationale des droits de l'homme* (3rd) (Larcier, 2014).
Lejeune, Y. *Droit constitutionnel belge. Fondements et institutions* (3rd) (Larcier, 2017).
Sottiaux, S. *Grondwettelijk recht* (Intersentia, 2016).
Uyttendaele, M. *Trente leçons de droit constitutionnel* (3rd) (Bruylant, 2017).
Uyttendaele, M. & M. Verdussen (eds). *Dictionnaire de la Sixième Réforme de l'Etat* (Larcier, 2015).
Van Damme, M. *Overzicht van het Grondwettelijk Recht* (2nd) (die Keure, 2015).
Vande Lanotte, J., G. Goedertier, Y. Haeck, J. Goossens & T. De Pelsmaeker. *Belgisch Publiekrecht* (8th) (die Keure, 2015) 2 vols.
Velaers, J. *De Grondwet. Een artikelsgewijze commentaar* (die Keure, 2019) 3 vols.
Witte E., J. Craeybeckx, A. Meynen & D. Luyten. *Politieke geschiedenis van België van 1830 tot heden* (Manteau, 2016).

§3. Publications in English

Alen, A. & R. Ergec. *Federal Belgium after the Fourth State Reform of 1993* (2nd) (Ministry of Foreign Affairs, External Trade and Co-operation for Development, Texts and Documents, 1998).
Bracke, S., G. Goedertier. & J. Vandelanotte. *Belgium for Beginners* (die Keure, 2006).
Brans, M.L. De Winter & W. Swenden. *The Politics of Belgium. Institutions and Policy under Bipolar and Centrifugal Federalism* (Routledge, 2009).
Craenen, G. (ed.). *The Institutions of Federal Belgium: An Introduction to Belgian Public Law* (2nd) (ACCO, 2001).
Fitzmaurice, J. *The Politics of Belgium. A Unique Federalism* (London, 1996).
Popelier, P. & K. Lemmens. *The Constitution of Belgium. A Contextual Analysis* (Hart, 2015).
Senelle, R. *Commentary on the Belgian Constitution* (Ministry of Foreign Affairs, Texts and Documents No. 301, 1974).
Witte E., J. Craeybeckx & A. Meynen. *Political History of Belgium from 1830 Onwards* (VUB Press, 2010).

Table of Legislative Instruments

Listed are legislative instruments, treaties, conventions, resolutions, and intergovernmental agreements discussed in the text. Only certain relevant national and international legislative instruments have entries for specific articles. All references include amendments to date. Numbers refer to paragraph numbers.

Table of Legislative Instruments

Table of Legislative Instruments

Table of Legislative Instruments

Index

The numbers here refer to paragraph numbers.

Index

Index

Index

www.ingramcontent.com/pod-product-compliance
Lightning Source LLC
Chambersburg PA
CBHW071421230926
51846CB00001B/101